Acclaim for Barry Werth's

31 Days

"[A] smart and artful account of the White House during the month following Richard Nixon's resignation. . . . Werth [shows] finesse in bringing the past to life."
— *Newsday*

"Werth brings a refreshingly personal tone [and] a sharp biographer's eye to the chronology of the Ford transition. . . . [His] day-to-day, real-time narration effectively conjures up the prevailing atmosphere—new promise mixed with the lingering baleful influence of Dark Lord Nixon—that made the Ford interregnum a unique moment of extreme contingency in the annals of the American Presidency."
— *The New York Observer*

"Barry Werth has written a crackling and instructive account of the tumultuous time when Gerald Ford moved into the Oval Office following the resignation of President Nixon. The power struggles, legal maneuvers, personality conflicts and big stakes all add up to a whodunit on a grand scale. I was there—and I was thrilled to make the trip again."
— Tom Brokaw

"A balanced fly-on-the-wall account of the byzantine intrigues that defined the first weeks of Ford's accidental presidency. Werth has talked to many of the players to build a well-crafted book. It's a story that has been told more than once—but rarely so well or in such depth as it is here."
— *Publishers Weekly*

"[A] runaway train of a read: I kept turning the pages as if I hadn't already lived through the event."   —Liz Smith

"An eye-opening tale of vicious interoffice warfare, implying that dog-eat-dog politics remain in place on Pennsylvania Avenue."
                                                        —*Kirkus Reviews*

"In this fast-paced narrative, Barry Werth has captured the excitement of the scary days just after Nixon resigned. It's a great inside glimpse at how government works, plus it reveals how some of today's power players, including Cheney and Rumsfeld, got their start."
                                                        —Walter Isaacson

Barry Werth
31 Days

Barry Werth is the author of *The Scarlet Professor*, which was a finalist for the National Book Critics Circle Award. He is also the author of *The Billion-Dollar Molecule* and *Damages*. His articles have appeared in *The New Yorker*, *The New York Times Magazine*, *GQ*, *Outside*, and other publications. He lives in Northampton, Massachusetts.

Also by Barry Werth

The Scarlet Professor

The Billion-Dollar Molecule

Damages

The Architecture and Design of Man and Woman
(coauthored by Alexander Tsiaras)

From Conception to Birth
(coauthored by Alexander Tsiaras)

31
Days

————

31
Days

GERALD FORD,
THE NIXON PARDON,
AND A GOVERNMENT IN CRISIS

Barry Werth

Anchor Books
A Division of Random House, Inc.
New York

FIRST ANCHOR BOOKS EDITION, FEBRUARY 2007

Copyright © 2006 by Barry Werth

The Library of Congress has cataloged the Nan A. Talese edition as follows:
Werth, Barry
31 days / Barry Werth.—1st ed.
p.   cm.
1. United States—Politics and government—1974–1977.
2. Ford, Gerald R., 1913–
I. Title: Thirty-one days. II. Title.
E865.W47 2006
973.925'092—dc22   2005053877

Anchor ISBN: 978-1-4000-7868-4

Author Photograph © Ellen Augarten

www.anchorbooks.com

Printed in the United States of America
10 9 8 7 6 5 4 3 2 1

In America,

no-one bothers

about what was done

before his time.

—ALEXIS DE TOCQUEVILLE,
Democracy in America

CAST OF CHARACTERS

Richard Nixon	President of the United States
Pat Nixon	Wife of the President
Gerald Ford	President of the United States; former Vice President under Nixon
Betty Ford	Wife of the President
General Alexander Haig, Jr.	White House Chief of Staff
Henry Kissinger	Assistant to the President for National Security; Secretary of State
Donald Rumsfeld	Ambassador to NATO: Transition team member
George H. W. Bush	Chairman, Republican National Committee
Philip Buchen	Counsel to President Ford
Robert Hartmann	Counselor to President Ford
Gerald terHorst	Press Secretary to President Ford
John Marsh	Counselor to President Ford
Nelson Rockefeller	Vice Presidential nominee: former Governor of New York
James Schlesinger	Secretary of Defense
Henry "Scoop" Jackson	Democratic Senator; leading opponent of détente
Ronald Reagan	Governor of California

William Saxbe Attorney General

Leon Jaworski Watergate Special Prosecutor

Fred Buzhardt Special White House Counsel for Watergate

Leonard Garment Counsel to the President

Jerry Jones White House Staff Secretary

Benton Becker Attorney for President Ford

Herbert Miller Attorney for President Nixon

William "Bill" Gulley Director of the White House military office

Melvin Laird Friend and adviser of President Ford: former Secretary of Defense

Bryce Harlow White House special adviser: chief lobbyist, Procter and Gamble

William Scranton Former Governor of Pennsylvania; Transition team member

Ronald Ziegler Press Secretary to President Nixon

John Sirica Judge; U.S. District Court for the District of Columbia

Lieutenant General Brent Scowcroft Deputy Assistant to the President for National Security; aide to Kissinger

Philip Lacovara Counsel, Watergate Special Prosecution Force

Alan Greenspan Chairman, Council of Economic Advisors

William Seidman Chief of Staff to Vice President Ford

Richard Cheney Deputy to Rumsfeld

John Dean II Former Counsel to President Nixon

Charles Colson Former Special Counsel to President Nixon

H. R. "Bob" Haldeman Former Chief of Staff, the White House

John Ehrlichman   Former Assistant to the President for Domestic Affairs

John Mitchell   Former Attorney General; manager of the 1972 Nixon campaign (Committee to Re-elect the President)

On his last morning in power, President Richard Nixon arose in the predawn darkness after just a few hours of sleep. He ordered his favorite breakfast of poached eggs and corned-beef hash served to him, alone, in the Lincoln sitting room, the same room where twenty-two months earlier he had retreated by himself to watch on TV as he and Vice President Spiro Agnew were reelected in one of the greatest landslides in American history. The most inward, solitary, and reclusive of presidents—who paradoxically was determined to ensure that every word he spoke, and that was spoken to him, was recorded for history—Nixon to a rare degree determined exactly what he hoped to do and say in public beforehand, by himself, by filling yellow legal pads with notes, arguments, talking points, and exhortations to himself. In a few hours he would say good-bye to the people whom he most depended upon, and whom he'd most let down, betrayed, disappointed, and infuriated—his top administration, who'd served and defended him through the agonies of Watergate and Vietnam.

As through much of this "impeachment summer," the morning sky was dull and overcast, a soggy heat blanketing the South Lawn and the

Ellipse, all but hazing out the Washington Monument less than a half mile away. A fire smoldered in Nixon's sitting room fireplace, one of several throughout the White House as aides tossed potentially troublesome documents into the flames. Already assistants had removed the contents of the president's three historic desks—Woodrow Wilson's, in the Oval Office; Dwight Eisenhower's, in room 175 of the Executive Office Building, which Nixon used as a hideaway; and the smaller Lincoln desk, in the president's sitting room in the residence—and packed them carefully into moving boxes now stacked for removal in the hallways. The office of retired General Alexander M. Haig, Jr., Nixon's chief of staff, was cluttered with oversized plastic bags stuffed with shredded files that Haig said were duplicates.

After finishing breakfast, Nixon took a pad from his briefcase, slouched down on the small of his back in an armchair near the hearth, and started writing. Haig, who for the past fifteen months had handled the business of the presidency while Nixon struggled to stay in power, knocked and entered. A tireless regent, whose prideful West Point bearing was never quite concealed by the dark business suits he favored, and whose tenure was circumscribed by a thankless choice between deserting Nixon or going down with him, Haig had defended Nixon even as he concluded that he had to resign and so engineered his abdication. "There is something that will have to be done, Mr. President, and I thought you would rather do it now," he said, apologizing. He took a sheet of thick White House stationery and placed it on the Lincoln desk. Nixon read the single sentence, addressed to Secretary of State Henry Kissinger—*I hereby resign the office of President of the United States*—and signed it. After Haig left, Nixon returned to his musing, then summoned him back.

"He was haggard and ashen," Haig would recall. "He thanked me for what I had done for him. I thanked him for giving me the opportunity to serve. Nothing of a personal nature was said . . . By now, there was not much that could be said that we did not already understand."

* * *

Gripping files and a briefcase, Vice President Gerald Ford stepped into a crowd of reporters in front of the brick split-level house in Alexandria, Virginia, where he'd lived since the early fifties, when he was a young congressman from western Michigan, and which his wife Betty said "kind of grew along with the children." He smiled cautiously—dazed, it seemed, no less than other Americans by the implications of Nixon's announcement during his previous night's prime-time speech from the Oval Office: that he, Nixon, would evacuate the White House for exile at his California compound before noon today. Ford, shortly after, would be sworn in, becoming the "new man on the television set in the living room," as his biographer James Cannon put it.

Now age sixty-one, Ford had never sought the position; he was handed it, more or less, by bipartisan consensus ten months earlier. At the time, he had been a likable legislative blocker and party workhorse—House minority leader—and he'd recently made up his mind to quit politics because he foresaw no hope in the reasonably near future of winning a majority that would elect him speaker. Then Agnew was forced to resign after pleading no contest to a criminal charge of tax evasion, and congressional Democrats assured Nixon that no one but Ford could win confirmation. Facing inflamed Democratic majorities in Congress as Watergate metastasized, Nixon had no alternative. He and Ford had worked together since the late 1940s, when they were junior congressmen in the Chowder and Marching Society, a conservative GOP forum and social club, and Nixon viewed him as someone who did what needed doing—as Seymour Hersh wrote, "who placed loyalty to Nixon and the Republican presidency above his personal ambitions and political well being." Little known outside official Washington, Ford was profoundly aware that he was about to become the only man in history to serve as president without having been elected to national office.

Haig thought the removal of a vice president and president little more than a "silent coup" by Nixon's enemies, and although Ford didn't doubt he had the constitutional authority to govern, others, both right and left, expressed serious concerns about having a president chosen solely by a disgraced predecessor and the warring partisan lawmakers who'd deposed him. Dressed in a medium blue suit and bold, blue and white, "good-guy" striped tie like those favored by bank executives back in Grand Rapids, Ford stood in front of a two-car garage converted into a family playroom and patiently fielded questions about becoming the world's most powerful leader.

"Mr. Vice President, when Harry Truman had the office suddenly thrust upon him, he said he felt that the stars and the moon and the planets had all fallen on him. How do you feel about all that responsibility being dumped on you?"

"I think that's a very apt description." Ford nodded, smiling. "I can tell you better this afternoon after it actually happens."

"Mrs. Ford has hoped you would get out of politics. What is her reaction to the heavy responsibility?"

"Well." He shook his head. "She's just doing her best and we'll wait and see about the other."

Ford climbed into the back of a Cadillac limousine with two advisers. So delicate was the matter of presidential succession, particularly in light of the impeachment proceedings that had forced Nixon to resign and would not simply abate because he stepped aside, and so unpredictable were Nixon's mental state and obsessive suspicion that he might be pushed from power, that Ford's former law partner from Grand Rapids, Philip Buchen, had organized a "secret" outside transition group to plan for the most crucial decisions of the next forty-eight hours, but precious little beyond that. Buchen had arrived at eight that morning accompanied by former Wisconsin congressman John Byrnes, an old Washington ally. As Watergate elevated the choice of a president's men to a matter of utmost national importance, Ford was happy to have his own counsel on how to establish a White House operation independent of Nixon's.

Ford had feared he could forfeit his legitimacy if he appeared at all to want to *be* president, and like Haig he had lived the last nine months "sitting on a time bomb," trying to support Nixon loyally while not being destroyed himself. Then, during the past two weeks, events in Washington soared to a crescendo in which all three government branches combined to drive Nixon from office. The Supreme Court, ruling 8–0, had ordered the White House to release to federal prosecutors tape recordings, secretly authorized by Nixon, on which the president could clearly be heard telling an aide to order the CIA to interfere with the FBI's probe into the 1972 break-in at Democratic headquarters—the infamous Watergate burglary dismissed by Nixon's men as "third-rate." The release of the tapes, indisputable proof that Nixon had lied to the American people, Congress, prosecutors, his staff, and his family, instantly caused his support among Republicans in Congress to evaporate, and three articles of impeachment were adopted by fateful margins. Special Watergate prosecutor Leon Jaworski, whom Nixon had appointed, believed the tapes "confirmed absolutely" that Nixon was guilty and should have to stand trial. At Nixon's last cabinet meeting three days earlier, Ford had stood up and declared he would have no further comment on the president's problems, as "I am a party of interest."

Crossing the Potomac into Washington, Ford studied the transition group's four-page memo on how to run the White House:

> We share your view that there should be no chief of staff at the outset. However, there should be someone who could rapidly and efficiently organize the new staff organization, but who will not be perceived or be eager to be chief of staff.

With a looping left hand Ford wrote, "Rumsfeld." At forty-two, Donald Rumsfeld had been part of Nixon's inner circle, a hard-charging administrator with a much-noted talent for impressing presidents and escaping political cul-de-sacs. The Illinois Republican had known Ford since they served together in the House, where Rumsfeld was one of the chief architects of Ford's rise to leadership. Brash and informal, and with barely concealed presidential ambitions of his own, Rumsfeld had conveniently been out of Washington during the unraveling of Watergate, serving as ambassador to NATO in Europe, but he had grown eager to return and continue his ascent. The job of top presidential aide, while powerful, was a staff position—not the sort of career plum that ambitious politicians like Rumsfeld ordinarily coveted.

Haig, the memo continued, should be asked to stay on to help with the transition but "should not be expected, asked, or be given the option to become your chief of staff." Ford wrote, "OK."

* * *

Under the startling intensity of the television lights in the White House East Room—America's gold-curtained, chandeliered "grand ballroom"—hundreds of cabinet and subcabinet members, prominent Republican lawmakers, staffers, and their spouses stood packed together and loudly applauded one last time for their leader. When Pat Nixon had heard shortly before that her husband's personal good-bye to those who'd followed him through the public hell of his second term would be televised, she'd been furious, but Nixon insisted. A crafter of historical moments, he saw one last opportunity to explain himself. "We owe it to our supporters," he told her. "We owe it to the people."

The president's face was drenched in sweat and his red-rimmed eyes fought back tears as he started to speak—the "nightmare end of a long dream," he wrote. His lips trembled and his head sagged into his hunched shoulders. Yet even after weeks and months living in what CBS newsman Howard K. Smith called the "meat grinder" of his undoing, he seemed utterly in command, the dominant political figure of his age delivering a final encore to those who, despite everything, still looked up to him and credited him with greatness. Kissinger, sitting in the front row, remembered Nixon's speech as an "elegy of anguish . . . Having devoted so much of his effort to self control all his life, Nixon seemed impelled to put on display the passions and dreams he had publicly suppressed for so long . . . It was almost too much to have to witness."

Wearing glasses in public for the first time, Nixon seemed to ramble, leaping from statements of gratitude to self-analysis to resentment, but he also managed to deliver a stirring and exquisite eulogy for his years in public life, a string of encomiums and lessons from a lonely virtuoso who saw himself as one of the select few whose vision could shape the fate of nations: a Churchill, a Mao. For him the "moment of truth" was when he sat alone with legal pads, and so what he said now, even as it revealed what he couldn't control, also displayed an adroit self-awareness. He thanked those who had served him and the country during the past five and a half years, jabbed once or twice at the press, defended his administration's scruples ("Mistakes, yes. But for personal gain, never!"), invoked his dead parents ("I remember my old man, I think they would have called him a sort of a little man, a common man . . . Nobody will ever write a book, probably, about my mother; my mother was a saint"), made a few Freudian slips ("This country needs good farmers, good businessmen, good . . . plumbers"), quoted Teddy Roosevelt on loss and redemption, neglected to mention Pat, who was standing and grimacing defiantly behind him, and vowed to survive. "We think that when we suffer a defeat that all is ended. Not true. It is only a beginning, always . . ."

"Greatness comes not when things go always good for you," Nixon said, "but the greatness comes and you are really tested when you take some knocks, some disappointment, when sadness comes, because only if you have been in the deepest valley can you ever know how magnificent it is to be on the highest mountain."

"Always remember," he advised, "others may hate you, but those who hate you don't win unless you hate them, and then you destroy yourself."

Nixon neither confessed to nor apologized for his role in Watergate. But he had disclosed "that amazing, mammoth insight," as his counsel Leonard Garment put it, that it was *his* hatred of his enemies at home, not theirs of him, that had finished him. Many were in tears; others reeled with fresh fascination at the strange, complex figure before them, and the shining tableau of the loving family that he had brought to grief—Pat, daughters Julie and Tricia, and sons-in-law David Eisenhower and Ed Cox. Kissinger, a Bavarian-born Jew whose family had fled the Nazis when he was a teenager, believed the tragedy originated in Nixon's straitened youth, with his pious, distracted mother and hardbitten, taciturn father. "Can you imagine what this man would have been had somebody loved him?" wondered Kissinger, a former Harvard professor whom Nixon had appointed both national security adviser and secretary of state, making him the world's most powerful foreign policy adviser and diplomat.

Others could be excused, as they joined the procession out to the South Lawn, where Nixon would depart by presidential helicopter, for worrying less about Nixon and more about themselves. Besides those who held elected office, Nixon was crucial to their hopes and ambitions. Yet in two hours Ford would control the government and the party. What was more, the "presidential timetable," especially for Republicans, had been upended. Under the constitutional arrangement that enabled Nixon to choose Ford, Ford now would nominate his own vice president. But because Ford had told the Senate during his confirmation hearings that he wouldn't run for president in 1976, an incumbent vice president would become the heir apparent for the party's nomination. A lifelong climb to the top politically was a combat version of the children's game Chutes and Ladders, normally taking decades. The GOP game board suddenly was rife with new battle lines and angles of attack—and accelerating opportunities.

No high-level appointee was more perplexed by the shifting political matrix than party chairman George H. W. Bush. Son of a Wall Street investment banker and former Connecticut senator, Bush, fifty, was a transplanted patrician oilman and former Houston congressman whom Nixon had rescued and elevated to national prominence with high-level assignments after Texas voters twice rejected him for the Senate. Bush had been among Nixon's staunchest defenders; then, at the last cabinet session, when Ford declared his independence from Nixon, Bush stood up and all but told Nixon he had to leave, for the good of the party.

"There is no way to really describe the emotion of the day," Bush wrote in his journal. "One couldn't help look at the family and the whole thing and think of his accomplishments and then think of the shame and wonder what kind of man is this really. No morality—kicking his friends in those tapes—all of them. Gratuitous abuse. Caring for no one and yet doing so much . . ."

Shortly after ten, the Nixons and Fords followed the long scarlet carpet onto the lawn. The women kept their arms around each other's waists as they walked past the statue-still honor guard. "You'll see many of these red carpets," Pat whispered, "and you'll get so you hate 'em." Then, in one of the most enduring scenes in American history, Nixon climbed aboard the helicopter, waved good-bye with a broad forced smile and his signature upstretched arms and double-V for victory, and left.

Walking back to the White House, a grim-looking Gerald Ford clasped his wife's hand. "We can do it," he said.

*   *   *

Ford took the oath of office in the East Room at noon, as Nixon hurtled thirty-nine thousand feet over Missouri in Air Force One. Not known for eloquence, he had crafted with his top assistant and speechwriter, the former newsman Robert Hartmann, a memorable twenty-five-hundred-word appeal for national unity in a time of urgency and crisis. The leaders of both parties in Congress sat together on one side of the aisle, the Fords' four handsome young-adult blond children on the other, and viewers at home couldn't tell which group looked more proud or pleased, or considered him more their own. Through a decade of Vietnam and two years of Watergate, America had torn itself apart. Yet in twenty-five years in Congress while the Democrats ruled and Ford toiled to reverse the tide, then more recently when relations between the White House and Congress had never been more sulfuric, Ford had won far more friends than enemies. With midterm elections less than three months away, and menaced by an angry snarl of problems—inflation, recession, a world energy crisis, and a quickening threat of war in the Middle East—his first priority was to bring them together.

"This is an hour of history that troubles our minds and hurts our hearts," Ford said, facing the camera and speaking to the nation. "I am acutely aware that you have not elected me as your President by your ballots. So I ask you to confirm me as your President with your prayers . . ."

He continued: ". . . neither have I gained office by any secret promises. I have not campaigned either for the Presidency or the Vice Presidency. I have not subscribed to any partisan platform. I am indebted to no man . . ."

"My fellow Americans," Ford recited, "our long national nightmare is over. Our Constitution works. Our great Republic is a government of laws and not of men. Here, the people rule . . ."

On the TV set in the living room, Ford looked shaky but characteristically stolid, still trim, his thinning blond hair combed neatly back from a strong, serious brow hooding a troubled albeit level gaze. His voice seemed adenoidal, quivery, pitched too high next to Nixon's gravelly baritone, but his delivery resonated. Only upon reaching the words the "wounds of Watergate, more painful and more poisonous than those of foreign wars," did he choke up.

"I ask again your prayers for Richard Nixon and for his family," Ford said slowly, red-eyed. "May our former President who brought peace to millions find it for himself . . ." On *peace*, Ford's voice cracked.

* * *

A football star in college, Ford hit the White House hallways running. From the East Room he strode to the nearby Red Room to ask the House and Senate leadership how soon he could address a joint session, then sped down one flight to the pressroom, which, as Sally Quinn reported in the *Washington Post*, "seemed just like a normal day . . . except that it was more crowded and hotter and smellier and dirtier and Walter Cronkite was there." As poisonous as relations with Capitol Hill had grown under Nixon, the enmity between the White House and the Washington media was far worse, crystallized by open mutual contempt between reporters and Press Secretary Ronald Ziegler, a former ad executive and the youngest presidential spokesman in history, who eighteen months earlier famously told reporters to consider "inoperative" all previous White House statements on Watergate.

"We will have one of yours as my press secretary," Ford announced,

"Jerry terHorst." Since the news had broken that Nixon would leave, the mood of the triumphal national press corps had plummeted from raucous euphoria to an existential "What now?" Steve Daley, bartender at the Class Reunion, a smoky bar where many reporters had drunk heavily and talked all night until they returned to work, thought they seemed "postcoital." Ford's choice of terHorst won immediate favor not only because he was a respected longtime colleague from the *Detroit News* but because he was soothing, not hostile, and understood their needs. "The transition of Presidents," Quinn wrote in her *Post* article, "was far less important in the press room than the transition of press secretaries."

"We'll have an open administration," Ford announced before leaving terHorst, who'd been offered the job less than two days earlier, to handle questions. "I can't change my nature."

Ford arrived next at the Oval Office, its desk and shelves and credenzas stripped bare of every book, picture, and memento, where he huddled for a few minutes with his family until Haig, who'd controlled who Nixon saw and when he saw them, interrupted. Determined to maintain that same authority with Ford, Haig had decided the first priority was a meeting with the White House staff. No one knew better than Haig that he had been acting president, keeping the White House going, making countless decisions Nixon was either too distracted or too out of sorts to make, and he worried that Ford wasn't up to the job. "We have to save Ford from his own inexperience," he told an aide. At the door to the Roosevelt Room, Haig handed Ford a list of talking points for his meeting with the Nixon loyalists. The memo concluded: "DO NOTS—At this time, do not commit yourself to dealing directly with anyone but Al Haig. DO—Ask each staff member to be alert to problems and to make suggestions to Al Haig or to Transition Team members."

The U.S. Army is a garrison force that trains its officers to seize and hold ground, and Haig, a decorated battalion commander in Vietnam, was determined not to yield his government's headquarters without a fight, especially against an unorganized and untested unit like Ford's transition group. Normally such teams prepare for months for an orderly takeover, but Ford's people had barely been recruited, much less trained, and that included Ford himself. While Ford hedged on some of the talking points, he told Nixon's people that Haig had "unselfishly agreed to stay on," leaving the impression that Haig would remain as chief of staff, and apparently reversing the decision he had made just hours earlier in the limousine with Byrnes and Buchen.

Watching, Bob Hartmann worried that Ford had been usurped by his palace guard. A gruff former reporter for the *Los Angeles Times*, Hartmann was Ford's closest political adviser and a much-needed alter ego for a politician whose career was fueled by trust and likability—dark where Ford was sunny, suspicious where he was naive, surly and combative where he was friendly and conciliatory. "You don't suspect ill motives of anyone until you're kicked in the balls three times," Hartmann told him. "In a human being, that's a virtue. But as a President, it's a weakness." Hartmann recognized in Haig both a Prussian sensibility and ferocious will to win, plus unswerving loyalty to Nixon. As soon as he could get Ford alone, he added: "I think your old friends ought to have some official status around here if we're going to be of any help to you . . . We aren't the President's staff—*they* are."

Ford's idea of an "open" presidency was diametrically at odds with the secretive, sphincterish Nixon staff model, in which the president consulted with a core group of minions before issuing "action memos"—edicts passed down through a single all-powerful chief who alone interpreted the president's real intentions and degree of will and who controlled all access to him. That system, Ford thought, made the president vulnerable. And indeed, Nixon's essential defense throughout Watergate was that he had been a victim of the "Berlin Wall" constructed around him by his first chief of staff, H. R. "Bob" Haldeman, and his powerful domestic policy adviser, John Ehrlichman; his "Germans," both now scheduled to go on trial in September on charges of conspiracy and obstruction of justice. Ford worried as well that during the transition "we'd end up with two 'White House staffs, two administrations,'" and that "chaos could ensue" as Nixon's opponents saw a chance to appeal to Ford through his new entourage, which had no official status.

Ford was torn. He believed Haig and his staff had performed heroically and deserved better than to be fired. Those who served Nixon most loyally in his first term were either in jail, facing charges, or at the very least tarnished by their service, and Ford didn't have the heart to put the rest out on the street. On the other hand, he knew he needed his own people in positions of authority or he couldn't govern. He immediately designated two counselors with cabinet rank: Hartmann and a former Democratic congressman from Virginia, Jack Marsh, one of Ford's most trusted aides. As vice president, Ford had chosen the forty-eight-year-old Marsh, a courtly, salt-and-pepper-haired defense hawk and then assistant secretary of defense, as his national security adviser. Marsh also was a small-town lawyer from a border state, skilled at reconciling foes. Smooth where Hartmann was rough, subtle where he was blunt, he more than anyone else would attempt to bridge the Nixon and Ford staffs.

Ford charged into the Cabinet Room to issue marching orders to the White House economists, telling them that the worst inflation in America's peacetime history was "public enemy number one" and that he would veto any spending bill that increased the federal deficit. Joining the group was a Wall Street consultant named Alan Greenspan, whom Nixon recently had appointed to chair his Council of Economic Advisors. Like other top-level appointments, Greenspan's confirmation was stalled by Watergate—twenty-four hours earlier Senate Democrats had been grilling him about his wealthy corporate connections and opposition to consumer protection laws—and he was fast growing disenchanted with the idea of government service, telling friends he was thinking about withdrawing his name.

Ford left for a whirl of ambassadorial calls arranged and directed by Kissinger and his staff. The message he and Kissinger agreed must be conveyed to other nations during the days ahead was that Watergate was a domestic political matter that had no bearing whatever on foreign affairs, and that while there had been a change at the top, all else was the same. In much of the world, Nixon was and would remain widely admired as the architect of a new and promising international order that, whatever its domestic controversies, was cause for hope and optimism. And Kissinger's diplomatic breakthroughs, "shuttle diplomacy," and aura of superstardom were celebrated by the global media; enthralled national leaders clamored for him to visit, to personally resolve stubborn issues in their regions. As one Ford aide observed, Kissinger *was* America's foreign policy.

Ford saw dangers in keeping Kissinger, especially from the political right, which viewed him as having exploited Nixon's vanity and incapacity to serve his own agenda—namely, European-style "realism" resulting in a sellout of American values and interests. But he saw far greater opportunities. Nixon and Kissinger had relaxed tensions with the Soviets at the height of the Cold War, negotiated the first nuclear arms reductions, opened relations with China, and ended the United States' longest, costliest, and most controversial foreign war in Southeast Asia. Ford hoped for further cooperation with the Soviets, especially in diffusing the flashpoint of the Middle East, and Kissinger, he wrote, was a "total pragmatist who thought in terms of power and national interest instead of ideology"—in Ford's view, a plus. Similarly, Kissinger regarded Ford's willingness to reach across ideological boundaries as a major asset in a world leader, a fund to draw upon. "Ford," he wrote, "was immune to the modern politician's chameleon-like search for ever new identities and the emotional roller coaster this search exacts."

Kissinger's deputy Brent Scowcroft, a pensive, soft-spoken air force lieutenant general with a Ph.D. in history from Columbia, ushered Ford through the diplomatic rounds—three regional groups consisting of ambassadors from fifty-five countries in Europe, the Middle East, and Latin America, and individual sessions with the representatives of the Soviet Union, Japan, Communist China, Israel, and Vietnam. Scowcroft explained that the Soviets tended to see Watergate as a domestic reaction to the thaw in the Cold War—détente—which made them uneasy about its effect on future relations, and that Communist leader Leonid Brezhnev had "acquired considerable stake" in his relationship with Nixon, with whom two months earlier he'd traded state gifts of a Cadillac for a Russian-built hovercraft. Brezhnev was bound to be in a sensitive position when many in Moscow saw his relationship with the Americans imperiled. At the same time, Kissinger and Scowcroft feared that Russian forces would see the United States in disarray and decide, in Kissinger's term, "to take a run at us"—force a crisis where the United States couldn't react. That concern had far from abated and would only intensify should Ford appear weak or uncertain.

"It was a very complicated period," Scowcroft recalls, "very complicated—because there were a number of trends that were changing. Vietnam was one of closing down an unfortunate chapter. Détente was moving in the wrong direction. Our China relations were positive. In the Middle East, we were on a rising tide—we'd produced these disengagements and stabilized the region. But it was a fast-moving train." Unlike Haig, Scowcroft, who had briefed Ford weekly on national security when he was vice president, had confidence in the new commander in chief.

* * *

While Ford reassured foreign emissaries that he would hew to Nixon's legacy, terHorst took questions at his first press briefing indicating that Ford would be held equally to account for Nixon's record at home. Washington was in a fever of tips, leaks, confabulations, and rumors: that Nixon had pardoned himself and all his aides before leaving; that he had spirited away the rest of the White House tapes with him to San Clemente; that Defense Secretary James Schlesinger had informed commanders not to take direct orders from the West Wing in case Nixon, said to be drinking and in a suicidal state of despair, refused to leave or ordered a nuclear strike. After twenty minutes, terHorst told the press he'd just been advised that Nixon hadn't issued any pardons, to himself or anyone else. A reporter followed up by asking if Ford would consider issuing a pardon himself.

Ford had been asked the same question ten months earlier at his vice presidential confirmation hearing in the Senate, answering, "I don't think the American people would stand for it." Without checking, terHorst said Ford still opposed granting Nixon immunity from prosecution.

"He is not in favor of immunity?" the reporter asked again.

"I can assure you of that," terHorst repeated.

*　*　*

At 5:40 Ford strode into the Cabinet Room to talk for twenty minutes with an ad hoc group of advisers "about being President of the United States," as journalist Richard Reeves wrote. Beyond filling—and healing—the breach left by Nixon, Ford's mid- and long-range goals were miasmic. Having stayed out of Washington as much as possible as vice president, promoting Nixon's innocence while keeping a safe distance, his grip on how the White House operated and was organized was uncertain. Hartmann observed that everyone but Ford seemed drained and exhausted; Haig, bearing the heaviest strains, looked the worst, tension creasing his pallid face as he chain-smoked Marlboro Lights. After thanking everyone and inviting Buchen to lay out the initial moves he had approved earlier, Ford announced that Marsh would be his counselor for national security—apparently forgetting that Kissinger already held that job. Marsh blanched. Responding to several more items on the transition team's checklist, Ford turned to Haig and said, "Al, what do you think of that?" "If you think it best, Mr. President," the general replied.

Power, loyalty, and the perception of power—which in Washington amount to the same thing—were nowhere more in play now than in this room. Within a period of hours, Buchen's secret team had spawned a top-level group to handle the transfer of presidential authority—an "interim government." Yet where Ford's embryonic presidency might lead, who would direct it, and how it would get there would be resolved far less by design than by the competing ambitions and maneuvers of those who served in it during its earliest days. And at the moment Ford hadn't one entourage but several, the nine men around him representing four distinct missions, each with a rival power base, agenda, timetable, and as many personal goals as members.

Of them all, he and Buchen knew each other best. Friends since college, they had opened a law practice together in Grand Rapids in 1941. But Buchen didn't know Washington well and was handing the transition planning to people who did, so that he could become Ford's personal attorney. Ford liked to have an outside eye and he trusted the scholarly, white-haired Buchen to bird-dog the White House legal staff, especially Nixon's special Watergate counsel, Fred Buzhardt, whose job was to advise the president and whom Ford planned to retain for now, but who until this morning had directed Nixon's legal team.

There were the two sparring, mutually distrustful staffs, Nixon's and Ford's vice presidential holdovers. Haig sat to one side of Ford at the table; Hartmann and L. William Seidman, a Grand Rapids businessman who organized and ran Ford's vice presidential staff, to the other. Much more than turf already divided them. As very few people outside this room, and only half those in it, knew, negotiations during the run-up to the transfer of power from Nixon to Ford already had placed these two entourages determinedly, fatefully at odds.

On August 1, just eight days earlier, Haig urgently had visited Ford in his Executive Office Building (EOB) office to tell him that Nixon planned to step down, and he had presented Ford privately a handwritten list, prepared by Buzhardt, of "permutations for the option of resignation"—ways that Nixon could relinquish the presidency yet avoid indictment. These included one that, as Ford put it, "Nixon could agree to leave in return for and agreement that the new President—Gerald Ford—would pardon him." Outraged that Ford hadn't thrown Haig out, Hartmann enlisted Marsh and together they had insisted that Ford phone Haig the next morning to state unambiguously, for the record, and in front of witnesses that Ford had made no commitments of any kind. Haig knew and liked Marsh—their kids went to school together—but he thought Hartmann was way beyond his depth. And Hartmann in turn considered Haig imperious and power hungry, an "asshole." The new ambiguity about Haig's role—whether or not he was Ford's chief of staff—stoked Hartmann to the boiling point.

Sitting opposite Ford was his transition team—the last mission group—four House veterans he liked and trusted. Three had already begun working: Marsh with Congress, the governors, business and labor groups; Interior Secretary Rogers Morton as cabinet liaison; and, directing recruitment, former Pennsylvania governor William Scranton, a moderate with bloodlines going back to the birth of the party, who'd retired from politics after challenging conservative avatar Barry Goldwater for the 1964 Republican nomination and who Ford knew wouldn't be promoting himself for a job. Rumsfeld, the putative leader, had been vacationing with his wife on the French Riviera when Buchen summoned him back to Washington. His flight from Brussels had arrived at Dulles Airport too late for him to attend Ford's swearing-in, but he'd been met on the ground by his former White House deputy, thirty-three-year-old Richard Cheney, and the two of them had arrived just hours earlier. Cheney, discreet and efficient, had agreed to leave his job at an investment firm, where he had lectured clients that Watergate wasn't a criminal conspiracy but a power struggle between Congress and the White House, to assist Rumsfeld during the transition.

Ford delivered no marching orders, although everyone but Haig hoped that he would. Unlike Nixon, Ford thrived on personal contact and collaboration. He didn't make decisions by himself after laying out the arguments and debating them in solitude; he liked to hear what others had to say.

"I'll have an open door to the cabinet," he cautioned Morton, "but when you come, talk about something. If you waste my time, it's going to be a long winter before you come back." Hartmann, anticipating problems, scribbled a note suggesting Ford describe his work habits and preferences. "I listen better than I read," he said, ". . . I like to see the alternatives."

Haig believed Ford should be able to do business as he chose, but he doubted an open door or hearing from a wide group of advisers would contain territoriality among factions; nor would they correct for Nixon's isolation. The problem with Nixon, he understood, wasn't that his chamberlains barred the door but that he was almost pathologically averse to personal conflict. More and more when people needed to see the president, or he them, Haig had had to "ramrod" them into Nixon's schedule.

Rumsfeld sat silently, taking notes. He believed Ford's first priority should be to establish a "legitimate government" insulated from the taint of the Nixon years—a difficult challenge at best, since Ford already had decided to keep Kissinger, the cabinet, Haig, Buzhardt, and the rest of the White House staff. Although a Nixon protégé, Rumsfeld thought Ford should clean house, and like Haig he doubted that Ford's open-door management style, a holdover from his days in the House, would work. But Rumsfeld agreed to do what Ford asked. Reporting to Ford afterward, Rumsfeld told him that the transition team members would help Haig and the West Wing staff adjust to Ford's decision-making style, then "go out of business" in a month. "Rumsfeld and the others were acutely aware of the dangers inherent in the role they played," Ford wrote. "They didn't want the transition team to 'take over' the government."

* * *

Air Force One, which Nixon had optimistically renamed *The Spirit of '76*, touched down at El Toro Marine Air Base, halfway between Los Angeles and San Diego, and rolled to a stop on the hot tarmac in front of more than five thousand cheering supporters. "Having completed one task does not mean we will sit back and . . . do nothing," Nixon told them. Pat and Tricia flanked him at the microphone, dressed in the same yellow and pink pastel outfits and white pumps as earlier, still clutching similar small white handbags, as if afraid they might lose them during the day's shocks and reversals. Standing in the sunshine, hands behind his back, Nixon seemed relieved to be rid at last of Washington and its people, whom he'd never much liked.

"In all the time that I have which can be useful I will continue to work for peace among nations," he said, met by wild screams of approval. "I'm going to continue to work for opportunity and understanding among the people of America."

Imperial stagecraft and campaign rhetoric aside, Richard Nixon was no longer president. Having destroyed all that he'd built and been forced to do the most distasteful thing he could imagine—acquiesce, *quit*—he was returning to California a private citizen: jobless, in debt, and threatened by federal prosecutors. A camouflage-brown marine Huey helicopter like those used in Vietnam evacuated the members of the ex–First Family to the twenty-eight-acre estate overlooking the Pacific Ocean that Nixon, financed by two wealthy friends, had bought during the first year of his presidency and had designated the Western White House.

The most remote of Nixon's hideaways, the fourteen-room villa he called La Casa Pacifica (the peaceful house) was also the most secure, heavily fenced with a guardhouse, windscreens, and bulletproof windows—improvements paid for by the government, also now under investigation. Volunteers from the University of Southern California maintained the grounds, which Nixon found "beautiful almost beyond description." When the chopper touched down at the coast guard station next door, Nixon got off shaking. The family climbed into a yellow golf cart for the three-minute ride to the house.

Inside at last, Pat went to the red-walled master bedroom to unpack her husband's things while Nixon walked straight to the phone to call Al Haig—to press him to start shipping all his White House records, papers, and tapes to California at once.

2

When Ford arrived at the Oval Office at eight thirty after taking a swim and toasting himself an English muffin at home, Haig met him and handed him a ten-page memo outlining how to organize his presidency. Nixon's "chief of staff" system was modeled after the army's: Eisenhower had employed it as supreme allied commander in Europe during World War II and first brought it to the White House in 1953. Having a single, dominant aide used to acting in the president's name enabled Ike to play golf in the afternoon, and Nixon, his marginalized, oft-maligned vice president, had admired its effectiveness. ("Nixon was world errand boy," Chief of Staff Sherman Adams explained. "I worked in the kitchen.")

Upon winning the presidency himself in 1968, Nixon ordered Haldeman to install the same system, not so he could relax with friends but so he could avoid confrontations and have more time alone. According to Jerry Jones, the Harvard-trained management consultant who stayed up all night preparing Haig's document, the pyramid-like structure was "absolutely essential to maintaining the integrity of the decision-making process—so some guy can't run in there with a pet project, sell the president on it, and go with it, without anyone else knowing, and then it craters in five other areas." It was Jones's job to make sure that every piece of paper Nixon—now Ford—saw was properly routed and vetted: to supervise his in-out box.

Ford knew what he had to have to take over the presidency and it wasn't a Haldeman or Adams, tireless, abrasive guardians who had caused his predecessors so much trouble. Sherman Adams, the bantam former timber executive and New Hampshire governor who could reach decisions and "move papers" faster than anyone in Washington, and who got priestly satisfaction from slaving like a dragon to serve his country, was a force of nature ruling over the operations of the Eisenhower White House—a virtual "co-president" until, after admitting to taking gifts from a shady New England businessman, he was attacked by conservative Republicans and dropped by Eisenhower, who sent Nixon to tell Adams the president would welcome his resignation. Bob Haldeman, who famously said that he was "Nixon's SOB," looked and acted like a marine drill sergeant. *Time* called him "spikey and glaring . . . the 'zero-defects man,' " and like nearly everyone in Washington, Ford regarded the former California ad executive as an overcompensating outsider with a fetish for order.

Ford wanted to see as many people as possible, hear a lot of opinions, he told Haig.

Haig—"with some amusement," he recalled—replied that he'd be happy to usher in as many visitors as Ford wanted. He thought Ford's opposition to a strong chief of staff "seemed to be more important to him than his own needs."

Seated at the Wilson desk, already buried under paperwork, Ford announced he would be his own chief of staff, with a half dozen or so co-equal advisers each meeting with him at different times during the day to report to him on separate areas of authority. He likened this office model to the spokes on a wheel. He would meet with Marsh to direct legislative affairs, Hartmann to talk about communications, Seidman to discuss the economy, and Kissinger for foreign policy. Haig's area of competence would be administering the White House.

Haig rejected the spokes-on-the-wheel system as clueless, naive. "Only a supreme optimist," he wrote, "could have believed that such an arrangement would work in a town in which ambition is mother's milk and every symbol of power from job title to parking space is the subject of fierce intrigue." He also thought Ford's real resistance to a powerful chief of staff concerned Hartmann, who'd commandeered the small anteroom to the Oval Office where Rosemary Woods, Nixon's faithful secretary, had been stationed until the day before. Ford depended too heavily on Hartmann, owed him too much, and was too loyal to get rid of him, yet no strong chief of staff could tolerate having him bivouacked next to the president, popping his head in whenever he wanted.

Ford asked Haig to stay on to direct White House operations. Haig replied that he would remain only on the condition that Ford maintain the chief of staff system, but Ford was "very reluctant. He refused to commit to it," Jones recalls. "I believe Ford said, 'I can't do that,' and Haig said, 'I'll have to go then.' "

Ford regarded Haig as a "very well organized person who had pushed himself unbelievably hard" for Nixon. Although they hadn't discussed it, he assumed Nixon's departure "had taken a big load off his shoulders" and that Haig was "tired and wanted to return to the military as soon as possible." "Al," he told Haig, who rose to leave, "Bob Hartmann is someone I'll handle."

* * *

Ford's first official act was to address the cabinet, a group that as a whole represented both the strangeness and half-realized hopes of Nixon's aborted second term. Nixon's victory at the polls in 1972—forty-nine of fifty states, a sweep of the south, half the youth vote, *35 percent* of Democrats—was, NBC anchor John Chancellor said, the "most spectacular landslide election in the history of United States politics." At eleven the next morning, Nixon had met with his top officials and said, "I believe men exhaust themselves in government without realizing it. You are my first team, but today we start fresh for the next four years. We need new blood, fresh ideas . . . Bob, you take over." Haldeman then asked each of them to deliver a letter of resignation by the end of the day. Back in the Oval Office, Nixon similarly brushed aside complaints from Republicans that he didn't do enough to support local candidates. "Cut that off," he told Haldeman. "Make sure we start pissing on the party before they begin pissing on me. Blame bad candidates and sloppy organization."

Now, two years later, except for Kissinger, seated at Ford's right, the current cabinet secretaries were all recent arrivals whose entire tenure had been marred by Watergate and the resulting White House paralysis. Poised on Ford's left, sucking on a pipe, forty-five-year-old James Schlesinger had taken over as secretary of defense in July 1973, a year earlier. By then U.S. involvement in Vietnam—and American casualties— had been reduced dramatically enough for the military to look beyond Southeast Asia to the strategic challenges ahead, and Nixon had assigned Schlesinger, a professional weapons systems analyst and formerly his CIA director, a dual mission: (1) to rebuild the demoralized, top-heavy service branches and faltering volunteer system that Nixon had installed to replace the draft; and (2) to manage the nuclear arms race alongside Kissinger as détente progressed. A classmate of Kissinger's at Harvard, Schlesinger was blunt, salty-tongued, and iconoclastic, a fierce anticommunist hard-liner who gave Kissinger fits by coming to arms control meetings with scale models of U.S. and Soviet missiles that showed the Soviets ahead. A father of seven, he wore rumpled suits and scrawny ties and was incorrigibly indifferent to niceties.

Quietly taking a seat behind Ford's right shoulder, against the wall and in the line of the television cameras, was Rumsfeld, his trademark oversized aviator glasses removed for the picture-taking. Framed by the portly, owlish Kissinger and the casual, determinedly unfashionable Schlesinger, he appeared sharp and competent—a polished, well-inserted aide-de-camp.

After greeting the secretaries by name, Ford got down to business. He told them he didn't want and wouldn't accept any resignations. "We need continuity and stability," he said.

Again, the extreme difficulty, if not futility, of Ford's situation arose; the more he needed to reassure the country that the Nixon period was over and that he was his own man, the more he also needed to show that he could govern competently and effectively, which meant above all keeping the machinery of government in motion. The result was confusing to everyone.

As the cameras rolled, Kissinger took on the job of responding for the secretaries. "Mr. President," he said, slowly, funereally. "We wish to express our unflagging support and total loyalty to you."

After the meeting, Ford took Kissinger back to the Oval Office—their first chance to speak alone since the swearing-in. They had known each other, though not well, since the fifties, when Kissinger had invited Ford, then a member of the House Foreign Relations Committee, to address his graduate seminars at Harvard. Ford was enormously impressed with Kissinger's understanding of the U.S.-Soviet relationship and thought Nixon's selecting him as national security adviser was a "masterstroke." Ford told him that he was giving serious thought to repeating his pledge not to be a candidate in 1976, and he asked for Kissinger's view. Ford believed his credibility in Congress and beyond would be substantially strengthened if he made clear that his tough actions as president bore "no relation to my political future."

Kissinger paused, deliberated, and said: "Mr. President, in my judgment that would be a mistake. A very serious mistake, especially as it relates to foreign policy. It would mean that for more than two years foreign governments—both allies and adversaries—would know they were dealing with a lame-duck President, and therefore our foreign policy initiatives would be in a stalemate."

Again the dilemma—continuity or change—reared up on Ford, who read the dangers. "Henry was right," he wrote. "The moment I said I wasn't going to run, the succession struggle would start. That would be divisive in and of itself, and what the country needed was a period of stability." Ford could no more allow Republican rivals to count him out than climb out on a diplomatic dead limb. First he'd have to persuade Betty, who felt yesterday was the "saddest day of my life"—not simply for their friends the Nixons, but also because as a political wife she had suffered secretly with depression and addictions and was scared and conflicted "about what kind of First Lady I would be," she wrote. But as he and Kissinger left for his first meeting with the National Security Council back in the Cabinet Room, Ford began to realize that despite his public and private vows to leave Washington after serving out Nixon's term, if he hoped to be effective he had to be a candidate in 1976.

* * *

Back in the Cabinet Room, the national security team—Kissinger, Schlesinger, Scowcroft, and CIA director William Colby—updated Ford on a decision that couldn't be delayed.

The CIA was conducting a secret $500 million deep-sea recovery effort in the Pacific, where six years earlier a Soviet submarine with nuclear missiles on board had sunk in more than three miles of water. Analysts believed the sub was a rogue, possibly headed to launch an attack against Hawaii. The Pentagon had its own advanced deep-ocean technology and could have carried out the search itself in complete secrecy. But Kissinger and Nixon had opted instead for a CIA plan to license the project to a corporate front—germophobic billionaire Howard Hughes's Summa Corporation. The cover story, which Colby had managed to keep from leaking out only by feeding Watergate-related leads to the *Times*'s Seymour Hersh, throwing Hersh off the scent, was, as Colby put it, a "farout experiment by the secretive . . . Hughes in the possibility of mining manganese nodules from the depths of the vast Pacific."

Summa had built a giant ship three football fields long and twenty-three stories high—the *Glomar Explorer*—and crammed it with computer-operated equipment and huge cranes and winches that, in theory, could drop a clawed arm weighing 2,230 tons down through seventeen thousand feet of swirling ocean currents to grab hold of the sub and pull it back to the surface. A hallmark of Kissinger's approach to nuclear deter-

rence was the "communication of uncertainty"—keeping potential enemies off balance by letting them think you're capable of retaliating with
far more force than you have. Possessing a renegade Soviet sub would be
a rare prize in a business—arms control—that was notoriously weak in
verification, a chronic problem for Kissinger not only in his negotiations
with the Soviets but also in his battles with Schlesinger and other defense
hawks.

Since June, the *Glomar* had been on site, manned chiefly by hundreds
of unarmed roughnecks—civilians. An armed Soviet trawler hovered
around her, taking photographs, and there was mounting concern that its
sailors might attempt to board—a "serious complication," Ford realized.
Several days earlier the crew had laid its tethered arm directly over the
sub and a piece of the arm had smashed and broken off. Now Ford had
to decide whether to go ahead with the mission, risking a clash with the
Soviets for the sake of, as Kissinger suggested, an "intelligence coup." His
first head-to-head dealing with Brezhnev, the decision would test them
both.

Ford had his own apprehensions about the operation. To lend credence to the underwater research story, the navy had kept supporting
ships far from the *Glomar*. Ford recalled painfully last time the communists had seized a U.S. ship in international waters. In January 1968, the
same month as the tide-turning Tet offensive in Vietnam, North Korea
attacked a spy ship, the USS *Pueblo*, capturing the vessel, the crew, and
everything the crew didn't have time to destroy. The eighty-two crew-
men were held for eleven months until the United States apologized and
then were released—a powerful victory for maximum leader Kim Il
Sung. The *Glomar* was a sitting duck if the Soviets attacked, yet if Ford
delayed and ordered naval ships to the area, Moscow would no doubt do
the same.

Ford raised two main concerns. He asked Colby how long the Soviet
trawler had been there; Colby replied about two weeks. He also asked
him to assess the chances of success and the risk that the Soviets would
board, since it would take days to get a navy warship and escort group to

the spot. Ford felt the *Glomar* action was a "gamble," but he decided to order the salvage operation continued. "I was convinced," he recalled, "we had to take the risk, in terms of what we stood to gain."

* * *

Watergate Special Prosecutor Leon Jaworski, a sixty-eight-year-old Houston dealmaker and former president of the American Bar Association, reportedly was "stunned and upset" by terHorst's declaration that Ford opposed presidential clemency for Nixon. By resigning from office, Nixon had forfeited the legal and traditional immunities that had shielded him from criminal prosecution, civil suits, and subpoenas to appear at the trials of others. His new status as a private citizen raised unprecedented questions about his legal liabilities—questions that Jaworski, a long-time crony of Lyndon Johnson and the 1972 chairman of Texas Democrats for Nixon, hoped strenuously to avoid. Jaworski suspected Ford, who evidently was renouncing his authority to put an end to Nixon's most urgent worries, of attempting to pressure him into making the first move.

It had been Jaworski's predecessor, Archibald Cox—"that fucking Harvard professor," Nixon called him—who precipitated Nixon's collapse. In May 1973, fifteen months earlier, Nixon's attorney general, Elliot Richardson, had nominated Cox after Nixon's top aides, H. R. Haldeman and John Ehrlichman, were linked to Watergate and forced to resign. Five months later, when Cox and his staff of militant young lawyers persisted in court trying to obtain transcripts of secret White House tape recordings, Nixon ordered Richardson to fire him. Richardson and an assistant attorney general both refused, quitting instead in protest, and Nixon ordered his solicitor general, Robert Bork, to fire Cox, close down the special prosecution force, and seal its records—a constitutional nightmare, bureaucratic bloodbath, and political disaster that commentators instantly dubbed the "Saturday Night Massacre."

Under extreme pressure, Nixon relented, and Haig then recruited Jaworski to resume the prosecution, which had branched into an all-out investigation of the White House. With impeachment talk suddenly ablaze in Congress, Haig had guaranteed Jaworski full independence and unfettered access. Yet when Jaworski arrived in Washington, his senior staff, loyal to Cox and suspicious of Jaworski's ties to the White House, shunned him, refusing to meet him at the airport. Jaworski, as a young military lawyer after World War II, had prosecuted major Nazi war crimes trials, and he preferred to be called "the Colonel." He met regularly with Haig in private to discuss legal developments before they became public—a situation so worrisome to his staff that they resorted to having him followed. Still, lately he had felt a "galling frustration" knowing that Nixon "continually twisted the facts while I, who knew the truth, had to remain silent," he wrote.

On Wednesday, six days after Haig presented Ford with the various options for pardoning Nixon, Haig had slipped through the media cordon ringing the White House by driving himself home at lunchtime. Meanwhile, his top aide, Major George Joulwan, picked Jaworski up a half block from his hotel and brought him to Haig's house. Haig wanted to tell Jaworski in person that Nixon was resigning, that his papers and tapes would be shipped out to California later, and that Jaworski would have access to them as needed. "There's no hanky-panky involved," Haig had said. Jaworski had noted the strain in Haig's usually impassive face. "I don't mind telling you," he recalled Haig telling him, "that I haven't the slightest doubt that the tapes were screwed with. The ones with the gaps and other problems."

Since that meeting, Jaworski had agonized whether to bring Nixon to trial. Never had a president been charged with crimes committed in office, and Jaworski took no pleasure in being the first prosecutor in American history to have to decide whether to do so. He'd been dismayed when Nixon didn't make his situation any easier in his resignation speech, with its carefully lawyered acknowledgment only that some of his judgments on Watergate had been "wrong." Over lunch in Haig's dining room, Haig had told Jaworski that Congress would pass a resolution to halt any legal proceeding against Nixon after he left. "Not after that speech, Al," Jaworski thought. Nixon hadn't given Congress "even a crumb of remorse to chew on."

Jaworski worried that the decision he now faced—Haig had told him that Nixon would refuse to testify at the cover-up trial or "any other proceeding" and implied that he was coming apart mentally and physically—should not be left to a lone prosecutor unaccountable to voters. Whatever Washington and the country decided to do about Nixon's future ought to be consensual, he thought. Jaworski had no shortage of ego, but he believed firmly in the sanctity of the presidency. And yet, with lawmakers eager to wash their hands of Watergate, finish up with Nixon, and go home, that now left either him or Ford to proceed.

At the special prosecution force headquarters on K Street, a fortress-like warren of offices equipped with multiple top-secret security systems to prevent spying and leaks, Jaworski huddled with his senior staff, most of whom were in their thirties and had long been certain of Nixon's guilt. The Watergate cover-up trial of Haldeman, Ehrlichman, former attorney general John Mitchell, and three others was scheduled for September 9. Although that date now seemed unlikely, most trial team lawyers assumed Jaworski would favor trying Nixon together with his aides, if at all. They were troubled when he was reluctant at first to agree to a delay, interpreting his hesitation as an attempt to evade any decision to indict Nixon.

When Haig had first approached him about replacing Cox, the general had told Jaworski the country was "coming apart" and that the "only hope of stabilizing the situation" was for Nixon to announce that someone in whom the country has confidence had agreed to serve. "I'm putting the patriotic monkey on your back, Mr. Jaworski," Haig said.

Now, as the special force discussed how to go forward, the "issue of who should properly share in the Nixon prosecutive problem—to put it bluntly, who should shoulder the responsibility and take the heat—was bruited about in our office as the 'monkey problem,'" prosecutors Richard Ben-Veniste and George Frampton wrote. "On whose back was the monkey going to end up: the prosecutors, Congress, the White House, the grand jury, the court?"

* * *

Among Ford's inner circle, Benton Becker distrusted Haig as much as Hartmann. Becker was a thickset, thirty-six-year-old former Justice Department lawyer whom Ford had gotten to know while in Congress and who'd counseled Ford during his confirmation hearings for vice president. One day as they'd been preparing for Ford's House testimony, Haig had telephoned Ford, and Becker, sitting across the desk, realized that Haig was leaking details from Ford's confidential FBI background check. Alarmed, Becker got up, grabbed the phone from Ford, and lectured Haig, warning him against compromising his client. "I said, 'General, before these confirmation hearings are over I guarantee you somebody is going to ask Representative Ford about this investigation,'" Becker recalls. "'And when he's asked that question, he's going to say, truthfully, "No." We . . . don't . . . want . . . this . . . information.'" Within hours after Nixon announced he would step down, Hartmann had asked Becker to help with the presidential transition, and for the past thirty-six hours he'd been investigating "top to bottom" the security of Nixon's papers and tapes.

Nixon, like all presidents, claimed everything—46 million pieces of paper, plus 950 reels of tape, packed in carefully marked and taped boxes piled throughout the White House, the EOB, and other locations. Ford wanted nothing to do with the documents and so far had resisted any White House offer to see or hear them—to be drawn deeper into Nixon's legal morass. But Hartmann had heard that some of Nixon's staff members were stuffing more than the usual fill of documents into burn bags, and Becker discovered that the White House burn room, where the bags were chemically macerated, was overflowing, with cartons stacking up unattended in the hallway outside. Fearful of any perception that he might allow the destruction of Watergate-related records, Ford ordered his staff to safeguard all of Nixon's materials until White House lawyers could resolve their status.

At dusk, Becker left the EOB, the post–Civil War, cast-iron-and-granite former war department headquarters next to the White House, where he and the other Ford loyalists set up makeshift operations while Nixon's staffers remained entrenched in the West Wing. An army truck stood at the entrance, and soldiers were loading boxes that Becker had seen earlier among the Nixon materials he'd examined. Becker asked the colonel in charge what was going on and the officer replied that they were "taking them to Andrews [Air Force Base] and shipping them to San Clemente, to the president," Becker says.

"President Ford has issued an order to the effect that nothing leaves the White House for California," Becker instructed. "Are you aware of that?"

"I take my orders from General Haig," the colonel said.

Becker had no official status—he had abruptly taken a leave from his Washington law practice and was volunteering his services—but he strode to the security gate, told the guards not to allow the truck to leave the grounds, then walked to the White House and upstairs to the Oval Office. The president was "really angry about it," he recalls. Ford called in and confronted Haig, who denied knowing anything about the shipment. "Haig adopted President Ford's indignation," Becker says. "President Ford's indignation was directed at Al Haig; Al Haig's indignation was directed at this poor colonel who, presumably, on his own decided to do this."

Whatever the truth—it's possible that another high-ranking officer loyal to Nixon had ordered the transfer—Becker's decision to interdict it on his own dubious authority, and Ford's to support him, put in play the *history* of the most secretive yet obsessively documented of all U.S. administrations. Barely one day after the Nixon White House went down in ruins, the struggle over Nixon's legacy was joined.

Gerald Ford, who hoped to escape any involvement, was not—and would not be—let go. Having assumed unwanted custody of Nixon's papers and tapes, he returned for the night to 514 Crown View Drive in Alexandria, where throughout the day the Secret Service had cordoned off the entire block and military helicopters now patrolled the black suburban airspace.

D A Y

3

Sunday, August 11

The Prize

Following a three-minute motorcade to church, the Fords prayed for courage and guidance. "We go to Immanuel-on-the-Hill in Alexandria," Betty wrote in a diary, "where we've been going for twenty-some years. There aren't going to be any more private services in the East Room for a select few." As always during a crisis, the president included among his prayers a favorite verse from Proverbs: *Trust in the Lord with all thine heart and lean not into thine own understanding.* Ford, an Episcopalian, in times of stress also consulted the Reverend Billy Zeoli, who produced and sold evangelical films and who like Ford was closely connected to Amway, the Grand Rapids–based cleaning- and household-products distribution empire. On the day that Spiro Agnew resigned, Zeoli later told an Amway Free Enterprise Day rally, "I said, 'Jerry, I believe you're God's man to be Vice President of the United States.' Two days later he was Vice President of the United States. So we went there and had Bible study and prayer."

Speculation about Ford's choice for vice president preoccupied official Washington, but no one who believed a candidate was "God's man" would say so aloud. Religion had vanished from national politics shortly after 1960, when John F. Kennedy, a Roman Catholic, beat Nixon, and a public official's relationship with a deity was considered private, like his sex life. As a moral force along the coasts and especially on campuses, the religious right had been eclipsed during the Cold War and Vietnam by the religious left, led by figures like Yale's William Sloane Coffin, who attacked privilege and injustice and counseled peace, tolerance, and nonviolent resistance.

What was certain was that Ford faced an urgent decision that arguably would affect the course of the battered, fractious GOP after Vietnam and Watergate more than anything else he might do in office. The Twenty-fifth Amendment, ratified in 1965 after Johnson served for fourteen months without a second-in-command following Kennedy's murder, required Ford to nominate a vice president; currently, Democratic House Speaker Carl Albert was next in line for succession. In selecting his vice president, Ford not only would be anointing an heir apparent, by picking the party's presumptive nominee for 1976; he also would choose someone with whom he thought he could win if, as now seemed inevitable, he ended up leading the ticket himself.

If not for Watergate, Nixon would have chosen former Democratic Texas governor John Connally instead of Ford to replace Agnew—to position Connally for the '76 Republican nomination. ("Nixon wasn't a Republican," counsel Leonard Garment recalls. "Nixon was a Nixonian.") Nixon held grand visions in his second term of a historic political realignment, on the order of the New Deal coalition that had been all but unbreakable since the thirties, and he wanted Connally, whom he admired more than anyone else in American politics, to lead it forward. The problem: Connally, Nixon's treasury secretary, was under investigation in connection with a secret Nixon campaign fund, and, as a turncoat Democrat, he had enemies on both sides of the aisle.

Ford arrived at the White House before noon and summoned his closest ally and strategist during his rise in Congress, former Wisconsin representative Melvin Laird. Bullet-headed and bluff, Laird had been Nixon's first secretary of defense and the chief architect of "Vietnamization"—the gradual withdrawal of U.S. forces, leaving South Vietnam to fight its own war with the North—and he had instituted Nixon's all-volunteer army. When Haig took over as Nixon's chief of staff, Ford and other congressional Republicans recognized that the former general was unlikely to have much political skill, clout, or judgment, and they had pressed Laird and veteran presidential adviser Bryce Harlow to return to the West Wing as Nixon's conduits to the party leadership and Capitol Hill. Before Laird would take the job as special counselor, he made Nixon sign a letter saying he wasn't involved in the Watergate cover-up—"to show my wife," he recalls.

It was Laird and Harlow who'd pushed Nixon to select Ford for vice president. Although better-known names were rumored—former New York governor Nelson Rockefeller, lame-duck California governor Ronald Reagan, Senate Watergate Committee co-chair Howard Baker, Senate Minority Leader Hugh Scott, Goldwater, Connally, Richardson, Bush, and Laird himself, among others—Nixon's ultimate constituency had shrunk drastically. If he was to survive in office, he needed to head off an impeachment vote by the House Judiciary Committee, and Ford, whom the White House used and often mistreated as an errand boy in Congress, was popular among the Republicans on the panel. Nixon had already done the math: He instructed Laird to phone Ford at home and sound him out. Laird says, "I said, 'Jerry, you're going to get a call from Al Haig. I don't want any bullshit from you. Don't hesitate. Don't talk to Betty. Say yes.' " Two days later, after Ford promised not to be a candidate for president in 1976, clearing the way for Connally, Nixon announced the nomination.

Ford now told Laird, who eventually had resigned his position as White House aide when he realized Nixon was guilty and jumped to a senior post at *Reader's Digest*, that he wanted him and Harlow to conduct the search for a vice president, someone to serve not as a fellow caretaker but as a strong, capable leader in his own right—a more than likely ticket-mate in two years. Other than Nixon's self-destruction and exile and his own surprising elevation, little about Gerald Ford's Washington had changed, especially the electoral calculus. The postwar bipartisan consensus that America was obligated to lead, but shouldn't try to dominate, world affairs, and that government programs were required at home to help correct social problems, remained intact. The Democrats, battered and divided themselves, still controlled Congress, but after Nixon's landslide no strong front runner had emerged for the presidency. Incumbency helped in winning elections, but not overwhelmingly.

Ford, a staunch Republican loyalist, marveled at the constitutional trap that befell him—an unelected president from a minority party choosing an unelected vice president requiring the approval of the opposition. Above all, he understood, the situation required him to think big, bigger than party and ideological needs, bigger than his own future.

* * *

Harlow arrived at the Oval Office just as Laird left to start making phone calls. In and out of government for the past two and a half decades, Harlow was a behind-the-scenes Washington icon—"Mr. Integrity"—and Ford thought he had "more common sense and political perception than anyone I know." Officially, he was chief lobbyist for household products giant Procter and Gamble, but when Hartmann and Marsh a week ago had become alarmed over the pardon document Haig had shown Ford, they'd at once contacted Harlow. Short and solemn-faced, Harlow warned Ford that it was "inconceivable that [Haig] wasn't carrying out a mission for the President" but that Nixon "knows he must be able to swear under oath that he never discussed this with you and you must be able to swear that you never discussed it with him." Following Harlow's advice, Ford had promptly set out to ensure that there were "no ambiguities." He wrote down in longhand what he wanted to say to Haig, then called Haig in Harlow's presence and read it, slowly: "I want you to understand . . . that nothing we talked about yesterday afternoon should be given any consideration in whatever decision the President may wish to make," Ford said. "You're right," Haig answered.

Now Ford asked Harlow to gather a list of vice presidential names, ranked according to three main criteria: national stature, executive experience, and the ability to "broaden my political base." Harlow, who'd advised every president since Eisenhower, both Republicans and Democrats, left the meeting with the understanding that Ford had begun to recast his presidency.

* * *

"Deep down inside I think maybe it should work this time," George H. W. Bush wrote in his diary. "I have that inner feeling that it will finally abort. I hope not. Another defeat in this line is going to be tough but then it is awful egotistical to think I should be selected."

An aide to Ford had asked Bush to meet with the president at three o'clock to discuss the vice presidency, one in a series of meetings with important Republicans scheduled throughout the afternoon. Bush tried to steady himself. Since Thursday, he'd quietly assembled a team to send out telegrams to national committee members, soliciting "input" as to Bush's chances. He had wanted the vice presidency badly when Agnew resigned, but with Connally, a much larger figure in Texas politics, in the running, he'd been in no position to pursue it. Ford warned that he wanted no campaigning, but Bush knew party members would be lining up early this time, and he was determined to be—and be perceived as—deep in contention.

In 1970, Texas voters had dynamited Bush's path to high office—or so it had seemed. Nixon had induced him, at age forty-six, to drop his safe seat in the House of Representatives to make a Senate run, and Bush lost, notably for a second time. "I'm looking introvertedly," he wrote in his journal, "and I don't like what I see. I must have done something wrong." His future clouded, unable to succeed in the arena of the paramount figure in his life, his father, who'd helped smooth Nixon's early career in the Senate and who played golf with Eisenhower, Bush returned to Washington deeply dispirited and uncertain of his future.

Nixon rescued him from political oblivion by appointing him ambassador to the United Nations, despite his having no experience in foreign policy. He and his wife Barbara—Bar—plunged into a life of diplomacy and regal entertaining in New York. China was then the most divisive issue facing the UN, and Kissinger, backed by Nixon, thwarted and humiliated Bush in his most crucial vote there. As Bush crusaded to keep Taiwan's seat when Red China was admitted, Kissinger secretly was traveling to Beijing and winking to allies that whatever Bush said in the General Assembly, the United States wouldn't punish them for voting with the communists.

Despite the betrayal, Bush remained loyal and Nixon promoted him, appointing him to lead the Republican Party, and providing a small, plum office near his own EOB hideaway. No national figure worked harder than Bush to defend Nixon in public during Watergate, but as it dawned on him that Nixon was covering up, he became both furious and miserable. In July, he'd concluded a bitter letter to his four sons: "I expect it has not been easy for you to have your dad be head of the RNC at this time. I know your peers must put you in a funny position at times by little words in jest that don't seem funny or by saying things that hurt you because of your family loyalty."

Bush was right: By now his sons had begun to pay a price for his failed ambitions and his loyalties, and he worried especially about his eldest, twenty-nine-year-old George W.—Junior to the family. On a night twenty months earlier, George W. had taken his fifteen-year-old brother, Marvin, to a friend's house, where they'd both drunk too much; on the drive home George W. had struck and dragged a metal garbage can down the street. "I hear you're looking for me," he shouted at his father from the driveway. "You want to go mano a mano right here?"

Now George W., who had avoided service in Vietnam by flying air national guard jets over Texas and Alabama, was trying to straighten out his life and get some career traction at what he liked to call the "West Point of Capitalism"—Harvard Business School. On the night Nixon resigned, a cheering, flag-waving throng of two thousand celebrants snake-danced through Harvard Square, blocking traffic a few blocks from Bush's apartment in a triple-decker. George W. avoided the "heaviness," as he called it, of Vietnam and Watergate by blaming the liberal culture of the sixties; classmates remember him as not saying much during class, except to challenge the New Deal. At home, he listened over and over to Johnny Rodriguez records, drinking Wild Turkey, while his peers stood in line for Bruce Springsteen, yet to release his third album, at Joe's Place, where the opening act was the unofficial house band Peter Johnson and the Manic Depressives. But neither he nor his father was immune to the fact that many people at Harvard, where he wore cowboy boots and a national guard bomber jacket and carried a spit cup to class for tobacco, knew about his family and found his pose laughable.

* * *

Nixon spent the morning of his third day in exile reading and rallying old California allies by phone from the turret-shaped den on the second floor of La Casa Pacifica, overlooking miles of shore break. "You don't realize until too late who your real friends are," he told Bob Finch, whom he'd ignored, then fired, as secretary of health, education and welfare. He called Herb Klein, his former director of communications, to apologize for what he'd said on one of the newly released tapes—that Klein "doesn't have his head screwed on right." Shortly before lunch, Patricia Hitt, national cochair of his 1968 campaign, visited briefly on Pat's suggestion. She found Nixon sluggish and worn out: rambling, albeit in good spirits, not bitter.

As he never tired of telling the world, Nixon thrived on crises. The crisis before him in the days and months ahead, the greatest of his life, wasn't the grandeur of his defeat and disgrace, nor that his "enemies," as he viewed all political opponents, still wanted to destroy him. It was that he'd lost his throne, his clout. "As president, even after I had been crippled by Watergate, I could still set the agenda to an extent," he later wrote. "But now without the powers of office I was utterly defenseless."

Ron Ziegler, now Nixon's de facto chief of staff, managed his isolation. Ziegler was a pugnacious, hard-charging former high school football star who after graduating from USC had gone to work as a jungle tour guide at Disneyland, and who could still recite his spiel from that job, forward and backward. As Nixon's "face" during Watergate, he had confronted a press in full roar as it discovered it was mightier even than the president. Like Nixon, Ziegler disdained reporters and took no pains to conceal it. His daily press briefings had "resembled a substitute teacher facing down a roomful of teenagers," historian David Greenberg wrote.

After Haldeman and Ehrlichman resigned in April 1973, Ziegler had joined Haig in manning the wall around Nixon: his new "Germans." While Haig ran the White House and managed Nixon's defense, Ziegler became his chief confidant and enforcer. After Nixon famously shoved him into a crowd of reporters in New Orleans after the Saturday Night Massacre, telling Ziegler to "get rid of them," Ziegler handed over the briefings to his deputy and focused on being Nixon's chief propagandist and keeper of his image, even as he understood the presidency was lost.

Since arriving in San Clemente, Ziegler had stationed himself a few hundred yards away in the warren of prefabricated buildings that had been the operations center of the Western White House, guarding access to Nixon as ferociously as Haldeman and Haig had. Late in the afternoon, Bill Gulley, director of the White House military office, arrived in a rented car, alone, and went straight to see him. The Pentagon presence in the White House is downplayed, but from operating the fleet of White House aircraft, to managing Camp David, to handling logistics and communications during trips, a ready force of several thousand officers and soldiers is available to do, as Gulley later wrote, "anything the president wanted, discreetly."

For instance, when Kissinger, who like Nixon fetishized secrecy, was still solely national security adviser, he had met covertly outside Paris with North Vietnamese negotiators while formal talks bogged down for eighteen months over the shape of the negotiating table. Gulley coordinated Kissinger's trips. Drawing from an off-the-books account, he arranged for Kissinger to be flown in and out of an old airfield 120 miles from the city by a pilot and crew who "wouldn't talk," filed international flight plans, complied with all immigration and customs regulations, and when Kissinger landed back at Andrews provided a Jet Star from the presidential fleet to fly him to New York so that he could be "seen by the Press wining and dining some beautiful woman"—all while maintaining such stealth that for months Defense Secretary Laird, with overall responsibility for fighting the war and his own special urgency about knowing what Kissinger was up to, didn't know what Kissinger was doing.

While Nixon had been bidding the staff farewell in the East Room last Friday, Gulley had collected a dozen cartons from the family residence. Amid Nixon's evacuation from the White House and flight to exile, which Gulley directed, his son got married, so he'd delayed bringing the boxes west. From the weight of them, Gulley, who also served Johnson and would serve Ford, assumed they contained documents that Nixon wanted hand-delivered.

Gulley, without mentioning the cartons, told Ziegler it was urgent that he see Nixon personally—to give him something. Ziegler said no, Nixon wasn't taking any calls. Gulley then went to Nixon's military aide, marine colonel Jack Brennan, and his appointments secretary, Steve Bull, who personally had collected the items on Nixon's Oval Office desk—his reading glasses, a picture of his daughters—and placed them on his desk in San Clemente, exactly as in Washington. They looked shell-shocked, he thought.

Gulley told Brennan and Bull about the cartons and what he suspected they contained. Before he left Washington, he'd consulted frequently with both Haig and Marsh, who worried chiefly that news would leak of his mission. Indeed, though part of Gulley's job was to serve as a go-between for the White House and former presidents, word of *any* official contact between the Ford Administration and Nixon would instantly arouse toxic speculation in the press. Gulley thought both Haig and Marsh were "dithering," and that while they "fussed" the situation had grown more pressing. What worried *him*, he told Nixon's aides, was the "shitload" of other materials not just at the White House and the EOB but at a government warehouse in Virginia.

Brennan and Bull shared his concern. As long as confusion over the decision-making structure at the White House persisted, the door remained open, albeit slightly. Once Ford consolidated control—once the Hobson's choice regarding Nixon's papers overtook him—he would halt any more shipments. Bull scheduled Gulley to meet with Nixon the next morning. Immediately after that, Gulley agreed, he would return to Washington and direct the remainder of the materials flown to California as soon as possible.

Monday, August 12

"I'm a Ford, not a Lincoln"

Benton Becker hadn't been the only one alarmed by the sight of soldiers hoisting boxes onto an army truck outside the EOB on a Saturday night. A reporter, on a tip, phoned press secretary Jerry terHorst to ask about it, and terHorst had consulted Haig's office. TerHorst couldn't reach Haig directly but recalls being told "nothing was leaving the White House without the president's OK." He wasn't informed of the unit's mission or Becker's interdiction.

Now, at noon, terHorst briefed the press, among whom he'd sat just days earlier sharing their "terribly bitter attitude" toward the person standing on his side of the rostrum. He intended to disarm them with candor, saying only, precisely, what he knew. Although he'd invited Ziegler's deputy Gerald Warren to stay on, terHorst arranged for Warren to steer clear of reporters, preferring to answer their questions himself.

Peter Lisagor, veteran special correspondent for the *Chicago Daily News* and a friend of terHorst's, started: Was there anything new on the status of Nixon's presidential materials? When Ford had first introduced terHorst, who was five feet five inches tall, to the press gaggle after his swearing-in, Lisagor had shouted, "Could you hold him up so that we can see him?" After years of docile frustration under Nixon, he and most other White House reporters tacitly agreed for now to remain amiable but feisty.

TerHorst told Lisagor the lawyers were still studying the question. He couldn't specify whether that meant Buzhardt and James St. Clair—Nixon's lawyers—or attorneys at the Justice Department.

"Are the papers and documents, as far as you know, still intact?" Lisagor followed up.

TerHorst said they were.

"Jerry," another reporter asked, "was former president Nixon blocked from taking the tapes out of storage here?"

TerHorst repeated what he knew: "No disposition nor movement of them has occurred."

TerHorst was "winging it"—all of Ford's people were, he thought—but he believed he had an advantage in knowing Ford's political instincts better than most of them. He recalls riding in the backseat of Ford's green Pontiac as a young reporter for the *Detroit News* covering Ford's first House campaign in 1948, listening to Ford and his campaign manager Jack Stiles discuss whether he should marry Betty, a department store model and former Martha Graham company member who'd divorced her first husband, before or after the primary. Grand Rapids and the surrounding farm communities where terHorst grew up were deeply religious and conservative, the buckle of the upper Midwest Bible Belt, and Ford worried he'd lose support either way. When the *News* sent terHorst to Washington in the late fifties, his wife and Betty babysat each other's kids. More recently, after Ford became vice president, terHorst, as the only Washington reporter who'd followed his career intimately, had contracted to write a biography of him, now nearly done. "I supported spokes-on-a-wheel," he explains. "I was one of the spokes."

"Has the president been in contact with the former president since Friday?" another reporter asked.

TerHorst recognized that Nixon, not Ford, was and would remain for some time the most compelling story in Washington. A press corps forged in the crucible of Watergate, whose members saw Nixon as an antihero deep in his own self-destruction, and who'd been systematically manipulated, misled, and punished by Ziegler and his staff, would not simply let go. TerHorst told the truth: He didn't know of any contact with San Clemente but hadn't asked Ford the question directly.

The "inquisition," as Hartmann called it, ground on: twenty-one questions in all about the custody of Nixon's tapes, their legal status, and possible secret dealings with Nixon in California. Reporters had spotted Attorney General William Saxbe earlier that morning in the West Wing. Question: Had he spoken with Ford?

TerHorst said no, that he thought Saxbe had met with Haig. What about? TerHorst didn't know. Well, could he specifically rule out the possibility that Haig and Saxbe met at Nixon's request? Again terHorst said he didn't know but would ask.

Newsday's Martin Schram asked the next question. Three years earlier, Schram had helped investigate the business dealings of Nixon's close friend and benefactor Bebe Rebozo, a South Florida banker who had arranged and bankrolled not just the purchase of the Western White House but a beachfront compound abutting his own in Key Biscayne— the Southern White House, also called the Winter White House. The six-part series had won the Long Island daily a Pulitzer Prize. From then on, Ziegler, as press chronicler Timothy Crouse wrote, "acted as if Schram did not exist." He all but refused to talk to him, barely acknowledging his questions at briefings. When Schram made an appointment to discuss the matter with him, Ziegler had made him wait all afternoon, then left by a back door without seeing him.

"Jerry," Schram asked, "does President Nixon still have any mechanism of contacting staff members back here and asking them to do one favor or another for him . . . and if so, can you tell us how that works?"

TerHorst recognized the damaging implications but again told the truth.

"There obviously," he said, "is continuing liaison between the former president and the present one, and the essential mechanism [for] that is of course Ron Ziegler and Steve Bull and Gerry Warren and anyone else to whom former president Nixon would care to talk."

* * *

Driving into the Nixon compound in California was an "eerie experience," Gulley later said, like boarding an abandoned ship. There was no guard at the gate and only two cars in the parking lot, not forty or more as when the buildings "had been a direct extension of the White House, with the same aura of importance, of powerful things happening." Like the darkened ballroom at the San Clemente Inn, where Gulley was staying, which had housed the press when Nixon was here, the place seemed desolate and deserted.

Nixon wore a suit and tie and was sitting in his office when Gulley arrived. He rose, and Gulley observed that he was "having trouble" with his leg. That June, two months earlier, Nixon had suffered a painful attack of phlebitis, an inflamed vein, during a trip to the Middle East. His left leg swelled to almost twice the size of his right, and his doctor, worried that a blood clot would form, break loose, and travel to his lungs, ordered him to wrap his leg in hot towels and stay off his feet as much as he could. But the trip for Nixon was irresistible—if not in the end the antidote to Watergate that he hoped, then a crowning international triumph, one of his greatest, he believed. Nothing could keep him off his feet.

A million people had lined the streets in Cairo, many chanting "Nikson! Nik-son!" as he and Egyptian president Anwar Sadat, who less than two years earlier had been solidly in the Soviet camp, stood proudly side by side in the back of a limousine. Their promising new relationship had grown directly out of détente and Washington's nuanced—and fractious—handling of the 1973 October War, which began with Egypt and Syria launching a withering surprise attack on Israel on the high holiday of Yom Kippur, and ended with Israel, assisted by a massive U.S. military airlift, winning the conflict, but not overwhelmingly so. For thirty-two days in the war's aftermath, with the world media tracking his every takeoff and landing, Kissinger had shuttled by jet between Tel Aviv and Damascus, negotiating a series of military disengagements along the Israeli-Syrian border. Despite stern rhetoric from the right, Nixon was at the height of his power and influence in the crucial region, rapidly restoring U.S. influence and prestige out of the still-smoldering wreckage of Vietnam. Though he limped noticeably, he stood beaming beside Sadat for long hours in the hundred-degree heat, ceremony after ceremony.

Nixon remained standing now. So, accordingly, did Gulley. "He was tense, strung out, demanding and combative," Gulley recalled. "He looked as if he hadn't slept; his eyes looked as though he hadn't rested in days—and I don't think he had his head together." Rumors about Nixon's declining health and state of mind, including reports of heavy drinking, were circulating furiously, and Gulley wasn't surprised that he seemed to be taking a sharp downturn.

Curt and direct, Nixon was primarily interested in his "entitlements." " 'Look,' he said," Gulley recounted in a book, *Breaking Cover,* " 'I'm entitled to anything that any other former President is entitled to. Goddamn, you know what I did for Johnson, and you know I did things for Ike and Truman, and goddamn it, I expect to be treated the same way. When I travel I expect military aircraft; I expect the same support I provided. I expect communications and medical personnel, everything they had. And goddamn it, you tell Ford I expect it.' "

Gulley, shaken, expected Nixon to show some understanding of Ford's situation, but Nixon forged on. He asked if Gulley knew what Ford was planning to do about his papers and tapes. Gulley answered that he didn't; all he knew was that as official White House liaison to former presidents, he would serve as go-between.

"Well, you tell those bastards that I'm going to keep my mouth shut," Nixon said. "I'm not going to be talking to the press. I'm not going to be making comments about Ford or the administration, but goddamn it, I want them to know I'm here. And I want them to know that there are certain things I expect from them. Briefing papers. Certain treatment."

Still standing fifteen minutes later, Nixon dismissed Gulley, coolly asking, "Is it going to present a problem for you, working with me?" Gulley, due to return to Washington, told him it wouldn't.

* * *

In the polished marble hallways and smoky, mahogany-paneled offices of the Capitol, Watergate and Nixon's unraveling had hit with earthquake force. Democrats controlled Congress with two-to-one majorities in both houses, were winning more races than ever, and still held the South. But the Nixon landslide over George McGovern had splintered the national party, already at war with itself over Vietnam, as well as over race, class, age, region, and, most recently with the rise of feminism, sex. Alabama governor George Wallace, a segregationist who'd won several northern primaries in 1972 and was angling to run again, was pulling the party rightward, but left liberals abhorred him. Senator Henry "Scoop" Jackson, a hawkish critic of détente, badly wanted the nomination, but he, too, had alienated the left. Among liberals, the biggest names, Hubert Humphrey and Ted Kennedy, were out. The stalemate offered an opening for a fresh face.

In his own caucus, Ford had been a down-the-line party man and strong conservative, rating 83 percent from the right-wing Americans for Constitutional Action and zero from its liberal counterpart, Americans for Democratic Action. He'd strongly supported all military spending requests and opposed federal welfare programs and Medicare. His positions were consistently pro-business, anti-union. He supported the major civil rights bills of the sixties but reluctantly and only after it was clear they would pass. On foreign policy, his internationalism and commitment to détente made him a moderate, more in the establishment mold of Scranton and Rockefeller than westerners Goldwater and Reagan.

Beyond the party infighting, Congress's aggregate might as a branch of government, which had risen and swelled with the War Powers Act of November 1973, enabling Congress to restrict a president's authority to make war indefinitely on his own, had crested with Nixon's removal and Ford's ascension. As Speaker Albert observed: "We gave Nixon no choice but Ford. Congress made Jerry Ford president."

Ford's motorcade arrived at the carriage entrance of the House side of the building at 8:45 P.M. The halls were mobbed with people reaching out to him. He was escorted to the speaker's office, where he shook hands warmly with the leaders of both parties. As he walked ahead of them into the packed House chamber, Ford was understandably moved, although, as the author Jimmy Breslin wrote, much of what might have felt like affection and admiration was simply exhaustion and gratitude:

> When the doors swung open and everybody in the chamber saw that it was not Richard Nixon walking in, the cheers that went up around me on the floor were merely perfunctory when matched with the feeling of relief, a feeling so intense that it could be felt, almost heard, as it rose from their chests and shoulders to leave them free of Nixon and all the name meant to their careers and their country. Oh, they liked Jerry Ford very much. He had been one of them; his success might mean their success. But for anybody who was standing up with the crowd, watching, listening, feeling, it was obvious that these men, who are in politics for a living, would have cheered for anybody.

Ford stood at the rostrum, under blazing television lights, acknowledging the thunderous applause, and seeking out familiar faces—down below, in front of him, the Supreme Court justices, the cabinet, the diplomatic corps, Hartmann, Marsh, and Haig; up in the gallery, Betty and the children, and Julie and David Eisenhower, looking pained. The men, and the few women, who were responsible for expunging Richard Nixon wanted nothing more now than to push him as far out of mind as possible. Ford, from a text crafted by a speechwriter and punched up by Hartmann, implicitly used his first prime-time speech to the nation to convince them he'd do everything to help the country forget the Nixon era.

"I do not want a honeymoon with you," he told Congress. "I want a good marriage."

Neither inaugural address nor state of the union, the speech needed to serve as both, and it gave Ford his first chance to tell the country what he planned to do to move ahead.

Gone, rhetorically, was partisanship. "The first specific request by the Ford administration is not to Congress but to the voters in the upcoming November election," he said. "It is this: Support your candidates, congressmen and senators, Democrats or Republicans, conservative or liberal, who consistently vote for tough decisions to cut the cost of government, restrain federal spending, and bring inflation under control."

Buried—with just Nixon's daughter and son-in-law to mourn him in the crowd—was Nixon. "There will be no illegal tappings, eavesdropping, buggings, or break-ins by my administration," Ford swore. "There will be hot pursuit of tough laws to prevent illegal invasions of privacy in both government and private activities."

Ford proposed a domestic "summit meeting" to attack inflation and pledged "continuity" in foreign policy—popular positions on both sides of the aisle. Other vice presidents before him, like Truman and Johnson, who abruptly became president in times of grave crisis, "have buried their predecessors and then gone on to reassure the people by wrapping themselves in the mantle of the men they followed," he wrote. "At the time of *his* departure, Nixon had no mantle left." Undaunted, and interrupted thirty times by applause, Ford now stitched together a new one: "the mantle of the Presidential center," the *Post*'s Lou Cannon wrote.

"I once told you that I am not a saint," Ford said near the end of his speech, returning his gaze to his former colleagues, "and I hope never to see the day that I cannot admit having made a mistake. So I will close with another confession.

"Frequently along the tortuous road of recent months, from this chamber to the President's house, I protested that I was my own man.

"Now I realize that I was wrong.

"I am your man, for it was your carefully weighed confirmation that changed my profession.

"I am the people's man, for you acted in their name . . .

"To the limits of my strength and ability," Ford pledged, "I will be the President of the black, brown, red, and white Americans, of old and young, of women's liberationists and male chauvinists and all the rest of us in between, of the poor and the rich, of the native sons and new refugees, of those who work at lathes or at desks, or at mines or in the fields, and of Christians, Jews, Moslems, Buddhists and atheists, if there really are any atheists left after what we have all been through."

* * *

Nixon, after an afternoon drive with Rebozo and a beach outing at the private oceanfront at Camp Pendleton, watched the address on TV with his family, then wired Ford his congratulations on a "splendid speech."

Ford knew he had done well. He had tried to "project a calmness, and a steady hand." A president, he believed, "has to go to the people with one hand and pull Congress by the other. He can't get Congress to move unless he has the people with him."

It would take time to know what the "people" thought—leading pollster George Gallup, for example, with strong ties to Republicans and an old college friend of Rumsfeld, usually needed more than a week to gauge public opinion. But the TV network commentators, the country's most powerful voices of opinion, witnessed Ford's steady delivery, and the wild reception he received, and were all but euphoric.

"A lot of people who would a year ago have regarded Gerald Ford lightly at the least . . . are surprised how easy it is to give this man the benefit of the doubt," ABC's Harry Reasoner exulted. "Mr. Ford has been on the minority side of a great many political issues all through his time in Congress. And unless his capacity for growth is as large as some of us think it is, he will be in the minority as president. But the feeling is very different, isn't it? The old saying may be being demonstrated again—that God takes care of fools, drunkards, and the United States."

As Ford set to work at eight o'clock on the first official business day of his presidency, he found his capacity for growth tested in all directions at once. The president isn't just the nation's chief executive, but also its head of state, commander in chief of the armed forces, and leader of his political party, and Ford had previously managed only a minority legislative caucus and his own office of a few dozen people. Meanwhile, Watergate had paralyzed Washington for more than a year, and Ford had assumed office, as Kissinger wrote, facing the most tortuous gamut of foreign policy challenges of any president since Truman, and the most "uncongenial domestic environment" of any since Lincoln.

Scowcroft briefed him on intelligence, including an update on the *Glomar Explorer*. The ship's crew had draped the octopus-like arm over the conning tower of the Soviet submarine, securing and lifting it from the seabed. But as they reeled the five thousand tons of waterlogged steel to the surface, the sub ripped apart from the force—scattering to the depths the missiles, codes, transmitters, and everything else of value. The CIA raised just the boat's nose, and the ship left the area unmolested.

Brezhnev hadn't taken a run at Ford, but he had ample other spots to choose from.

More urgent was an unfolding crisis in Cyprus. In July, a Greek military junta had engineered a coup on the Mediterranean island, where ancient ethnic rivalries between Greeks and Turks had neared the breaking point for more than a decade. The junta installed as president a former guerrilla leader who called for enosis—unification with Greece. Kissinger, distracted by Watergate and with no good options, initially cabled both capitals that the United States rejected enosis, and he warned away the Soviets. Beyond that, the U.S. position, oddly aloof given the dangers to the Western alliance and international stability, supported the junta—until it was ousted eight days after the coup.

"The overwhelming concern," Kissinger wrote, was to prevent a war "between two NATO allies that would destroy the Alliance's eastern flank and open the way to Soviet penetration of the Mediterranean."

Turkey had reacted to Washington's pro-junta stance by invading Cyprus and pushing far inland. Yet as Greece mobilized its forces, Washington's position shifted. The United States regarded Turkey as far more important to the western alliance and adopted a more pro-Ankara line. On July 22, a day before the release of the White House tapes, the countries agreed to a cease-fire while their diplomats tried to negotiate a settlement in Geneva, urged on by the United States, Britain, and the UN.

On Saturday morning, Kissinger had told Ford in his first full national security briefing: "We're having some developments on Cyprus." The Geneva talks were continuing, the cease-fire holding—barely. Kissinger said Turkey now controlled 15 percent of Cyprus but might try to grab more. "I have talked to the prime minister of Turkey," he reported. "He was a student of mine, and I have told him that we could not—really in the first forty-eight hours of your term in office—be very relaxed about unilateral military action." "We sure can't," Ford had said.

Now Kissinger discussed the diplomatic state of play, putting ideas to Ford, who puffed on his pipe, listened, and nodded his support. The ideas would be sketched later into a State Department statement supporting greater autonomy for the Turkish community in Cyprus while warning that the "avenues of diplomacy have not been exhausted and therefore the US would consider a resort to military action unjustified."

That Ford was a neophyte in foreign policy went without saying, and Kissinger had wasted no time extending his sweeping authority. He'd drafted a memo for Ford that guaranteed him supremacy in foreign affairs by putting the National Security Council in charge of all decision making. Kissinger, as under Nixon, chaired all top-level meetings: If Schlesinger or the Joint Chiefs wanted to advise the president, they had to go through Kissinger. As *Newsweek* reported: "While Kissinger cleared each move with the new President, Ford's essential reaction was to listen and say, 'That's a good tack, Henry,' and even, once, a familiar 'Make that perfectly clear.' "

Ford's main concern was Congress, where the sentiment favored Greece. "Instead of blaming the former Greek government for starting the incident," Ford recalled, "Congress moved to embargo delivery of American arms to Turkey." Healing rhetoric and warm handshakes aside, Ford knew that Congress, with its recently gained upper hand in foreign policy, would oppose—even overrule—him if he tilted too far toward Ankara. "They didn't want to know the facts; they simply wanted to punish the Turks."

Kissinger stayed for an hour and a half, going over the week's schedule. Ford had planned to ease into foreign policy under Kissinger's tutelage, including a special fifteen-minute report each day on a new issue. But he faced a rapid-fire round of meetings within the next seventy-two hours with Soviet ambassador Anatoly Dobrynin, Egypt's foreign minister Ismail Fahmy, and Jordan's King Hussein, for whom he and Betty would host their first state dinner in the East Room on Friday night. He counted himself fortunate to have Kissinger, who had strong relationships with all three, to guide him through.

* * *

Between sessions with Scowcroft and Kissinger, Ford huddled for forty minutes with Haig and Rumsfeld. Since Saturday, the transition team had clashed hard, again and again, with the Nixon holdovers; Hartmann wrote that he and Marsh had to lock arms to muscle a forward position in Ford's entourage before his speech to Congress. Haig's people, hunkered in the West Wing, kept the White House running, while the transition group studied their activities, focusing wholly on domestic policy. Cheney, whom the Secret Service would name "Backseat" for his low-key persona, willingness to stay behind the scenes, aura of invisibility, and stealthy efficiency in getting done even the most mundane tasks, recalled that Ford's "marching orders were to go and view the Office of Management and Budget and the White House domestic operations and relations with the White House and the Cabinet and report back to me, but stay out of the national security area . . . the National Security Council, State, Defense, they're off limits."

Haig, who'd been Kissinger's top aide before he was Nixon's, knew the situation and ceded any major policy role in foreign affairs, except for Vietnam, where Nixon and Kissinger, ever distrusting each other, each relied on him to spy on the other and stiffen administration resolve when the other weakened or wavered.

Two years earlier, for example, when Haig was Kissinger's deputy, Nixon had allowed Kissinger to hold his first press conference just days before the 1972 election—to announce that after ten years and more than fifty thousand American dead and hundreds of thousands of wounded, of nightly television reports from the battlefield and increasingly violent uprisings at home, a secretly negotiated treaty to end the Vietnam War was finally in reach. "Peace is at hand," Kissinger declared. It was the first time TV audiences heard his German-accented baritone, and he was celebrated for bringing the war to a close. Then, within weeks the talks broke down, embarrassing the White House.

As Nixon fumed at Kissinger, and Kissinger raged at North Vietnam's "insolence," it was Haig who urged using the most forceful option available—unrestricted strategic bombing of the North's main cities—to shock the communists back to the bargaining table before Congress returned in January and shut down the entire process under the War Powers Act. While Nixon and Kissinger squirmed over the political costs of the "Christmas bombing"—forty thousand tons of bombs dropped over eleven days; several times more explosive power than the atomic bomb that felled Hiroshima—Haig pressed them to "stand tall and resume the bombing and put those B-52 mothers in there and show 'em we mean business."

Rumsfeld, too, had tested Kissinger under Nixon, but ostensibly from the left, as an antiwar social moderate who saw Nixon's slow withdrawal from Vietnam as a brake on the administration's—and his—domestic ambitions. Midway through Nixon's first term Rumsfeld tried to interest Nixon in sending him as a special presidential envoy to postwar Southeast Asia as hostilities wound down, in order to "focus attention and emphasis on Indo-China *peace* instead of Indo-China war." Kissinger, through Haig, first sat on the request, then rejected it. Six weeks later, Rumsfeld openly challenged Kissinger at a staff meeting, pressing for an explanation why the White House couldn't move faster to end the war. "I think Rumsfeld may be not too long for this world," Nixon told Kissinger and Haldeman after the session. "Let's dump him."

Nixon was especially peeved that Rumsfeld, a fast-witted speaker who appealed to younger audiences, wouldn't speak out to defend the administration. "I don't want somebody who's just with us, God damn it, when things are going good, you know what I mean," he told Haldeman. "If he thinks we're going down the tubes, and he thinks he's going to ride with us, maybe he's going to take a trip to Europe occasionally—then screw him, you know?"

Instead of firing him, Nixon sent Rumsfeld to Europe as ambassador to NATO, and thus Rumsfeld couldn't help now being involved in the Cyprus situation. Otherwise his job was to deliver the spokes-of-the-wheel management system in the White House that Ford requested and that he, like Haig, doubted would work. "Rumsfeld," Hartmann observed, "had an enormous advantage over Haig and the other Praetorians. They had been meticulous students of Nixon and Haldeman, but Rummy was also a student of Gerald R. Ford." While other Nixonians held Ford in "almost open contempt, Rumsfeld knew better. He knew he would have to carry out 90 percent of what Ford wanted in order to get 10 percent of what he wanted."

What Rumsfeld wanted, beyond serving Ford, remained unclear. Nixon believed he had the "charisma for national office" but not the "backbone." Kissinger saw him as the vanguard of a new breed of a "special Washington phenomenon: the skilled full-time politician bureaucrat in whom ambition, ability and substance fuse seamlessly." Ford recognized all this, but his concerns were more immediate. He had called Rumsfeld back from Europe for many reasons, but surely chief among them was that Rumsfeld was a maverick, which was how Ford viewed himself, and what he considered most necessary for leading now.

A decade earlier, Goldwater's humiliating loss to Johnson had spurred Rumsfeld to spearhead an insurgent group of House Republicans who dumped Minority Leader Charles Halleck, replacing him with Ford. Ford loved to talk about this victory in upsetting the political order, and he credited "Rummy" as its architect. Rumsfeld, as transition manager, now believed the main task before the country was to restore the presidency; and since presidents "lead by consent, persuasion, and trust, not by command," that meant building upon Ford's most valuable assets, not just his solid, open character but also his knowledge of Congress and mastery of the budget process. He argued that Ford must above all be, and be perceived as, his own man, at all times in control of the office.

Haig regarded Rumsfeld as a "strong personality and fine administrator," if a novice in inner-circle politics. Haig listened apparently without disagreeing, although he believed Ford needed him and Kissinger now more than ever, as the country faced the next battle—surviving, and learning the lessons of, Vietnam and Watergate. He noted Rumsfeld's proximity to Ford and Ford's obvious reliance on Rumsfeld, a former navy pilot and flight instructor. If Ford was to be his own man, someone would have to propel him there, and Rumsfeld, a wrestler in his college days at Princeton, had demonstrated in Congress and with Nixon that he was unafraid to move hard against his opponents and shake things up. Ford, Rumsfeld wrote, "had to provide sufficient change to make the transition from what many perceived to be an illegitimate White House and administration to a legitimate administration. It was a bit like climbing into an airplane, at 30,000 feet, going 500 miles per hour, and having to change part of the crew."

* * *

Speculation on who Ford would pick for vice president quickly narrowed to two names, Rockefeller and Bush. Laird, touted as an early favorite, dropped out to run the search process for Ford and to press for Rockefeller, whose name he started leaking three days before Nixon left office, and who he believed was the only party leader who could help Ford win in 1976. "I thought we could carry New York, California and maybe Florida," he recalls. On the day Ford was sworn in, Los Angeles car dealer and Reagan financial backer Holmes Tuttle requested a half hour with the president to promote Reagan, a former movie star and corporate pitchman finishing up a second term as governor, and the chairman of the California GOP had sent telegrams to the forty-nine other state chairmen urging Reagan's candidacy. But Reagan, too, failed to catch on. Walking down the White House drive after telling Ford his preferences, Goldwater, himself being promoted by conservative North Carolina senator Jesse Helms and others, told reporters he was too old for the job, but would accept it if offered. Asked whom he'd recommended, Goldwater turned and said, "I imagine . . . George Bush."

Bush's campaign had swung into high gear. Nebraska national committeeman Richard Herman established a boiler room operation in a suite of rooms at the Statler Hilton, where he and two assistants churned out a cascade of phone calls to Republicans around the country urging support for Bush—cajoling, calling in favors, making promises. Some Republicans in Congress, and at least one Democrat, started wearing leftover buttons from Bush's last senatorial campaign. Bush kept his distance from the overt campaigning, but there was little doubt about his eagerness for the job, or his involvement: "We got out our telegrams asking for input from the National Committee," he wrote in his diary on the day Nixon resigned. After Ford's speech to Congress, House Minority Leader John Rhodes offered a room to one of the networks for interviewing political leaders with reaction, a primitive ad hoc "spin room." As soon as Ford was done, the doors opened and in rushed Bush.

The case for Bush, as Herman put it, was that he was the "only one with no opposition. He may not be the first choice in all cases, but he's no lower than second with anyone."

Rockefeller remained far from the politicking—officially aloof, above the fray. On the day he'd been informed by an aide that Laird was promoting his name to reporters, he was set to board a private jet for a monthlong vacation at his sprawling wood-and-fieldstone summer home in Seal Harbor, Maine. "I don't know what to make of this," he told the aide, Hugh Morrow. "You know Mel, he's so devious. He's usually in business for himself." Speaking finally with Laird, Rockefeller feigned lack of interest: "You know what I think, Mel," he said. "Jerry ought to name you as vice president. You're the ideal person. Why are you talking with me?"

Rockefeller, at age sixty-six, had quested harder for the presidency, with more energy, outsized charm, and money, than perhaps anyone else in U.S. history, losing the party nomination in 1960, 1964, and 1968. Like Bush, he had campaigned—and been privately disappointed—when Nixon chose Ford, and now saw his last, best opportunity to vault to the Oval Office, although he was skeptical of Laird. For Ford, Rockefeller would bring depth and experience, but also incite the right, which reviled him. Ford had been startled when, leaving a prayer meeting with Rhodes in his old House office two days before he became president, crowds on the Capitol steps met him shouting "Don't pick Rockefeller! Don't pick Rockefeller!" The protests had been organized by Helms, an incendiary, far-right, one-term senator from North Carolina who was leading the anti-Rockefeller charge.

Rockefeller was one of the country's richest men, grandson of Standard Oil founder John D. Rockefeller. A fiscal liberal and social moderate, he'd grown more conservative—notably ordering state police units to force a bloody end to the Attica prison uprising and pushing through the country's harshest drug penalties—during four terms as the nationally popular governor of New York, until recently the country's most populous state. In 1972, despite a long-standing mutual disdain, he and Nixon had buried the hatchet, and Rockefeller, an enthusiastic supporter of rapprochement with China and détente with Russia, stumped for him with genuine admiration. Rockefeller saw the vice presidency as "not much of a job." Still, when Agnew had resigned, it became a "major test as to whether his loyalty was cutting any ice with Nixon," as his former speechwriter Joe Persico wrote. After Rockefeller wasn't selected, he'd explained his feelings to a reporter: "Anyone who is interested in public service, as I have been all my life, wants to be of service where he can. I leave it right there."

Rockefeller flew to Maine, but not before having all his phone numbers changed so he could be reached there and bringing along senior aides. "I figured if the White House wanted to find me," he said, "they could find me. I didn't want to discuss the thing or do anything about it."

Wednesday, August 14

Distant Drums

During the early morning hours, Ford came face-to-face with his first foreign crisis. Kissinger woke him by telephone to say that Turkish forces had launched heavy air and ground attacks and appeared to be on their way toward seizing most of northern Cyprus. The Geneva peace talks had collapsed. Thousands of Greek Cypriot refugees were pouring southward after Turkish planes bombed Nicosia, the capital.

Kissinger phoned Ford from the windowless basement Situation Room, where the crisis was being coordinated and where on a night ten months earlier, at the height of the Yom Kippur War, a rump meeting of the National Security Council—Kissinger, Schlesinger, Colby, and Chairman of the Joint Chiefs Admiral Thomas Moorer—came to a momentous decision, without consulting Nixon, to send a threatening military signal to Moscow. With Kissinger in the chair, the group placed American nuclear forces and troops worldwide on a higher state of alert. Nixon was upstairs in the Lincoln Sitting Room, drinking, desolate over the impeachment talk arising from the Saturday Night Massacre: His enemies wanted to kill him, he told Kissinger, "and they may succeed. I may physically die." There was no vice president—Ford had been named but not confirmed. Kissinger, thinking better than to present Nixon with a serious international matter, preserved what his biographer Walter Isaacson calls the "fiction of presidential control" by arranging with Haig to chair the meeting as the president's assistant rather than as secretary of state.

Now the overnight dispatches from the eastern Mediterranean were grim. Washington's attempts to get the Turks to compromise had failed; America was having no effect. Kissinger believed Cyprus foretold a radical new type of global danger—ethnic conflict. Unlike other recent world events—Vietnam, East-West détente, the China opening, the October War—that "had been played out against the backdrop of the Cold War and a tacit reliance on the essential rationality of the superpowers . . . [the] calculus of deterrence and détente simply did not apply in Cyprus," he wrote.

Kissinger's style, like Nixon's, was to posture grandly in public while negotiating through back channels so hidden that the rest of Washington didn't know what the White House was doing. He believed Turkey had seized advantage of the American presidential transition to swiftly expand its area of control. And so he advised Ford that the United States should put out a formal statement "deploring" Turkey's actions while calling for an immediate cease-fire and resumption of peace talks. Kissinger, meanwhile, would continue mediating personally with both sides.

In the Oval Office by eight o'clock, Ford met with Marsh to map the plan of battle with Congress. He needed Marsh to persuade Democrats that if the United States stopped delivery of arms to Turkey—which the Turks had already paid for—they would probably respond by closing vital U.S. intelligence facilities near the Soviet border. He also believed a weakened Turkey would risk the future of Israel—a point Marsh would make to Jewish lawmakers in particular.

Soon after Marsh left, Ford telephoned Schlesinger, asking him to review the strategic impact if Greece, as expected, withdrew its armed forces from NATO. Since the alliance hadn't prevented Turkey's military advances in Cyprus, the new regime in Athens felt it could no longer rely on it for security. Schlesinger feared Greece's decision would weaken

U.S. defenses by imperiling important military operations, including deployment of tactical nuclear weapons and the use of support facilities for the Sixth Fleet.

Here, suddenly writ large, were the limits of the faltering Nixon-Kissinger approach to East-West relations—Kissinger's "calculus of deterrence and détente." The policy of détente, which had eased U.S.-Soviet tensions and given Nixon and Brezhnev each a stake in the other's standing at home, had wide national appeal. But as Nixon's power collapsed and Ford took over, a surprising coalition had emerged to oppose it: defense hawks like Schlesinger, who believed the treaty between the United States and the USSR on the limitation of strategic offensive arms (SALT I) gave Soviet nuclear forces the edge; pro-Israel groups and human rights activists protesting restrictions on Jews and others who wanted to emigrate from the Soviet Union; union leaders opposed to freer trade; and Cold War triumphalists who felt the policy cynically shorted human values and American ideals at the expense of accommodating Soviet power. "Conservatives who hated Communists and liberals who hated Nixon came together in a rare convergence, like an eclipse of the sun," Kissinger remarked.

Under current conditions, and with few other alternatives, Ford felt he had to try to keep both Greece and Turkey in the western camp. But he faced an array of opponents, not only in Congress but also within Ford's administration, who would be strengthened by the degree to which they now could show themselves repudiating Nixonian realpolitik and Kissinger. Détente, Scowcroft recalls, "was not sustainable anymore; it didn't match the state of affairs. It was a tactical decision to reduce tensions, and it did that well. But it didn't reflect a real improvement in the relationship between the two powers. Nothing fundamental had changed. We just agreed to be decent to each other."

Soviet ambassador Dobrynin, Moscow's man in Washington since before the Cuban missile crisis a dozen years earlier, arrived at eleven for his introductory meeting with Ford. Superpower relations overarched America's role throughout the world, and as field managers of détente, Kissinger and Dobrynin had grown close, often speaking privately on a secure phone line to avoid having to share their conversations with the State Department. Dobrynin had been in Russia during the transition, and Kissinger, in a phone call before Dobrynin left, noted rumors that he was to be named foreign minister. "Well, Anatoly, I would be very torn," Kissinger had told him. "On the one hand, I would like to see you in a higher position, on the other . . . I would also hate to lose a personal friend here."

During his consultations at the Kremlin, Dobrynin had faced shock and incomprehension about Nixon's removal. "They thought, 'How could the most powerful person in the United States, the most important person in the world, be legally forced to step down for stealing some silly documents?' " he recalled. Less than seven weeks earlier—just weeks after Nixon's triumphal visit to Egypt in June—Nixon had met with Brezhnev at a summit that had begun in Moscow and continued at Brezhnev's dacha near Yalta, and the two leaders talked in private for an hour in a grottolike building cut inside a rock along the Crimean seaside. The "Meeting in the Grotto" produced no strategic breakthroughs, nor did it save Nixon's faltering grip on power, but it was a swan song for détente.

Brezhnev, who as much as Nixon contended with attacks from hard-liners and liberals alike, first raised the issue of the Middle East, insisting that the Soviets had tried everything to restrain Egypt and Syria during the October War but were "unable to do so." Nixon countered with the problem of Jewish emigration and most-favored-nation trade status for the Soviet Union, two issues that along with the next phase of nuclear disarmament talks (SALT II) framed the central indictment of the gathering anti-détente forces in Washington. Democratic senator and presidential hopeful Henry "Scoop" Jackson, Schlesinger's closest ally in Congress, had brought the issues together, linking support for a major trade bill to the plight of Soviet Jewry. Nixon, eager to defuse the right, urged Brezhnev in their private discussion to "make some sort of gesture on Jewish emigration if only to pull the rug out from under Jackson."

"If détente unravels in America," Nixon warned him, "the hawks will take over, not the doves." In the past five years, Nixon and Kissinger had prodded Jewish immigration up from four hundred to thirty-five thousand annually. Angrily, Brezhnev protested to Nixon that that was enough; he promised that Dobrynin would get Kissinger the statistics.

Now, in the Oval Office, Dobrynin delivered Brezhnev's personal regards as Ford and he took matching yellow armchairs before the empty hearth. Photographers jostled and snapped pictures. After the media left, Ford got down to business. "I told him," Ford wrote, "that I would consider it a personal favor if his government would agree to release Simas Kudirka, a Lithuanian seaman who had jumped aboard a U.S. Coast Guard vessel, only to be turned back to the Soviets by an American captain. Dobrynin said he would see what he could do."

The conversation then turned to the plight of Soviet Jews. Dobrynin said the Kremlin would orally guarantee an annual release of fifty-five thousand. But, he said, seeming to heed Nixon's warning to Brezhnev, "it wouldn't put that guarantee on paper and let Jackson use it for his own political purposes."

* * *

Ford had been introduced to what Kissinger called the "cauldron" of Middle East diplomacy on Saturday, when Schlesinger used the first National Security Council meeting to ask Ford's guidance on a $40 billion Israeli long-term military-aid request. To give the Israelis the advanced aircraft and weapons systems they wanted, Schlesinger warned, would draw down on American reserve stocks, making the United States more vulnerable. "Do they understand that that's the case?" Ford asked. "Yes, sir," Schlesinger said, "but they consider that their needs take priority." "That certainly is an unselfish attitude," Ford said. Rare sarcasm aside, Ford didn't plan to begin his presidency by dampening optimism about a nascent peace process in the Middle East. He delayed, saying, "I think we should hold them off until we see their attitude. This is a hole card we can control. I'm not sure Congress would jump at something like this with the current inflation."

After more than twenty-five years of silence between Arab capitals and Jerusalem and four wars, the White House in July had begun hosting a "negotiating process" in which Israel and its neighbors spoke to each other for the first time—through Kissinger. The October War and its aftermath had plunged the Middle East, and America's first Jewish secretary of state, deeply, suddenly, into America's consciousness. Israel won the war but had been bloodied, alarming American Jews and their allies. The Arab countries, unified behind Saudi Arabia, responded by unsheathing the "Oil Weapon"—an embargo on shipments to the West, which quadrupled energy prices and forced Americans, who for thirty years had risen to world dominance and unprecedented prosperity on a sea of cheap petroleum, to wait in line for hours at gas stations. Kissinger, meanwhile, visited the Middle East and negotiated a pullback of Israeli forces from the Suez Canal, then in May converted the Boeing 707 that Johnson had used as vice president into a diplomatic "shuttle," visiting Jerusalem sixteen times, Damascus fifteen times, and six other countries in between to win a military disengagement between Israel and Syria. "Within months," Walter Isaacson, author of *Kissinger*, observed, "every state in the region would regard America as the paramount force there, and Kissinger would become the personification—and to a large degree the cause—of that heightened influence."

With the disengagements—and Kissinger's star—in place, Kissinger had recommended to Nixon a step-by-step method toward negotiating a more lasting peace in the region. Dismissing the goal of a comprehensive settlement between Israel and its neighbors as beyond reach, each believed the best hope was to persuade Israel to withdraw from captured territories in exchange for security guarantees—land for peace. But Israel had suffered perhaps the most traumatic year in its history. Elected by a fragile coalition, its new prime minister, former general Yitzhak Rabin, was demanding the massive long-term military-aid package as Israel's price to sit down and bargain.

Ford met briefly with terHorst and Rumsfeld about planned changes in the White House. He saw Rhodes and Laird to discuss the vice presidential search, and Kissinger and Scowcroft on Cyprus, and then spent a few minutes with Kissinger and his daughter and son, who on Saturday would be having his bar mitzvah outside Boston. At about one thirty, Ford, Kissinger, and Egypt's foreign minister Ismail Fahmy retreated to the first-floor Family Dining Room for a working lunch. It had been Egyptian President Anwar Sadat who chose Kissinger, during Kissinger's first trip to Egypt, to mediate between Egypt and Israel, but only after Fahmy had sized him up. A dapper, nimble diplomat—a "professional's professional," Kissinger wrote—Fahmy had arrived in Washington on Sunday to deliver Sadat's proposal for negotiating a separate peace with Israel.

The problem, from Egypt's point of view, was the fate of the Palestinians living in the West Bank, which Israel had seized from Jordan in 1967. With the Arab states increasingly focused on the Palestinian struggle, and oil moving to the center of U.S. relations in the region, Kissinger favored a next step with Jordan. But the Egyptian leaders, he recognized, "had no intention of miring their hope to recover at least part of the Sinai in the bottomless morass of West Bank haggling." In 1972, they had expelled Soviet military advisers, and other Arab leaders viewed Fahmy especially as pro-Western.

Addressing Ford now, Fahmy delicately foreclosed "all options save a separate Egyptian-Israeli agreement," Kissinger wrote admiringly. "His jovial manner was a great hit with Ford and obscured the indirect threats he kept putting forward the way a doctor might present an unfavorable diagnosis—as events beyond his control. Absent some early progress in the Sinai—say, by November—he would claim, the Middle East would erupt again . . ."

With Jordan's King Hussein already en route to Washington in preparation for Ford's first meeting with a visiting head of state, Ford made no commitments. But the lunch set the direction for subsequent peace efforts, with a U.S.-brokered separate agreement between Egypt and Israel emerging as the most probable next step.

Ford met throughout the afternoon with a delegation of state governors and a group of big-city mayors, mostly Democrats. During a three-minute ceremony in the Oval Office, he signed into law an act to permit ordinary U.S. citizens for the first time in decades to buy and sell gold, a move prompted by inflation fears. Leaving the White House after a twelve-hour day, he was asked by a reporter about the Cyprus crisis. "I think we handled it all right," he said.

On the White House lawn, NBC News correspondent Tom Brokaw, age thirty-four, interviewed some of the departing mayors and governors. In keeping with the times, sweeping brown hair obscured Brokaw's ears and collar, and his sideburns ended near his chin. Speaking to the camera, he summed up the public mood in the capital. "When it was all over," he said, "there was a bipartisan spirit of goodwill on the White House grounds."

Brokaw said Ford might have to delay appointing a vice president until after the weekend as he devoted more time to the Cyprus situation. "Sources close to President Ford," he added, referring, it seems, to Rumsfeld, "were saying today that he will replace about half the cabinet by the end of the year, and that General Alexander Haig is expected to leave his job as the White House chief of staff, as the new president moves to establish a Ford administration."

* * *

At terHorst's press briefing, most questions again were about Watergate and, in particular, the fate of the thousands of hours of tape recordings Nixon secretly had made of his conversations with aides, associates, and advisers. Every president since Franklin Roosevelt had secretly recorded meetings. Eisenhower told Nixon, in 1954, that he thought "it a good thing, when you're talking with someone you don't trust to get a record made of it." Kennedy hid microphones in the Oval Office and had a dictabelt system for recording telephone calls, and when Johnson wanted a phone conversation recorded, he would signal one of his ubiquitous secretaries to "take this," and she would activate a tape machine.

Nixon's voice-activated taping system differed qualitatively from his predecessors'. With hidden microphones installed in the lamps and fix-

tures, embedded in furniture, wired behind pictures, and placed in tele-
phones in the Oval Office, Nixon's EOB hideaway, the Cabinet Room,
and Aspen Lodge at Camp David, he had recorded more than thirty-
seven hundred hours of meetings and conversations—five months'
worth. Everyone he'd spoken with—or about—from July 1971 through
July 1973 was recorded on them, including Haig, Kissinger, and the
other Nixonites in the White House, as well as the leaders of Congress.
And the tapes were critical evidence in the court proceedings against
dozens of former employees of the Nixon White House and the 1972
Committee to Re-Elect the President (CREEP), not to mention indis-
pensable to Jaworski and the Watergate prosecution force investigation
of Nixon himself.

Reporters grilled terHorst on the tapes' legal status. "I can't give you
much on that . . ." he said. "As I mentioned the tapes are in the protec-
tive custody of the Secret Service, but they have been ruled to be the personal property of former President Nixon."

By whom? a reporter asked. TerHorst said the decision was based on
a "formal," although unwritten, opinion by White House lawyers Fred
Buzhardt and James St. Clair, with whom Buzhardt had coordinated
Nixon's Watergate defense, and who terHorst now announced was resigning to return to private practice in Massachusetts. Historical precedents reaching back to Washington applied, he said. Unaware of a
brewing and toxic legal dispute, terHorst, who'd gotten the information
from Buzhardt's office, said the judgment was a "collective one."

TerHorst scarcely knew the half of it. On Monday, while he had been
telling reporters no decision had been made, Buzhardt had preemptively
instructed Staff Secretary Jerry Jones to box up all the tapes as an air
force truck waited outside. Haig had recruited Buzhardt from the Pentagon, where he'd been chief counsel, and ever since the White House
had disclosed in November that an eighteen-and-a-half minute section
of one tape had been "accidentally" erased, Jones, a lumbering Texan, was
the only person authorized to enter the guarded, un-air-conditioned
basement vault in the EOB where the recordings were kept. Jones be-

lieves Philip Buchen, Ford's private counsel, gave Buzhardt approval to send Nixon the tapes.

His jacket off, sweat-soaked in the stifling heat, Jones had packed and cataloged the five drawers of eight-inch reels while Buchen and Buzhardt continued to talk. Then, after two hours, Buzhardt called and told him to stop. "I think what happened is Buchen changed his mind," Jones recalls, "and then Fred had a problem. I think we probably could have shipped them after Buchen told him not to. But Fred felt that being the case, we simply couldn't do it . . . It was a trust thing. We were all in the position that if we did the wrong thing, or if I relied on Fred and he did the wrong thing, or he relied on me and I did the wrong thing, or we both relied on Haig and *he* did the wrong thing, we could go to jail."

On Wednesday, two days later, Jones says, "nobody knew what in the hell to do with these things."

"Did the president have anything to do with this decision?" a reporter asked terHorst.

"No, he did not," terHorst said. "This was made independently of President Ford."

"Does he concur in it?"

"Yes, he does."

Little versed in the issue, with scant information and no one but Buzhardt for guidance, terHorst followed the press inquiries onto an unsteady limb. Asked how Ford could conclude that the tapes weren't vital to the ongoing Watergate investigations, terHorst said: "I presume that was a judgment made by the respective legal counsels, both those who served President Nixon and those who served in the Special Prosecutor's office."

"Are you saying," a reporter asked, "there was an agreement among the different staffs, the Special Prosecutor, the Justice Department and the White House legal staff?"

"I assume there would be," terHorst said, "because I'm sure neither one would just take unilateral action."

* * *

Lawyers at the special prosecution force headquarters on K Street were less concerned about who had physical custody of Nixon's tapes and more interested in whether to bring him to trial and, if so, when. It had been the defeat over the tapes—and what was on them—that brought Nixon down as president. But the legal, constitutional, and policy issues regarding whether to indict him had evaporated on Friday over Missouri, while Nixon, sipping a martini and picking at a lunch of shrimp cocktail, prime rib, green beans, tossed salad, and cheesecake, became a private citizen. Since the White House ruling was based on precedent, rather than law, and since it didn't affect the status of the tapes now in the possession of Watergate judge John Sirica of the U.S. District Court, some sixty-two conversations, Leon Jaworski protested that he'd been "advised" but not "consulted" about the decision, but raised no other public objection. The statement sent reporters scurrying back to their phones to call terHorst for clarification.

Jaworski had received a telephone call from Senator James Eastland, Democratic chairman of the Judiciary Committee and a longtime friend of Nixon's, who told him that Nixon had phoned, crying, from San Clemente. "He said, 'Jim, don't let Jaworski put me in that trial with Haldeman and Ehrlichman. I can't take any more . . . ' He's in bad shape, Leon," Eastland said. Meanwhile, Senator Edward Brooke, a liberal Massachusetts Republican and the first black senator since Reconstruction, dropped his plan to ask for a congressional resolution opposing prosecution, which, while not binding, would have provided cover either for Jaworski or for Ford if either decided to take action to keep Nixon from facing trial. Jaworski had asked Eastland if the Judiciary Committee might consider something similar. "We'll think on it," Eastland told him. "We'll be in touch."

In his game of chicken with Congress and the White House, Jaworski again found himself disadvantaged. His jurisdictional grant required him to pursue Nixon. Prosecutors at times sacrificed underlings to get to the top of criminal pyramids, but never the reverse—leveraging prosecution by offering immunity to the top man. Jaworski believed he could argue that Nixon couldn't receive a fair trial in the District of Columbia, the epicenter of Watergate media publicity, but under what interpretation of the law, what prosecutorial logic, should citizen Nixon escape facing charges?

"The whole premise of this exercise called Watergate was to follow the facts wherever they lead, and if they led into the Oval Office, to apply the law to those facts in the same way that the law would apply to any other person," special prosecution force counsel Philip Lacovara, whose job it was to advise Jaworski on the scope of his duties, recalls. ". . . It would be fundamentally inconsistent with the idea of equal application of the law to prosecute people who had acted on President Nixon's behalf, and indeed under President Nixon's *direction,* and to give him a pass."

Ford met for breakfast in the White House with Senate negotiators on the Soviet trade and emigration standoff—Jacob Javits of New York, Abraham Ribicoff of Connecticut, and Jackson—and he conveyed Dobrynin's offer of an oral guarantee to allow fifty-five thousand Jews to exit each year. "I presented Brezhnev's promise and warned that if they insisted on a written guarantee, the agreement would come unstuck," he wrote. He cautioned that if the Senate persisted in holding up the trade bill granting the USSR the same terms and conditions as more than a hundred other countries, the Soviets, who regarded the legislators' interference as a dangerous attempt to meddle in their nation's domestic affairs, would most likely cut the number. Ford, Kissinger wrote, raised the hope that "freed of the accumulated resentments of the Nixon era, we could now all work together to find a solution."

Diplomatic language aside, there was friction in the meeting, especially between Kissinger and Jackson, a key member of the Armed Services Committee, who, along with his provocative young pro-Israeli aide Richard Perle, had since the October War become Kissinger's most persistent adversary in a city awash with them. Despite the hopeful aftermath, Jackson and Perle depicted Kissinger's handling of the war as dangerous proof that détente was weakening America, and that the U.S. mood of retreat in the wake of Vietnam, combined with an eagerness to work alongside Moscow, imperiled Israel. "There was a strong sense the Israel was doomed unless U.S. power in the world was maintained," Perle said.

That the president and the nation's three ranking Jewish political figures—Kissinger, Javits, and Ribicoff, all with deep ties to Israel—favored a quiet, nonconfrontational approach to the fate of Soviet Jews failed to impress Jackson, who didn't need a fervent, aggressive aide like Perle to motivate him. A sturdy Lutheran of Norwegian stock, Jackson was thoughtful but recalcitrant in his beliefs, in particular his faith that the survival of the United States and its friends depended on unswerving antipathy to global communism. He saw the Soviets, not the Israeli conflict with the Palestinians, as the chief threat to America's accelerating interest in the region and its oil, and thus regarded a militarily supreme Israel as essential not only to its own future but to the West's.

Javits and Ribicoff seemed to accept Dobrynin's compromise, but Jackson resisted. Telling Ford he was being too soft on Moscow, Jackson countered by saying he would drop his target from one hundred thousand to seventy-five thousand emigrants per year, although he continued to insist on a written pledge. "It made no sense to me because it was sure to be counterproductive," Ford recalled, "but he would not bend, and the only explanation is politics."

Jackson had found in the plight of Soviet Jews a human face for his dual crusade against communism and détente, but he was little known outside the Beltway, and his presidential aspirations hinged on becoming a major voice in foreign policy by forging an alliance between anti-Nixon former liberals—neoconservatives—and old-line hawks, and so he had no incentive to compromise. Ford's anticommunist and pro-military credentials were strong—as strong as Nixon's, possibly stronger. But Jackson and the defense intellectuals with whom he collaborated saw Kissinger as both weakened and a liability now that Ford was president. In the new issue of *Foreign Affairs*, the nuclear strategist Albert Wohlstetter, Perle's mentor and an oracle for the younger generation of pro-Israeli neocon-servatives, had thrown down the gauntlet. Asking rhetorically "Is There a Strategic Arms Race?" Wohlstetter raised, as he'd done in 1957, alarms of a growing "missile gap." Contrary to the fashionable belief that the Pentagon systematically overestimated Soviet programs to win bigger budgets, he argued, it actually *underestimated* Soviet forces. In effect, East-West parity was, and had been for decades, a "myth," he wrote.

Kissinger thought Wohlstetter a "brilliant analyst," and he respected Jackson's ability to play havoc with the defense budget, but he was plagued and baffled by the neoconservative attacks on him, especially by Perle, whom he considered "ruthless . . . a little bastard." Nixon had cut his teeth politically as a passionate anticommunist, coming to national attention as the dogged young California congressman who exposed State Department mandarin Alger Hiss as a perjurer, if not a Red. As the architect of détente, he had come to believe that in light of Vietnam, superpower contention had to be moderated, and he and Kissinger had tried to build a "structure of peace" relying on linkages: If the Soviets did something we liked in one area, say by choosing not to meddle in the Middle East, we would reward them with agreements in another, such as trade subsidies. As Nixon told Mao Tse-tung, the leader of China, at their first meeting in 1972, "What is important is not a nation's internal political philosophy. What is important is the policy towards the rest of the world and towards us."

Kissinger anticipated that Ford in his first weeks as president, like Nixon, would be "assaulted from two opposite directions: from the still-dominant liberal end, for being too geopolitical and Cold-Warish; and from the conservative side for being too tactical and non-ideological." But Vietnam and the overarching threat of nuclear war had changed the calculus in world affairs: As Kissinger would soon tell the Senate, "Where the age-old antagonism between freedom and tyranny is concerned, we are not neutral. But other imperatives impose limits on our ability to produce internal changes in foreign countries. Consciousness of our limits is recognition of the necessity of peace—not moral callousness. The preservation of human life and human society are moral values, too."

What Kissinger and Nixon and now Ford would chronically underestimate was the neoconservatives' argument that the United States should not so much seek to coexist with the Soviet system as to overthrow it through direct confrontation. Or the extent to which the neoconservatives would go to exaggerate a foreign threat and stir up fear.

After the meeting, "to show our good intentions," Kissinger assigned the State Department counsel to work with Jackson and his staff to draft a letter summarizing the assurances from Moscow, but he wasn't optimistic. Shuttling between Jackson and the Kremlin, he said, "made me long for the relative tranquility of the Middle East." Comparing Gromyko and Jackson, he judged the Soviet foreign minister the "easier party."

* * *

Back in the Oval Office, Ford turned to the problem of the tapes. The morning front-page headlines were a "disaster," Hartmann recalled, uniformly suggesting that Ford "was trying to pull a fast one" on Nixon's behalf. After reviewing the full transcript of terHorst's briefing the previous day, Ford was livid and upset, but not with his press secretary. He blamed St. Clair and Buzhardt and, in part, himself. The decision to bar Nixon's materials from being airlifted on Saturday night somehow hadn't leaked; thus it appeared that Ford was trying to spirit the tapes past the special prosecutor when in fact he'd done the opposite, assuming custody of Nixon's papers despite his urgency to be rid of them. Ford realized belatedly that he could not take advice from Nixon's lawyers, no matter their intentions. He needed his own legal team. He told terHorst to announce that Buchen would be named immediately as counsel to the president, replacing Buzhardt, "who hasn't resigned but will be leaving," and that Buchen would consult fully with Jaworski, Attorney General Saxbe,

Nixon's lawyers, and constitutional experts before he—Ford—decided the status of Nixon's papers and tapes.

Ford's decision to oust Buzhardt dealt Nixon a severe blow—Nixon no longer would be able to influence Ford's deliberations, plus he'd lost an irreplaceable mole—but ultimately it struck hardest at Haig, who recoiled when Ford told him and Rumsfeld about it in the Oval Office. Haig would write that he had hired Buzhardt, whom he "had known slightly at West Point (he graduated a year ahead of me) and later at the Pentagon," to represent Nixon "without enthusiasm" after Nixon rejected his advice to hire a top Washington criminal lawyer. But that description belied a deeper reality—that Haig had been seeking not only someone to defend Nixon but also to advise and protect *him*, and that Buzhardt had kept him out of trouble before. "It was one of the wise things I did," Haig recalled. "I decided I would never touch a thing about Watergate unless I had a lawyer's opinion on whether it was appropriate or not appropriate." In short, despite extreme complications for them all, Buzhardt not only had served the past fifteen months as Nixon's lawyer, but—unofficially—as Haig's, too.

Haig's own legal situation—and thus his political future, in and out of the military—remained treacherous, far from resolved. Though he hadn't been chief of staff when the secret White House apparatus for domestic spying and political disruption known generically as "Watergate" was in operation, he had understood from the moment he took over from Haldeman that he "would inevitably be drawn into the day to day management of the Watergate crisis unless [Nixon] immediately put someone else in charge." He had turned unhesitantly to Buzhardt, a former top aide to segregationist South Carolina senator Strom Thurmond, who proceeded on a crash basis to get to know Nixon as he sat with him for hours in seclusion going over the minutiae of an ever-widening criminal conspiracy—what the previous White House counsel, John Dean, famously called a "cancer within, close to the presidency."

Complications from their three-sided relationship erupted nearly from the start. A month after Haig and Buzhardt arrived in the West Wing, Dean alleged during riveting televised Senate hearings that suddenly turned Watergate into true national theater that Nixon was directly involved in the Watergate cover-up long before he—Dean—informed him of it. Nixon rebutted Dean's charges by having Buzhardt secretly supply a Senate lawyer with highly detailed, near-verbatim accounts of their private meetings together. Buzhardt understood that Nixon had recorded some private conversations, but the extent of the taping system remained among the most closely held secrets in the White House—Kissinger and Ehrlichman didn't know—until early June, when Nixon, reassuring himself "not even Buzhardt knows," told Ziegler and Haig about it. Haig immediately corrected him, saying Buzhardt also knew about the voice-activated system. "All right," Nixon said. "No further. He shouldn't tell anyone. I don't want it put out."

With the president and Dean, a telegenic thirty-four-year-old with a comprehensive memory, stalemated, and with Nixon retaining the powerful legal advantage of "executive privilege"—the idea that a president's private conversations are inviolate and therefore can't be subpoenaed—Nixon had strong reasons to believe he would survive the hearings. It was Dean's word against his. "Nobody in Congress likes him," Haig encouraged Nixon. "We can take the son of a bitch on."

The problem, inevitably, was the tapes. How soon Haig and Buzhardt each learned about the hidden taping system remains in dispute. More certain are their actions during the five crucial days surrounding former White House aide Alexander Butterfield's shocking disclosure of it the next month to Congress and the nation—days that would doom Nixon. Haldeman had instructed the handful of White House employees who knew about the taping system to say it was covered by executive privilege and refuse to talk about it. However, a week before Butterfield, a former air force intelligence officer, was called to testify, Haig instructed another aide, former Deputy Chief of Staff Larry Higby, to "tell the truth" if asked about the taping system. Then, on Friday, July 13, Butterfield sat down with investigators, who asked how the White House could have such detailed accounts of Nixon's discussions with Dean. "I was hoping you fellows wouldn't ask me that," Butterfield said, volunteering. "Well yes, there's a recording system in the White House."

Nixon was then in Bethesda Naval Hospital with viral pneumonia, after awakening the day before with severe chest pains and a high fever. Haig and Buzhardt learned during the weekend—maybe Saturday, certainly by Sunday—that Butterfield would be compelled to testify on Monday, but they decided not to inform Nixon, even though there remained time for the White House to take action, by claiming executive privilege. "I was shocked by this news," Nixon later wrote of the Butterfield revelation. Haig, remarkably, would also claim to be stunned—not only by Butterfield's testimony but also by the political and legal bombshell that Nixon had a secret taping system in the White House. "I had no foreknowledge of Butterfield's appearance, let alone the nature of his testimony," he wrote, adding of Nixon: "It never occurred to me that anyone in his right mind would install anything so Orwellian as a system that never shut off, that preserved every word, every joke, every curse, every tantrum, every flight of presidential paranoia, every bit of flattery and bad advice and tattling by his advisors."

An instant sensation, the tapes unleashed the climactic, yearlong battle for Nixon's presidency, which Haig and Buzhardt commanded. Neglecting to inform Nixon about Butterfield's testimony wasn't the last time they made a tactical error in the struggle for the tapes that raised doubts about which side they were on. In Nixon's hospital room, Nixon and Haig spent several hours discussing what to do. Nixon, supported by Buzhardt, suggested destroying them, and Haig later wrote that he told the president, "You'll take a tremendous amount of heat, but, whatever happens, it'll be over fairly quickly." Alternatively, Haig said, "The process of disclosure will last forever. It will reach into history."

* * *

Rushing to stem a sudden Watergate backwash, Ford also removed Haig from any responsibility for dealing with Nixon. From now on, he said, Buchen would have custody of Nixon's papers and tapes, and Marsh would be the liaison officer with the former president and his California staff on other matters.

Back in his office with Jones, Haig took stock of his reversals. "Haig knew his supremacy in the White House was over," Ford's biographer James Cannon wrote, "but he was not yet ready to leave." Not a man to back down in battle, Haig was ambitious and soldierly, and he had his own urgent stake in how Ford handled the tapes and the rest of the Watergate legacy. In a sense, Ford had now taken over from him the "day to day management of the Watergate crisis" that he had taken over from Haldeman, yet there was no one else in the White House who would, as he and Haldeman had for Nixon, lift that burden from Ford's shoulders. No spoke on a wheel could protect Ford from the full frontal assault of Congress and the media once he was in the fray. "I've lost the battle," Jones says Haig told him. "But I'll stay long enough to get Nixon the pardon."

Now that Ford had no recourse but to guard the tapes—plus the 15 million cubic feet of files that Nixon left behind and that Gulley, unknown to Ford's people, had started to ship to California—he asked Buchen for guidance. Buchen had handled sensitive legal affairs for Ford since 1941, when they went into practice together in Grand Rapids. Silver-haired, stooped, a compulsive worker who had been crippled by polio as a junior in high school, Buchen navigated Washington's steepest staircases by handing off his cane without complaint, flopping down, and shinnying up a step at a time. Officially located in the EOB as director of a study on citizens' privacy rights, Buchen had secretly directed Ford's orderly elevation to the presidency, and had done much to set the centrist, healing tone of his first address to Congress. "The gentle, crippled man that Jerry Ford trusts," *PeopleWeekly* proclaimed him.

Within hours of replacing Buzhardt, Buchen met with Jaworski, with Buzhardt present, to begin pursuing a consensus on the tapes. He said he needed time to consult with Ford, Congress, and the attorney general on an unprecedented array of issues. Despite Nixon's correct claim that every president since Washington got to own all his files from office, the

Constitution said nothing about presidential ownership of materials. Jaworski told Buchen that he had agreed to request a delay in the start of the cover-up trial, but he gave no indication whether he would seek to indict Nixon. Yet even if Nixon avoided indictment, both knew, pressure for the tapes would mount from all over—the courts; the special prosecution force; Congress; the lawyers for Haldeman, Ehrlichman, Mitchell, and the others still to be tried; the press; historians.

After the meeting, the White House abruptly reversed position on Nixon's materials. Ford, acting through Buchen, ordered that all Nixon's files be held in White House custody until legal issues involving Watergate were resolved. Jaworski announced that none of Nixon's files would be moved "pending further discussion" and that the special prosecution force was "satisfied with these arrangements." Buchen, carefully choosing his words, said that the reversal "in no way constitutes a denial" that the files belonged to Nixon.

"The crucial concern," Hartmann later wrote, "was not that Nixon wanted his records back, nor that Jaworski and Nixon's even more implacable press pursuers wanted to prevent Nixon from getting them. The key factor was that *Ford wanted to get rid of them.* He had no desire to be the daily arbiter of this no-win contest. Nixon's files were a millstone hung around his fledgling presidency; he desperately wanted to cut himself free."

* * *

Buzhardt's value to Nixon and Haig—and the sudden, sharp loss of it—became clear in the afternoon, when Judge Sirica issued a subpoena for Nixon to appear as a witness for Ehrlichman at the Watergate cover-up trial. Nixon's former domestic affairs adviser had listened to the tapes the prosecutors intended to use at trial. Two weeks earlier he had been convicted of conspiracy and lying in connection with a second break-in at the office of a California psychiatrist who treated Daniel Ellsberg, a former marine captain in Vietnam and Kissinger protégé who turned against the war and leaked a secret Pentagon history to the *New York Times*. Ehrlichman, who Nixon claimed initiated the cover-up of the Watergate break-in and lied to him about it, had been sentenced to a minimum of twenty months in prison.

Readying for that first trial in June, Ehrlichman's lawyers had demanded that Jaworski's office hand over their client's White House files. But the special prosecutor provided an affidavit from Buzhardt saying there was "nothing in them" material to Ehrlichman's defense. Then Buzhardt suffered a heart attack and was hospitalized, in intensive care, and Ehrlichman was thwarted from asking how Buzhardt had determined that in tens of thousands of files there was nothing to help Ehrlichman's case. "I have no idea how Jaworski persuaded poor Fred Buzhardt to sign it before he had his heart attack," Ehrlichman wrote.

As a tune-up for prosecutors—and the genesis of Ehrlichman's "strategic disagreement" with Haldeman, Mitchell, and the other defendants: that is, to try to force Nixon to testify in court at the upcoming trial—the first break-in trial highlighted just how explosive the issue of Nixon's tapes had become; how ominous, even lethal, it must have appeared to both Ford and Nixon. Predating the burglary at Democratic headquarters in the Watergate office complex in Washington by eleven months, the first break-in was the "seminal Watergate episode," as Ehrlichman put it. And like all original sins, it held the complete DNA of subsequent misdeeds.

Nixon's name had appeared nowhere in the seventy pounds of documents—the Pentagon Papers—showing how the Democrats under Kennedy and Johnson secretly escalated the war in Southeast Asia, and he at first thought they would do him more good than damage. But Kissinger, deep in arranging his secret trip to Beijing, exploded. "This will destroy American credibility forever," he ranted to his staff. "We might as well just tell it all to the Soviets and get it over with." In a phone call to Nixon, Kissinger appealed to his masculinity: "It shows you are a weakling, Mr. President . . . if other powers feel we cannot control internal leaks, they will not agree to secret negotiations." Kissinger feared that his association with Ellsberg and another former aide, Leslie Gelb, who had left government to head the liberal Brookings Institution, would hurt him with the president. Days later at a meeting in the Oval Office, Ehrlichman recalled, Kissinger railed about Ellsberg: "He said he knew for a fact that Ellsberg had slept with his wife and another woman at the same time." Kissinger added that Ellsberg was a "known drug user."

The White House obtained a temporary restraining order that blocked publication for eight tense days while the *Times* appealed directly to the Supreme Court, which ruled 6–3 to let the paper resume publication. Nixon was in the Oval Office with his aide Charles Colson when he heard the decision. "We've got a countergovernment here and we've got to fight it," he said, the recording system, as ever, bearing silent witness. "I don't give a damn how it's done. Do whatever has to be done to stop these leaks . . . I don't want to be told why it can't be done." He then called in Mitchell, Kissinger, and Haldeman—but not Ehrlichman. He compared Ellsberg to Alger Hiss, instructing, "Don't worry about his trial. Just get everything out. Try him in the press, try him in the press . . . leak it out." Finally, the president lashed out at Gelb and Brookings, telling Haldeman, "I want the break-in. Hell, they do that. You're to break into the place, rifle the files, and bring them in . . . Just go in and take it. Go in around eight or nine o'clock."

To remove any doubt, Nixon repeated—on tape—the next day: "Get it done. I want it done. I want the Brookings Institute's safe *cleaned out* . . ."

Born in these discussions was the "Plumbers" unit, formed to plug leaks—the criminal enterprise that would engulf the Nixon White House. Two weeks later, Ehrlichman, a college friend of Haldeman's who joined Nixon's entourage as an advance man because he was bored with practicing real estate law in Seattle, updated Nixon—alone—on its progress. Ehrlichman had created, he said, a special investigations unit, and its first target would be Ellsberg. Within days, the two young lawyers assigned to run the operation were reporting back to Ehrlichman that they had assembled a black-bag team and recommended a "covert operation" to steal Ellsberg's files from the office of Dr. Lewis Fielding, a California psychoanalyst. Ehrlichman approved the project, writing: "If done under your assurance that it is not traceable." Conducted by the same team of burglars, the break-in was a tune-up for Watergate.

Ehrlichman, having lost access to his papers in mounting a legal defense, and facing prison, was "deeply pessimistic" about the impending cover-up trial. In deciding to subpoena Nixon to testify, he hoped to set in motion a confrontation between Jaworski and Nixon's lawyers— though with St. Clair gone and Buzhardt on notice to leave, Nixon was temporarily without criminal counsel.

In San Clemente, Nixon worried that Ford was double-crossing him. When Haig had shuttled between them in the final days of Nixon's presidency, shading him toward resigning, Nixon had come to expect that as a private citizen he would escape prosecution and retain his papers. Haig and Buzhardt had made the arrangements: Ford and Jaworski, he felt assured, had agreed on both issues. The guarantee of a future, however costly in legal fees, and secure access to the sources from which he could write his own history and make an income, had uplifted him during his departure, when at certain times he appeared remarkably buoyant, even giddy. Sitting, for instance, behind the Wilson desk one week earlier in the minutes before he would announce his resignation, he'd bantered with the CBS crew, which was handling the pool broadcast for all three networks. "Blondes, they say photograph better than brunettes," he said to a technician doing a light check. "My friend Ollie always wants to take a lot of pictures of me," he said, pointing to the White House photographer. "I'm afraid he'll catch me picking my nose."

Nixon's former special counsel, Leonard Garment, whom Ford had decided for now to retain, recalls of Nixon's pre-broadcast warm-up: "It's so fucking interesting. He's on top of the world. He looks good . . . He's merry. It solidifies what I always felt, which is that he was happy to be done with it. He knew that if he didn't resign that he was going to die— his phlebitis or something else would kill him. Now, finally, the moment had come, the hour had struck, and he was gleeful."

Nixon now instructed Haig to increase the pressure on Ford, but he seemed to realize that his situation was lost. He no longer held the power to affect the course of events. Ehrlichman's subpoena had been mailed to

U.S. marshals in California with instructions to serve Nixon with it as soon as possible; included was a check for $302 for witness fees and travel expenses. Down below, the miles of beachfront that had been kept private for his use as president swarmed with surfers, sunbathers, gawkers, and news crews. On CBS, reporter Leslie Stahl commented that unnamed "defense lawyers" said Jaworski's seeking a trial delay "was a tip-off that he has indicted Mr. Nixon." The special prosecutor's office refused to comment.

"One after another," Nixon wrote piteously, "the blows rained down."

Friday, August 16
Ghosts of Watergate

Kissinger and Ford formally received King Hussein of Jordan in the Oval Office, which still looked as if Ford had just rented it. The recessed, scallop-crowned bookshelves were bare, and Ford, whose family wouldn't be moving into the residence until Monday, so far had planted only a pipestand and a few other personal items on the credenza behind the Wilson desk. In June, after leaving Egypt, Nixon had visited Hussein in Amman, in his tiny landlocked kingdom surrounded by mightier Arab states and Israel, and at a state dinner had toasted his endurance. Since taking the throne at age eighteen, Hussein, thirty-nine, had survived more assassination attempts than perhaps any other world leader. "I do not know where this journey will end," Nixon conceded, offering hope for a Jordanian option—a pullback of Israeli forces along the West Bank of the Jordan River in exchange for increased Jordanian involvement in finding a homeland for the Palestinian exiles there. "I cannot tell you when it will end. The important thing is that it has begun."

With Egypt now eclipsing Jordan as Israel's most likely negotiating partner in the next phase of the nascent Mideast peace process, Ford and Kissinger had little to offer—the king less. Hussein believed that Sadat, scorned by other Arab rulers for bargaining unilaterally over the Sinai, couldn't afford to go it alone this time, and needed progress on the Palestinian front as political cover. But Egyptian foreign minister Fahmy had ridiculed that notion over lunch on Wednesday. "Jordan can't move without the solid support of President Sadat," he said. "No Arab leader can support King Hussein. As I told you, he is a very good man, a courageous man, but what happened in Black September . . . precludes him from acting without the support of Egypt."

Seminal events four years earlier—in September 1970—had drawn Kissinger, Hussein, and Israel into a secret and fateful alignment, now approaching a decisive stage. In an attack that marked the start of international terrorism on a grand scale, militant Palestinian nationalists first had hijacked four western commercial jets and flown their passengers to a desert airstrip near Amman. Then, after negotiating the release of all hostages, they blew up the emptied aircraft in front of news cameras. Hussein responded by mobilizing his troops for a showdown with the Palestinian Liberation Organization (PLO), then mostly a guerrilla organization based in Jordan.

When Kissinger got a cable indicating that Hussein might request U.S. military support if Iraq or Syria intervened on the PLO's behalf, he persuaded the White House crisis group that it would be better to encourage *Israel* to come to Hussein's aid. Nixon, meanwhile, took the confrontation as an opportunity to challenge the Soviets, announcing that if Syrian tanks rolled into Jordan, he would prefer the United States stop them alone. Nixon never minded letting the Soviets think he was capable of irrational or unpredictable acts—the "madman theory," as both he and his critics called it. Kissinger eventually convinced Nixon that it was better to let Israel handle the job, and, after Hussein secretly cabled the British government requesting an Israeli air strike and the cable was routed through Washington to Prime Minister Golda Meir, Israel moved in decisively with Nixon's approval. Three thousand Jordanians and Palestinians died in the conflict.

Since Black September, as the events came to be known, Hussein had lost influence and prestige throughout the Arab and Muslim world. At the same time, the PLO took up operations in Lebanon, its leader, Yasser Arafat, vanquished all rivals for control of the Palestinian struggle, the oil states found it good domestic politics to support the Palestinian cause, and international terrorism and Muslim fundamentalism began to ignite. Then came the October War and the subsequent oil embargo, shaking the world balance. As *Time* noted in its Man of the Year article, on Saudi Arabia's King Faisal and oil, "Few noted the considerable historic irony that the world's most advanced civilizations depended for this treasure on countries generally considered weak, compliant and disunited."

Kissinger, adding it all up, had concluded that Israel's best tactic for avoiding having to negotiate with the PLO, which vowed the destruction of the Jewish state, was to let Hussein do it. "The best way to deal with the Palestinian question," Kissinger told the Senate Foreign Relations Committee in May, the same month Hussein and Meir reportedly twice met in secret, "would be to draw the Jordanians into the West Bank and thereby turn the debate . . . into one between the Jordanians and the Palestinians." To Israel's Foreign Minister, Yigal Allon, another former Kissinger protégé, he was blunter: If Israel didn't deal with Hussein now, Arafat would be recognized within a year as the spokesman for the West Bank.

In the Oval Office, Hussein now sought renewed support from Ford for the Jordanian option, or, barring that, parallel Israeli negotiations with both Jordan and Egypt.

"We would like to know, sir, where we stand now," the king said. "If we are not to be involved, we are prepared to turn over our responsibilities to the PLO and let them try to deal with the problem." According to Kissinger, Jordanian prime minister Zaid Rifai jumped in to clarify: "We don't mind being used, but we want a piece of the cake."

Hussein suggested that the Palestinians should be given the choice of joining Jordan or seeking autonomy in a loose federation with his kingdom. "Had we been in a position to allow our sympathies to guide our policies," Kissinger wrote, "both Ford and I would have concurred eagerly." But both understood that with the PLO on the verge of international legitimacy, there was little left but to discuss the larger goal—what

Hussein called the "common desire to see the establishment of a just and durable peace in our part of the world." Egypt and Israel would dictate the timetable, and the fragile Rabin government was not about to dismantle its security outposts and withdraw its tanks from the unsettled West Bank.

Kissinger and Hussein left for a red-carpet reception at the State Department and a working lunch as Ford returned, head-snappingly, to the domestic front, discussing with his staff his economic package and a controversial school aid bill that included a limited busing provision. As all week, he anticipated conservative opposition, especially from within the administration, where resistance to many Nixon-Ford positions was vehement if still muted. Right-wing speechwriter Patrick Buchanan, for example, despite his pugnacious loyalty to Nixon, believed conservatives had become the "niggers" in the Nixon White House and that "there is no substitute for a principled and dedicated Man of the Right in the Oval Office." Of Ford and his men, Buchanan would write:

> They never fought for the Presidency; they never forged a national victory; they feel no obligation to the mandate President Nixon's men believed they had won . . . Like some brash Fortinbras with his retinue arriving in the final scene of Hamlet, to take charge of the disposition of affairs, the President and his Hill and Michigan counselors appear at times not even to understand what the bloodshed and carnage were about.

Yet Ford's mantle of the "Presidential center" so far had yielded glowing results, especially in Congress and the media. The nightly network news commentators, the most powerful voices of mainstream political opinion in the country, lauded him in their broadcasts and pleaded for steadiness, openness, honesty, and a break from the psychic tremors of the past decade, when the last three presidencies ended in tragic, or at least painful, circumstances. "Our recent history suggests that the best way for a political leader to get along with the American people," NBC's David Brinkley said in his nightly *Journal,* "even if politically they don't agree with him, is to play it straight, stay out of other people's wars, and tell the truth, good or bad."

Ford, now confronted by his first tough decisions, planned more or less to follow Brinkley's prescription, despite being well aware that his positions "seemed certain to leave [the right] sputtering."

* * *

His survey with Laird complete, Harlow handed Ford a list of recommendations on the vice presidency.

"It would appear the choice narrows to Bush and Rockefeller," he wrote. "For party harmony, plainly it should be Bush. But this would be construed primarily as a partisan act, foretelling a Presidential hesitancy to move boldly in the face of known controversy. The Rockefeller choice would be hailed by the media normally most hostile to Republicans . . . the best choice is Rockefeller."

Knowing the importance Ford placed on being seen as his own man, Harlow added that choosing Rockefeller "would encourage estranged groups to return to the Party and would signal that the new President will not be captive of any political faction."

All but decided, Ford strongly agreed, but the vetting had hit a snag. On Sunday, Buchen received a phone call from an elderly right-wing activist and author from Philadelphia named Hamilton Long, who claimed to have information linking Rockefeller to Watergate. A retired army major, lawyer, lecturer, and self-publisher in the fifties of tracts like "Permit Communist-conspirators to Be Teachers?," Long told Buchen that documents missing from the office of convicted Watergate burglar E. Howard Hunt proved that Rockefeller money was earmarked to hire thugs to disrupt the 1972 Democratic National Convention. He said the papers were in two lockboxes in a bank vault outside Washington.

Buchen met with Long at his EOB office to assure himself the "man wasn't off his nut," he said, and became sufficiently impressed to assign Benton Becker to look into the allegation. Becker reported back that seven boxes of Hunt's papers had mysteriously disappeared from the White House two years earlier and that a trove of new revelations "might indeed exist." Buchen promptly reported the information to Ford, who directed him to pass it on to Jaworski.

Long's story had leaked to syndicated columnist Jack Anderson, whose scoops about the trail of illegal money flooding into Nixon's 1972 campaign had made him the country's favorite investigative reporter, and terHorst began fielding questions about the White House's response at his late-morning briefing. Unaware of Buchen's contact with Long, ter-Horst told reporters he'd look into the matter and get back to them.

Ford now met for twenty minutes with FBI director Clarence Kelley to discuss the situation. Long had told Buchen that he came forward in order "to avoid President Ford's being caught in another 'Eagleton Affair,' " referring to George McGovern's ruinous decision in 1972 to nominate, then drop, his running mate, Missouri senator Thomas Eagleton, after it was learned he had received electroshock treatments for depression. Ford himself had undergone probably the most thorough government investigation of any vice-presidential nominee in U.S. history—three hundred fifty special agents interviewed one thousand witnesses, including a former football player from Union High School in Grand Rapids whom Ford had hit with a late tackle during the Depression: "like undergoing an annual physical exam in public view," Ford described it. He wanted Kelley to ensure that by the time he announced his choice, most likely early next week, there would be no other surprises.

As rumors spiraled that Ford was dumping Rockefeller—indeed, that Rockefeller's lead in the "Veepstakes" had already passed to one of the other contenders on Ford's list—Ford privately gave Kelley three names to investigate: Rockefeller, Bush, and—an apparent standby—Rumsfeld, who coincidentally began to attract notice from network news crews as something of a mystery man in Ford's retinue, the angular, blunt-spoken NATO ambassador notably nearer the president's side than his age, duties, experience, or title seemed to explain.

Rumsfeld possessed none of the national stature, executive experience, and base-broadening political appeal that Ford had instructed Harlow to look for; a former congressman from a neighboring state, Rumsfeld offered no geographic balance as a ticket-mate in 1976. But like the other finalists, he too was campaigning, promoting his availability as a dark horse. He had scant popular or party support, but he was strongly positioned—with Cheney alongside, doubling his capabilities—in an undisciplined, confused, and fractious White House environment, and he skillfully exploited his temporary billet in the West Wing. Noted Hartmann, who'd begun to clash with Rumsfeld, as he did with Haig, over access to Ford, "The only overt activity by Rumsfeld supporters was the clearly coordinated planting with Washington reporters of the fact that Rumsfeld was one of those under consideration."

* * *

A week after Nixon resigned, public opinion over the question of whether he had suffered enough showed Americans less agitated about his fate since he left office, but deadlocked over whether he should be penalized further, now that he was an ordinary citizen. On *NBC Evening News,* John Chancellor reported the results of the network's latest poll, taken since Wednesday morning:

NIXON SHOULD BE PUNISHED

AGREE	46%
DISAGREE	46%
NOT SURE	6%

Chancellor said that a majority of Southerners felt Nixon shouldn't be prosecuted. But as elsewhere, opinions about whether losing his presidency was penalty enough seemed mostly to reflect where people stood amid a clash of values—equal justice under the law vs. special mercy. In sweltering Demopolis, Alabama, a small former cotton city at the confluence of the Tombigbee and Black Warrior rivers, most residents told the network's Tom Pettit that they were relieved, but also saddened, by Nixon's resignation.

"Putting him in jail would be an empty, meaningless thang," a blond businessman in his thirties said, standing outside a brick church where white families clustered. Next to him, his skinny teenage son—wearing lank, shoulder-length hair, braces on his teeth, and a sky-blue bowtie the size of a pinwheel—responded: "In all honesty I do believe he ought to be punished for what he's done." A thickset man on a patio said: "Leave him alone. Let him rest now." Pettit reported that all that remained of Nixon's black-and-white portrait in the post office "is a fine layer of dust. And when we found the portrait, on the floor of the postmaster's office, he told us, 'Why don't you stop persecuting the man.' "

At its annual meeting in Hawaii earlier in the week, the American Bar Association (ABA), the country's most powerful and prestigious lawyers' group, unanimously approved a resolution calling for impartial application of the nation's criminal laws "without fear of favor arising from the position or status" of the accused. Though the ABA carefully avoided mentioning Nixon by name, most attorneys believed he ought to be open to stand trial alongside his former advisers. But when NBC asked 1,543 "scientifically selected" households whether Nixon should receive immunity, Chancellor told viewers, they again revealed a sharp split:

MADE TO STAND TRIAL	
YES	45%
NO	47%
NOT SURE	6%

The public's ambivalence terminated with Nixon's guilt. Nearly two thirds of those surveyed believed there no longer was any question of it:

IS NIXON GUILTY?	
YES	65%
NO	16%
NOT SURE	16%

Similarly, Chancellor said, "An overwhelming number of people . . . feel that all the Watergate tapes and papers in the White House should be turned over to the courts":

TURN OVER MATERIALS	
YES	74%
NO	23%
NOT SURE	2%

Nixon feared that his countrymen were in a dark, retributive mood. But instead, the poll suggested, that having got rid of him at last, most Americans hoped only to let him go—to consign him, to borrow the indelible phrase his domestic adviser Daniel Patrick Moynihan used to describe Nixon's racial policies, to a "period of benign neglect." Asked if Nixon deserved his $60,000 government pension, another large majority answered that he did:

ENTITLED TO PENSION	
YES	60%
NO	32%
NOT SURE	7%

* * *

Standing at the North Portico of the White House at about 8 P.M., wearing grosgrain-bowed pumps with his dinner jacket, Ford seemed stiff and nervous as he waited to start the formal greeting of King Hussein and his third wife, Queen Alia. Betty, in a long-sleeved white crepe dress trimmed at the neck and wrists with floating white feathers, smiled gamely. "Queen Alia told me she'd been worried about whether or not I was going to make it through the evening," Betty recalled in a memoir. "Poor, beautiful Queen, she later died in an air crash."

The Fords escorted the royal couple as they descended the grand staircase to the East Room, but any resemblance to state dinners of recent years, as the *Times* pointed out, was "purely protocol." To show that the White House social whirl would be more open and less formal than the Nixons', they'd invited who they wanted, including five press and TV reporters who normally covered the White House, a bipartisan assortment of congressional members, a large State Department contingent, Kennedy's and Johnson's defense secretary Robert McNamara, columnist Art Buchwald, and California representative Pete McCloskey, Jr., one of Nixon's earliest and most ardent critics within the Republican Party.

The party dined on cold salmon and standard political-dinner-cut roast beef, and afterward Ford made a rambling and personal toast to Hussein's courage and "superb understanding of the Middle East." In deference to the Muslim ban on alcohol, Hussein toasted Ford with a champagne glass half-filled with ice water. Routinely under Nixon, guests at state social occasions were herded after dinner into rows of tiny stiff-backed gilt chairs to be entertained, and the Nixons often left right after the show. "Betty and I wanted our dinners more relaxed," Ford wrote. After coffee and the arrival of another fifty guests, the party returned to the East Room—for champagne and dancing.

The Fords and the royal couple took the floor at about ten thirty, and for the next hour the president danced nearly nonstop. "People danced and laughed and onlookers laughed and shook their heads and said things like, 'Isn't this something?' " the *Times* reported, adding a "tinge of incredulity . . . seemed to heighten the enjoyment . . . the Queen of Jordan doing a little discreet jitterbugging, a member of Congress cutting in to dance with the President's wife, a President laughing. It was, someone said, like a celebration at the end of a war." As an amplified orchestra swung between presidential requests like the University of Michigan fight song and standards such a "Mack the Knife," "C'est Si Bon," and "Tea for Two," Oregon senator Mark Hatfield and his wife brushed near CBS commentator Eric Sevareid on the dance floor. "Happy New Year!" Hatfield yelled, and Sevareid called back, "Happy New Year!"

Ford was rolling, ebullient, plainly pleased. As the party went on, he and Betty ushered the king and queen to their limousine, kissing Alia good-bye, then returned to the dance floor. Alone amid a circle of on-lookers, Ford and Cindy Nessen, wife of NBC reporter Ron Nessen, stomped to "Bad, Bad Leroy Brown," a new dance hit about a six-foot-four-inch Chicago gambler with a custom El Dorado whom ladies called "Treetop Love" and who got cut up in a barfight after leering at another man's wife. It was the "high point, in terms of things no one would have believed possible," the *Times* reported. "The crowd grinned, the President grinned, the orchestra blared away, and he finished to applause."

"Betty and I stayed up until 1 am," Ford later wrote. "As they were leaving, the McNamaras came up to us and said, 'Boy, what a change.'"

D A Y

9

Saturday, August 17

Two Steps Forward, One Back

A few minutes before 9 A.M., Ford called Haig into the Oval Office and asked him to phone Rockefeller in Seal Harbor. While he and Betty had been hosting last night's state dinner, investigators from the prosecution force had located the safety deposit boxes that Hamilton Long said held Hunt's papers and had found them empty; Jaworski promptly dismissed the charges against Rockefeller as baseless and telephoned Buchen to say that the matter was closed. Ford had arrived from Alexandria at eight, and since then had sat alone, listing nine discussion points on a sheet of yellow foolscap. When Haig got Rockefeller on the line, Ford picked up.

"Nelson," Ford said—the president knew the former governor, but not well. "I want you to be vice president and I'll tell you why. I think the country needs you, a person of your stature, both domestically and internationally. I think it'll strengthen my administration at a traumatic time."

Ford's accidental presidency raised anxieties, in others if not himself, about whether he could command sufficient respect in Washington and among the people around him. The country knew little about its new leader except for a few scattered facts: Born Leslie King, Jr., in 1913, Ford had taken the name of his stepfather, a paint and varnish salesman; he'd pulled himself up through a combination of hard work and sports heroics, graduated in the top third of his class at Yale Law School, and served in World War II, a pillar of what NBC's Brokaw would later dub "The Greatest Generation." A Midwesterner, he was a staunch party workhorse who in twenty-five years in Congress introduced no significant legislation but who rose steadily to the top. The country liked his plain, open character, but was he strong? Could he handle the infighting unleashed by Nixon's departure?

Rockefeller, conversely, possessed independent power and stature, a man whose birth on the same date as that of his grandfather was reported on page one of the *Times*. He represented an establishment that was dying out, but his name, wealth, connections, ego, ambition, and widespread experience in and out of government made him a world figure of rare influence and standing. Nixon said in 1970, "Only three men in America understand the use of power. I do. John Connally does. And, I guess Nelson does." Some of Ford's advisers—principally Rumsfeld—feared that Rockefeller, Kissinger's first patron in government, would overshadow Ford on domestic affairs as Kissinger appeared to be doing in foreign policy, diminishing Ford's presidency at a dangerous juncture.

Ford continued reading from his notes: ". . . I'll give you meaningful assignments; I don't intend that you would just preside over the Senate and go on ceremonial trips . . . I believe your input, whether in the Cabinet or in the National Security Council, will be invaluable."

With the grand passion that he was famous for, Rockefeller had burned for the presidency—and disdained the vice presidency—ever since he'd first arrived in Washington in 1940 and witnessed both jobs up close. Franklin Roosevelt gave him his first job outside the family empire, appointing him at age thirty-two to direct inter-American affairs. "Are you sure you want me for this job?" Rockefeller had asked Roosevelt in the Oval Office, as Roosevelt prepared to take the country to war against European fascism, rather than communism, which conservatives of both parties considered the graver threat. "There's my family's connection with oil companies in Latin America. And I'm a Republican." Roosevelt replied, "I'm not worried." After appearing on the cover of *Life*, Rockefeller rapidly outgrew his duties, and Roosevelt named him assistant secretary of state for Latin America. Many mornings before work, Vice President Henry Wallace arrived at Rockefeller's Foxhall Road estate at 7 A.M. for tennis, and Rockefeller began to see and hear what it meant to be what he called "standby equipment." "You have to be pretty frustrated to do that," he recalled.

Truman replaced him, but Rockefeller returned to Washington under Eisenhower, who appointed him to chair a committee on government organization. "He [Eisenhower] said, 'Make a study of what might be given to Dick Nixon as a job,' " Rockefeller said. "We studied for about three months and decided there was nothing for the Vice President in the Constitution except presiding over the Senate." Rockefeller became undersecretary of the new department of health, education, and welfare; served as special White House assistant for Cold War strategy; and chaired the secret "Forty Committee," a group of high government officials charged with overseeing the CIA's clandestine operations, before returning to New York in 1958 to challenge the popular Democratic governor Averell Harriman. Rockefeller had been governor barely six months before he put to work a privately financed task force of seventy people to analyze his chances of winning the 1960 party nomination for president, which went to Nixon. Unable and unwilling to appeal to party loyalists, Rockefeller instead summoned Nixon to his Fifth Avenue triplex and dictated terms for a more liberal party platform. Goldwater denounced the pact as the "Munich of the Republican Party," launching Rockefeller's estrangement with the right, which more recently had worsened when he divorced his wife of thirty-two years and remarried a younger woman named Margaretta Fitler Murphy, better known as "Happy," with whom he had two young sons, ages ten and seven.

Ford had not announced publicly—nor had he and Betty yet agreed— that he was going to run in 1976, but he clarified his intentions. "I will run, Nelson," Ford said, "and your loyalty is important." Rockefeller thanked Ford and asked for a day to think it over and to consult with his family.

* * *

Since the embarrassment over Nixon's tapes, terHorst had tried to rein in the White House press operation, with uneven results. Haig, furious over Buzhardt's sudden public dismissal, confronted him, calling him the "little executioner." "Do you feel good," Haig asked, alluding to Buzhardt's heart trouble, "executing a sick man?" TerHorst countered by "keeping things closely held to 5 or 6 people" in the news office and channeling sensitive documents to Marsh, whose secretaries handled the stenciling and who he trusted to "make sure all the copies got back," he says.

Ziegler's assistant Diane Sawyer had accompanied Nixon to California, leaving terHorst largely alone to manage the outpouring of official statements, proclamations, corrections, clarifications, denials—and unofficial, often conflicting, feints and whispers. Up each day before five, he wrote feverishly for an hour at home, pressing hard to finish his suddenly now awaited first biography of Ford, before getting to work at six thirty to review the morning papers, overnight dispatches, and presidential schedule. After meeting with Ford, usually for fifteen to twenty minutes at midmorning, he faced reporters.

Miscues were common, and costly. At about the same time that Ford was on the phone with Rockefeller, terHorst—speaking on background, in response to the Jack Anderson column—told a wire service reporter that Ford had asked the special prosecutor's office to investigate allegations that Rockefeller had helped finance a project to disrupt the Democratic National Convention in Miami. Ford had confirmed to him that the probe had been opened but not, apparently, that it had been closed. Thus the White House appeared to credit the charge while discrediting Rockefeller. The wire service dispatched the story by teletype under the heading "Urgent," literally sounding bells in newsrooms, and the *Times* and other newspapers assigned bullpenned reporters to pursue the "Rockefeller Papers."

After meeting again with Ford, terHorst sped to the press room, now ablaze with mounting speculation about Rockefeller's chances as a contender, to clarify events. "President Ford," terHorst announced, "has advised me that Governor Rockefeller has been and remains under consideration for the vice-presidential nomination." The allegations, he said, were an "attempt by extremists who wished for reasons of their own to discredit Governor Rockefeller." To remove any ambiguity about the motive behind the earlier White House statement, terHorst identified himself as the source of the earlier wire service dispatches quoting an unnamed White House official to the effect that Rockefeller was under investigation.

"It would appear on the basis of the special prosecutor's office report that the original information given Mr. Buchen was without foundation," he said.

The briefing raised more questions than it answered: What extremists? What "reasons"? Would the allegations affect Ford's decision? Was the White House satisfied with the special prosecutor's report? Had Ford delayed his announcement of his vice presidential choice pending completion of the probe? Why didn't terHorst know the investigation was over when he'd confirmed it earlier in the day? Implicitly: Was terHorst out of the loop? TerHorst struggled to respond. Meantime, in Maine, Rockefeller huddled with his advisers, issuing a statement that "members of the Rockefeller family, including the governor," had donated money to Nixon's campaign, but only after three months of haggling to ensure it could be used exclusively in New York State.

As doubts continued to rise about Rockefeller's standing, terHorst returned to the pressroom to try, not for the last time, to clear up the confusion. "This matter should have no bearing on President Ford's consideration of a vice-presidential nominee," he said.

But it seemed that it already had, and the press, smelling a return to the obfuscations of Watergate—the "modified limited hangout" and "non-denial denial," terms of art coined by Nixon's men—suddenly was back in full cry, demanding a swift and full accounting.

* * *

After lunch, Ford called in Schlesinger, Hartmann, Marsh, Buchen, and terHorst—but notably not Haig—to plan for his first out-of-town trip, set for Monday, to Chicago to address the annual convention of the Veterans of Foreign Wars. A year earlier, Nixon received several roaring ovations from thousands of VFW delegates meeting in New Orleans when he insisted that the 1969 secret bombing of Cambodia, which started the violent destabilization of a neutral country that would lead to a communist takeover and ultimately a holocaust, was "absolutely necessary" and that it had forced the communists to the negotiating table and saved American lives. Nearly 30 million veterans, together with their families, accounted for half of the U.S. population, and the VFW was a bulwark of Americanism, anticommunism, and support for the Vietnam War. Ford, a VFW member himself, as well as a member of two other veterans' organizations, welcomed the excursion, which also would serve to keep him and Betty away from the commotion of moving day.

Unlike Watergate, Vietnam had begun to recede in the national memory, although just barely, and with an acrid residue of rage and recrimination salting a variety of still-open wounds. Ford wanted to do something quickly to heal the breach. One of the most painful wounds was the more than two thousand Americans still listed as North Vietnamese prisoners of war or reported as missing in action; the VFW had taken up the POW/MIA crusade in 1970. Another was the fate of some fifty thousand draft resisters and deserters, who were barred from entering the United States and who Ford, despite his solid support for the war, believed were victims also.

Nixon had run in 1968—the most polarized and violent year of an increasingly anxious decade—on a general theme of law and order, and in office he continued to hold a hard line against amnesty for draft resisters, especially as Watergate began to engulf his presidency. "Certainly I have sympathy for any individual who has made a mistake," he said in his first second-term news conference, one day after the first court convictions in the burglary case. "We have all made mistakes." He continued:

> But also, it is a rule of life, we have to pay for our mistakes. The war is over. Many Americans paid a very high price to serve their country, some with their lives, some as prisoners of war for as long as six to seven years, and of course, two or three million gave two to three years out of their lives, serving in a country far away in a war that they realize had very little support among the so-called better people—the media, intellectual circles and the rest . . . Amnesty means forgiveness . . . Those who served must pay their price. Those who deserted must pay their price . . . The price is a criminal penalty for disobeying the laws of the United States. If they want to return to the United States they must pay the penalty.

It wasn't surprising, given Nixon's choice of rhetoric, that the issues of amnesty for draft resisters and presidential pardons for the Watergate defendants—including, quite likely, Nixon himself—by now had gotten conflated, and that many people, most notably Haldeman, were suggesting that they be linked more purposefully. As Ford and his men knew, Haldeman and his lawyers had tried during Nixon's last forty-eight hours in office to present Nixon with a petition to grant clemency to everyone already convicted or facing conviction for Watergate crimes, and they had urged him to pardon Vietnam draft resisters and evaders at the same time, ostensibly to provide Ford with a clean slate. Nixon, however, had refused to take Haldeman's calls, leaving it to Haig to call him back and tell him "that the idea has been rejected as impossible; it can't be done," Haldeman recalled. "It was not a little ironic that Haldeman's own screening system was working so well to keep his calls from the President," Ehrlichman would note.

It was Schlesinger who first proposed that Ford "do something" on the amnesty issue, both to accelerate national reconciliation and to "draw a real distinction between the Nixon and Ford administrations," Ford wrote. Laird agreed, and so had Ford's three sons. Ford, as always, was concerned primarily with conservative reaction, and the discussion in the Oval Office focused now on the complex terms for allowing war re-sisters, most of whom lived in Canada, to return home. "All of us agreed that any proposal I made should be conditional and that the draft re-sisters and deserters should have to 'earn' their amnesty," Ford wrote.

As the forty-five-minute meeting wound to a close, Ford asked Marsh to work with the Pentagon, the Justice Department, and the Veterans Administration to put together a Vietnam amnesty "package." The group then talked briefly about an appropriate forum for announcing the plan. Plainly, a liberal audience would be most receptive, but Ford said he wanted to announce the change on Monday, in Chicago. "The more conservative VFW would be very disturbed," he recalled, "but announc-ing it to them would indicate strength on my part."

"The Chicago address," Ford wrote, "was the right occasion."

* * *

TerHorst launched his third briefing of the day with a statement from Ford that clearly kept Rockefeller in the running. TerHorst said:

> The president regards the inaccurate information given to Mr. Buchen . . . as a deplorable example of the lengths to which cer-tain persons will go to discredit Mr. Rockefeller and thereby at-tempt to remove him from consideration . . . What's been going on in the last week or so is a grave effort on the part of supporters of persons deemed to be under Mr. Ford's consideration to influ-ence his choice.

The sharp infighting among Republicans since Nixon had announced his resignation eleven days earlier now heaved into open view as terHorst delivered the impression that Hamilton Long, identified in news accounts only as "Mr. Long," an elderly right-wing activist from Philadelphia, was working on behalf of Goldwater or Reagan—maybe even Bush. Long, who made it a point of pride not to belong to any political organization, claimed to be acting only for himself. Nonetheless, the White House position that evolved throughout the day was, as one unnamed source told the *Times,* that the "Rockefeller Papers" were a hoax contrived by a "group of right-wing extremists who decided it would be useful to blacken the name of Gov. Rockefeller."

"There is no clear indication," terHorst continued, "that those responsible were connected in any way with one of the other men said to be under consideration for vice president, and the real identity of the tipster, Long, is still unknown."

Ricocheting around the pressroom, the story refused to die down. Reporters and columnists generally agreed that Rockefeller, despite being the victim, had been damaged by the smear, and in particular by the White House response, and sources throughout Washington obliged them with names of other candidates whose chances were now assumed to have improved. Ford's thinking on the matter remained, of course, a mystery. As the *Times* reported, "There was no evidence that the clearing of Mr. Rockefeller's name at the White House had improved his chances for the Vice-Presidency."

At terHorst's fourth and final briefing of the day, he took full responsibility for the confusion. Attempting to explain why Buchen hadn't informed him that the special prosecutors couldn't find Hunt's papers and considered the case closed, terHorst suggested there had been a brief lapse in communication in the White House. The wire service, he added afterward, had misinterpreted him; Buchen had referred Long's tip to Jaworski but never requested an investigation or a report.

Hartmann, as ever, watched the day's disparities with mounting frustration, viewing them as chiefly damaging to Ford, who had all but chosen a nominee who through no fault of his own now looked not only as if he'd been sullied by a rival but also inadequately supported by the president—if not done in by the inexperience of the staff. "This was unfortunate," Hartmann wrote, "but we were all babes in the White House. We had done the right thing and truthfully told what we had done, but it was unfair to Rockefeller to give Presidential credence to Long's hearsay. And, of course, the press castigated us for that the next day, by which time a counterrocket had been launched."

10

Sunday, August 18

Signs of Normalcy

The throng lining the driveway at Immanuel Church-on-the-Hill waved greetings as the presidential motorcade rolled up for the ten o'clock communion service. Cameras clicked and whirred when the Fords stepped out of a black limousine bearing the presidential seal. Dressed in a gray checked suit and wide, diagonally striped tie, Ford yelled to the crowd, "Good morning, everybody. How are you all?" as Betty, wearing a blue polka-dot dress, red carnation, and white shoes, stood by. An onlooker told a *Post* reporter, "He's very friendly. He's very approachable. He waves. He says, 'Nice to see you.' He comes and goes like anyone else. It's really thrilling."

Congregation members since the early fifties, both Fords looked uncomfortable at the attention, and Secret Service men shepherded them inside. Taking their seats in the last pew under the choir loft, they appeared "more relaxed in the solemn confines of the church," the *Post* reported. Betty wrote that their daughter Susan, their last child, had gone off to the beach for a week, "leaving me with her cat, Shan, and mixed emotions." Ford had plans to play golf in the afternoon with Laird and two old friends from Congress.

Nixon in his first inaugural address had spoken of a national "crisis of the spirit," and Ford had inherited that crisis, too—a crisis lately grown worse, less because of Watergate than because the thirty-year economic boom after World War II had ended, startlingly, with the Arab oil embargo. Few realized that with the quadrupling of oil prices by countries most Americans had long viewed as minor powers, the epoch-making mass upward mobility of Americans was over, most likely forever. But many felt gripped by an inchoate and long-repressed dread. According to a Gallup poll conducted the week before Ford took office and reported this morning in the *Times,* nearly half of all Americans believed the country was now headed toward a depression "such as the one experienced in the 1930s."

Sharing a hymnbook, the Fords joined in singing "Hallelujah, Sing to Jesus" and recited the day's prayers. The waning years of the boom had also spewed up, as Tom Wolfe observed, the "upward roll . . . of the third great religious wave in American history." Both the Catholic Church and the mainstream Protestant denominations were confronted by an upsurge of fundamentalism, evangelism, cults, and therapies that owed more to the ecstatic spiritualism of the youth and drug culture of the sixties than the Reverend Norman Vincent Peale or the Vatican. Suburban churches like Immanuel Church-on-the-Hill, hoping to attract disaffected young people, countered with attempts to update Christianity through social activism and liberal advocacy.

The Reverend William Dols, Jr.—known to everyone as Bill—gave the sermon, a meditation on Jesus' entering Jerusalem. Dols, forty-one, "hadn't slept a wink," he recalls. Immanuel, though historically progressive and liberal, had among its parishioners several other congressmen, the commandant of the marine corps, and other ranking military men and women, and as rector he walked a fine line. Recently Dols had sponsored as a deacon the cochair of the Coalition for Women's Ordination, a group fighting for the installation of women as priests, and the episode had been controversial. The new human potential movements heavily influenced Dols's theology, and he used sensitivity training and human relations techniques in his Bible study groups.

Dols told how, according to Luke's gospel, Jesus burst into sobs when he entered the holy city, heartsick over what he saw. With Ford in mind, Dols told the worshipers that the purpose of learning more about themselves and God in Christ was to get involved in the social and moral problems of the times—"common humanity," he called it.

"So much that passes for living is in retrospect the dying times of the moment missed—the cry not heard—the hurt unrecognized—the opportunity ignored—all the might have beens and could have beens and if onlys," Dols said. He spoke of the "dares not taken and the risks sidestepped by people, like cities, who are forever backing away and making excuses.

"Jesus wept over a city that did not recognize God's moment when it came and would not grasp it . . . The weeping is about the dares not taken—the risks side-stepped—those awful moments when the ante is there and we are not."

Dols's homily neatly if unintentionally evoked a soaring event etched in recent memory and linked symbolically to Ford's own elevation to power. Early on the morning of August 7, just hours before Nixon summoned Ford to tell him that he would become president, people on their way to work near the foot of Manhattan looked up to the wedge of sky between the two shimmering behemoths of the still-unfinished, largely unrented World Trade Center, a Rockefeller family–led project courting financial ruin and facing a fusillade of social and architectural criticism, and saw a man walking. Six years earlier an eighteen-year-old Paris street performer named Philippe Petit had come across an article with an illustration of the project in model form. Petit perfected his skills as a wire-walker and studied and scouted the towers, and the previous evening he and two teams of friends had set to work, slipping to the tops of the towers with a disassembled balancing pole, wire for rigging, two hundred fifty feet of one-inch steel cable, and a bow and arrow. When the people below saw the tiny figure walking on air between the towers, a Port Authority police sergeant dispatched to bring him down could only look on.

"I observed the tightrope 'dancer'—you couldn't call him a 'walker'—

approximately halfway between the two towers," the policeman later reported.

> And upon seeing us he started to smile and laugh and he started going into a dancing routine on the high wire . . . He was bouncing up and down. His feet were actually leaving the wire . . . Unbelievable really . . . everybody was spellbound by the watching of it.

Petit's heroic skywalk was eclipsed in the news by Nixon's fall and Ford's emergence, but it had managed briefly to pierce the national gloom. Ford, working hard to bear the burdens of office but knowing that bigger tests lay ahead, listened intently to Dols's sermon. "The minister," the *Post* reported, "drew a smile and a brief laugh from the President with a quote from a man who said, 'When you tell me what I could be, it terrifies me.' "

After the gospel, Ford pulled out his collection envelope and waited for the plate to be passed around, though the ushers skipped the presidential pew. Finally, a smiling woman in front of the Fords turned and held out the plate for his donation. When Ford took communion, he stood in line behind the crippled and the halt, awaiting his turn.

* * *

While Ford returned to Crown View Drive for lunch, twenty thousand emotional Greek American protesters massed on the Ellipse, chanting "Turks out of Cyprus" and "Killer Kissinger," who was burned in effigy as many cheered. Many Greek Americans blamed Kissinger personally, bitterly, for not preventing the Greek coup that led to the Turkish invasion, then betraying Greece by asserting America's neutrality. Schlesinger, speaking on *Face the Nation,* buttressed their anger with a warning to Turkey, whose forces in the past twenty-four hours had broken a cease-fire and were pushing further south.

"We understand the desire of the Turks to protect the minority Turk population," Schlesinger said. "But the Turkish moves at this point have gone beyond what any of its friends or sympathizers would have anticipated, and are prepared, I think, to accept." Schlesinger also warned that the United States couldn't undergo sustained annual cuts in the defense budget and still remain a "first-class military power."

Ford viewed the mixed signals from his conflicting cabinet secretaries with mounting concern, particularly as he surveyed Capitol Hill, where Democratic Idaho senator Frank Church was calling on Congress to choose between the administration's "divergent" nuclear arms policies. Church, a liberal member of the Foreign Relations Committee who, like Jackson, had presidential hopes and planned to use upcoming public hearings on détente as a forum, said that Nixon's "debilitating ambivalence" in the Kissinger-Schlesinger debate that preoccupied U.S. military strategists had crippled foreign policy, and that the country had to choose between them. "Great as the President's responsibility is," Church cautioned, "Congress too has the responsibility to choose [and] . . . the power to enforce its choice through binding legislation."

News crews captured Ford, wearing a golf cap with his suit and tie and clutching an armload of papers to work on in the car, coming out of his front door for the half hour ride to Burning Tree Golf & Country Club in Bethesda, Maryland, an old wooded course on hilly terrain that on weekends served as a nexus of politics and deal-making. Reporters asked him about the vice presidency, and Ford said he would announce his selection on Tuesday.

The press had reinserted Rockefeller in the race, but *Newsweek* had released a story earlier in the day saying that George Bush had "slipped badly because of alleged irregularities in the financing of his 1970 Senate race." The magazine quoted unnamed White House sources as saying "there was potential embarrassment in reports that the Nixon White House had funneled about $100,000 from a secret fund called the 'Townhouse Operation' " into Bush's losing Senate campaign and that $40,000 "may not have been properly reported as required by election law."

Here was the "counterrocket" Hartmann referred to—an internecine attack among vice presidential rivals, fired this time anonymously from within the White House. Bush, at his family compound in Kennebunkport, reeled at the news. Broad party and congressional support had built for his candidacy; his public eagerness and the novelty of his lobbying for the vice presidency had brought cries of foul from Rockefeller supporters, but no indication that it had hurt him with Ford.

The "Townhouse Operation," like the Fielding break-in, was an early Nixon White House prototype, a precursor of Watergate. A year after Nixon had taken office, he sent Haldeman an action memo stating: "One of our most important projects for 1970 is to see that our major contributors funnel all their funds through us . . ." Meeting in the White House, Haldeman and Secretary of Commerce Maurice Stans set up a secret fund-raising organization designed to bypass the Republican National Committee. The idea was to allow Nixon to pick candidates who would be loyal to him—and reliably opposed to the Eastern Establishment he never got over resenting. "A total Nixon man, first," Nixon once described Bush. "Doubt if you can do better than Bush."

Receiving from Texas contributors a total of $106,000 earmarked for his campaign, Bush became the main beneficiary of the Townhouse fund—a "dress rehearsal for the campaign finance abuses of Watergate, as well as for today's loophole ridden system," as the *Wall Street Journal* later wrote—which was now under investigation by Jaworski's staff. Even had Ford wanted to nominate Bush over Rockefeller, picking Bush surely would reopen Watergate as well as lead to the disclosure of up to eighteen more secret Townhouse donations to Republican Senate candidates.

Bush had no comment, leaving his Texas supporters to fend for him in the press. "There is absolutely nothing irregular about George Bush in any fashion," Harris County finance chairman James Bayless told the AP. "There are absolutely, unequivocally no grounds for this report. It makes me want to vomit." Bush's state finance chairman also denied the report. But the damage was done. Bush's name and his loyalty now both tied him to everything Ford most wanted to keep out of the White House. Though Jaworski eventually excluded him in his final report, the smear, unlike Rockefeller's, would not wash off.

As Ford arrived at Burning Tree, reporters ambushed him again. He knew very little. The Bush smear would not have come from Harlow, for whom discretion was power. But a "White House source" could be anyone from any of the rival contingents surrounding him. Bush himself believed it was Laird, a "master's voice from behind the scenes," he wrote. "I felt his hand on the VP situation very clearly and coolly. But I felt it on the back, not on the front." James Cannon, a former national affairs editor and chief correspondent at *Newsweek,* and special assistant to Rockefeller who would soon become Ford's top domestic affairs adviser and still later his biographer, suspected Rumsfeld. "No doubt about it," he says. "I'd bet money on it."

Clearly, with Rockefeller still dusting himself off and mulling a decision, Rumsfeld stood to gain the most if Bush stumbled. Rumsfeld had notified Ford that he needed to return to Europe due to the Cyprus crisis, and Ford agreed: He'd be leaving for Brussels in a day or two, when Cheney would return to his mid-tier job in the private sector. Ford, in the meantime, was coming rapidly to see that his "spokes on a wheel" staffing system needed improvement, and that someone would have to assert control over it even at the risk of rebuilding parts of Nixon's "Berlin Wall." Rumsfeld's window of opportunity to affect Ford's decision was rapidly dropping.

As the motorcade swung past Burning Tree's gate and up the winding drive, Ford looked forward to his first golf game in three weeks, since he and several congressional leaders took the vice presidential jet to play a charity tournament with host Tip O'Neill, then House majority leader, in Worcester, Massachusetts. During the flight O'Neill had told him Nixon would be impeached and Ford refused to believe him. Paired this afternoon with Minority whip Les Arends and Texas Democrat George Mahon, chairman of the House Appropriations Committee, whom Ford would need in his budget battles, he and Laird, regular golfing partners, thought they could win.

* * *

In Kansas City, the Democrats, as they had every time they had convened since 1968, tore themselves apart. If Nixon's downfall was an opportunity to reunite after the schismatic 1972 convention in Miami—which didn't need Rockefeller to send thugs to disrupt it—few noticed it. Seizing control with McGovern's nomination, reformers had mandated a midterm "mini-convention" in December to ratify the party's first constitution, which Chairman Robert Strauss and many other officials feared was a disaster-in-the-making. One hundred twenty-five delegates had come to Missouri for the weekend to hash out the new charter.

Tensions had first erupted on Saturday afternoon, when party regulars and AFL-CIO representatives maneuvered to block major reforms that would guarantee more authority over state and local branches and more independence from elected officials. Angry blacks, women, and leftists threatened to walk out. Late into the night, various caucuses met to avert a crisis as the commission prepared to decide the fate of the party's anti-discrimination rules.

Chairman Terry Stanford, a former North Carolina governor, delayed the start of the second-day session for almost two hours, hoping to find a compromise on a section requiring state Democratic parties to take affirmative action in selecting delegates. Then Washington representative Thomas Foley, Jackson's closest ally and chair of the labor-regulars group, proposed striking a statement that the goal of affirmative action was "to encourage participation by all Democrats as indicated by their presence in the Democratic electorate"—what Foley and a string of labor delegates called "implied quotas."

The reaction, David Broder of the *Post* wrote, "was violent." California assemblyman Willie Brown, leader of the black caucus, denounced the Foley amendment for "driving blacks and women out of the party." White liberals complained, too, about what one called the "final rape of this document." For several hours, a showdown loomed while commission members offered compromises . . . until midafternoon, when the wife of an AFL-CIO staff member proposed eliminating a ban on "unit voting"—a rule requiring that a state's entire vote must go to the candidate with the majority of delegates. In other words: Winner takes all.

Brown, a lawyer from San Francisco, approached the microphone and shouted: "I am walking out. This is a travesty on the whole process . . . This is the nail that closes the coffin on the Charter Commission." Joined by up to twenty black delegates and a scattering of whites, he went to the foyer and before the TV cameras repeated his denunciations. Stanford, short of a quorum, was forced to adjourn the meeting, leaving unresolved several issues, including the antidiscriminiation program.

The rift—one of those who left with Brown instantly dubbed it the "Sunday Afternoon Massacre"—"virtually guaranteed" an emotional scene when six hundred elected grassroots delegates and eight hundred party and public officials returned in three months for the mini-convention, Broder wrote. Like Republicans, Democrats were emerging from Vietnam, Watergate, five and a half years of Nixon, and the traumatic transfer of power deeply, perennially at war with themselves.

For Ford, whose immediate task as party leader—and as a candidate in 1976—was to help the Republicans win in November, the Democrats' meltdown offered a welcome burst of assistance, a windfall. As one distraught swing member on the commission, New York Democratic chairman Joseph Crangle, pleaded with Brown just before he and the others walked out, the televised spectacle in Kansas City was the "best thing the Democratic Party could do this year to help elect Republicans in 1974 and 1976."

* * *

Ford stopped by the Oval Office for a half hour before heading home for his last night in Alexandria, where Betty had taken charge of the packing. Through his years in Congress he had traveled relentlessly. Late most weekday afternoons he had taken a car from his House office to the airport, then flown to remote districts to speak, scout candidates, raise money, and make contacts with local Republicans before flying back to D.C. and arriving home around midnight. Betty recalled finding him one night in his sleep repeating "Thank you . . . Thank you . . . Thank you"—she realized he was dreaming about campaigning, standing on a receiving line and shaking hands. Living in the White House, he'd persuaded her, meant they would see each other more, and when he traveled, she could join him.

Ford reviewed his amnesty speech with Hartmann and spoke by phone with Rockefeller, who told him that, if offered the vice presidency, "I would be honored to serve." Ford repeated his promise that Rockefeller would be a working vice president. "He wanted me to give him support in the domestic field and wanted me to head it up as Henry would in the foreign field," Rockefeller recalled. "And he wanted me to help him on recruitment, which, he said, could be very helpful, as I was known for having attracted good people."

Ford hoped to preserve the suspense and secrecy surrounding his decision until he announced it on Tuesday; he told Rockefeller to be prepared to come to Washington but didn't make the offer definite. Yet he had now set his administration's course. By choosing Kissinger and Rockefeller as his chief policymakers in world and national affairs, two men who each not only could overshadow him but were deeply allied with each other, he had opted for the strongest possible partners instead of relying on the usual Washington traits of familiarity, loyalty, ideological purity, and party service. No synergy could be more troubling to conservatives, or to those on his transition staff like Rumsfeld, who argued that Ford could grow into the presidency only by shrinking those around him, but Ford seemed unconcerned.

Laird had made the case to him that Nixon inadvertently diminished himself by choosing as his running mate the unaccomplished, little-known Agnew, a statehouse politician from Maryland with no foreign policy experience who was a favorite among the law-and-order right, and that Ford couldn't afford to make the same mistake. Nixon plainly had had similar feelings about *him,* chortling to Rockefeller shortly after Ford's vice presidential swearing-in: "Can you imagine Jerry Ford sitting in this chair?" Rather than fearing the presence of strong advisers with large public agendas, Ford believed his willingness to have them close by in itself indicated strength.

Nixon, in his pep talks to himself on his legal pads, often had prodded himself to project characteristics he believed showed his remarkable side. On an undated page discovered in the Oval Office on the day he left Washington, he wrote:

> Foreign Policy=Strength . . . Must emphasize—Courage,
> Stands Alone . . . Knows more than anyone else. Towers
> above advisors. World leader.
>
> Restoration of Dignity. Family man—Not a playboy—respects
> office too much—but fun.
>
> Extraordinary intelligence—memory—Idealism—Love of
> country—Concern for old—poor—Refusal to exploit.
>
> You must be personal and warm.

Yet by reminding himself over and over of the disparities between who he was and how he hoped to be seen, Nixon seemed forever masked, forever dissembling. Ford, by comparison, seemed nothing if not "normal"—solid, guileless, his own man. "Ford asked the American people to take him at his word," the *Post*'s veteran White House reporter Jules Witcover wrote, "and they did." It had been just ten days since his inauguration, but nearly everyone in Washington, and particularly the media, had begun to regard Ford as maybe just the right man to satisfy the public's longing to forget not only Nixon but Johnson, whose credibility by the time he left office had been equally shattered by Vietnam.

"Almost perfect," Witcover judged Ford, applying only slight hyperbole:

> He had the look of a strapping steelworker, dressed—even over
> dressed—in his one slightly noisy Sunday suit. He spoke haltingly
> and plainly; reporters found that they could speed up his voice on
> their tape recorders and still hear the words distinctly. Best of all

he spoke frankly, and was not afraid to laugh at himself. . . . That Ford's politics were not far removed from Nixon's in any important respect, and that he was himself a politician with a survivability record of a quarter century, were facts lost or at least temporarily overlooked in the euphoria of a return to normalcy in the White House.

Home by seven-thirty, Ford pitched in and helped Betty with the last of the packing. The house was in chaos, crates and cartons everywhere—"chunks of our lives uprooted and labeled for storage," she would write. "It had been," she recalled, "a very traumatic experience for me."

D A Y

11

Monday, August 19

Moving

Before flying to Chicago, Ford composed a list—*Bush, Rumsfeld, Richardson, Rockefeller and Raeygon* (sic)—and handed it to Hartmann. "While we're gone," he said, "have Phil [Buchen] check these names out with Jaworski." The three names Ford had given FBI director Kelley on Friday already had leaked, and Hartmann warned that Goldwater and other Republicans in Congress might be miffed when, inevitably, this list, too, got out. Ford agreed: "Well, let's say that I narrowed it down to six. We won't ever tell who the sixth one was and they'll all be happy." The mangled spelling of Reagan's name was unsurprising if not bluntly dismissive; Ford had met the California governor on occasion at party functions and didn't "take Reagan seriously," as he later wrote. "Several of his characteristics seemed to rule him out . . . One was his penchant for offering simplistic solutions to hideously complex problems. A second was his conviction that he was always right in every argument; he seemed unable to acknowledge that he might have made a mistake."

Quietly, Ford's staff had ordered Nixon's *Spirit of '76* removed from the fuselage of Air Force One, so the new president wouldn't appear to be using the "Flying White House" as a campaign prop during his first official trip. Onboard, the Fords reviewed their accommodations, decorated by Pat Nixon basically in blue—muted blue plaids, blue-gray marbled carpeting, Wedgewood-blue crushed velvet upholstery in the First Lady's sitting room and the presidential lounge. The president's chair was deep solid blue, as was his desktop, which added to the regal effect of the deep blue suits favored by Nixon because they set him off from others on the podium. Squeezed behind the family quarters and the staff compartment were the press and Secret Service.

As the plane approached Chicago, Ford told Haig he planned to announce a limited amnesty for draft exiles in his speech to the VFW. "Because I had always believed that some draft evaders were genuine conscientious objectors," Haig wrote, "I had no argument to make against selective forgiveness." But Haig warned Ford that the audience reaction would be hostile; he might even be booed. Other than objecting to Ford's choice of audience, he believed Ford's "scheme" was motivated by Christian charity and a patriotic desire to grant a second chance to flawed young men, and that it had the added merit of "decoupling clemency from political considerations (a generous and courageous thing, given the times) and opened for him the opportunity of arguing from the general (the draft evaders) to the particular (Nixon)."

Onboard, news reached Ford and his staff about an attack on the U.S. Embassy in Nicosia. Greek Cypriots protesting American neutrality had marched on the compound, shouting anti-American slogans and waving blood-spattered banners saying "Kissinger Murderer." A few men scaled the gate, took down the U.S. flag, and burned it. The crowd then overpowered the guards and swarmed the compound, overturning cars and setting them ablaze. When police hurled tear gas at them, some demonstrators, a few with machine guns, opened fire, killing the new U.S. ambassador, Rodger Davies. Initial dispatches said Davies and an aide had been killed by stray bullets as they sought safety in a hallway.

In Chicago, before a crowd of local dignitaries, a public address announcer at O'Hare airport mistakenly welcomed the First Couple as "The President and Mrs. Nixon." The city's powerful Democratic mayor

Richard Daley was absent from the reception—he'd suffered a stroke and was in the hospital—but he had ordered a spectacular display along the motorcade route of fireworks, fireboats, banners, and bands. Standing, Ford waved and smiled to packed crowds from an open limousine . . . until several thousand Greek demonstrators rallying in front of the Conrad Hilton Hotel, where the VFW was meeting, forced him to duck back inside. In 1968 the twenty-eight-story hotel had been headquarters for both the candidates and the press during the tumultuous Democratic National Convention. While Daley erupted and shook his fist at dissenting delegates inside the convention hall, the lobby and lower floors had filled with tear gas during the "Battle of Michigan Avenue," the worst of five days of rioting in which Chicago police clubbed not only protesters but reporters and doctors offering medical help. Chicago still wore a black eye from that violence, and it was hoped locally that Daley's warm welcome for Ford would help repair the city's image.

Ford stumbled slightly through his opening thank-yous. He guffawed warmly after he introduced himself as a "proud member of old camp post VFW 830" and a delegate in the back of the hall let out a whoop, and he got an enthusiastic laugh when he pointed out for the sake of "national unity" that he was also a proud member of the American Legion and AMVETS. Their colored VFW hats covered with pins and patches, many of them in uniform, many more with their wives sitting next to them, the thirty-nine hundred delegates were mostly middle aged; Vietnam veterans, sharply divided over whether to be proud of their service, were joining in historically low numbers. Many murmured and groaned when Ford announced that Ambassador Davies had been killed that morning on Cyprus, saying sadly, "He, too, gave his life in foreign wars." They cheered and whistled wildly when he told them he was appointing former Indiana representative Richard Roudebush, a former VFW commandant, to head the Veterans Administration.

Departing from the official text, Ford turned, indirectly, to his amnesty proposal—specifically, a cabinet-level study of options for alternative service. "As minority leader of the House and recently as vice president, I stated my strong conviction that unconditional blanket amnesty for anyone who illegally evaded or fled military service is wrong," Ford said. Again the audience burst into thunderous applause.

"But all, in a sense, are casualties," he said, "still abroad or absent without leave from the real America. I want them to come home—if they want to *work* their way back.

"In my judg-a-ment," Ford said, "these young Americans should have a second chance to contribute their fair share to the rebuilding of 'peace among ourselves and with all nations.' " Hartmann had borrowed the last phrase from Abraham Lincoln, who decided as his first act toward Reconstruction and reconciliation to offer amnesty to Civil War Confederates, provided they swore loyalty to the United States.

"So I am throwing the weight of my presidency into the scales of justice on the side of leniency. I see their earned reentry—*earned* reentry—into an atmosphere of hope, hard work, and mutual trust . . . As men and women whose patriotism has been tested and proved, I want your help."

A stony silence followed: The convention would vote unanimously to oppose Ford's idea. But Ford felt he had achieved what he set out to do, showing the country his courage, independence, and ability to change—to lead by moral example. On the return flight to Washington, he climbed in the back with Hartmann and terHorst to talk with reporters about why he'd chosen to make his announcement before the audience most likely to reject it. Calmly, he explained that the decision was one he'd calculated carefully.

"Five or six people in the cabinet, in my staff, and others, said to me last week, 'Well, at some point we have to do something on this,' " he began. "And the more I thought about it, the more I thought the right audience would be an audience that . . . might be difficult. And rather than going to speak to some hand-picked audience, I thought it would be better to talk to people who I hoped might have some understanding, which I think they did. It would be a little . . . cowardice, you know, if we'd picked some audience that would have been ecstatic. But these people were, I thought, wonderful."

* * *

Lawyers for the six defendants in the Watergate cover-up conspiracy case smiled encouragingly as they arrived at Judge John Sirica's courtroom to seek a trial delay. All agreed that they didn't have enough time— less than four weeks—to review the more than sixty newly released Nixon tapes, and that the explosion of publicity surrounding the impeachment hearings and Nixon's resignation would prevent their clients from getting a fair trial, especially in the nation's capital. Jaworski, pressed by his trial staff and facing the decision whether to try Nixon along with his advisers, also wanted more time, meaning the government, too, supported a postponement.

The lawyers' smiles vanished as they rose to present their arguments to Sirica, age seventy, who'd handled the case since it was still about a botched burglary. Chief district judge by dint of seniority, Sirica had assigned the break-in case to himself, and, as Watergate historian Stanley Kutler wrote, he "caricatured the type of judge that candidate Richard Nixon loved." A former prizefighter, he had been a faithful Republican since the party first helped him land a job as an assistant U.S. attorney forty years earlier. He'd double-dated with Senator Joseph McCarthy, who offered to make him chief counsel to his subcommittee investigating communist influence in government; Sirica, who recently had taken a lucrative job with a private firm, declined, and McCarthy hired Roy Cohn instead. After campaigning for the Eisenhower-Nixon ticket, mostly among Italian American groups, he was appointed to the federal bench. Unapologetically tough on sentencing, his courthouse nickname was "Maximum John."

In spite of his political loyalties, it was Sirica's threatening to hand out the stiffest possible punishments that broke the Watergate scandal open. Until March 1973, near the end of the break-in trial, Nixon and his aides had successfully kept the investigation from reaching higher than the Plumbers unit. They had induced then–minority leader Ford, whom

Nixon's aides disparaged as a "wind-up dog," to kill an investigation by the House Banking and Currency Committee into the money trail; the Senate Judiciary Committee probe remained easily deflected as a jealous and partisan attempt to reverse the results of the Nixon landslide; and Cox's young prosecutors were having little success penetrating the White House, which blamed the affair on the CIA. No one talked seriously about impeachment.

Sirica, unable to believe that no higher-ups were involved, pounded at the burglars to break ranks and come forward until one did, a former CIA employee named James McCord, Jr., who three days before his sentencing delivered Sirica a letter outlining a far-reaching conspiracy to obstruct justice and asking to meet privately with him in chambers. The next day, John Dean went to Nixon to tell him about the "cancer" on the presidency, which as Dean explained was the lethal fact that too many people knew too much and couldn't be silenced. As McCord had predicted earlier in a letter to the White House, "Every tree in the forest will fall."

Defense lawyer William Hundley, representing former attorney general John Mitchell, argued first, complaining that Mitchell "had pretty much been written off as guilty" by every member of the House Judiciary Committee during televised impeachment hearings. He suggested that the trial be delayed until after the first of the year, "when we can look forward to an abatement of the prejudicial climate."

"I think the climate is right now," Sirica said. "If you pick up the *Washington Post* you hardly see [Watergate] on the front page any more."

Haldeman's lawyer John Wilson rose next to claim that the case was "deluged" with negative publicity, noting that Haldeman's name had appeared "hundreds of times" in recent issues of *Time* and *Newsweek*. "If any juror doesn't know who Haldeman is, I regret the state of his intelligence . . . Most of the co-defendants don't want to be tried with us now," Wilson said. Ehrlichman's lawyer Andrew Hall echoed the point, telling Sirica that serving a subpoena on Nixon had convinced him that the Watergate story hadn't receded. "Much to my surprise," Hall said, "it made the headlines." The subpoena ordering Nixon to testify as a witness had arrived that morning in Los Angeles, where a U.S. marshal told reporters he would serve it personally to Nixon, who still had no lawyer, in San Clemente "within a reasonable time, possibly today."

Sirica said he sympathized with their arguments, conceding it was an unusual case. But, he added, it's "not the type of case that arouses the passions of hatred . . . not a case of a woman being raped or murdered, say, where pretrial publicity would be an obvious problem.

"Millions of people," Sirica said—including himself—"feel very sad about what happened to Richard Nixon."

Sirica seemed impatient. He noted that there had been heavy publicity when Robert G. (Bobby) Baker, a former Senate aide to Lyndon Johnson, was tried for attempted income tax evasion, conspiracy, and fraud. "That was peanuts compared to this," Wilson said. "Just a small, little peanut. You are not giving us a fair trial if you put us to trial in the next three months."

Hall, speaking for Ehrlichman, told the judge that he and his client needed more time to review the new tapes, and Associate Special Prosecutor James Neal agreed. Despite launching an around-the-clock operation, using skilled FBI clerks to make first-draft transcripts for the trial team, Neal said the government couldn't hope to examine all the tapes in time.

But Sirica said, "I'm not impressed. I don't think it's going to take too long to listen to those tapes." Sirica and an assistant had been the first people outside of the White House to hear them, in a small soundproof room adjacent to his courtroom, and from that moment he had known there was no question of Nixon's guilt. (As he later wrote: "I'll never forget hearing the President tell his aides on the March 22 tape, 'And, uh, for that reason, I am perfectly willing to—I don't give a shit what happens. I want you all to stonewall it, let them plead the First Amendment, cover-up or anything else, if it'll save it—save the plan.'" March 22 was two days after Sirica opened McCord's letter and a day after Dean's dire warning. "A lifetime of dealing with the criminal law," Sirica wrote, "of watching a parade of people who had robbed, stolen, killed, raped, and deceived others, had not hardened me enough to hear with equanimity the low political scheming that was played back to me from the White House offices.")

Sirica refused to budge. Back in March, he'd scheduled the trial date so that they could be done by Christmas, and he warned the lawyers to prepare for long sessions, possibly until 6 P.M. "I want to see the end of this case sometime," Sirica grumbled. Wilson replied, "You're not going to give us a fair trial. There's not the slightest doubt in my mind."

"That's your opinion," Sirica snapped. "There's no better time to try this case than the present time. The case will be called to trial at nine-thirty A.M. on September ninth."

With that, the attorneys' indignation flared. Hall slapped down a standby notice of appeal on the prosecutor's table—anticipating Sirica's decision, Ehrlichman already had decided to pursue a delay to the Supreme Court if necessary. Haldeman's lawyers believed Sirica wanted the case over mainly for "purely personal" reasons; he'd been mired for two years in Watergate and was eager to retire. Deep mutterings filled the courtroom, but outside, mindful of Sirica's gag order, the lawyers said little.

"Mr. Wilson," a television reporter asked. "You've known Judge Sirica for many years. Both sides wanted a delay in this trial. Why do you suppose he wanted to go ahead with it at this time, September 9?"

Wilson laughed. "Boy, that is a question I wouldn't attempt to answer."

* * *

Ford instructed Kissinger to conduct the State Department briefing on Cyprus in person, both to underscore American concern about events in the region and to show that he and Kissinger were in strong accord. The attacks on Kissinger had been among the sharpest of his career, and he was adjusting to Nixon's downfall—a "fate of almost biblical proportions," as he later wrote—with his own fate, yoked to Nixon's, also hanging in the balance. The unlikely Nixon-Kissinger relationship—the "grocer's son from Whittier and the refugee from Hitler's Germany, the politician and the academic," in Nixon's words—had turned inevitably darker and more complex during the two years of Watergate. Kissinger's star had risen just as Nixon's fell, and it didn't take as resentful a figure as Nixon, or one as labyrinthine and paranoid as Kissinger, to see that Ford's and Kissinger's problems on Cyprus, the first test of America's global strength after the Watergate era, carried implications for all three of them.

The flash point, in fact, had already occurred. Last Friday, the White House had erroneously expressed confidence that the Turkish advance had halted. Then, over the weekend, Turkish forces seized more territory, now totaling 40 percent of the island. After a phone conversation with the Turkish prime minister on Sunday morning, Kissinger announced that it was his "understanding" that the territory held by Turkey "can be reduced in size." Thus while Kissinger and Schlesinger had spent the weekend warning Turkey not to advance, its armies grabbed more territory than it really wanted in order to cede some back. Negotiations were set to resume.

"We believe," Kissinger told a packed pressroom, "it will be necessary for Turkey, as the stronger power on the ground, to display flexibility and concern for Greek sensitivities, both in terms of territory and the size of military forces on the island."

The State Department now believed Ambassador Davies had been assassinated, in a carefully coordinated attack in which snipers with .50 caliber automatic weapons used the march on the embassy compound as cover. From the angle of shots that crashed through his office windows, it was clear that the gunmen had fired from an upper floor of a nearby building. The fifty-three-year-old career diplomat had been felled by a freak hit, but the murderous assault was premeditated, making Davies the third U.S. ambassador murdered since 1968 while serving abroad. As Ford dispatched a plane to Beirut to pick up Davies's children, whose mother had died a year earlier, Davies's seventy-eight-year-old mother went on TV to criticize Kissinger's monthlong policy on Cyprus. "I think the United States should have stepped in, I really do," she said.

Kissinger, expressing shock and grief over Davies's killing, defended his own handling of the crisis. "We are disappointed by the outcome, by the actions of the parties at various times on Cyprus," he said, but "our judgment was that under the circumstances, that quiet diplomacy" would be the best course. As Eric Sevareid summed up in his newscast: "The official reasoning here is that the basic choice was between intervening at the start, with the double risk of getting stuck there for years plus Soviet reaction, or taking for a while the lumps we've been taking."

Yet the damage to Kissinger's standing had been done. He had failed to stop a murderous invasion of one ally against another; Greece had withdrawn from NATO, leaving a hole in the transatlantic military alliance; Congress now threatened to cut off U.S. arms aid to Turkey in order to halt its forces; a U.S. ambassador had been assassinated; and in the streets of Nicosia, Athens, Washington, Chicago, and other cities he was being vilified more bitterly than at any time since the height of the Vietnam protests three years earlier—a large target shielding an unfamiliar new president.

On Sunday, Kissinger had told reporters, "There is a limit to what diplomacy can achieve . . . The United States has never claimed, and could not accept the proposition, that it must stop every local war between smaller states." He appeared to be justifying reduced superpower intervention in a world beset by rising ethnic tensions. An inveterate background briefer, Kissinger meanwhile also labored behind the scenes to line up public support for the upcoming battle in Congress, and friendly, familiar voices soon weighed in on his side.

"The Russians also did nothing," Sevareid noted in his CBS commentary, "but there are no demonstrations outside the Kremlin, no Russian diplomat has been shot by Greek Cypriots. An old story: Governments open to persuasion are hammered at; those presumed not open are left alone. The crowd in the bullring, after all, does not shout its protests and advice to the bull, but to the bullfighter."

* * *

After the press conference, Kissinger returned to his office to address another urgent problem—Vietnam—where the fighting had grown the
heaviest since the peace accord ending American military involvement
was signed in January 1973, and where recent communiqués from the
communists indicated, he later wrote, an "arrogance which suggested
that Hanoi was feeling the wind at its back."

The agreement that had ended the longest war in U.S. history, for
which Kissinger and North Vietnam's Le Duc Tho received the Nobel
Peace Prize, provided for the total withdrawal of U.S. forces in exchange
for the North Vietnamese release of U.S. POWs, while allowing the
communists to govern South Vietnamese territory that they already controlled—"peace with honor," Nixon called it. (Tho, saying "peace has not
yet been established in South Vietnam," rejected the prize and his share
of the money.) As John Negroponte, an aide to Kissinger, noted, these
were basically the same conditions Kissinger had rejected three months
earlier, before the Christmas bombing: "We bombed the North Vietnamese into accepting our concession," Negroponte lamented. Now,
nineteen months later, communist forces were sixteen miles from Saigon,
the capital of South Vietnam, the first time since the cease-fire went into
effect that North Vietnamese regular troops had been so close to the city
and the closest they'd ever brought their Soviet-made tanks.

Nixon and Kissinger had proclaimed the Paris accord as the best deal
possible for ensuring the survival of the South Vietnamese government,
but the battle raging on the southern tip of what Americans used to call
the Iron Triangle fueled rising speculation that they secretly had adopted
a "decent interval" exit strategy, one designed to delay South Vietnam's
collapse long enough so that its defeat wouldn't appear to be Nixon's
fault. Nixon and Kissinger vigorously denied this, but Kissinger in fact
had assured China—twice—that once the POWs were returned, and a
decent amount of time for negotiations between North and South Viet-

nam had elapsed, the United States was "much less likely" to intervene in a civil war.

Believing that North Vietnam, like Turkey, was now testing America's ability to react after Nixon's collapse, Kissinger wrote his longtime interlocutor Tho a message warning against treating the transition as a military opportunity and expressing Washington's desire for improved relations with Hanoi. "President Ford, as you must be aware, has been a firm supporter of President Nixon's policy in Indochina for 5½ years," he wrote.

Kissinger's frustrations were typically huge. Though he and Nixon had ended Kennedy's and Johnson's misguided and tragic war of communist containment in Indochina, they had done so with such characteristic duplicity that the inevitable outcome was fast looming—too late for Nixon to take the blame while in power, but not too late for Ford and Kissinger. Meanwhile, Congress was chafing to tie Ford's hands on Turkey. During the Vietnam War, Congress had been reluctant to bind the president to specific courses of action, but the restraints had come off with Watergate, and the legislative branch now had the power to prescribe the tactics of Cyprus policy.

Kissinger, who had all his phone calls recorded and transcribed by teams of secretaries, voiced his pessimism in an end-of-the-day phone call with British Foreign Secretary James Callahan, who was equally melancholy about the prospects for diplomacy in the post-Vietnam period.

> **CALLAHAN:** . . . I think life is getting worse, Henry.
>
> **KISSINGER:** I think you are right.
>
> **CALLAHAN:** I don't know what sort of age we're passing through or going to pass through, but historians like yourself ought really to give us the rundown on it and tell us how you think this next half century is going to look.
>
> **KISSINGER:** I'll tell you . . . I'm glad I'm not going to be running part of it. It's going to be brutal.

*   *   *

When the Fords returned for the night to their new living quarters, Betty
wrote, everything was in "perfect order," their clothes, knickknacks, and
other personal items placed precisely where she'd asked. Most of their
furnishings—"good Grand Rapids decor," she called it—had gone into
storage, but on CBS Connie Chung reported that the Ford's king-sized
bed had been moved and that the Fords, unlike the Nixons, would share
a bedroom. Betty wrote:

> Our bed and bedding and pillows are in the First Lady's Bedroom,
> and the room usually referred to as the President's Bedroom has
> been made into a private sitting room for us. There are Jerry's fa-
> vorite blue leather chair and footstool, and his exercise bike, and
> all his pipes and his pipe rack, and our old television set. The pic-
> tures of the children—from babyhood through Mike's and Gayle's
> wedding—are hanging on the walls. So Jerry and I will have one
> room in that great big White House that isn't all stuffed with im-
> portant furniture. Besides, at the end of the day, no matter how
> marvelous the help is, I'm going to want a place to escape to, a cor-
> ner I can crawl into, someplace where I can shut a door. I am not
> going to want to sit out in some dumb hall.

12

The cabinet and leaders of both parties in Congress stood along the wall of the Oval Office, mingling as they waited for Ford to enter with his choice for vice president. Gold drapes blocked the windows and a row of standing battle flags partly disguised the still-bare bookshelves. Rumsfeld, stationed nearest the closed door through which Ford would emerge, was the lone member of his entourage among the standees. He'd also been seated prominently at the VFW convention, fueling the nightly newscasts, which noted his dark horse candidacy and Ford's knack for surprises.

Ford spoke by phone with Nixon in the adjoining private office, a courtesy call before the formal announcement. "He seemed very pleased," Ford wrote. "He said Nelson's name and experience in foreign policy would help me internationally, and that he was fully qualified to be President should something happen to me. The extreme right wing, he continued, would be very upset, but I shouldn't worry because I couldn't please them anyway."

Ever since Rockefeller had challenged him for the nomination in 1960, then turned down Nixon's urgent appeal to be his running mate,

Nixon had considered Rockefeller his chief rival. After he'd lost for California governor in 1962, bitterly telling the press they wouldn't have "Dick Nixon to kick around anymore," Nixon fled California for New York—the "base of my major opponent," he would write. Whatever his pleasure at a lifetime of besting Rockefeller and the Eastern Establishment, Nixon bore him no grudge and indeed before he resigned had recommended that Ford choose him, telling Ford, "There are a number of good people," but failing to mention any other names.

Ford then phoned Bush, in Kennebunkport, where Bush had retreated with an aide to spend a few days playing golf and riding the choppy Atlantic waters in *Fidelity,* a Cigarette racing speedboat that he had bought in the wake of the oil crisis. They had brought a television out on the porch and were waiting for the announcement with Bush's family. "It was a very hard call," Bush recalled Ford telling him. "You had tremendous support and I just wanted you to know that." "Yes . . . well, Mr. President, you've made a fine choice," Bush said, "and I appreciate your taking the time to call. You really didn't have to . . ." When Bush hung up, he told aide Pete Roussel, "You'll never guess who that was. Watch. It's not going to be me." Despite his apparent calm, Bush wasn't comforted, writing to his long-time associate James Baker that being passed over was an "enormous personal disappointment. For valid reasons we made the finals (valid reasons I mean a lot of Hill, RNC and letter support) and so the defeat was more intense—".

Rockefeller had flown down from Maine in his family's fifteen-passenger, $4.5 million Grumman Gulfstream 2, a jet with international range, and had met briefly with Ford, who told him as vice president he would have to live in the official residence on Admiral's Hill, smaller by far than any of Rockefeller's five houses, instead of his sprawling estate on Foxhall Road. Rockefeller grimaced, but he agreed.

As the cameras whirred and clicked, the door to the Oval Office opened a crack and the assembled leaders turned toward it to see whom it would reveal. Just as abruptly, the door shut, and there was laughter at Ford's apparent tease: He'd already announced his decision in private to both groups. When a minute later the door reopened and the Fords strolled in accompanied by Rockefeller, it was the liberal, moderate, and pragmatic conservative Republicans, looking ahead to the fall elections and to 1976, who applauded loudest. Only 23 percent of voters in the most recent Gallup poll identified themselves as Republicans. Settled on what seemed to be a Ford-Rockefeller ticket in two years, euphoric party leaders saw the GOP's first opportunity in two decades to overcome its status as a permanent minority in American politics.

"After a great deal of soul searching," Ford said stiffly, eyes ahead, "after considering the advice of members of the Congress, Republicans as well as the Democratic leadership, after consulting with many, many people within the Republican Party and without, I have made a decision which I would like now to announce to the American people.

"It was a tough call for a tough job. A number of people who were considered by me in the process were all men of—and women of—great quality.

"But after a long and very thoughtful process, I have made the ch . . . the choice, and that choice is Nelson Rockefeller of New York State. It is my honor and privilege to introduce to you a good partner for me and a good partner for our country and the world."

Rockefeller stepped forward. Shorter than Ford by several inches, he wore a black chalk-striped suit spouting a white pocket handkerchief and the enormous black-framed rectangular eyeglasses favored by Hollywood moguls—power glasses. He spoke not to the cameras but to Ford, in the familiar honking voice that meshed scrappy New Yorkese with broad Brahmin vowels.

"You, Mr. President, through your dedication and your openness, have already reawakened faith and hope, and under your leadership we the people and we as a nation have the will and the determination and the capability to overcome the hard realities of our time. I'm optimistic about the long-term future. Thank you, sir."

* * *

Within a half hour after the ceremony, Rockefeller plunged into a whirl-wind of press encounters and political calls, beginning with a testy exchange with Washington reporters over his refusal to estimate for them his net worth, assumed to be several hundred million dollars. "I haven't been confirmed and I haven't gone before the committee, and my understanding is that you don't discuss matters that are going to be taken up by a committee before you get to the hearings," he said. He met with Kissinger for a briefing and lunch at the State Department, then with Democratic senator Howard Cannon of Nevada, chairman of the Senate Rules Committee, which held jurisdiction over his confirmation hearings. Cannon told him he would request full financial disclosure of Rockefeller's holdings and trust to determine whether there was any possible conflict of interest. Rockefeller pledged to turn over his tax returns and anything else the committee wanted.

Met in a hallway by news crews, he was asked whether he and Ford had discussed a Ford-Rockefeller ticket in two years.

"Well," he said, "I think it would be fair to assume that as President of the United States that he is bound to be a candidate, and I totally urge and support his candidacy for 1976. But equally, it would be totally inappropriate for me to in any way consider or suggest anything about his Vice-Presidential candidate."

"Did he say anything to you about 1976, one way or the other?" a reporter asked.

"About himself, but not about me—no sir. And I didn't ask."

The press persisted: Did Ford say he would be a candidate?

"Well, he has every intention," Rockefeller said.

"He has every intention of running in '76?"

Rockefeller swung around, seemingly for effect. "That was my impression," he said. "That's what I heard. That was my assumption."

The political calculus in Washington shifted seismically with the implication that Ford and Rockefeller were thinking beyond the short term—triggering even before Rockefeller left Congress to fly back to Maine the first serious rumblings of complaint from the right since Ford had taken office. "We have to see what this team does," Goldwater announced before the cameras, withholding comment on Rockefeller's confirmation. "If in the next year and a half they do a bang-up job, then I think the question is answered." Incredulously, House Minority Leader John Rhodes, an old Ford ally, countered: "I can't believe conservative Republicans feel broadening the base of the party is a bad thing—unless they want to keep on losing and keep being a minority—and I just can't subscribe to that way of thinking."

If Ford's VFW speech had shown he would challenge traditional allies in order to steer the country toward the center—as he'd first hinted a week earlier during his joint address to Congress and the nation—Rockefeller's answers were the strongest hint yet that Ford aimed to use the power of the presidency to lead the country more permanently in that direction. The network commentators, as near to a national Greek chorus as any group during Watergate, unanimously praised Ford's choice of Rockefeller and all that it seemed to forecast. "He [Rockefeller] will add something to the new atmosphere the Republicans are trying to create in Washington, so far with great success," NBC's Brinkley said, "—the atmosphere of a break with the recent past, an open, casual government looking with friends to work with rather than enemies to punish."

On CBS, Sevareid—often criticized as "Eric Severalsides" for his elliptical, prismatic views, his zero-sum "on-the-one-hand-on-the-other-hands"—rhapsodized: "A funny thing has happened to the whole American process of selecting its presidents and vice presidents. We're doing better by the undemocratic procedure of appointment by one man than we were doing recently by the procedure of general election.

"Clearly the key to President Gerald Ford is common sense. The common sense thing to do in these transition days is to feel generously, think big, and act decisively.

"As things look now," Sevareid told viewers, "the Democratic Party, more deeply divided than the Republicans, will have to lay in stocks of water and Pemmican for a long stretch in the presidential wilderness. Their only savior, one no patriot can pray to, would be a severe recession, making Mr. Ford the Herbert Hoover of this period. The Democrats ran against Hoover for twenty years. They thought they could run against Mr. Nixon for the next twenty. But as things now stand they can't run against Nixon even this year."

* * *

After the Rockefeller announcement, Ford met in the Cabinet Room with the bipartisan leaders of Congress to discuss the economy. Both Hoover's and Nixon's gyrations in trying to keep the nation from sliding into a depression, as they simultaneously focused on reelection, plainly haunted him. A former commerce secretary, Hoover had won in a landslide in 1928, taking power soon after America had emerged as the richest nation in history. The stock market was roaring, optimism was rampant; Republicans dominated national politics. Then, seven months later, Wall Street crashed, sparking hysteria and panic, although little worse than during previous, periodic busts in the business cycle.

Hoover, who had earned a fortune as a mining engineer before setting out to apply his expertise to the nation's challenges, at first bucked his party's conservative wing, asserting a more aggressive stance in battling economic decline than any previous president. He convinced business leaders and bankers not to cut jobs or wages, and encouraged Congress and the states to launch public works projects. But when those steps faltered a year later, the "Great Engineer" reversed tack. He raised tariffs to their highest levels ever and shored up the banks while fiercely rejecting federal relief for the unemployed and ordering troops to disperse tattered, hungry World War I veterans who came to Washington seeking early war bonuses. Blamed for the Depression and appearing insensitive to misery, Hoover engineered, without intending to, the New Deal coalition that elected Roosevelt four times and had controlled Congress ever since.

When Nixon lost to Kennedy in 1960, he concluded that he'd been beaten by a recession that most people blamed on Eisenhower, and that memory had stalked him into the White House eight years later. In

August 1971, faced with the alarming rise of "stagflation"—wages and prices were going up, but the economy wasn't growing and new jobs were scarce—he retreated to Camp David with Secretary of the Treasury John Connally and his top economic advisers. The economy was hardly Nixon's passion, but he and Connally devised the most massive program to intervene in the marketplace since the New Deal—the curiously Leninist-sounding New Economic Policy (NEP)—which then–Ford Motor Company president Lee Iacocca observed "makes Nixon's trip to China look like child's play."

Wildly popular at first, the NEP was a sweeping array of monetary and domestic measures; the most controversial was a mandatory ninety-day freeze on wages and prices. The Cost of Living Council—a new federal bureaucracy chaired by Rumsfeld—managed the controls, reimposing them a second time after Nixon's reelection. Most of the system finally expired in April, five months after the start of the Arab oil embargo and as the endgame erupted over Nixon's tapes. Since then, with the White House reeling, wholesale prices had spiraled, jumping 3.7 percent in July alone—a compound annual rate of more than 54 percent. "Latin American style inflation," Sevareid warned ominously.

Before Nixon resigned, Congress had proposed an economic "summit meeting," a national conference at which all major economic sectors would work together in a spirit of "discipline, compromise and a sacrifice for the common good." Most economists agreed that Nixon's on-and-off controls made inflation worse than it would have been under consistent controls, or no controls at all, and in fact the second round of freezes simply had collapsed: Ranchers halted shipping cattle to market, farmers drowned their chickens, and consumers hoarded food, emptying supermarket shelves. On Ford's first day in office, General Motors announced a 9.5 percent average increase—$500—on its 1975 models, and Ford phoned GM's chairman and "pleaded for restraint," he wrote. "I knew the rise would stimulate other industries to raise prices, pushing the inflation rate even higher." Following suit, his first request to Congress was $1 million for a new wage-price monitoring agency in the White House, the Council on Wage and Price Stability, to help him jawbone industries and unions but with no authority to impose mandatory curbs. The House had quickly accepted the Senate version of the bill Monday night, after Iacocca announced that his company might boost prices on its new cars by 10 percent.

Ford now reassured the leadership that he had no plans to ask for any legislation for either standby or mandatory wage and price controls. And he said he aimed to head off any "anticipatory" raises by business and labor. Meantime, he said he would take Senate Majority Leader Mike Mansfield's recommendation: He announced that the White House would organize a televised summit conference on the economy in late September or early October, preceded by a series of mini-conferences on smaller issues like agriculture or banking and finance, some of which Ford planned to chair personally. Ford placed in charge William Seidman, the Grand Rapids accounting executive who had served as his chief of staff as vice president and had been out of a job since Ford decided to keep Haig, and he proposed that the leaders of the House and Senate name four members to work with top administration figures on a steering committee.

If Ford seemed deferential and cautious, failing to lay out any specific direction or requests, he had good cause. In his speech to both houses of Congress eight days earlier, he hadn't pledged to meet Nixon's goal of reducing the federal budget by $5 billion to $300 billion, and the omission was presumed deliberate. "It may be that Mr. Ford simply did not wish to set goals unilaterally from the White House," *Times* analyst Eileen Shanahan wrote. "Or it may be that he has a greater concern than Mr. Nixon felt, in his final days in office, that too much budget cutting could bring on too much contraction in an economy that already may be in a recession. Or it could be both." Ford himself later wrote, "nothing . . . was more important than holding the line on federal spending and keeping the budget . . . at or under $300 billion." But he was confronting a new law, the Budget Reform Act, denying the White House independent control over spending once an appropriation was approved. His hands were tied. A president could ask Congress to defer or rescind decisions, but, as he wrote, "isn't likely to succeed."

After the meeting, terHorst released a statement announcing Ford's moves. The statement said that business and labor leaders could be assured that Ford would do his "best to see that the new wage and price monitoring agency works effectively to combat inflation." Ford recalled later: "The economic proposals that I submitted to Congress in the first weeks of my Administration were fairly similar to the ones Nixon proposed. But while his relations with Capitol Hill were terrible, mine were excellent, and I hoped this good will might help get those proposals through."

* * *

Ford huddled for fifty minutes late in the day with his transition advisers over their final report. They urged him to reduce "substantially" the overall White House staff; cut the Office of Management and Budget's "foreman's role" in domestic policy-making; reduce the power of the chief of staff so that he "coordinates but does not control" the work of other senior officials; deal directly with six top aides responsible for foreign policy, domestic policy, economic policy, the budget, personnel, and legal problems; name the Treasury secretary to head the White House economic team; and take the vice president out of his "standby role" and make him a major presidential adviser.

The proposals formalized Ford's ideas for a spokes-on-the-wheel system, but as Haig had predicted, Ford by now had begun to doubt whether such a system could work in the West Wing. The ground war between the Nixon holdovers and Ford's new people was intensifying, with the president, as terHorst observed, "spending an inordinate amount of time soothing his own loyalists and placating the sensitive feelings of Haig."

When matters touched on Watergate, the clashes exploded. A few days earlier, after Hartmann was tipped off that several unconnected microphones remained embedded in the Oval Office, including two in the Wilson desk, Ford had confronted Haig, who formerly had assured

Ford that they'd been removed. Haig claimed to know nothing about them and had them dug out and delivered in a plastic bag to Becker, who handed them over to the Secret Service as possible future evidence. Hartmann, furious, railed that Haig either knew or should have known about the bugs and the "calamitous embarrassment" they might cause. Ford began to detect Hartmann's handprints on stories in the press that Haig had tried to ramrod the appointment of Patrick Buchanan as ambassador to South Africa's apartheid regime and had issued staff memoranda to bypass Hartmann. "The storm drain," Haig wrote, "filled up with leaks."

The transition team advised Ford to put his own people in top positions as soon as possible, and Ford realized that he needed, if not a regent, a disciplined, headstrong gatekeeper to keep order and get done what needed doing. "Because power in Washington is measured by how much access a person has to the President, almost everyone wanted more access than I had access to give," Ford wrote. "Someone, I decided, had to be responsible for scheduling appointments, coordinating the paper flow, following up on decisions I had made and giving me status reports on projects and policy development. I didn't like the idea of calling this person chief of staff, but that in fact was the role he would fill."

Ford thanked them all for their work. Marsh would remain in the White House, Morton at Interior, Scranton available for special assignments. Rumsfeld, a Nixon insider now with as much access to his successor as Kissinger and Haig, was happy to be flying back to Brussels. Having made it onto Ford's short list for vice president, he had achieved what only he and Bush among Nixon's loyalists could now claim—future viability as a candidate for national office. He gladly might have headed a major federal department, but Ford had made clear he was keeping Nixon's cabinet. Rumsfeld recognized the growing dysfunction in the White House, and he had no desire for a staff position that, however exalted, was unlikely to be a promising career move. He offered Ford his loyalty but wasn't eager to remain in the acid and unstable climate around him. "Don," his wife Joyce recalled, "believed he would be signing up for oblivion."

On the night of Nixon's landslide twenty-two months earlier, the consuming ambition of Ford's life—the speakership—came to a bleak end when Republicans failed to win a majority of seats in the House. Ford had flown to Grand Rapids to vote, then returned home to Alexandria to watch the election returns with Betty, eating steak, baked potatoes, and butter pecan ice cream on TV tables in the family room. "If we can't get a majority against McGovern, with a Republican President winning virtually every state," he told her as the returns were reported, "when can we? Maybe it's time for us to get out of politics and have another life." Betty, who said later that she'd been "waiting and waiting for the day that we could have a life together," told him she'd support whatever he chose to do, and Ford decided to stay on through the end of Nixon's term. After calculating his pension against the costs of sending their remaining children to college, he quietly began sounding out his friends in business about becoming a lobbyist.

If Ford was the right man now for the presidency because he had never lusted for it, Rockefeller's disclosure that Ford would be a candidate in 1976 recast him overnight as more than an accidental figure, a place-filler. He had not burned to become president, but once he had all but announced his desire to be chosen over others who had, he believed he needed to wage a determined, muscular, *inclusive* campaign.

Ford burst from the blocks, launching a day of frenetic, scripted, campaign-style activity, of seeming to be anywhere and everywhere in Washington. He started with a forty-five-minute meeting in the Cabinet Room with the Congressional Black Caucus, sixteen liberal Democrats. Only one of them had voted for his confirmation as vice president, and several had opposed the decision to accept Ford's invitation because, as the *Times* reported, a "meeting so soon after his taking office could only be a political gold mine for Mr. Ford." The caucus had met just once with Nixon, in March 1971, after thirteen months of asking to sit down with him. Two months later Nixon returned a barbed point-by-point critique of their sixty recommendations. Relations since had been toxic.

Ford told them he was seriously considering public service jobs programs for high-unemployment areas and that his budget cuts wouldn't just affect social programs but also the Pentagon, though he warned not to expect across-the-board cuts in military spending. He also promoted his decision to consider amnesty for draft resisters as an example of his flexibility and willingness to change. Ford listened to their concerns, frequently interrupting to ask questions or clarify his views, and they gave him a variety of position papers, mostly on domestic and urban issues. He vowed to read and consider them. Other than that, he pledged only to assure them continuing access to the White House.

Smiling caucus members cautiously lauded Ford's openness to reporters gathered outside on the lawn. "The important thing is not that we got commitments," California representative Yvonne Braithwaite-Burke said, "but that we established a way of negotiating, and that's so important to us. You see we've had no input whatsoever. We've been having to face a President who acted as if we didn't exist." Representative Barbara Jordan of Texas predicted a "more open door, sensitive kind of administration under President Ford," adding, "It remains to be seen whether we can translate that openness into substance."

Ford flew by helicopter to Andrews Air Force Base in Maryland, where he joined Kissinger for a ten-minute ceremony for slain ambassador Rodger Davies. A blue, white, and silver air force jet bearing Davies's coffin and family touched down and rolled to a whining stop on the tarmac. Ford and Kissinger escorted Davies's children past an armed service honor guard to a plane-side platform. Then a black-uniformed military band played the national anthem and five howitzers a hundred yards away boomed a nineteen-gun salute, white smoke from the fusillade wafting skyward on a light breeze. Moments later, Ford eulogized Davies, calling him a man who "lost his life in the search for peace in America and all the world."

"He had judg-a-ment, he had dignity, he had wisdom, and he had humor," Ford said, solemnly and slowly, as many of the three hundred State Department workers, members of the diplomatic corps, and other government officials openly wept. "His services to our country embodied the best of time, of effort, and competence." He presented the U.S. ambassador's flag that had been displayed in Davies's Nicosia office to his older child, Ann, then kissed her on the left cheek.

Joined by Kissinger, Ford climbed back into the helicopter, and by noon the two were in the Oval Office for a series of courtesy calls and photo opportunities with the ambassadors of Pakistan, Iran, and India, countries still safely within the détente-era calculus, restrained appreciatively by their reliance on the superpowers for weapons, aid, and diplomatic favors. Ford ate lunch, then met with his personal photographer, David Kennerly, a thin, brash, twenty-two-year-old photojournalist who had covered him as vice president for *Time* and whom Ford increasingly liked to have around in part because Kennerly seemed determinedly unawed by Ford's new status. Kennerly's close-ups of Ford climbing out of his pool at 7 A.M. on his first morning in office, carried worldwide, already had established a new patina of presidential intimacy, an impression of a man at home with himself and distinctly unlike Nixon, who when he felt he needed to be pictured as more relaxed and Kennedyesque famously exchanged his suit jacket for a presidential windbreaker and went for a walk on the beach in gleaming black street shoes. Dressed in tennis sneakers and scruffy jeans, Kennerly joined Ford in the backseat of the limousine during the brief motorcade to attend a bill-signing ceremony at the Department of Health, Education and Welfare (HEW).

The bill, a $25 billion education package, contained a school-busing provision, part of which Ford opposed but which, overall, he found acceptable. Throughout the summer, busing children from their neighborhoods as a remedy for segregation had reached a critical stage. A federal judge in Boston, W. Arthur Garrity, Jr., had ruled in June that the city's school committee had actively and secretly maintained a segregated system. Upheld on appeal, Garrity ordered the city to begin integration, and the city had hastily begun reassigning students from Roxbury, the heart of the city's black ghetto, to primarily Irish Catholic South Boston, an antibusing stronghold. Boston was volatile, braced for violence. Meanwhile, the Supreme Court had ruled in *Milliken v. Bradley* against a multidistrict desegregation plan involving Detroit and two affluent suburban school systems. The decision, handed down the day after the Court's unanimous decision to force Nixon to surrender his tapes, marked a turning point for the high court in racial matters. With all four Nixon appointees voting with the 5–4 majority, the decision left central cities to cope alone with the problem of de facto segregation of their schools. In effect, the constitutionality—and social costs—of busing now ended at the city limits, with suburbs receiving judicial permission to remain white.

Ford, who in Congress had opposed federal spending for public housing, rent subsidies, Medicare, mass transit, model cities, urban renewal, and even rat extermination, signed the bill, which provided for cross-district busing unless a court determined otherwise. "I think it's fair to say," he said, "that this legislation places reasonable and equitable restraints upon the problem of busing, and in conjunction with the Supreme Court decision will hopefully relieve that problem and make the solution more equitable and just." Met outside the building by an enthusiastic, biracial crowd, Ford stopped and mingled, bending down to shake hands with a line of kindergartners.

Ford motored from HEW to the Capitol, a three-minute ride. "Enroute, he greeted representatives of special interest groups and Members of Congress attending the ceremony," according to the daily White

House log. No moment was wasted as he returned to charm old friends and foes alike.

He had his work set out for him. The Senate throughout the morning had debated defense cuts, slashing $5 billion from Pentagon spending by a vote of 85–6 as a first step toward balancing the budget. A Democratic amendment to cut weapons aid to Vietnam by $150 million to $550 million—about one third of what Nixon had requested and half of what Ford was seeking—was narrowly defeated only after Goldwater, who opposed any cut, offered an amendment to reduce the figure to *zero*. Goldwater wanted to demonstrate that the overwhelming majority of the Senate opposed abandoning South Vietnam entirely—that the United States would sustain a besieged ally—but, in truth, those who wanted to cut support to the corrupt and crumbling Saigon regime were, as Kissinger observed, "gaining ground because no one was left to contest the field. The conservatives had lost heart . . . the Nixon supporters were demoralized by Watergate; and the new White House staff had no stomach for the brutal fight they had heretofore watched from the sidelines." Ford believed it would be hopeless to undo the vote on cutting defense, contenting himself to try to get part of the money back when committee leaders met in conference.

Speaking to the Senate, Ford was conciliatory, thanking members for "going more than halfway" in helping him get action on several major pieces of legislation. He described his visit as an informal effort "just to say hello and officially inaugurate Pennsylvania Avenue as a two-way street." His decision to clarify his intention to run for election was widely construed on Capitol Hill to serve two main purposes: to assure conservative Republicans upset about his choice of Rockefeller that he intended to lead the party himself in 1976, and to head off any possible insurgency in which a splinter group might field a candidate against him. In effect, he now stated his election platform; he appealed to all sides for support "so we can march towards the center in achieving good results for the country as a whole."

Ford shook every hand, reaching out also to the pages, before heading over to the House, where Speaker Albert introduced him as a "beloved friend of every member of this chamber." He redeclared the "two-way street" between the White House and Congress to a standing ovation, and repeated—as he spoke to them about moving from Alexandria to his new address—Harry Truman's comment on leaving the White House in 1953: "If I had known how much packing I would have to do I would have run again."

Gathering Congress with one hand, Ford reached out with the other to the country, projecting a new tone and speaking in language so bipartisan as to be nonpartisan. Instinctively coy, he appeared to relish the balancing act. By letting it be known that he would seek the nomination, but not announcing the decision himself, he also gave the postcoital Washington press something to stir fresh excitement: a suddenly alive fight for the Oval Office. Their main perpetual story line—the juggernaut of presidential politics—rumbled back to life.

* * *

While Ford swept around the city, terHorst explained to reporters Ford's reasons for reversing his position not to run. "Well," he said, wearing a white sports jacket, powder blue shirt, and black tie, "the president told me in answer to Governor Rockefeller's statements on Capitol Hill yesterday that he has changed his view towards running in 1976. In the past he always talked of not running. But those were views expressed as a nominee for vice president. Now that he's president, his position has obviously changed, and so his views have changed."

TerHorst had survived the missteps over the tapes and the Rockefeller smear with mixed, if affectionate, marks from the press. Asked what seemed to have changed Ford's mind, he answered in careful generalities. "He realizes his duty, as he sees it, is to bind up the wounds of the country, try to put the country back on its feet, to lead it in a new and wholesome and healthy direction after years of travail and agony for many. I think he feels the job may take him on beyond the present term.

"He is now of the opinion he will probably run in 1976, assuming of course he is nominated by delegates to the Republican Convention," ter-Horst said. Asked if he wanted to keep the word "probably" in his statement, he said he definitely did.

Ford returned to the White House shortly before four. An ABC news crew followed him as he walked from the car to the Oval Office. "Your press secretary said today that you were planning to run in 1976," reporter Steve Bell importuned. "Can you put that in your own words?"

"Well," Ford said, "I think the governor well expressed that yesterday."

"Was he right?"

Ford hesitated, smiled. "I want you to worry about that for a bit."

Ford and an aide ducked inside for his final legislative meeting of the day, with House Ways and Means Chairman Wilbur Mills, an Arkansas Democrat who in three days of open hearings had failed to muster enough support for a national health insurance bill. Ford had made national health insurance one of his two legislative objectives for this Congress, and he had reignited hopes of passage when he told both chambers to get together on a compromise in his August 12 speech to the joint session. On Monday the committee staff had brought back a version specifying that no family would have to pay more than $1,000 in medical expenses beyond insurance premiums. But members balked, especially at a provision to use a payroll tax to finance coverage for catastrophic illness and provisions that would require all Americans to participate in the plan. Mills believed a health bill was dead for the year unless Ford could save it, by persuading Republicans on the committee to compromise.

Ford committed his staff to help out. He still wanted a bill, but he knew Congress would do nothing before the election. After the meeting, Mills told reporters he thought Congress should hold a lame duck session, recessing until after the November election, then returning to Washington to finish work on trade, health insurance, and other important legislation. He insisted the suggestion had not come from Ford, but in the new rhetorical atmosphere, he expressed hope. "Anything's possible," Mills said.

The promise that Gerald Ford might serve in the White House beyond Nixon's unexpired term capsized the country's political balance and whipped up a froth of new wisdom. Far from being sundered by Nixon's downfall, Ford and the Republicans now seemed, leading into the vacation weeks of late August and Labor Day, notably better positioned and prepared to benefit from the changeover in power than the fractious Democrats. "This country's problems, divisions and violence have lately become destroyers of presidents," NBC's Brinkley commented. ". . . Nobody can predict anything. But just two weeks ago the Democrats could have seen their prospects as pretty good. Now in that short time it has all turned around."

* * *

Betty fretted that the White House employees didn't like her. "I feel terribly uncomfortable here when I speak to one of the guards or the White House police," she told the head usher, Rex Scouten, "they never answer me, they just sort of back off." On Scouten's order, staff members immediately began to return her greetings. "The Nixons," she explained in her diary, "preferred more formality, and the staff, trained to be as silent and invisible as possible, didn't know how to act with us."

Ford arrived upstairs at the Residence—he had told the staff to stop calling it the Mansion—at a few minutes before seven thirty, and with Susan still away at the beach, he and Betty had a drink and ate dinner alone. During his long absences as a congressman, she had become dependent on a five o'clock cocktail at a neighbor's house, or at home while talking on the phone with a friend. She routinely took "another while I was fixing dinner, and then, after the kids were in bed, I'd build myself a nightcap and unwind by watching television," she wrote. In 1964, she suffered a pinched nerve, was in traction for more than a week, and began taking pills to wipe out the pain. A year later, she "snapped. I packed my bag one afternoon, and decided to drive to the beach, take Susan with me, and let my whole ungrateful family worry about where I was and whether I was ever coming home." The "crack-up," as she called it, got the family's attention, and she saw a psychiatrist, who diagnosed her problem as low self-esteem, the result of an overbearing, perfectionist mother. Ford blamed himself for her misery. At one point, she began pouring vodka into her morning tea.

No one, perhaps Ford least, wanted to admit that Betty had a serious problem, but her close friends now worried about her: Her neck problem had gotten worse, her pills were always with her. As one put it, "Nobody ever gave a damn how is the congressman's wife doing, and she couldn't unload her problems on him, and then all of a sudden, he became President, and she was pushed into the public eye, and that is the cruelest eye anywhere, and it frightened her." Standing next to Ford as he recited the oath of office, Betty wrote, nearly had unnerved her: "The words cut through me, pinned me to the floor. I felt as though I had taken the oath with him." Since then, their two older sons, Mike and Jack, had returned to their own lives, and their third son, Steve, had graduated from high school in June and would soon be out of the house, leaving only Susan at home.

Despite all this, Betty discovered, life "was *better* in the White House. I flowered. Jerry was no longer away so much. And I was somebody, the First Lady. When I spoke people listened."

"I did not drink alcoholically in the White House," she recalled. "There was too much at stake, too much responsibility. I was too heavily scheduled. What little drinking we did was confined to Camp David on a weekend, or drinks upstairs—there was a bar in the President's quarters—before we went to bed."

Ford took the day to catch up on domestic affairs. At six thirty, he went for a physical in the White House doctor's office and was pronounced in "excellent health," though his weight was up to 200¾ and Dr. William Lukash told him to lose five pounds. Ford sorely missed his pool and rode his exercise bike instead. In between his regular morning meetings with Scowcroft, Haig, Kissinger, and terHorst, he phoned and thanked GM chairman Richard Gerstenberg, who announced Wednesday that the carmaker would cut its planned price increase by $54—about 10 per-cent—in response to Ford's appeal for voluntary controls. He also called Massachusetts senator Ted Kennedy, who in a speech to the VFW the day after Ford's, had backed Ford's appeal for limited amnesty for draft resisters. "It is wrong to turn him down without even hearing his pro-posal in full," Kennedy had told the conventioneers. When Kennedy asked the veterans if they had "faith enough to be generous and the strength to be, as he [Ford] said, lenient," many jumped to their feet and shouted, "No! No! No!"

Ford met for twenty minutes with Buchen and Attorney General Saxbe to discuss Nixon's tapes and papers, which, as the boxing and crating continued, were accumulating primarily on the third floor of the EOB. "There were so many boxes yielding such great weight that the Secret Service expressed concern that the floor of the Executive Office Building might cave in," Becker recalled. Nixon continued to press Haig for them, and Gulley managed to ship an unknown amount. But the Watergate tapes and the core documents of the Nixon Administration remained in Ford's custody, and his impatience to be rid of them yielded to the cautions of his lawyers. "I suggested to President Ford, not too diplomatically . . . ," Becker wrote, "that American history would record his transmittal of the records and tapes to California as the final act of the Watergate cover-up—an act initiated and carried out by Gerald Ford."

Ford told Saxbe he wanted the Justice Department to review the entire matter. Who owned the materials? he asked. Were they the property of the U.S. government? Did Ford possess any legal right to retain them? What were his obligations with respect to subpoenas and court orders?

"Bill," he said, "I need you to give me an official opinion before we do anything."

Saxbe was a former Republican senator from Ohio whom Nixon had appointed after the Saturday Night Massacre. Like Ford, he was far from Nixon's first choice, a frequent critic on Vietnam who said after the Christmas bombing that Nixon "appeared to have left his senses," but one whose confirmation during the early days of the impeachment debate was easily assured after he told his colleagues he'd made a "covenant with myself" to "vigorously support" Jaworski's probe. When Ford at last distanced himself from Nixon at Nixon's last cabinet meeting three weeks ago, Nixon had oddly thanked him, then said he wanted to take up the most important issue confronting the nation—inflation. It was Saxbe who burst his reverie. "Mr. President," he said, "I don't think we ought to have a summit conference. We ought to be sure you have the ability to govern."

Watergate had tainted and traumatized Saxbe's department more than any other in government. John Mitchell—captain of John Kennedy's *PT-109* and a hero in World War II; a top municipal bond lawyer and Nixon's former law partner—had personally controlled a secret White House fund for spying on the Democrats while serving as attorney general, and he eventually approved the Watergate break-in. (When *Post* reporter Carl Bernstein called Mitchell for a comment, he famously threatened the *Post*'s publisher: "Katie Graham's going to get her tit caught in a big fat wringer if that's ever published.") Mitchell's successor Richard Kleindienst had been forced to resign along with Haldeman, Ehrlichman, and Dean and had pleaded guilty at trial for failing to tell the Senate during his confirmation hearing that Nixon had ordered him, as assistant attorney general, to drop an antitrust suit against International Telephone and Telegraph Company, which donated heavily to Nixon's campaign. During the Saturday Night Massacre, Nixon had to enlist the number three official, Bork, to fire Cox.

But Ford realized, after the Buzhardt debacle, that he needed independent legal advice from someone who presumably wouldn't be swayed by loyalty either to him or to Nixon. He sympathized with Nixon's claims, but with Jaworski, the various Watergate defendants, and lawyers in a growing number of civil suits issuing subpoenas to the White House to produce Nixon's tapes and records, he was a party of interest. He needed to know whether he had any legal authority to retain them. "Somehow," Ford wrote later, "we had to satisfy these competing claims and do so in such a way as to reassure the public . . . that nothing would be altered or destroyed."

Following the meeting, Ford went to the Cabinet Room to sign a proclamation designating August 26, the anniversary of women's suffrage, as Women's Equality Day. He had invited all thirteen women in Congress, most of them Democrats, to attend, and all of them did, although like members of the Black Caucus, some worried about giving Ford a symbolic victory before he'd disclosed his true intentions. A paramount issue was the Equal Rights Amendment, which in the early seventies overwhelmingly passed both houses of Congress and thirty state legislatures before being stalled by right-wing opponents. The proposed measure to guarantee women's rights under the law had been written by suffragists in 1923, three years after they won the right to vote, and had been introduced in each session of Congress since. Though Ford had not been enthusiastic about its passage, Betty was a staunch proponent, and she "kept pushing, trying to influence him," she wrote. "I used everything, including pillow talk at the end of the day, when I figured he was most tired and vulnerable."

Betty proudly peered from behind the lawmakers as Ford, seated, handed out ceremonial pens. Over his shoulder, applauding warmly, stood a matronly representative in a straw hat and billowing polka dot dress who'd become a national icon of liberal, feminist rage and outspokenness against Nixon, and who often said she was "born yelling."

"Even Bella Abzug smiled," Ford wrote.

* * *

On Capitol Hill, the House Judiciary Committee released its final impeachment report. The 528-page document stated unanimously that there was "clear and convincing evidence" that Nixon "condoned, encouraged . . . directed, coached and personally helped to fabricate perjury" and had abused his power, and should have been removed from office had he not resigned. Even the ten Republicans who stood by him up until the release of the June 23 tape now agreed that he had admitted obstruction of justice. They warned in a minority statement that while some people might say that Nixon was

> hounded from office . . . we feel constrained to point out that it was Richard Nixon who impeded the FBI's investigation of the Watergate affair . . . it was Richard Nixon who created and preserved the evidence of that transgression . . . and concealed its terrible import, even from his own counsel, until he could no longer do so. . . . It is striking that such an able, experienced and perceptive man . . . should fail to comprehend the damage that accrued daily to himself, his administration, and the nation, as day after

day, month after month, he imprisoned the truth about his role in the Watergate cover-up so long and so tightly within the solitude of his Oval Office that it could not be unleashed without destroying his Presidency.

The House voted 412–3 to approve the report. When the inquiry had begun back in October, experts had counted 125 votes at most for impeachment. Now, few Democrats gloated. "I feel tremendously relieved," Judiciary chairman Peter Rodino told reporters after the vote. "The country can get moving again."

The House also voted to turn over transcripts, memoranda, and notes from the inquiry—for review, but not to copy—to Haldeman, who requested the impeachment evidence for his defense in the cover-up trial. In the open season that now beset him, Haldeman, like Nixon, faced not one legal proceeding but many, with more surely to come. Like Nixon, he lived in California, though the two seldom spoke. Before traveling to Washington in the afternoon to start examining the impeachment material, he stopped over in Charlotte, North Carolina, to give a deposition in a civil suit filed by protesters who had been barred from an appearance by Nixon at Billy Graham Day ceremonies in the Charlotte Coliseum three years earlier.

Members of the Red Hornet Mayday Tribe, radical leftists who were suing Haldeman, two other administration officials, and the Secret Service for alleged civil rights violations, taunted and jeered him as he walked from his car to a lawyer's office. "People hate you as much here as anywhere else, H.R.," one shouted. Haldeman personally had approved tough security measures for Nixon's Charlotte visit, during which police and members of a local VFW chapter ejected people from the Coliseum on the claim that they held forged tickets. "Yes," he had written in a planning memo. "As long as it is local police and local volunteers doing it—not our people." Now, Red Hornet leader Marvin Sparrow shouted as Haldeman walked inside, "Bob, I want you to tell the truth in there and don't lie."

"I've never lied in my life," Haldeman answered.

*   *   *

Rebuked by the U.S. Circuit Court of Appeals, which "advised" that he grant a three- or four-week delay, Sirica reluctantly put off the start of the cover-up trial until September 30. As much as he insisted upon keeping to his schedule, he understood the higher court would hear any appeal by the defendants if they lost, and so he had no choice but to accept a postponement. Ehrlichman's lawyers, hoping to delay jury selection until January, readied their threatened appeal to the Supreme Court.

The extra time gave Jaworski breathing room to decide whether to indict Nixon. He no longer could rely on Congress to adopt the "monkey problem"—the decision to prosecute. Senate Judiciary chairman James Eastland, who'd promised to see if Congress had any color of authority to grant Nixon immunity, never called back, and indeed Congress had neither the power nor the slightest will to decide Nixon's fate in the courts. Meanwhile, the grand jury, whose foreman was clamoring to reconvene, "would indict him in a minute," Jaworski knew. The grand jurors had voted to indict Nixon earlier along with top aides, but named him instead an "unindicted co-conspirator" after Jaworski advised them he didn't think they could charge a sitting president.

"Columnists and cartoonists depicted me as a lonely man, deserted by Congress and the President, left to deal with a heavy burden," he wrote. "It was all interesting, and I was touched by the concern, but the chief question occupying my mind was this: could Richard Nixon receive a fair trial? That was the true dilemma."

Jaworski hadn't publicly decided whether to seek an indictment, but the 38–0 House vote on the charge of obstruction of justice spoke directly to the problem of finding jurors so uninformed as not to realize that Nixon was engaged in the cover-up. "We had ample time to decide whether to prosecute," he recalled. "I had concluded that if Nixon was to be indicted, it would come only after the jury had been sequestered in the cover-up trial. To indict prior to that would mean an indefinite delay in the trial."

As Sirica noted, the problem of whether to indict Nixon once he was out of office was a "question not of law, but of judgement." Jaworski polled his staff and without exception they argued that Nixon had to be at least indicted, if not actively prosecuted, or else history would condemn the entire work of the special prosecutor's office. George Frampton, who had mapped out the case against Nixon, wrote a memorandum summarizing their views:

> Those capable of making a "political" decision on this issue—the Congress, political leaders, President Ford—have not done so. Neither they nor the country can expect you now to abandon *your* mandate and responsibilities to the administration of justice in order to assume *their* burden. . . . I wonder if ten years from now history will endorse the notion that Mr. Nixon has "suffered enough." The powerful men around him have also lost their jobs and been disgraced, but many of them will have lost their liberty and their livelihood. Mr. Nixon, on the other hand, will be supported in lavish style with a pension and subsidies at taxpayers' expense until his death. He may reenter public life, however morally crippled.

To Jaworski, the Watergate cover-up charges represented his best chance for a conviction, but Nixon's alleged misdeeds were encyclopedic, spanning a yawning expanse of criminal conduct. While Sirica was announcing the delay, for instance, another U.S. district court judge in another courtroom ordered new information turned over to prosecutors in a separate case involving the alleged use of campaign contributions for, among other things, improvements to the houses in Key Biscayne owned by Nixon and "First Friend" Bebe Rebozo. Prosecutors believed the money, in hundred-dollar bills, had come from Howard Hughes and the chairman of a Jacksonville food store chain and had passed through as many as seven bank accounts. There also was a question of whether Nixon would be compelled to testify; for undetermined reasons, the U.S. marshal in California had failed to serve him Ehrlichman's subpoena. If

Jaworski was to proceed against Nixon, he would not be goaded into haste.

Above the Pacific, Nixon—venturing out less, seeing fewer visitors, not answering as many calls—brooded alone. Pat, according to a friend, reported the Nixons had received four hundred flower arrangements when they first arrived in San Clemente. But now only Rebozo and another friend and personal financier, Bob Abplanalp, got through to see Nixon, who, besieged and still lawyerless, recalled darkly, "I was utterly defenseless. My public standing was driven so low that I do not think that there was any allegation about me, however horrendous or base, that would not have been believed if it was aired or published . . . It was not enough for my critics to say that I had made terrible mistakes. They seemed driven to prove that I represented the epitome of evil itself."

* * *

Bush, meanwhile, plummeted to his lowest ebb since his defeat for the Senate in 1970, when he realized he wouldn't reach the White House by winning elections in his adopted state. He'd kept up his climb by making himself useful to Nixon, working diligently at the expense of his family and fortune. Back in Houston, his friends and associates were riding the upheaval in the petroleum market by increasing business with the Saudis as "suddenly, Saudi Arabia took on the position Texas itself had once had and became the swing oil producer for the great industrial nations of the world," journalist Craig Unger wrote. While Bush had pursued his ambition, Bar had supported each decision and moved around with him, raising five children, now all teenaged or older, and she felt a growing isolation as friends and acquaintances drifted away, repulsed by what George called the "stench" of Watergate. When Ford called him on Monday to tell him about Rockefeller, Ford had encouraged him to expect a high-level appointment—soon. As he had with Nixon the last time his prospects had fallen this low, Bush flew to Washington both eager to please and focused on the larger prize.

After Bush lost his election for the Senate, Nixon had offered to make him an assistant to the president, with unspecified responsibilities, but Bush had other ambitions and broached them with Nixon. Haldeman took notes on that meeting: "Bush told the President he would be delighted to take on this assignment, although he did still prefer the opportunity of going to the United Nations as U.S. Ambassador," he wrote. According to Haldeman, Bush explained that "for too long the President had not been represented there by anyone who was a strong advocate"; also "that there was a dearth of Nixon advocacy in New York City and . . . that he could fill that need in the New York social circles . . . The President was very much impressed with Bush's arguments."

Now, with his options severely limited in light of the Townhouse connection, Bush arrived at the Oval Office to have a similar discussion with Ford. Ford knew and liked him from his days in Congress, and he told Bush the decision on the vice presidency had been "very close," according to Bush, who detailed the meeting in his diary. Bush wrote that Ford said to him: "You should have been very complimented by the support," and "What do you want?" Bush also noted that "Haig had indicated that the President had told him that George can have anything he wants . . ."

"We discussed my being chief of staff if there was some real substance," Bush wrote. "I brought it up. Ford seemed very interested in that." When Ford explained that the chief of staff job had changed, that he planned to see more people and deal with them himself, Bush "told him I could see a role where I could deal with the embassies, special interest groups, etc., but only if there were some stature or substance involved in this deal." With Kissinger firmly in control of foreign policy, it was hard to imagine such an arrangement.

Ford had suggested on the phone that he might offer Bush a top diplomatic posting. London, the most coveted, required congressional approval and substantial personal wealth, as ambassadors were expected to entertain lavishly and largely at their own expense, something Bush already had done in New York with help from his Connecticut relations, yet at a cost to his own finances. "We went back and talked more about England," Bush reported. "He wondered if it was substantive enough—

so did I. We talked about the money. I told him I had lost a lot of money and didn't know if I could afford it. He indicated there were some outside ways of doing this. I told him I was aware of this from my UN days."

"I will mention it to Kissinger," Ford told him. "I see no problems there." They also discussed China, where Bush's earlier efforts to prevent the communist government from being seated at the UN had failed and embarrassed him. Ford and Bush both recognized that Mao's government could kill Bush's appointment to head the liaison office there—without formal relations, the United States had no ambassador, which not incidentally meant that Congress didn't have to confirm Ford's choice. Bush reassured him. "I told him the UN vote conceivably could be against me although I got along with them once they were there. I told him that I was very interested in foreign affairs . . . I indicated that way down the line, maybe 1980, if I stayed involved in foreign affairs, I conceivably could qualify for secretary of state.

"The President seemed to agree," Bush wrote. As with the Nixon and the UN post, Bush was pursuing a difficult and uncharted career agenda necessitated by his election losses—trying to rise to the White House through a succession of appointments in an area still dominated by Kissinger. Nineteen-eighty, it went unsaid, marked the end of Ford's elected term if he could win in 1976—a period of succession. If Bush was eventually to become vice president, then president, a hiatus in China would afford both him and Bar the chance to establish loyalty to Ford's administration while escaping Nixon's shadow and the political, financial, and social cul-de-sacs in which they found themselves as runners-up to Nelson and Happy Rockefeller.

Ford, he wrote, "was very warm, very grateful, very friendly. I told him that if he appointed me to England the party people would think he was moving me over and out—or kicking me upstairs. I told him this was perfectly OK with me though because I thought it was a great challenge. I told him, 'You don't owe me a thing. I could very easily go back into private life.' Indeed we discussed it. He said, 'I don't want you to do that. I don't want you to lose your talents.' "

D A Y

Friday, August 23

"What do you think I'm doing here?"

The parade of Arab and Israeli envoys through the Oval Office resumed with the arrival of Syria's foreign minister, Abd al-Halim Khaddam. Syria faced being excluded from Middle East diplomacy unless Khaddam could persuade Ford that no peace process could ignore the Golan Heights, the Israeli-occupied mountain region where for two and a half months the killing had stopped but not the buildup for another war. The Soviet Union had shipped Syria more than $2 billion in arms, including supersonic MIG-23 fighters and a sophisticated air defense system, and Jerusalem now feared Damascus could fight a war with Israel on its own. Meanwhile, U.S. impotence on Cyprus and the assumption that Ford, unlike Nixon, had no incentive to put strong pressure on Israel, helped stiffen Israeli intransigence.

Khaddam had met Kissinger on the tarmac the first time Kissinger had flown to Damascus in December, and he had wasted no time asserting that Syria opposed any partial settlement in the Middle East. "Nor," Kissinger wrote, "did he give the impression that the survival of Israel ranked high among his priorities." During the thirty-four-day shuttle, they had shared daily car rides to meetings with President Hafez Assad.

Khaddam wasn't part of Assad's inner circle, and was generally called in only after Kissinger and Assad, Israel's most implacable neighbor, met alone first. But slowly, reluctantly, Assad and Khaddam had both come to embrace a diplomatic process that accepted Israeli statehood.

All sides credited this historic turnabout to Kissinger, who in eighty-five hours of talks with Assad and forty with Israel's President Golda Meir forged close personal associations that made them willing to trust, if not each other, him. The Israeli/Syrian agreement signed on May 31— the only agreement ever between the two countries, it was delayed for fifteen minutes while newsmen and photographers were cleared out at Syria's request so there would be no pictures of the signing—returned three hundred square miles of treasured farmland captured by Israel during the October War in exchange for a pullback in Syrian forces. Suddenly, Egypt's Sadat no longer was the only Arab leader to have negotiated with Israel, and Syria, like Egypt, had emerged tantalizingly from the Soviet tent—a major reversal in the calculus of the Cold War. "By all measures," Sadat declared, "Dr. Kissinger has again done a miracle." Israeli deputy prime minister Allon concurred: "What Henry has achieved now is the impossible."

Nixon seized on the breakthrough, hastily revving up his triumphal tour of the Middle East, which he hoped to parlay into some sort of agreement at his June summit meeting with Brezhnev that might derail the impeachment juggernaut. In fact, the moment had crested, far less to his favor than to Kissinger's. Kissinger returned home a symbol of renewed American strength and power: a "national treasure," liberal historian Arthur Schlesinger, Jr., called him. "It's Super-K!" *Newsweek* trumpeted over a cartoon cover of a muscled-up Kissinger in horn-rimmed glasses and a cape soaring above the world. A record 85 percent of participants in a Harris poll rated Kissinger good-to-excellent, compared with 32 percent for Nixon, and three out of four people said they wanted him as secretary of state no matter who was president. "Indeed," the magazine gushed, "there seems to be no limit to Kissinger's phenomenal rise to a place of unparalleled esteem in the hearts and minds of his fellow Americans and many abroad."

Kissinger's bruising return to earth—accelerated by Cyprus and his battle with the neocons and the Pentagon over détente—had started almost the same minute he stepped off the plane in Salzburg on his way back to Washington. Instead of being bathed with glory at his first press conference, he was asked about wiretaps linking him to the White House scandals. A trickle of leaked evidence from congressional hearings showed that he had been more intimately involved with surveillance of some of his top aides and several newsmen during Nixon's first term than he had let on, and that he may have misled the Senate in his confirmation hearings for secretary of state. In May 1969, to prove to Nixon that news stories that the United States was secretly bombing neutral Cambodia were not being leaked by liberals on the National Security Council staff, Kissinger had called FBI director J. Edgar Hoover and urged the wiretaps—which he later denied. Now in Austria, his voice quaking, hands trembling, and eyes watering, Kissinger railed at the attacks, demanding his name be cleared, threatening to resign if it wasn't.

Few in Congress had the stomach to diminish Kissinger during Nixon's final days, but singed by Watergate, he began to shed the aura of a miracle worker. Khaddam understood, too, that Washington's influence over Israel had deteriorated sharply. Yitzak Rabin, the new prime minister, was asserting, as *Newsweek* reported, a "muscular" hard line: "the Golan Heights would remain an inseparable part of Israel; and Israel's 'right' to settlements in Judea and Samaria, the West Bank of the Jordan River that Israel seized from Jordan in 1967, goes back to 'ancient times.'" In Israeli polls, Kissinger's popularity had dropped for the first time below 50 percent, and his close working relationship with the Arabs disturbed many Israelis and American Jews. This had complicated his position with Nixon, who in one of many anti-Semitic comments on the tapes could be heard boasting to Egypt's Fahmy about "my Jewboy." As for Ford, Khaddam knew little but that he had been a strong champion of Israel in Congress.

Khaddam now joked lightly that he would invite Kissinger to the next Arab summit, since his colleagues were telling Kissinger everything anyway. He lodged no opposition to Jordan's negotiating over part of the

West Bank as, alone among Arab leaders, Assad didn't equate Palestinian sovereignty with the PLO; a Palestinian state interfered with his vision of a greater Syria. "Khaddam," Kissinger recalled, "indicated that Syria might be prepared to work with Jordan on developing a special form of Palestinian self-determination not tied to the PLO."

Kissinger knew that King Hussein distrusted Syria too deeply for anything to come of the proposal; indeed, the entire peace process was deflating fast, largely if inadvertently due to Ford's ascension. "A mood of black despair has now taken hold in all Arab capitals since Kissinger's last Mideast success," Chicago *Sun-Times* columnists Rowland Evans and Robert Novak wrote in their syndicated column. "Because of his extreme political weakness at home, a desperate President Nixon needed diplomatic successes in the Mideast as fast as Kissinger could get them and so leaned hard on Israel. Mr. Ford is under no such pressure." Contrarily, Jews feared that Kissinger might try for a quick new triumph by forcing Israel into fresh territorial concessions. The stalemate led many to worry about a bloodier, longer war to come, more apt to involve a full-blown superpower confrontation than last October's. "The upshot of Khaddam's visit," Kissinger wrote, "was—inevitably—procrastination: we agreed that we would continue the dialogue in Damascus." Kissinger, adept at stepping in and solving crises when they peak, played for time. Letting pressure mount was a favorite diplomatic ploy of his.

Ford, according to a statement issued by terHorst, assured Khaddam during the meeting of his "determination to continue the deepening and strengthening of Syrian/American relations" and pledged to be "as helpful as possible" in getting a special $100 million aid bill through Congress. Ford then spent the rest of the day closing out the week's affairs, attending to phone calls, proclamations, and political chores. He went to the Rose Garden briefly to meet with the 1973 national Farm Family of the Year, taped a message for the Michigan Republican state convention, met in the Cabinet Room with representatives from senior citizens' groups, and late in the afternoon rode to Bethesda Naval Hospital to get fitted for new contact lenses.

* * *

Rockefeller, back at his summer estate in Seal Harbor to begin preparing for his confirmation hearings, held a noontime press conference at the end of a boat dock near his house. For thirty-five minutes he and Happy sat on a bench, taking questions amid the snapping halyards and squawking gulls. Secret Service agents, veiled in pale fog, patrolled the rocky shoreline and stood lookout on the roof of his boathouse. Wearing a matching yellow sport shirt and socks and a pair of green slacks, Rockefeller put his arm around his wife, joked, laughed, and shook hands with visitors. For the benefit of reporters unable to make the first conference, Rockefeller later met alone with the press again under the trees near a guesthouse at a neighboring estate, put to use as a press center.

He appeared to have convinced himself, once he accepted Ford's nomination, that he prized being designated for a job he had long disdained. His top aide, Robert Douglass, recalls that despite his extreme privilege, Rockefeller revered the presidency: "His eyes used to glisten when they played 'Hail to the Chief,' " Douglass recalls. Nothing if not aware of the near-universal perception that he would find it difficult, if not impossible, to adjust to being Ford's understudy, he set out to prove his sincere enthusiasm.

"I just want to be useful," he told the reporters. "I would like to help in any way I can President Ford, who, in my opinion, has reestablished faith and hope in this country. He has opened the doors and windows and there is a great feeling of confidence and optimism growing. He drops in on the Senate, the House of Representatives. The Black Caucus meets with him . . . to see Bella Abzug standing right next to the president and [black Congresswoman] Shirley Chisholm near her clapping— my goodness, this has got to be a new era!"

Saying he had accepted Ford's nomination because he felt "there is a national and worldwide crisis of very serious proportion," he declared himself "extremely optimistic" about the country's future.

A reporter asked Rockefeller to react to Ford's proposal for leniency for draft evaders and deserters. Rockefeller said he thought it was an "excellent statement" that "showed great courage." Well, another asked: What about "amnesty" for Nixon?

"Shouldn't that be a matter for the courts?" he asked. Rockefeller wasn't asked and didn't say whether he had consulted the White House, although it was fair to assume that he had, and that he wouldn't comment on the Watergate prosecutions without doing so first. "Congress said that they don't have the power," he said. "I listened to Senator Hugh Scott on the air, and as Senator Scott said, he's been hung, and it doesn't seem to me that in addition he should be drawn and quartered."

Rockefeller was asked if he planned an "independent" vice presidency, wherein he would air any disagreements with the president. "If I had any disagreements or any thoughts, my tendency would be to give them to him privately," he said.

Inevitably the questions returned to Rockefeller's own ambitions. Twice at the first session, reporters asked him if he was reconciled to the idea that, failing Ford's death or disability in office, he was unlikely ever to sit in the White House. Both times, according to the *Times*, Rockefeller "talked around the question."

"Politics at this time are totally irrelevant," he said. "The question of ideologies—liberal and conservative, Democratic and Republican—really has no place. In times like these we can't afford the luxury of some of these traditional activities."

When the question was put to him again at the second session under the trees, he answered: "To be perfectly frank, this is not a matter of any concern to me at all. I have wanted to serve this country. I now have an opportunity to serve this country. I can't ask for any more." But then, asked if seventy-two—his age in 1980—would make him too old to run for president, he first called the question irrelevant, then spoke admiringly of Golda Meir, who in June had stepped down at age sixty-eight, and the late West German chancellor Konrad Adenauer, who retired from office when he was eighty-seven.

Rockefeller, it seemed, was willing to shrink himself to become what he called "a No. 2 type of guy" but not to forego his dream of being number one. As he would later tell reporters, who long remained skeptical of his motives, "I'm not going to kid you that I came down here with no thought of the presidency in mind."

"What," he would ask, "do you think I'm doing here?"

16

Saturday, August 24

State of Alert

TerHorst got to his office about six thirty, lit a pipe, and sampled the morning papers. "They had them ready on my desk," he recalls. "The *Post*, the *Times*. The *New York Daily News* and *New York Post*—you want the tabloids." A small story on page eight of the *Washington Post* caught his attention. Under the headline "Pentagon Kept Watch on Military," the paper stated that during Nixon's last days in office, Schlesinger and the Joint Chiefs had "kept a close watch to make certain that no orders were given to military units outside the normal chain of command." Extraordinary if not unprecedented, the alert was "based on hypothetical situations that could arise during a period when President Nixon's hold on the Presidency was not clear," the paper said, adding: "Specifically there was concern that an order could go to a military unit outside the chain of command for some sort of action against Congress during the time between a House vote for impeachment and a Senate trial on the impeachment charge."

According to the *Post* story, the Defense Department said it had no evidence to indicate that the White House had plans to use military units on its own, but lines of communication were tightened between the civilian and military leadership and "word was passed" to ensure that no military commander took an order that came from the White House or elsewhere that didn't descend through military channels. The Pentagon was said to be particularly interested in the air force, known to have a "special loyalty" to Nixon for his efforts to bring home captured pilots shot down in Vietnam, and it "paid close attention to the atmosphere in meeting places of military officers during the period."

Schlesinger, asked about the decision, was quoted as saying: "In keeping with my statutory responsibilities, I did assure myself that there would be no question about the proper constitutional and legislated chain of command, and there never was any question."

TerHorst wasn't the only one alarmed by the story, which appeared to confirm rumors percolating through the pressroom since before Nixon went into exile. Media interest spiked. Scenarios about Washington coups and countercoups were a popular Cold War staple. The 1964 hit film *Seven Days in May,* based on a bestselling novel, told the story of General James Mattoon Scott, chairman of the Joint Chiefs of Staff, who leads a Pentagon plot to overthrow the government after the president and Congress enter into a treaty with the Soviet Union in which each side agrees to destroy its nuclear arsenal. The generals believe the Soviets plan to break the pact and attack the United States, and the coup is crushed, but the film plumbed deep national fears of annihilation, treason, and betrayal. You didn't have to be an editor at the *Post* through the anxious years of Vietnam, détente, the opening of China, and Watergate to grasp the strong visceral distrust between Nixon and the Pentagon brass, who thought he had gone "soft on communism," and the rare opportunities for circumventing the Constitution because of his collapse.

Indeed, deep strains between the White House and the Pentagon had spawned the seminal crisis of Nixon's first term, which remarkably still remained secret despite Watergate's storm-tide of disclosures. In December 1971, Nixon learned of a Pentagon spy ring within the White House. A young navy stenographer assigned to Kissinger, Yeoman Charles Radford, had confessed that for more than a year he'd been systematically rifling through burn bags, interoffice envelopes, and even

Kissinger's briefcase and passing thousands of top-secret documents to his superiors. The espionage was provoked by what Admiral Elmo Zumwalt, chief of naval operations, described as the "deliberate, systematic and, unfortunately, extremely successful efforts of the President, Henry Kissinger, and a few subordinate members of their inner circle to conceal, sometimes by simple silence, more often by articulate deceit, their real policies about the most critical matters of national security."

When Nixon had learned about the spy ring, he pounded his desk in anger, speaking gravely about prosecuting Chairman of the Joint Chiefs Admiral Thomas Moorer and others. He especially voiced deep suspicion about Haig, then Kissinger's military aide. "I'm afraid Haig must have known about this operation," he told Ehrlichman. "It seems unlikely he wouldn't have known." Two days later, however, Nixon reversed course, apparently deciding that Haig was more valuable to him as a bridge to the Pentagon and a force to rein in Kissinger. "We're going to continue to handle the chiefs . . . through Haig," he told Ehrlichman. Nixon decided to let Moorer know that he knew about Moorer's role in the spying, an unprecedented case of espionage by the military leadership against the White House in wartime, but didn't fire him. "Moorer's our man now," Ehrlichman said. When Kissinger heard Moorer would be reappointed, he'd exploded at Haldeman: "They can spy on him and spy on me and betray us and they won't fire him! . . . I can assure you this tolerance will lead to very serious consequences for this administration."

In burying the scandal, Nixon helped seal his subsequent fate by maintaining at the helm of his national security apparatus a cast of characters whom he distrusted and who distrusted him. Now, that distrust— and renewed concerns about Nixon's lust for power and mental state during his final days in office—burst into the open and ignited yet another flash fire for Ford, who as terHorst understood, first needed to know if the story was true and, second, how the paper got it.

* * *

Criminal defense lawyer Herbert "Jack" Miller was at home at his Maryland horse farm when the phone rang. A discreet former aide to Attorney General Robert Kennedy, and a pallbearer after Kennedy was
assassinated during the 1968 presidential campaign that Nixon won,
Miller, age fifty, had become "almost a one man conglomerate of Watergate clientele," the *Post* observed. He had represented former attorney
general Richard Kleindienst during the ITT scandal, plea-bargaining a
suspended sentence on a reduced charge and keeping Kleindienst out of
jail by telling how he had admirably resisted pressure from Nixon to drop
the government's antitrust case. Miller's stirring leniency plea had
swayed the sentencing judge to attribute Kleindienst's perjury before the
Senate to a "heart that is too loyal" rather than to mendacity.

The caller—a Nixon appointee and former client of Miller's named
Richard Moore—phoned from "somewhere in the woods, up in Maine I
believe," Miller says. Moore, a friend of both Nixon and Mitchell, had
provided legal "white hair" for Nixon during Watergate, bird-dogging
Dean and inevitably becoming entangled when it came down to Nixon's
word against Dean's during the Senate hearings. It was Moore's two and
a half days of testimony, during which he quoted apparently verbatim,
with Miller beside him, private conversations with Nixon that finally
prompted investigators to ask about the existence of a White House taping system. As Stephen Ambrose noted: "Nixon's defense team were not
just playing with fire, they were shoving their hands into it."

"I have a question to ask you," Miller remembers Moore saying.

"Fire away."

"If you were asked to represent Richard Nixon, what would your answer be?"

"If I answered that no," Miller said, "I'd resign from the bar tomorrow."

"That's what I thought," Moore told him. Assured that Nixon
wouldn't be turned down and/or embarrassed, Moore added, "You'll be
getting a call later today."

* * *

Surrounded by the leaders of Congress, Ford beamed as he sat at the head of the ellipsoid table in the Cabinet Room and signed into law the first bill he'd sent them—authorizing a council on wage and price stability. Unlike Nixon's Cost of Living Council, empowered to impose controls, the new agency would give "guidance in very broad terms to management and labor so they don't take advantage of a free economy in this critical situation," he told them. Ford planned to do whatever he could to get America moving again, chiefly with a stern dose of Republican "old-time religion"—tight budgets and tight money—and by cajoling inflation down from its ledge through public pressure on companies and unions. "We have learned from experience that in today's economy, controls lead to disruption and new troubles," he said.

Wall Street meanwhile verged on despair. Savaged by soaring prices, high interest rates, worldwide shortages of food and dozens of key commodities, uncertainty over the supply and price of its main energy source—oil—and fears of a global recession, stocks had plunged throughout the week to their lowest level in more than four years, bringing serious comparisons for the first time in decades to 1929. Not one new stock offering had been floated in nine weeks, and brokers, it was said, were "happy only that the windows can't be opened in these fancy new buildings." A day earlier, Pan American World Airways, the country's largest international carrier, appealed to Washington for a $10-million-a-month subsidy, retroactive to April. Whipsawed by stagflation—plummeting passenger loads combined with stratospheric fuel costs—the company said that without the money it would either have to slash service and unload many of its assets or seek bankruptcy.

Ford agreed with his treasury secretary, William Simon, and the new chairman of his Council of Economic Advisors, Alan Greenspan, that it would take between two and five years to bring inflation down to a reasonable level—say, 2 to 3 percent—and that, initially at least, he needed to hold the line on spending. He indicated he wanted to be the first president since Eisenhower to balance the budget and would be unafraid to use his veto. "We can do it," he said. "We are going to do it. And that ought to be reassuring, I think, to the American people."

"It would be unrealistic to expect this [wage-price] council to bring any immediate relief from inflation," he told the leadership. "We face an uphill road, and we will make it through only if we all pull together . . . This battle has to be won and will be won."

Successful persuasion would be harder outside this room. Yet so far Ford had sent comforting signals on the economy, and across the nation most people felt he was off to a good start—Wall Street's desperation aside. Business leaders felt relief over Nixon's departure and were generally elated about Ford's choice of Rockefeller. The problem, as always, was time. Ford was hoping that events would free him to get his feet under him before tackling the economy, the most difficult problem he faced. He expected his honeymoon with Congress and the public to last until the fall election, about three months, the usual duration. But with hyberbolic Wall Street the most visible and troubling measure of the nation's economic ill-health, he was starting to see that the markets might not be able to wait until after the September summit conference—a " 'let's reason together'-type gathering," as *Newsweek* called it—for Ford and his economic advisers to "make their stand." "By last week," the magazine reported, "it appeared that the rate of economic decline was outrunning the Presidential timetable."

Ford had planned to play golf in the afternoon at Burning Tree but he canceled, working in the Oval Office until six thirty, when he went upstairs for dinner with Betty and their son Steve. Their third child, Steve had decided to put off entering Duke for a year while he headed west to work as a wrangler on a ranch, and he was champing at the bit to get out of Washington. Daredevil Evel Knievel planned to leap fifteen hundred feet across the Snake River Canyon in Wyoming on a 350-mile-per-hour rocket-powered motorcycle on the Sunday after Labor Day, and Steve Ford, who Betty described as the "charmer in the family . . . [who] . . . bounced in and out of schools like a Ping-Pong ball," wanted to be there for the show.

* * *

Ronald Reagan, serving his eighth and final year as governor of California, was in the thick of wrangling with a Democratic-controlled legislature in the final week of its session. But Reagan, at age sixty-three, flew overnight to the Eastern Shore of Maryland to appear at a party fund-raising bull-roast. Officially undecided whether to run for president in 1976, Reagan had been catalyzed overnight into a candidate by Ford's choice of Rockefeller.

Conservatives, infuriated at the prospect that Rockefeller might inherit the presidency from Ford, and believing the nomination was designed to stop Reagan, abruptly galvanized around his candidacy. Major Republican misfortunes had benefited Reagan twice before: Nixon's 1962 loss for governor, which enabled him to challenge an incumbent Democrat four years later, and Goldwater's landslide defeat, which for the past decade had left the GOP "especially bereft" of promising stars on the right, as the *Post*'s Lou Cannon wrote. Reagan's trip to within fifty miles of Washington was a rapidly organized shot across Ford's bow.

Nixon had thought Reagan "strange" and not "pleasant to be around": "Reagan on a personal basis," he told Haldeman, "is terrible." Like Bush, Reagan had been hurt by his stalwart support for Nixon, yet unlike most Republicans he had been strangely buoyed by Nixon's downfall. The day after the resignation, he'd urged young Republicans meeting near Lake Tahoe to forget Nixon and put their faith in conservative ideology. Now, he warned the Ford Administration to reassert the "mandate of 1972," as he called it. He told the crowd of more than two thousand that in re-electing Nixon overwhelmingly, the "voters rejected an invitation to Utopia and reaffirmed the basic values from which our system was built. They voted for fiscal responsibility and individual determination of their own destinies.

"They repudiated the idea that government should grow bigger and bigger . . . ," he went on, "that we should embrace more costly programs to alleviate human misery—programs that somehow never succeed no matter how much money is spent on them. The mandate of 1972 was a matter of the people vs. big government.

"The people, I believe, have given the government a mandate which they expect to be enforced."

During a hurried twenty-five-minute press conference, Reagan left open the possibility that he would be a candidate for the White House. "My plans remain the same," he told reporters. "I want to get around the country, especially the campuses, and talk to the young people." Earlier, an aide had told them that Reagan was concerned that Ford was drifting to the left and that there might be an accommodation with liberal policies rejected two years earlier. Asked what about Ford so far concerned him, Reagan said he opposed Ford's broad grant of amnesty for Vietnam deserters. A reporter asked if Reagan would nonetheless accept a position in a Ford cabinet.

"No." Reagan nodded. "I feel I'd rather remain independent."

Sunday, August 25

Friendly Fire

Schlesinger's cryptic comment to the *Post* about military precautions during the White House transition morphed overnight into page-one news, leaving Ford to react to the impression that in the days surrounding his taking office, the top commanders of the U.S. armed services took measures to thwart a possible coup d'état. The *Times*, quoting a "senior Pentagon official," revealed that Schlesinger had been worried about two main possibilities, however unlikely. The first was that Nixon or one of his aides might order military units to block Congress from the "constitutional process" of formally removing him from office, or else that some other official might try to oust Nixon; the other, that a real emergency might develop in which U.S. forces might have to act and that Schlesinger and air force general George Brown, who had replaced Moorer as chairman of the Joint Chiefs, could be called on publicly to justify taking military action. The above-the-fold story was headlined "Pentagon Kept Tight Rein in Last Days of Nixon Rule."

Schlesinger's second concern—the Pentagon's credibility—stemmed from the general skepticism arising in October when Kissinger, Schlesinger, Colby, and Moorer placed U.S. units on high nuclear alert after it seemed the Soviets might send in forces to help Syria and Egypt against Israel. Reporters afterward had questioned Kissinger at a press conference whether that alert was linked to some desire to distract public attention from Agnew's resignation, the Saturday Night Massacre, and the rising chorus of Democrats calling for impeachment proceedings. Though Kissinger stressed then and since that the October alert was legitimate, a Pentagon "senior official" now voiced concern that if a similar crisis had developed while Nixon was losing the presidency, and the secretaries of state and defense were spurred to act, the public might not believe them. As the *Times* reported, Schlesinger "decided he wouldn't leave Washington during the White House crisis so that he could be at the center of Pentagon command."

Ford, furious, wondered who would leak such a story now—and why. What Schlesinger might have known, or feared, or been correct in taking precautions to prevent, paled next to what Ford believed was a profound act of disloyalty—to him, Nixon, the country, and the officer corps. To suggest, he later wrote, that "our military commanders—men who are controlled by civilians under the Constitution—might take some unilateral and illegal action at a moment of grave national crisis was to stab our armed forces in the back. And that, in my opinion, was inexcusable."

The White House traced the leak with special urgency. Deputy Defense Secretary William Clements, Ford later would learn, was "in California at the time. His telephone began to ring about 4 A.M., Pacific Daylight Time. What was going on? Everyone wanted to know," Ford recorded. Clements canceled his appointments, flew back to Washington immediately, and huddled with Brown.

"What in hell is this all about?" Clements demanded, according to Ford's account.

"Nothing," Brown replied. "There was no alert."

"Are you sure?"

"Absolutely," Brown said. "I've checked at headquarters. There are no recorded messages coming out of the Secretary of Defense's office. Furthermore, if there had been a call, it would have been referred back to the

National Military Command Center here at the Pentagon. We have no record of that. I've checked every record and it's all pure fabrication."

"You've checked it yourself, George?"

"Yes, there's no question."

During the first days of the October War, when Nixon's preoccupation with Agnew's resignation kept him out of the decision-making and Israel was stunned and weakened by the surprise invasion, Kissinger and Schlesinger jointly had managed U.S. policy. Clements, a self-made Texas oil-drilling contractor, handled the operations. Israel urgently requested military supplies, and for the next week the three of them waged a sharp, underhanded battle to determine how to respond. Kissinger, eager to help Israel but fearing Arab and Soviet reaction to U.S. planes ferrying weapons into the region, wanted a covert airlift, using chartered transports, but with Nixon distracted, he was isolated. Schlesinger and Clements, reflecting the Pentagon's view, warned that a major rearming of Israel would poison relations with the Arabs, especially the Saudis, who might unleash the "oil weapon" in retaliation.

More than a week went by as the situation turned more ominous. The Soviets began their own airlift; Israel, in trouble, put its nuclear-armed missiles on alert. "As Israel began to fall apart, Henry began to fall apart," Schlesinger recalled. Finally roused to action by the Soviet resupply effort, Nixon discovered that five phantom jets he'd ordered sent to Israel two days earlier had not gone out. He exploded, and Kissinger, though he too wanted Israel sufficiently bloodied so it would have to make diplomatic concessions after the war, blamed the Pentagon and especially Clements for the delay. He told Nixon: "They think there is a special relationship with the Saudis." Nixon announced, "Do it now!" and Kissinger enlisted Scowcroft to stop the foot-dragging at the Pentagon. He also phoned Haig: "Could you stiffen Schlesinger's back?" he said. "The guy is totally panicked. Clements is beating after him. If the Egyptians win, we will lose our position."

The schisms in the national security group had only sharpened under Ford, particularly between Ford himself and Schlesinger, whose "aloof, frequently arrogant manner" put Ford off. "Our personal relationship, which had never been good, slid downhill after I became President," he wrote. Schlesinger had been delegated a secondary role on Cyprus, was serving in effect as weapons merchant in the Middle East peace process, and was further marginalized by Kissinger's assumption of even greater power over foreign policy since the transition. Ford credited him with the idea to consider leniency for draft resisters, although Schlesinger opposed any form of amnesty. Meanwhile, Ford wrote, Schlesinger "kept telling me that I should get rid of Clements," and Ford had become irked by his approach—which consisted of suggesting to Ford that Clements's involvement in Pentagon deals related to the Saudis and other Arab oil producers could blow up into a scandal, and that it was in Ford's best interests to ask him to leave. Ford had the allegations checked out and discovered there was nothing to them—"which didn't exactly enhance my confidence" in Schlesinger, he wrote.

On Friday, within hours after Ford and Kissinger met with Syria's Khaddam in the Oval Office, Schlesinger had held a background briefing with Pentagon reporters over lunch. According to Ford, after General Brown told Clements that there had been no alert and the story was "pure fabrication," Clements confronted the defense secretary. "Shaken," Ford recalled, "Clements walked upstairs and entered Schlesinger's office. He mentioned the 'scare' stories in the press and that they had obviously emanated from Schlesinger's lunch with reporters, then asked, 'Why did you say all this?'

"At first Schlesinger didn't reply," Ford wrote. "Finally, he looked up and said, 'I don't know.'"

* * *

In what Kissinger termed an "insolent reply," Hanoi's Le Duc Tho rebuffed his warning against treating the presidential transition as a military opportunity. The scholarly top politburo member and negotiator, whom Kissinger had nicknamed "Ducky" behind his back, not only took credit for Nixon's collapse but threatened Ford with a similar result: "Mr. Nixon met with failure in the enterprise and had to leave the White House. Should Mr. Ford continue doing so, he would certainly and inevitably fail too."

Saigon was abandoning military posts throughout the country, and no one in Washington had the will to revisit the question of whether the United States should do more to help forestall a rout. In the past twenty-four hours, fierce fighting left a hundred government and communist soldiers dead or wounded. With roughly two hundred thousand North Vietnamese Army troops in the South, Hanoi appeared to be marshaling for a general offensive, maybe as early as November, the beginning of the dry season.

For weeks, the decency of Nixon and Kissinger's interval in withdrawing U.S. forces from Vietnam had been reduced to its blind essence—military spending. By slashing aid to Saigon to $700 million, Congress had provoked a spasm of recriminations. All sides were inflamed. A former top-ranking military officer in South Vietnam, General John Murray, accused Congress of "sacrificing blood for the lack of ammunition." Another veteran testified, "Today the South Vietnamese are forced to hoard their air power and artillery and so they get more people killed and wounded. It's not only sadistic, it's racist." After Murray was dressed down, a fellow general anonymously denounced the "fiscal whores" in the Pentagon for juggling the defense budget to deprive the South's forces of what they most needed. One third of the request was slated either for new fighter planes, even though the South couldn't maintain the ones it already had, or else for overhead and handling costs that should have been charged elsewhere.

Kissinger would strain to argue that without Watergate, Washington's will to stand by South Vietnam would not have been sapped. But the country was riven and beleaguered by his and Nixon's four-year war to gain a cease-fire that had allowed the government of President Nguyen Van Thieu to retain authority in Saigon, which in the end had been the North's primary concession in the Paris peace accord. All other major points—cease-fire conditions, prisoner exchanges—were identical to proposals made by Hanoi back in 1969. Nixon's goal of Vietnamization—training the regime's forces to take over the war effort themselves—had achieved little beyond the withdrawal of U.S. troops: a "camouflaged bugout," Asia expert Richard Holbrooke called it. As Walter Isaacson wrote: "The deal would turn out to be costly: an additional 20,552 Americans dead, and the near unraveling of America's social fabric, a breakdown in respect for government authority, the poisoning of America's reputation abroad (especially among an entire generation of youth), and the spread of the war to Cambodia and Laos."

Kissinger fumed at Tho's letter, though he realized Ford could do little to show that he or the United States would do anything to reverse an inevitable communist takeover. Even the Pentagon's staunchest supporters on Capitol Hill were balking. When Ford appealed to Mississippi Democrat John Stennis, chairman of the Armed Services Committee, to restore $300 million to Saigon's military assistance budget, Stennis told him he was "getting information from some military people that we could cut down." He advised Ford to send someone to South Vietnam to get his own appraisal.

Reading the same signals, Tho concluded his message with a terse counter-warning:

> In case the U.S. continues the implementation of the Nixon Doctrine without Nixon and the use of the Nguyen Van Thieu group to pursue the war and to undermine the Paris Agreement on Vietnam, then the Vietnamese people will resolutely carry on their struggle to defend peace and the Paris Agreement until complete victory.

* * *

Ziegler ushered in Jack Miller to meet with Nixon, whose seclusion fueled rumors about his state of mind—rumors that seemed to be confirmed by reports that Pentagon officials were concerned about his potential for erratic behavior as he faced resignation. A "Congressional source" told *Newsweek* that the former president had "taken to wandering around his estate in need of a shave and looking so rumpled that it seemed he had slept in his clothes." One of his California lawyers announced he was experiencing a "severe cash flow problem." Miller understood that Nixon's unpopularity would cost his eight-lawyer firm business—even as the complexity of the case would swamp his associates and staff—but he'd flown to San Clemente on the first plane he could get. He'd talked with Ziegler into the wee hours, slept briefly, then returned by noon to Casa Pacifica, where he found Nixon subdued but "alert," he says.

Despite having been recruited, Miller feared Nixon might not hire him. A lifetime Republican—he'd run and lost for lieutenant governor of Maryland on a GOP ticket—he retained affectionate ties to the Kennedys. As head of the Criminal Division at the Justice Department under Bobby Kennedy, he'd been a central member of the legal team that had investigated corrupt Teamsters union boss Jimmy Hoffa, and he'd campaigned for Kennedy in California before his assassination. Miller tried to put to rest any concerns Nixon might have by volunteering that he had worked very closely during the highly publicized Hoffa probe with associate Watergate prosecutor James Neal, now in charge of the cover-up trial. Miller also brought up, preemptively, recent statements by one of his law partners, Nathan Lewin, who'd railed in print that Nixon should be fully investigated and prosecuted.

Lewin argued in the newest issue of *The New Republic* that criminal action against Nixon was crucial to achieving a firm historical judgment about his presidency, since by resigning he had "robbed the Senate" of the chance to render one. He also noted "the probability that Richard Nixon knows of or participated actively in crimes related to Watergate that have not yet been made the subject of a formal charge.

"What possible explanation will there ever be," Lewin wrote, "if history records that those who acted on Nixon's instructions, express or implied, were charged and convicted of crimes and went to jail while their chief spent his retirement years strolling the Pacific beaches, writing about his accomplishments in foreign policy and lecturing to college audiences."

Most troublesome for Miller, Lewin attacked the plea-bargaining process that Miller had used so successfully on behalf of Kleindienst, calling it "most unfair to those accused criminals who have no public trust to barter for leniency."

Nixon appeared unfazed by either connection. At once immensely complex and enormously simple, his legal situation had narrowed to a single immediate goal—"to try to persuade Leon Jaworski not to seek an indictment of Nixon," as Seymour Hersh reported in the *Times*. And for that, Miller's reputation as a savvy plea bargainer and his relationship with Neal could only help.

Related intimately to the question of indictment was how Nixon would answer a growing number of subpoenas. Hiring Miller moved him at once a step closer to being served with court papers, not just by Ehrlichman but also by the Red Hornet Mayday Tribe, which had gotten a court order for him to testify in their civil rights suit in Charlotte—the suit in which Haldeman had been deposed four days earlier. Service of both subpoenas had been delayed largely by the inability of U.S. marshals and Nixon's staff to agree on a seemly formula for delivering them, and a media watch had intensified outside the compound gates.

As Miller flew back to Washington to begin talking with Jaworski, he blocked out his legal strategy for defending private citizen Richard Nixon. He narrowed it to a single claim—that no court could guarantee Nixon his constitutional right to an impartial jury. "From my standpoint, analyzing the situation, I didn't see how it was possible to get a fair trial—because of the massive, overwhelming publicity," Miller says. "Where could you find a jury, unless it was in some isolated place in Idaho, that hadn't been flooded with the press outpouring—television, radio, newspapers, magazines—proclaiming his guilt?"

Later, Nixon in his first interview after resigning would say: "I brought myself down. I gave them a sword. And they stuck it in. And they twisted it with relish. And I guess, if I'd been in their position, I'd have done the same thing." Now, confronting the nearer term, he decided to put his future in the hands of a lawyer who would claim in effect that he couldn't be judged impartially by his countrymen because he had incriminated himself too publicly and too well.

DAY

18

Monday, August 26

"Deep breather in front of the open window"

Ford had scheduled his first White House press conference for Wednesday, hoping to focus the nation's attention on the economy. Midmorning, he discussed inflation for ninety minutes with the cabinet, laying out goals for the September summit, promising to act sooner if needed. Agriculture Secretary Earl Butz reported that retail food prices in July jumped at an annual rate of 30 percent but asserted that food supplies remained adequate despite a severe drought in the Midwest. "There is no reason for panic buying," Butz said, adding, "and there has been some of that."

Flanked by Schlesinger and Haig, Ford returned to the Oval Office to discuss his growing alarm over the military's reported fears of a coup. "I talked to Haig about it," he recalled, "and we concluded that it had been leaked deliberately from the highest level of the Pentagon." Ford didn't know about Brown's confrontation with Schlesinger. Nor did he know the subterranean history between Nixon and the Joint Chiefs going back to the Moorer-Radford spy affair, or the full array of Haig's connections and overlapping loyalties beginning with that period, when he worked under Kissinger out of the cramped National Security Council office in the White House basement and still wore his army colonel's uniform on the job.

Ford was "furious," he wrote, because Haig had assured him that no such measures had been taken. Even if the leaker's main target was Nixon, the news stories fostered the impression that he—Ford—became president in a climate of dangerous instability, and that his presidency might be the product of a secret power shuffle. That such a story had been planted in the press less than three weeks into his term by someone in his top echelon could only be read as a direct affront to Ford's leadership.

"Jim," Ford said. "I'm damn disturbed about these rumors . . . Obviously, they came from the top, and I want the situation straightened out right away."

Schlesinger denied that he was the source of the stories. Far from deferential—he alone among the cabinet secretaries had smoked a pipe throughout Nixon's farewell speech in the East Room—he was vague about their accuracy. Yet if he and the Joint Chiefs had ordered the precaution on the basis of distrust for Nixon and Kissinger, or if concerns had risen to such a pitch that, as the newspapers were reporting, Schlesinger had taken to sleeping on a cot in his office to bar against a coup by—or against—Nixon, he hadn't operated by himself. Haig would have been intimately aware and involved. A four-star general after a quick series of promotions during his White House tenure, Haig, albeit retired, was the ranking military officer in the White House. Nixon had used him to control Moorer, and Haig had coaxed and enabled Nixon's resignation. Indeed, according to Nixon's former counselor, convicted Watergate felon Charles Colson, Haig was the one who initiated the Pentagon watch, asking the military to disregard any order from Nixon.

Haig publicly distanced himself from the Pentagon's precautions. "The suggestion," he wrote, "that a military coup was even a possibility not only was a fantasy, it was an insult to the armed forces." He thought the only real plot to seize the White House came from what Nixon called the "countergovernment"—Congress, the courts, the press—and that it had succeeded, driving both Nixon and Agnew from office. But he also, as the *New Republic* found, "hinted darkly" about "dangers to the country deeper than Watergate" and he spoke to a reporter at the *Los Angeles Times* about the threat of "extra-constitutional" steps during Nixon's last days. Seated at the helm of the executive branch, negotiating the terms that would allow Nixon to resign, Haig had held more power in those days than the president. "Similar circumstances in other countries resulted in bloodless coups," Colson wrote. Vietnam and Watergate had made the notion of a general taking charge of the government sadly plausible.

Ford dressed down Schlesinger as Haig, who "greatly admired" Schlesinger and had recommended him for his job but also thought that "something about the post of Secretary of Defense seems to attract and amplify intellectual arrogance," looked on. During the half-hour session, Schlesinger confirmed that no orders for a heightened watch had been given as the crisis intensified over Nixon's resignation, but he was ambiguous about whether he had requested that such an order be given. Finally, he and Haig stood, left, and were replaced two minutes later by Hartmann and terHorst, summoned to help Ford craft a public statement about the episode.

Minutes later, terHorst read Ford's announcement to reporters: "I had a meeting today with the Secretary of Defense. We discussed the matter and I have been assured that no measures of this nature were actually undertaken." Sticking only to what Ford told him, terHorst refused to confirm or deny accounts that Schlesinger asked for a tight watch to ensure that no extraordinary orders went out from the White House during the succession. He referred all further questions to the Pentagon, where officials maintained that Schlesinger and Brown had discussed between themselves how they should be aware of any illegal orders being issued to military units, and that the word was spread to commanders not to carry out orders from the White House, or elsewhere, outside normal channels. Schlesinger never feared that a coup would be successful, these officials said, even had one been attempted.

"That was pure Schlesinger," Scowcroft recalls. "How much that was Schlesinger actually acting or making statements I don't know. But I

would call it bizarre. First of all, the notion that Nixon would have anything like that in mind. Second, he wouldn't know who to call—he'd ask
me. I mean it just wasn't going to happen. Until I heard what Schlesinger
said he had done—the precautionary measures that no one was to take
orders from the White House—it never crossed my mind. And I'm sure
it never crossed Nixon's mind."

* * *

While Attorney General Saxbe handed off the question of Nixon's ownership of his files and tapes to a combative young Justice Department
lawyer named Antonin Scalia, Saxbe took to the airwaves as Ford's main
surrogate on the subject of leniency for draft exiles.

"What we're talking about," Saxbe told a TV interviewer, "is that we're
going to give these people a chance—if they want it. And it's not going
to involve prison. We're going to say, 'You come back and you're not going to prison.'" Instead, the administration would insist on an "act of
contrition." A "draft dodger"—Ford hadn't yet come to an opinion on
deserters—would "have to come either into the draft board, the U.S. attorney, the state Selective Service headquarters, or a special commission,
and say, 'I'm sorry, I want to take my medicine,'" Saxbe explained. Penalties could run from an extreme of two years of "substantial assistance to
some hospital, some public works, some good works of various kind" to
attendance at a quasi-judicial hearing at which charges would be
dropped for a promise of good behavior. Cases would be considered in-
dividually.

More than 200,000 young men had been formally accused of violat-
ing draft laws during the Vietnam War. Twenty-five thousand had been
indicted, 8,750 convicted, and about 4,000 served jail time. Among the
50,000 or more who'd moved to Canada—the largest politically motivated migration from the United States in two hundred years, since
British loyalists voted with their feet to oppose the American Revolu-

tion—Ford's "earned amnesty" proposal evoked throughout the week no less frigid a reaction than among veterans.

Network reporters trudged to Toronto, heart of the exile community. The Vietnam War's dirty secret at home had been the inequity of sacrifice. Some 16 million men took shelter from military conscription by staying in school or taking advantage of other deferments. Some, like Cheney, who received five deferments (four for being a student and one for being a new father), went to notable lengths to pursue what Cheney later called "other priorities." Millions more like George W. Bush became "sunshine patriots," joining reserve or national guard units shielded from active service by the draft. The New Canadians, as they were called, had sacrificed—if not all that Vietnam veterans had—their citizenship, homeland, and the right ever to return to the United States, to go home and see loved ones.

The politicized exiles were to the antiwar movement what the POW/MIAs were to the VFW, and Ford's and Saxbe's vow not to make them go to jail was thin consolation—as reporters quickly found who made their way through the American ghetto in Toronto to *Amex*, the militant news magazine for resisters. Housed in a smoked-filled donated room in a building shared with the student newspaper at the University of Toronto, *Amex* stridently championed unconditional amnesty for exiled resisters and thousands of deserters alike, finding no moral inequivalency between those who refused to fight in Vietnam before they got drafted and those who fled the military rather than to go into combat for a cause that their leaders already understood to be a mistake.

Jack Colhoun, who'd gotten a doctorate in history and politics while editing *Amex*, gave the publication its moral and political tone. Colhoun had grown to doubt the military's role in Vietnam as a member of the Reserve Officer Training Corps at the University of Wisconsin, when a respected instructor candidly told cadets that he had seen South Vietnamese soldiers torturing prisoners. With bloodlines dating back to the *Mayflower*, Colhoun—ponytailed, mustached, and wearing black-framed Coke-bottle glasses like Trotsky's—bristled with what exile historian John Hagan called "strains of indignant patriotism." "If I didn't feel so strongly about America," he said, "I wouldn't be here in Toronto. I'd have sold out like everyone else."

Colhoun dismissed out of hand Ford's and Saxbe's "middle ground" on the amnesty issue. "I wanted in 1967 to get the army to allow me to work with mentally retarded children, as I was doing, as an alternative to service in the military, but the Army wouldn't allow it," he said. "Now, seven years later, I'm not being asked but apparently being told that I must do that to earn my way back. That's not justice. The President should realize that those seven years in exile is punishment enough."

The common understanding among the New Canadians was that amnesty was purely a U.S. political issue: As another *Amex* activist, Gerry Condon, told CBS's Steve Young, "It's obviously a play-off—amnesty for Nixon and amnesty for war-resisters—which is a play-off we don't really appreciate, because we maintain that we have acted correctly and we maintain equally that Nixon is a criminal."

* * *

After addressing 160 Little League players in the State Dining Room, Ford had a fifty-minute fitting with his tailor, Harvey Rosenthal, who owned a fashionable Washington men's store and who had also, as he put it, "taken care of" Eisenhower, Johnson, and former Supreme Court chief justice Earl Warren. Rosenthal had been fitting Ford for six years, gradually recasting his image. "I really had to get on his back to stop wearing those narrow lapels," he recalled. "We switched him off the suits he was wearing. They came from Grand Rapids, I think, and were a little too sharp."

Ford's beloved plaids were yielding to muted soft-shoulder two-button suits with slightly flared, uncuffed trousers, and Rosenthal endeavored to make him "look like a president," telling him: "It has to be plain blue, plain gray, brown." Ford cared about how he looked; after being named vice president he got his teeth capped and traded his glasses for contact lenses. His image-making with David Kennerly, the intimate photos of the open, confident, casual man, reassured the public. But Ford's heartland, at-home fashion sense—hip-flared pants, Pat Boone white bucks, superstriped ties—created problems by exposing a too-friendly persona. "Ford wore clothes exactly right for minority leader . . ." New York clothing consultant John Molloy noted, "a nice guy who wouldn't offend anyone. But he's still dressing like a guy who slaps you on the back. Nobody is going to follow Ford until he dresses like a leader and sounds like a leader. Dressed as he is, when the President says, 'Let's sacrifice,' people say, 'Aw, c'mon Jerry.' "

Ford was finding that likability, like continuity, was a two-edged sword. Where Nixon with his angular features appeared sharp and weaponized, Ford with his broad brow and thinning blond hair seemed bland. Menswear designer John Weitz, author of a how-to guide for middle-aged men called *Man in Charge*, thought dark horn-rimmed glasses might give Ford more authority. "Contact lenses," Weitz observed, "are part of the traditional athletic hang-up . . . you can't wear glasses and play ball." And yet Ford's stolid athleticism also defined his appeal. He seemed a "deep breather in front of the open window," *Playboy* fashion director Robert Green wrote. "I get the feeling he enjoys getting dressed in the morning . . . that he looks in the mirror, pulls in his gut and realizes that he has held on to his football player charisma."

Ford had been thirteen years old—five feet eight inches, 130 pounds—when he started to play the sport, and in particular the position, that would help form his character and catapult him beyond the circumstances of his youth. His mother Dorothy's remarriage to Gerald Ford, Sr., had placed him as the lone stepson and the eldest of four boys in a loving but stern household. Gangly and blond, he first tried out for football among a hundred eighth-graders on a dirt playground in 1926, and the coach picked him out, saying, "Hey, Whitey, you're a center." Ford, headstrong though earnest and shy in school, relished instantly the brute contact and competition and the precision involved in hiking a football. "I spent hours learning," he would recall, "how to snap the ball back, leading the tailback in the direction he was going to run, putting it high and soft for a fullback coming in to the line, getting it on the right hip for the punter. And then after you centered the ball, you had to be quick to block the opposing lineman who had the jump on you."

As a fifteen-year-old, Ford was named all-city; two years later he won a contest to pick the most popular high school senior in Grand Rapids. Relentlessly industrious, he worked hard in class, was an eagle scout, and made pocket money mowing lawns, handling concessions at an amusement park, and slapping hamburgers and washing dishes at a diner across from his high school. One day during his sophomore year, a tall, handsome, middle-aged stranger with a big open face and wide shoulders drove up to the diner in a new Lincoln and asked Ford if he was Leslie King. When Ford said no, the man said, "I'm your father," and invited him to lunch, after which King gave his son $25 and drove off with a wave. Ford, staggered, had known Gerald Ford was not his real father, but "we really hadn't discussed the situation at home," he wrote. "That night was one of the most difficult of my life . . . nothing could erase the image I gained of my real father: a carefree, well-to-do man who didn't really give a damn about the hopes and dreams of his first-born son. When I went to bed that night, I broke down and cried."

Dorothy and Gerald Ford consoled him, although his younger brothers weren't told until much later, leaving Ford unable to talk with anyone at home about his quandary. Whatever aggression he felt—whatever the demons of discovering as an adolescent what Duke historian Peter Wood has called the "unshared secrets of those he should have been able to trust the most," his parents, who might have saved him the shock by telling him much sooner—was channeled with renewed intensity onto the football field. Ford estimated that in high school and college he snapped the ball a hundred thousand times—bending over, gunning or feathering the ball into the arms of a moving target twenty or more feet away, then smashing into an onrushing opponent. A linebacker on defense, most games he played all sixty minutes. At Michigan, he made All–Big Ten and was named most valuable player, rare for a lineman, while keeping up a B average. After college, the Packers and the Lions both approached him about playing professionally, but first-year players earned $100 to $200 a game, and Ford had decided he wanted to go to law school. Entering politics already had crossed his mind.

Long on determination, Ford was short on means, having worked his way through college during the grimmest years of the Depression by washing dishes, then serving as a paid house manager at DKE fraternity, the clubby masculine society where he met Buchen. In 1935, he graduated with $1,000 in debt. Ford hoped to stay in Ann Arbor for law school, working as an assistant football coach, and with the Grand Rapids furniture industry collapsing, and his parents struggling to keep their paint company going, he wrote to Leslie King to ask for financial help. King never answered. Again football and Ford's work ethic pulled him through. Yale, which trained both fall and spring, hired him as an assistant coach, provided he also coached boxing in the winter.

In New Haven, Ford impressed Yale's players, but the law school, where 80 percent of freshmen had graduated Phi Beta Kappa from college, rejected him for admission. Rebuffed, he returned to Ann Arbor for the summer, took two courses at the University of Michigan Law School, got Bs in both, and presented his grades back at Yale, which then accepted him on a trial basis. "I cheated a little bit," he recalled. "I didn't tell the athletic department that I was going to take two courses. And I didn't tell the law school that I would continue my full time coaching . . . I knew I could do both—coach and go to law school at the same time. But I must say I worked my ass off." A year later, he was able to leave coaching and study full-time after Dorothy finally received a lump sum court settlement of long-neglected child support payments from King.

In all of this Ford displayed a relentless obduracy and optimism— strong up the middle—reflected now in his character and his presidency. But his taste for plaids and wide stripes worked against the image he needed to project. So, too, the fact that, as Molloy put it, he seemed like a man who wanted to have an over-the-fence chat. "Ford has excellent credibility as a person but he's not credible as a leader," he said. "Sometimes in industry a man who has been promoted will be given $1,000 to dress himself in clothes to separate himself from the pack he's been elevated above. It may be easier for him to lead when visually disassociated from them. Americans want their leaders to be larger than life . . . to be gods." It was a lesson that Nixon, a second-string tackle in college who sat on the bench for four years, had learned well and took pleasure in asserting with his well-tailored blue suits.

During Ford's fittings with Rosenthal, they often kibitzed about the economy. Ford was bow-legged, requiring his tailor to double-check the legs of his new suits to make sure the crease didn't jut outward. Ford told Rosenthal the economy would improve, and Rosenthal shot back, "I'm in the retail business. Show me!" Later, in an interview, Rosenthal sized up the country's new leader, saying, "I have seen him with his pants down. I have talked to him in down-to-earth fashion. The American people need this type of man."

Hartmann sat at his desk a few feet from the Oval Office, flipped through his phone messages, and found two from Clark Mollenhoff of the *Des Moines Register and Tribune* and formerly of the Nixon White House. Even among Washington reporters, Mollenhoff nursed a special fury toward Nixon, though he liked Ford and called Hartmann a friend. Bullnecked, Mollenhoff had a reputation as the toughest investigative reporter in Washington: When Teamsters boss Jimmy Hoffa was led off to jail in 1967, Hoffa spat on him. Two years later he became Nixon's ombudsman, assigned to ferret out and address abuses and problems before the press got hold of them. Shunted into secret Nixon projects like the Middle America Committee, a staff group assigned to counterattack antiwar protests by reaching the "large and politically powerful white middle class," Mollenhoff quit after a year, then returned to the *Register*'s Washington bureau, where in a series of tough columns he called on Nixon to set up a bipartisan panel to investigate Watergate and battled with Ziegler to a point other reporters found embarrassing.

Five days after the transition, Mollenhoff had been extolling Ford's record to conservative Iowa Republican representative H. R. Gross when

Gross interrupted him, saying, "Come off that cloud. Ford will probably be better than Nixon, and that's only because Nixon made such a mess of it, but I have seen Jerry Ford operate for twenty-five years. Jerry Ford will deal on anything, and don't forget it." Since then, the pardon dilemma had fallen out of the news, but Mollenhoff remained aroused. He wondered why else Ford would try to offer leniency to draft resisters, or Scott and Rockefeller would urge mercy for Nixon, except to set the stage for a "compassionate act" of immunity for Nixon. An aide had defended Rockefeller's opinion as "simply political posturing"—a bid for support from Nixon's few remaining friends in Congress—but when Mollenhoff heard Ford would hold his first press conference, he began dialing Hartmann. "I questioned him about Ford's position on a pardon for Nixon and on the large number of stories and columns that saw his comments on amnesty as a ploy to soften the liberal Democrats for a pardon," he recalled.

Hartmann told him the Vietnam amnesty had nothing to do with Nixon or with Haldeman's eleventh-hour appeal for blanket forgiveness for Nixon's former aides and draft exiles alike. There had been no such deal, he said. Mollenhoff then suggested that at the news conference someone was bound to ask about pardoning Nixon and that the question would give Ford an excellent opportunity to "put speculation to rest and say in no uncertain terms that he would let justice take its course," as Hartmann recalled. Mollenhoff warned if Ford didn't, his "good start on the presidency would be sorely crippled."

Hartmann stalled by asking what was the urgency: "Nobody had suggested that Ford planned to pardon Nixon, so why should he deny it?" he wrote. But he couldn't say with absolute certainty that Ford hadn't given Haig ample reason to think that he would do so, and that Haig hadn't conveyed that to Nixon, which led Nixon to resign. He also wondered why moderate Republicans like Scott and Rockefeller were pleading against indictment, and whether their comments weren't trial balloons, released to test the winds for Ford.

Hartmann promised Mollenhoff he would try to convey his views to Ford, who was scheduled for sparring sessions with his staff all afternoon and several hours on Wednesday to prepare for his press conference. Nixon had held only thirty-eight news conferences, the last time in March, and Ford observed that they "often turned into belligerent, surly confrontations which . . . demeaned both the President and the press." Ford, hoping to do much better, cloistered himself most of the morning, poring over briefing books and cramming with his advisers, urging them to hit him with what Hartmann called "every dirty question we could think of." "I assumed," Ford recalled, "that the reporters would zero in on the economy. Then there was the reorganization of the White House staff. Surely, they'd want to know what personnel changes I intended to make. Finally, there was the Cyprus issue, the pending SALT [Strategic Arms Limitation Talks] negotiations, and the omnipresent possibility of renewed warfare in the Middle East. The press would want to know what initiatives I planned to take in foreign policy."

At midafternoon, Hartmann, terHorst, Haig, and Marsh took up places around the Wilson desk for the first dress rehearsal. One by one they peppered Ford on inflation, Rockefeller, and his proposal to go easy on Vietnam war resisters. Ford, *Newsweek* reported, "sat with his feet on his desk, mildly sucking at a pipe, sipping iced tea and brainstorming answers with his counselors." When Hartmann's turn came, he asked Ford if he would put a stop to all the talk about his pardoning Nixon or his Watergate confederates.

Ford declined the bait, saying it was inappropriate for him to comment when such matters were still pending in court. Besides, he said, Nixon hadn't been charged with anything.

Did that mean Ford disagreed with Scott and Rockefeller that Nixon had suffered enough? Not at all, Ford said, but they didn't have the legal responsibility of the president and were entitled to express their opinions. Everyone seemed satisfied with Ford's answers. Hartmann noted, "Very good, we all felt. He in effect was putting further legal questions out of bounds. He should just stick to that line." But terHorst kept at Ford, saying that Nixon reportedly had been phoning friends in Congress to complain about Jaworski. Had Ford gotten any such calls or talked with Nixon about immunity? "Ford said flatly that he had not talked to President Nixon since he left the White House except, as had been announced, to tell Nixon of his choice of Rockefeller," Hartmann recalled.

Ford answered each question dutifully, but he seemed persistently naive about the press corps' interest in Nixon. "I simply couldn't believe that the press would focus entirely on these matters," he wrote. As far as he was concerned, Watergate should have ended—*needed* to end—with Nixon's resignation. Ford believed he had annulled any commitment implied to Haig and Nixon on August 1, when Haig presented him privately with Buzhardt's "permutations" on the terms by which Nixon could resign and not face prosecution. He "hadn't given any thought to Nixon's legal status" since becoming president, he would write. Pressure from Nixon's staff and Jaworski aside, Ford was holding open his options. He delivered the impression that he would decide what to do about Nixon if and when he had to, and not before.

Hartmann suspected differently, although he didn't speak up. Distrusting Haig, he had pressed Ford early on August 2 for details of the previous day's meeting, and had discovered that Ford and Haig had spoken again by phone that night, in strict confidence. Ford would write that Haig called him at about 1 A.M. to assure him that "nothing has changed . . . the situation is as fluid as ever." But in recounting events to Hartmann and Marsh later that same morning, Ford told another story. According to Hartmann, Ford told him: "Betty and I talked it over last night . . . We felt we were ready. This just has to stop; it's tearing the country to pieces. I decided to go ahead and get it over with, so I called Al Haig and told them they should do whatever they decided to do; it was all right with me."

Ford may not have promised Nixon a pardon in exchange for the presidency, but he had examined just such a proposal from Haig without explicitly turning it down, then phoned Haig late that night and told him to "do whatever they decided to do." Hartmann and Marsh, after lighting into Ford, immediately called in Harlow, who advised Ford to phone Haig and read him a written statement asserting unambiguously that nothing they had discussed should be construed as a deal. Yet even that statement by Ford—carefully lawyered, designed to control the damage, and anticipating subsequent review—referred only to what he and Haig had said to each other "yesterday afternoon." It failed to mention the late-night phone call. As a former reporter, Hartmann didn't need to be told what conclusions Mollenhoff and the others would likely draw from such facts should they ever put them together.

After the others left the Oval Office, Hartmann told Ford that if he recognized Mollenhoff during the press conference he should expect a question about ruling out any pardons for Nixon and the other Watergate defendants.

Ford nodded sadly.

"Clark is very bitter," he said. "It's too bad."

*   *   *

Nixon's old friend Leonard Garment, still White House counsel, also wondered if Ford should announce at the news conference whether he would pardon Nixon. At lunch with columnist John Osborne of the *New Republic* at the Federal City Club, a favorite hangout of liberal establishment journalists and their sources, Garment sought Osborne's opinion. "I asked John what is his view whether Nixon should be tried or be pardoned," he recalls. "And he said, 'He should be pardoned. Who needs it?' I mean, this was a tough-minded journalist . . . *enough, enough,* he was saying.

"I called Eric Sevareid," Garment adds. "And he said the same thing."

Spurred by agreement from such unlikely sources, Garment decided to visit former Supreme Court Justice Abe Fortas at his house in Georgetown. A fifty-year old Brooklyn Law School graduate and former jazz clarinetist, Garment had been a successful Wall Street lawyer when, in 1967, he found himself arguing a Supreme Court case alongside his new law partner, Nixon, who then was springing back from the humiliating election defeats of the early sixties. A notable invasion of privacy case, *Time Inc. v. Hill,* forged Garment's connection both to Nixon and

Fortas, a New Deal liberal and successful Washington litigator who two years earlier, in 1965, reluctantly had accepted Johnson's appointment to fill the high court's "Jewish seat."

In the case, the Supreme Court ruled that the media could convey false impressions so long as they did so unknowingly and without "reckless disregard" for the truth. Nixon and Garment had argued on behalf of a family who'd been held captive in their home by armed intruders— an episode later depicted far more luridly than it actually occurred in a Broadway play *The Desperate Hours,* then publicized nationally in a *Life* magazine photo spread in which the cast staged made-up reenactments from the play, including invented scenes of sex and violence, of the family's ordeal. Nixon and Garment lost the decision 5–4. "I always knew I wouldn't be permitted to win a big appeal against the press," Nixon told Garment, adding, "Get this absolutely clear: I never want to hear about the *Hill* case again." Yet Fortas, too, was stirred by the damage to the family and wrote a scathing dissent. "Needless, heedless, wanton and deliberate injury of the sort inflicted by *Life*'s picture story," he wrote, "is not an essential instrument of responsible journalism."

Lyndon Johnson thought Fortas was the best lawyer in the country. In 1948, when Johnson first ran for senator from Texas, charges of voting fraud in the Democratic primary led his opponent to win an injunction preventing his name from appearing on the ballot, and Fortas, an immigrants' son from Memphis who graduated second in his class from Yale Law School, managed to have the injunction overturned. In 1968, a year after the *Hill* ruling, Johnson nominated Fortas for chief justice. During his Senate confirmation hearings, however, *Life* revealed that Fortas had accepted an annual $20,000 honorarium from a convicted financier. Though Fortas returned the money, he was forced to resign from the Court. Nixon had authorized his surrogates to attack Fortas in the 1968 campaign, but he never attacked him personally: Staunch political opponents, the two shared a festering hostility toward the press and, now, disgrace and financial worries. Unable to return to the powerful Washington law practice he had built before succumbing to Johnson's insistence that he take a high court seat, Fortas had lately started what he described to Garment as a "tiny law firm but an interesting practice."

Now, Garment put his questions to Fortas: Should Nixon be pardoned? Was it feasible? Should he try to convince Ford?

Fortas, too, thought the country had experienced enough trauma. This is "Ecclesiastes time," he told Garment—a time to cast away stones, a time to heal. A trial for Nixon, Fortas said, would be a "horror."

Convinced that Ford could anticipate sympathy, even political cover, from those presumed to hate Nixon the most, reporters and liberals, Garment returned to his office in the West Wing. Unlike Buzhardt, he'd been kept—and kept himself—at a distance from defending Nixon during Watergate, concentrating on cultural and other policy issues. At the same time, he was a close personal observer of Nixon, proudly psychoanalytical, perhaps the one remaining member of Nixon's inner circle of legal strategists who continued to have standing with Ford. He phoned Haig, asking if he should propose to Ford, as special counsel to the president, a pardon for Nixon.

"Yes," Haig told him. "It's time to get something in."

* * *

At the special prosecution force barracks on K Street, Jaworski kept his own counsel, seeking—and weighing—a round-robin of opinion about Nixon but disclosing little of his own bias to the prosecution staff. His counsel, Phil Lacovara, recommended in a lengthy memorandum that he move swiftly to indict Nixon and try him alongside his aides, but that would mean asking Sirica for another postponement. Jaworski still hoped to pressure one or more of The Big Three—Haldeman, Ehrlichman, and Mitchell—into pleading guilty rather than stand trial, and he believed that "Mitchell and the others are not apt to plead if they know there will be months of delay," he said.

Lacovara, thirty-one, called it "extraordinarily unjust" that Nixon's men faced prison and personal and professional ruin while Nixon him-self might escape indictment and live out his days with the same lavish perquisites as other presidents who left office honorably. And he thought Nixon could receive a fair trial despite the extensive publicity about his role in Watergate. That Lacovara—a Goldwater conservative in a regi-ment of liberals, whose job it was to tell Jaworski how to interpret the Constitution and his responsibilities—went on record with his opinions was a "fact of some consequence with which [Jaworski] would have to reckon," prosecutors Ben-Veniste and Frampton wrote.

Jaworski also began to hold private discussions with Miller. On his own initiative, he invited Nixon's lawyer to submit legal arguments showing why prejudicial pretrial publicity would make it impossible for his client to receive a fair trial in the reasonably foreseeable future. As this, in essence, was the sum of Miller's defense strategy, Miller was only too happy to oblige, although the invitation disturbed members of the trial team, who argued that there were many legal techniques available to deal with publicly celebrated cases.

Lawyers for the cover-up defendants, too, were arguing that Sirica couldn't find an impartial jury, but there was ample legal precedent for dealing with such concerns: delaying jury selection, interviewing a large enough jury pool to find twelve people who would be objective, gag or-ders, careful questioning of prospective jurors, transferring trials to other jurisdictions where press coverage was less pervasive. "To do otherwise here," Ben-Veniste and Frampton wrote, "was to admit that the enormity of Nixon's crimes and the importance of his office automatically guaran-teed him immunity from prosecution . . . Here was something a prose-cutor might hang his hat on if he were searching for a plausible reason to justify avoiding an indictment."

Miller also spoke with Jim Neal, fellow veteran of the Hoffa task force, phoning Neal even before Jaworski told Neal that Nixon had hired Miller, and joking with him about "bringing his client in on a misde-meanor." Neal, too, wrote Jaworski a memorandum setting out his views. An ex–marine officer and former U.S. attorney from Nashville, he argued that prosecuting Nixon "would not be in the country's best interest" and that "such a prosecution would divide the country for a considerable period of time" and could lead to an unspecified "tragic event." He proposed that Jaworski go before the grand jury personally, let it review the new tapes, give Nixon a chance to appear, then leave it to the jurors to decide. Despite Neal's own inclination not to indict, he wrote, "the manner in which this issue is decided is more important than the decision itself."

As Jaworski played for time, he worried that events would overtake him, forcing on him a decision he hoped to avoid. As his deputy Henry Ruth wrote in his own memorandum: "Indictment of an ex-President seems easy to many of the commentators and politicians. But in a deep sense that involves tradition, travail, and submerged disgust, somehow it seems that signing one's name to the indictment of an ex-President is an act that one wishes devolved upon another but one's self. This is true even where such an act, in institutional and justice terms, seems absolutely necessary." Within hours of receiving the memorandum from Neal, whom Jaworski understood most likely was the lone exception among the 110 lawyers on the force, he sent each prosecutor in the office a short memo in a plain white envelope stamped "Personal/ Confidential." In it, he invited their opinions about what to do about Nixon. He said he considered this course "far superior to the holding of staff conferences because in this manner I will be able to give study to any views that are expressed."

Later, he wrote: "But with all the advice, all the suggestions, with all the study I did myself, I knew in my own mind that if an indictment were returned and the court asked me if I believed Nixon could receive a prompt, fair trial as guaranteed by the Constitution, I would have to answer, as an officer of the court, in the negative.

"If the question were then asked as to how long it would be before Nixon could be afforded his constitutional rights, I would have to say in fairness that I did not know."

* * *

Even in seclusion, Nixon continued to make headlines. He had stopped going out, largely to avoid being slapped with a subpoena, although U.S. marshals in California had no intention of staging an ambush. They told network crews camped at their headquarters that they had been ordered by their superiors in Washington to "cool it"—to avoid any move that would seem discourteous to the former president. Prosecutors believed the order originated with Jaworski, who was searching for a way to serve Nixon discreetly at home. As ABC's David Schoumacher reported from the around-the-clock press watch at the gates to Nixon's compound, "Serving a subpoena on Nixon, unless carefully prearranged to dodge reporters, would only create more publicity."

As Miller arranged for both subpoenas to be hand-delivered within the next couple of days, Nixon hunkered down: reading, writing on his legal pads, and making phone calls to members of Congress who had supported him until the end. He tracked down three-term Memphis representative Dan Kuykendall, who was vacationing at his ranch in Texas. There were no black congressmen in the South, but Kuykendall, who grew up a hundred miles from Austin and moved to Memphis to work for Procter and Gamble, was in danger, due to extensive "white flight," of losing his seat to Democrat Harold Ford, Sr., scion of a prominent family of black funeral-home owners. Within hours, all three networks caught up with Kuykendall in front of a small single-engine plane at a hot scrubby airstrip in San Saba County.

Kuykendall told reporters Nixon "sounded sad and sounded lonely." The former president's voice and diction were clear, he said, but there was no small talk, and Kuykendall couldn't discern his mental state.

"I asked him very personally and very pointedly—How are *you*?" Kuykendall said, sweltering. "He said, 'Well, we're gonna be all right. We certainly have problems—you know about them—with the prosecutor's office.' Then he said, 'Dan, what I'd like to know is what do the people think? Do the people want to pick the carcass?'

"That was the only direct question he asked me."

Kuykendall continued: "I said, 'Well, instead of trying to judge the people at the moment, I didn't find any mood for that in the Congress.

Whether it be the liberals on the Democratic side who are my friends, I don't find that they have any more mood for revenge than the Republicans do.' "

In March, Kuykendall had traveled to Nashville to greet Nixon at the airport as he flew in on Air Force One to help dedicate a new wing for the Grand Ole Opry. Tennessee's two Republican senators and its Republican governor also attended, and crowds and banners pumped up the aura of a campaign stop. Nixon joked with singer Roy Acuff, tried to spin a yo-yo, and played "God Bless America" and "Happy Birthday" for Pat on the piano, after which Pat rose from her chair and crossed the stage, her arms outstretched, as Nixon, already turning away, indicated to the MC that he was done. The miscue reinforced the impression that Nixon was indifferent to his wife.

Now, Kuykendall, a politically vulnerable junior lawmaker, was asked to speak as Nixon's interlocutor, his proxy. He weighed his words carefully, pleased, it appeared, to have been anointed yet astonished as to why. "I couldn't have expected anything but a sad conversation," he reflected. "After all, when we were through . . . I was saying to myself, 'A few months ago that was the most powerful man in the world.' " Later in the day Kuykendall would pose for photographers symbolically brandishing a noose.

Wednesday, August 28

Apotheosis

After staying up all night to write, in longhand, successive drafts of a three-page memorandum summarizing the case for pardoning Nixon, Garment arrived at the White House at 6 A.M. He handed it over for typing and gathered from speechwriter Raymond Price, who'd composed Nixon's resignation announcement, a draft presidential statement for Ford's use at the two thirty press conference. By eight, Garment submitted both documents to Buchen, for delivery to Ford, in a blank brown envelope. He sent Haig a carbon copy. Garment wrote:

> My belief is that unless the President himself takes action by announcing a pardon today, he will very likely lose control of the situation . . . The national mood of conciliation will diminish; pressure from different sources of prosecution will accumulate; the political costs of intervention will become, or in any event seem, prohibitive; and the whole miserable tragedy will be played out to God knows what ugly and wounding conclusion . . .
>
> For President Ford to act on his own now would be strong and admirable, and would be so perceived once the first reaction from

the media passed. There would be a national sigh of relief . . . The country trusts President Ford and will follow him in this matter at this time.

Garment also suggested that Nixon's mental and physical condition couldn't withstand the continued threat of criminal prosecutions and implied that, unless Nixon was pardoned, he might commit suicide. "For it to continue would be to treat him like a geek—a freak show," he says. "It was an awful thing to contemplate." Having last heard from Nixon, who'd called to thank him, at 2 A.M. on the morning before he resigned, Garment believed Nixon was relieved to be alive but suspected that his fire burned dangerously low.

Garment returned to his office while Haig met alone with Ford. "Haig was for it too, although he never flatly said as much," Ford recalled. "He laid out the pros and cons, then stepped back and said, 'It's your decision, sir.' " Buchen, meanwhile, held on to his copy of the proposal: Believing it was premature, he decided not to present it to Ford, who nonetheless seemed suddenly swayed. "About ten o'clock, Haig called me and said, 'Don't leave. It's a done deal,' or words to that effect," Garment says. Haig told Garment that Ford was planning to go ahead and make the pardon announcement at the press conference, and instructed him to stand by for a meeting to go over the details.

Ford agonized. He didn't think the country wanted to "see an ex-President behind bars." Nixon, he believed, had "already suffered enormously. His resignation was an implicit admission of guilt, and he would have to carry forever the burden of his disgrace." But whatever his sympathy for Nixon's plight or the state of his health and sanity, what vexed him most was the widespread obsession with Nixon and with Watergate, which retained a fevered hold on the national psyche. "It was the state of the *country*'s health at home and around the world that worried me," Ford wrote. "As army major Bob Barrett, one of my military aides, said:

"We're all Watergate junkies. Some of us are mainlining, some are sniffing, some are lacing it with something else, but all of us are addicted. This will go on and on unless someone steps in and says that we, as a nation, must go cold turkey. Otherwise, we'll die of an overdose."

While Garment waited for the staff to meet to iron out details, Haig called back around ten thirty to say that the afternoon announcement was off. "They're lawyering it now," Haig said, "so there's going to be a delay." Haig would long deny making any effort to intervene in Nixon's legal fate: "I played no role at all," he wrote. He later told the *Post*, "No one was more sensitive than I for the reasons not to become involved in this. I couldn't have been a credible advocate for a pardon anyway." Still, after the second phone call, Garment believed Haig was implying that it was his personal intervention with Ford that secured a commitment to pardon Nixon, if not now, soon.

"All of these people [Nixon, Haig, Kissinger, possibly Ford—political men pursuing intricate agendas at the pinnacle of power] are too complicated, unable to do other than to manipulate the environment endlessly," he says. "So that when Haig said, 'It's a done deal,' I think he was reflecting something, that it may have been the result of my memo or other interventions. Then he called back to say that they're not going to do it today. But of course what he did do, through the garble, was to reflect that the pardon was on track, although it was diverted temporarily. He indicated that something was cooking."

* * *

In a kind of pregame rite, Ford talked and prayed in private with his friend and spiritual adviser Billy Zeoli, who on fall Sundays conducted locker room chapel services for professional football players. After Ford was nominated for vice president, Zeoli started sending him weekly devotionals—memos containing a passage of scripture and a personal prayer. A "large man in black with white tennis shoes," as one parishioner described him, Zeoli tapped deeply into Ford's trinity of politics, football, and faith. Ford felt strongly about keeping his religious beliefs private because he thought it might look like he was using them for political gain, but he had begun to rely on one-on-one counseling sessions with the flamboyant Zeoli at critical times; adding, *Time* reported, a "dash of evangelical fervor to the President's restrained Episcopalianism."

Zeoli ministered on the importance of the gospel and of being ready in life, and he liked to invoke the last-minute heroics of Roger Staubach of the Dallas Cowboys, first dubbed America's Team during the era of Staubach and Coach Tom Landry. Early in Staubach's career, when he didn't yet start as quarterback, Zeoli had stood with Landry on the sidelines during a play-off game. The Cowboys trailed by 16 points with two minutes to go. Landry turned to Staubach and said, "Roger, go in," a fair indication that he might be throwing in the towel. Instead, as Zeoli liked to say, Staubach led Dallas to two touchdowns and a field goal and won the game . . . "because this young man, fresh out of the Navy, was *ready.*"

At two thirty, all three networks interrupted their broadcasts to carry Ford's press conference live from the packed East Room. Hundreds of reporters from around the world chattered with anticipation. Entering briskly, eyes ahead, Ford strode to the podium in a blue chalk-striped suit with wide lapels, a blue-and-white pinstriped shirt, and blue tie with white floral insignias. The stagecraft was purposefully changed and unfamiliar: Nixon's regal blue backdrop was replaced by the open doors to the red-carpeted Grand Hallway; a narrower, tapered rostrum stood in front of the president, accenting his physicality. Unlike Nixon, Ford wore no makeup. He appeared relaxed and comfortable.

"At the outset," Ford said, "I have a very important and a very serious announcement." Ford's voice—an "Anglo-Saxon voice . . . thin, pitched too high, without range unless deliberately trained," as the writer Richard Rhodes observed—bore a quality of strain, as if his voicebox was too small for a man his size. Absent any prepared text, it was hard to know where he was headed.

"There was a little confusion about the date of this press conference. My wife, Betty, had scheduled her press conference for the same day.

Obviously, I had scheduled my press conference for this occasion. So, Betty's was postponed."

Ford's eyes scanned the room. "We worked this out in a calm and orderly way," he said, leaning into his punchline, one of several prepared for him by a speechwriter, Bob Orben. "She will postpone her press conference until next week, and until then I will be making my own breakfast, my own lunch, and my own dinner."

There was light laughter. "Helen," Ford said. From the front row rose Helen Thomas of UPI, often invited to ask the first question ever since she had begun showing up unassigned at Kennedy's press conferences a dozen years earlier.

"Mr. President," she said, "aside from the special prosecutor's role, do you agree with the Bar Association that the law applies equally to all men, or do you agree with Governor Rockefeller that former president Nixon should have immunity from prosecution, and specifically, would you use your pardon authority, if necessary?"

"Well," Ford began, "let me say at the outset that I made a statement in this room in the few moments after the swearing-in, and on that occasion I said the following . . ." Ford paused, looked down, shuffled through some cue cards, then read, slowly . . . "that I hoped that our former president, who brought peace to millions, would find it for himself.

"Now the expression made by Governor Rockefeller, I think, coincides with the general view and the point of view of the American people. I subscribe to that point of view. But let me add, in the last ten days or two weeks I have asked for prayers for guidance on this very important point." Standing along the wall, Hartmann felt his stomach drop as he sensed Ford skip away from the careful position rehearsed the day before. "In this situation," Ford declared, "I am the final authority. There have been no charges made, there has been no action by the courts, there has been no action by any jury, and until any legal process has been taken, I think it is unwise and untimely for me to make any commitment."

"Mr. President." Another wire service reporter stood up. "You have been in office nineteen days now, and already some of your naturally conservative allies are grumbling that you are moving too far to the left. Does this trouble you?"

Ford smiled tentatively. "I don't think I have deviated from my basic philosophy nor have I deviated from what I think is the right action. I have selected an outstanding person to be the vice president. I have made a decision concerning amnesty, which I think is right and proper—no amnesty, no revenge—and that individuals who have violated either the draft laws or have evaded Selective Service or deserted can earn their way, or work their way, back. I don't think these are views that fall in the political spectrum right or left.

"I intend to make the same kind of judg-a-ments in other matters because I think they are right and I think they are for the good of the country." Responding to the next question, Ford confirmed that he would "probably be a candidate in 1976. I think Governor Rockefeller and myself are a good team, but, of course, the final judg-a-ment in this matter will be the delegates to the national convention."

"May I just follow up on Helen's question?" someone asked from the back. "Are you saying, sir, that the option of a pardon for former president Nixon is still an option that you will consider, depending on what the courts do?"

"Of course, I make the final decision," Ford said. "And until it gets to me, I make no commitment one way or the other. But I do have the right as president of the United States to make that decision."

"And you are not ruling it out?"

"I am not ruling it out. It is an option and a proper option for any president."

Several voices rose at once. Ford had created an opening, and the reporters, accustomed to doing battle with Nixon, blitzed. Scanning the expectant faces, he found Tom Jarrell of ABC.

"Do you feel the special prosecutor can in good conscience pursue cases against former top Nixon aides as long as there is the possibility that the former president may not also be pursued in the courts?" Jarrell asked.

"I think the special prosecutor, Mr. Jaworski, has an obligation to take whatever action he sees fit in conformity with his oath of office, and that should include any and all individuals."

"Mr. President, what do you plan to do as president to see to it that we have no further Watergates?"

"Well, I indicated that, one, we would have an open administration." Ford's cadences were controlled, his litany ready. "I will be as candid and forthright as I possibly can. I will expect any individuals in my administration to be exactly the same. There will be no tightly controlled operation of the White House staff. I have a policy of seeking advice from a number of top members of my staff. There will be no one person, nor any limited number of individuals, who make decisions. I will make decisions and take the blame for them or whatever benefit might be the case.

"I said in one of my speeches after the swearing-in, there would be no illegal wiretaps or there would be none of the other things that to a degree helped precipitate the Watergate crisis."

"Do you plan to set up a code of ethics for the executive branch?"

"The code of ethics that will be followed will be the example that I set." Ford gunned a firm look and an outstretched finger at the next questioner, a woman in a yellow suit.

"Mr. President, do you have any plans now for immediate steps to control and curtail inflation, even before your summit on the economy?" she asked.

Ford spoke numbingly, fiduciarily, about the budget, relieved, it seemed, to showcase his expertise. "We have announced that as far as fiscal control is concerned, we will spend less in the federal government in the current fiscal year than $300 billion. That is a reduction of 3, er, $5 billion 500 million at a minimum," he said, chopping the air for emphasis. "This, I think, will have two effects: Number one, it will be substantially beneficial, it will make our borrowing from the money market less, freeing more money for housing, for the utilities to borrow, and in addition, I think it will convince people who might have some doubts that we mean business . . ."

Scouring the room, he nodded to NBC's Brokaw: "Mr. President, as you know, a number of people have questioned your opposition to a return to wage and price controls . . . Can you foresee any circumstances under which you would be willing to do that and make them work?"

Ford gazed directly at the cameras. "I can foresee no circumstances under which I can see the reimposition of wage and price controls . . . wage and price controls are out, period." Did Ford plan, then, to replace Nixon's economic advisers—the team that implemented controls yet failed to slow inflation? "There is one significant change," he said, eyes brightening. "Just within the last forty-eight hours, Herb Stein, who did a superb job for President Nixon, is going back to the University of Virginia, and Alan Greens*pahn* is taking over and he has been on board, I think, two days. That is a distinct change. I think Mr. Greens*pahn* will do an excellent job."

Ford promoted his September economic summit, urged government and individual belt-tightening, pledged to work with all parties, and vowed to rely on Rockefeller both to help prepare new domestic legislation and "make a significant contribution to some of our decision-making in the area of foreign policy." His eyes alight but his tone deadpan and circumspect, he added that Rockefeller, "can be helpful, I think, in the political arena under certain guidelines and some restrictions"—implying that Rockefeller would be of limited utility against incumbent Democrats in the fall election, lest they retaliate by holding up his confirmation.

Ford appeared upbeat as a reporter asked how he would try to stop the oil states and commercial cartels from restricting supplies in order to keep fuel prices artificially high. A national energy policy was perhaps the most damaged and neglected legislative casualty of Nixon's self-destruction. During the oil embargo, Nixon had proposed that citizens turn down their thermostats and carpool and that utilities switch from oil to coal, and he'd called grandly for a new crash program, Project Independence, on the scale of the atom bomb and moon-landing projects. "Let us set as our national goal," Nixon pledged, ". . . that by the end of this decade we will have developed the potential to meet our own energy needs without depending on any foreign energy source." Ford, sidestepping the immediate problem, now picked up on the all but stillborn idea.

"I think," he said, "this points up very vividly the need and necessity for us to accelerate every aspect of Project Independence. I think it highlights the need and necessity for us to proceed with more oil and gas drilling, a greater supply domestically. I believe it points up the requirements that we expedite the licensing processes for new nuclear reactors. I think it points up very dramatically the need that we expand our geothermal, our solar research and development in the field of energy."

Nixon usually answered about fifteen questions at his news conferences. Up on the balls of his feet, hands clasped behind his back, Ford, after twenty-four, pointed to another reporter, ensuring further opportunities to probe his earlier ambiguities, contradictions, feints, and dodges.

"Mr. President, you have emphasized here your option of granting a pardon to the former president."

"I intend to," he said. The reporters scribbled in their notebooks.

"You intend to have that option? If an indictment is brought, would you grant a pardon before any trial—" Ford interrupted here "—took place?"

"I said at the outset that until the matter reaches me, I am not going to make any comment during the process of whatever charges are made."

Squelching a flurry of noisily raised hands, Ford, visibly annoyed, pointed to a face at his far left, inviting still another question: "Mr. President, two questions related, how long will the transition last, in your opinion, and secondly, how long would it be proper and fair for Democrats on the campaign trail this fall to hold you accountable for the economic policy this fall and the economic problems the country faces?"

"Well, I can't judge what the Democrats are going to say about my policies. They have been very friendly so far and very cooperative," he said. "I think it is a fair statement that our problems, domestically, our economic problems, are the joint responsibility of government. As a matter of fact, I think the last poll indicated that most Americans felt that our difficulties were caused by government action and that, of course, includes the president and the Democratic Congress. So we are all in this boat together, along with labor and management and everybody else. I don't think that making partisan politics out of a serious domestic problem is good politics."

"Thank you, Mr. President," terHorst injected. Ford picked up his cue cards and terHorst escorted him out. After cutting back briefly to their anchors, who praised Ford's performance as strong and well informed, if workmanlike, the networks returned to their normal programs—*Another World, General Hospital,* and *The New Price Is Right.*

* * *

Ford charged back to the Oval Office, seething. Of the twenty-nine questions, only eight referred to Nixon; the network summaries emphasized his statements on the economy, not Watergate. But Ford felt besieged, and angry with himself for the confusion he knew he would cause with his answers. "God dammit," he recalled telling himself, "I am not going to put up with this. Every press conference from now on, regardless of the ground rules, will degenerate into a Q&A on, 'Am I going to pardon Mr. Nixon.' "

"It would come after he was indicted, which he was going to be," he wrote. "It would come after he was convicted, which he was going to be. It would come after his appeals, probably up to the Supreme Court. It was going to be a never-ending process. I said to myself, 'There must be a way for me to get my attention focused on the major problems before us. There must be a way to get the American people's minds off this terrible experience.' "

By declaring first that he had "asked for prayers for guidance" about whether to grant Nixon immunity, then that he wouldn't intervene with the legal system "until the matter reaches me"—implying he might have to wait until just minutes before Nixon went to prison—Ford had staked out positions utterly at odds with each other. Yet he didn't know any way to avoid it. For him to say Jaworski shouldn't do his duty would be illegal and would undermine the entire Watergate prosecution by signaling that Ford wanted him to give preferential treatment to one potential defendant. The impending criminal prosecution of his predecessor held profound complications not only for Nixon and the cover-up defendants but also for Haig, Buzhardt, Kissinger, and everyone else with whom Nixon worked closely while and after the tape machines were running— including Ford. How, he wondered as he huddled with a clutch of his top advisers, could he and the country not be incrementally swallowed by his dilemma?

Ford groped his way toward a firm decision, fighting, as Hartmann wrote, "for a little more time." He already was struggling with the question of jurisdiction over Nixon's papers and tapes, which Saxbe was reviewing, but he needed someone to research, in utter secrecy, the scope of his pardon authority. He didn't consider what Haig told him during the August 1 meeting definitive, and Garment's memo and Price's speech, which he said afterward he never received, raised several specific questions. "Did I, as President, have the legal right to pardon someone who had not been indicted, or convicted, yet? Could I issue a pardon that didn't contain a reference to a specific crime? Could it be a general pardon?" Ford wrote.

He summoned Buchen: "Phil, I don't know what I'll decide but I've got to have information." He told Buchen he also needed his own secret conduit to Jaworski, to find out whether Jaworski planned to indict Nixon, and if so, when and on what charges. Since prosecutors weren't supposed to reveal who they planned to indict, any public communication between Ford's staff and the special prosecution force would embarrass them both. Buchen, who wasn't a criminal lawyer and was highly visible as a member of Ford's inner circle, explained that he would be of limited value.

"OK, I'll try to find the answers for you," he said, "but I'm going to need some help. I can't take the responsibility for the research and get everything done that I have to. And I'm not sure I have anyone in my office who can handle it." He paused. "Well, there is one person you can trust. How about my approaching Benton Becker?"

In the two and a half weeks since Becker had stopped the military truck with Nixon's papers, he had stayed on as an unpaid volunteer, meeting during the past few days with Buchen and Miller to discuss what he called "mutual problems" relating to Nixon's materials. He'd met privately with Sirica, suggesting that Sirica himself decide the final disposition of the records, papers, and tapes, to which Sirica politely answered, "No thank you, Mr. Becker." Just under six feet tall, stolid and blond, a former trial attorney in the fraud section of the criminal division of the Justice Department whom Ford had hired on both personal and constitutional business and who aggressively shepherded Ford through his vice-presidential confirmation hearing, Becker had the twin virtues of being relatively obscure and nondescript. He was under investigation stemming from charges that he'd advised a client in a Maryland stock fraud case to lie, but he'd been cleared of eight of nine allegations with the last one pending, and Ford had full faith in him. Ford jumped at Buchen's suggestion, calling Becker a "prodigious worker . . . shrewd . . . tough . . . discreet."

"I thought he would be ideal," he wrote.

* * *

About 5 P.M. Pacific Daylight Time, a black limousine bearing, in the backseat, a figure appearing to be Nixon with his head buried in a newspaper, sped away from the gate of the former Western White House in San Clemente, followed by a station wagon with what looked like Secret Service radio equipment inside. Hundreds of cars a day turned off Avenida del Presidente in a futile attempt to see Nixon's house, obscured behind a high white wall and lush vegetation, and as the two-car motorcade dissolved from view, startled reporters and cameramen raced to reach their own vehicles, parked about three hundred yards down the road. No one remained to notice whether or not it was Nixon who apparently returned sometime within the hour.

At about six, a U.S. marshal arrived from Los Angeles, presented credentials to a treasury agent and a coast guard sailor at the gate, entered the compound, served two subpoenas directly on Nixon, and left, exposing him for the first time as an ordinary citizen to the power of the courts to force his testimony. Miller, in Washington, declined to comment on whether he would seek to have the subpoenas quashed.

* * *

"After that press conference," Ford announced as he welcomed a hundred or so guests to an evening of dinner and dancing at the White House, "I was ready for a little relaxation." Ford confessed with a grin that he had been jittery when he stepped up to the podium but got over it after the first five minutes. "It was just like any football game," he said. "After all, I've had fifty-five press conferences in eight months. This was just a little different format . . . I haven't been playing in the minor leagues." Ostensibly an informal meet-and-greet for cabinet officers and senior White House officials and their wives, the party also served as a coming-out for the Rockefellers, who had jetted in and were staying overnight in the Lincoln Bedroom.

After cocktails upstairs in the Yellow Room, guests walked on through to the Truman Balcony, to gaze at the panorama of the Washington Monument bathed in lights—a warm, reassuring midweek glow in the waning days of "impeachment summer." Like the Fords, they were dressed as if for a semiformal at a country club; and as the First Couple stood for handshakes, passing them through the doorway, their gaiety—and gratitude—seemed natural and unforced. Ford hadn't struggled for the presidency, hadn't *won* it, but it was hard for anyone, especially those who had survived Nixon's collapse, not to admire his faith and determination that he would not fail at it, even as a good number of them distrusted his abilities, goals, and politics. He and Betty were warm and comforting hosts.

Downstairs in the Blue Room, before a dinner of gazpacho and prime rib, Ford issued a toast, and Kissinger, speaking on behalf of the cabinet, replied that while they didn't always agree on everything, they were unanimous in their "great support for President Ford." The *Post* described the scene: "Recalling decades past, Kissinger noted that the country had passed through periods when it thought it 'could do everything': and, with a reference to the Watergate-plagued Nixon Administration, noted that the country had passed through times 'when it thought it could do nothing.' He envisioned the country now as being 'back on a positive track.' "

Was it? Certainly it was for the men in this room, who drank together and danced with one another's wives and lavished their praise on their new boss. Saxbe complimented Ford's relaxed, informal mood, which he said was being reflected throughout government. "I can feel it in the staff that it's altogether different," he said, joking that in a few short weeks Washington had become "just like Ohio," his home state. "They got me on a short ration," he added, sounding a note of humility in tune with Ford's ethos. "The only one who makes less money is the waiter, and I wasn't sure about him."

Interior Secretary Rogers Morton, a member of the transition team, described Ford as "totally dedicated," adding he had "never seen this cabinet as performance-conscious as they are now . . . I've spent more time with President Ford in the last two weeks than with President Nixon in the last four or five months."

Ford's prodigious energy, gift of access, and example of not taking himself too seriously had set a new tone, a new standard—and for a few hours even his warring entourages laid down their arms and relaxed their guard in one another's company. "It was supposed to promote camaraderie between the Nixon and Ford people, though we were grossly outnumbered," Hartmann recalled. "Everybody but Rocky, Buchen, Marsh, Seidman, and terHorst and me was a Nixon retread. But it was a fun party, anyhow."

After dinner, the Marine Dance Combo struck up in the Great Hall, and Ford swept Happy Rockefeller onto the floor, followed by Rockefeller and Betty, who, dressed in a belted, long-sleeved, closed-back gown, danced with a purse dangling from her elbow. Ford led the dancing through a medley of Rogers and Hart foxtrots with Betty and Happy and what *Newsweek* described as a "decorous frug" (to the rock song "Proud Mary") with society columnist Betty Beale.

Minutes before heading upstairs at eleven, Ford was asked if he was tired after another long day. "Why should I be?" He laughed. "It's only ten-thirty, quarter of eleven. As long as you enjoy it, the hours don't make any difference."

"Like many others," Jaworski would write, "I couldn't determine exactly what the President had meant in his replies to the reporters." Jaworski flew home to Houston on weekends, but Monday to Friday he resided at the Jefferson Hotel, an eight-story Beaux Arts former residence four blocks from the White House, where in the vaulted lobby guests gathered in overstuffed wing chairs around a hearth, and the rooms were crammed with antiques—canopy beds, grandfather clocks, marble bathtubs and busts, Federal-era portraits, massive armoires, oriental rugs. Conveniently, so did Buchen, who, after Ford told him he needed more information about his authority to pardon Nixon, began holding nightly private discussions with the special prosecutor.

Soon after Jaworski arrived at work, Lacovara handed him a confidential memorandum detailing his own response to Ford's news conference. Lacovara looked the part of the young Watergate prosecutor—short, stocky, with a black mustache and a helmet of black hair obscuring his ears—but his responsibilities included directing research on a staggering array of legal matters, and his conservatism, militant grasp of detail, and brilliance on his feet marked him for special status among Jaworski's senior staff. He had been working as a top aide to Solicitor General Bork when Cox hired him, and Jaworski, impressed by his ferocity (Lacovara was first in his class all three years at Columbia Law School) and energy (he had seven children), took stock at their first meeting of Lacovara's mental agility and healthy self-regard and made a point to let him know at once how much he wanted him as his counsel. "Such men, I had learned over the years, sometimes need assurances of their value more than their lesser, plodding fellows," he wrote. In July, the two had argued *U.S. v. Nixon* together before the Supreme Court, and Lacovara's rebuttal of James St. Clair on why Nixon was not above the law was generally considered the day's strongest presentation.

Now Lacovara wrote that Ford had placed Jaworski in an "intolerable position." By declaring that he reserved the right to pardon Nixon, yet also citing the special prosecutor's "obligation to take whatever action he sees fit," Ford had forced Jaworski's hand, telling him to make up his mind about—and take the heat for—indicting Nixon. From Lacovara's point of view, Jaworski needed to retaliate in kind. He wrote:

> I see no reason why the matter should not be put squarely to [Ford] now whether he wishes to have a criminal prosecution of the former President or not . . .
>
> Since President Ford is now publicly on record as having expressed willingness to assume the responsibility for the exercise of the ultimate Constitutional powers that are his, I believe he should be asked to face this issue *now* and make the operative judgment concerning the former President, rather than leaving this matter in the limbo of uncertainty that has been created.

Less than five weeks remained until jury selection in the cover-up trial—arguably the most important criminal case ever to be tried in U.S. courts—and Jaworski had pressing concerns about how Ford's comments would affect the prosecution, especially of The Big Three. Lacovara thought that the longer Ford waited to clarify his position, the greater the risk to the government's case against Mitchell, Haldeman, Ehrlichman, and the other defendants. "The worst thing in the world for us—for the principle we were trying to establish, which is equal justice, as well as the practical impact on the trial—was to go forward, get an indictment, and then on the eve of trial, or in the midst of trial, have the president, as a co-defendant, pardoned," he says. Such a situation would both generate enormous publicity and highlight the inequities between Nixon's treatment and that of his subordinates.

"So I said in my memo," Lacovara recalls, "if President Ford is seriously considering pardoning President Nixon in order to spare him from criminal prosecution, he ought to make the decision now, as early as possible, before there's an indictment, and before we got onto the eve of trial."

Jaworski also worried that Nixon might die and that he, the Colonel, would be blamed. Ever since Nixon had vanished from public view, speculation had grown about the toll on his health and how much longer he could bear up. "You have to understand, throughout this period Leon and General Haig were having daily conversations about what was going on, and Miller was making his point about pretrial publicity, and both he and General Haig were making the point to Leon . . . that the president was mortally ill, suffering from phlebitis, which was likely to lead to his imminent demise, and that he wasn't likely to survive very long," Lacovara says.

"Why should the special prosecutor put this man into his grave? He'd suffered horribly enough and been forced to resign in disgrace. Just as a matter of human decency this fatally ill man should not be called before the bar."

Lacovara's office was next door to Jaworski's, but he put his arguments in writing to ensure a historical record. Jaworski weighed Lacovara's advice, sharpening his dilemma. "On this ultimate subject—what to do with the former president—Leon was being pushed not only by the junior staff, people like Ben-Veniste and Frampton, but by me, as his counsel," Lacovara says. "That was something he didn't want to do. He was persuaded that it might complicate the prosecutions that were already under way and might actually lead to the president's death. He didn't want to buck the staff and make a decision to pass up the opportunity to prosecute. He also didn't want to prosecute."

What Jaworski hoped, flatly, was to pass the buck. "Leon was a very skilled trial lawyer and a pretty skilled negotiator, although many people in the office felt that at every step Haig outmaneuvered him," according to Lacovara. The Colonel's regular meetings with Haig dismayed Lacovara as much as the other prosecutors. But now Jaworski wanted to communicate a message not to Nixon but to Ford, and Haig was vitally positioned to deliver it. After considering his memo, Lacovara recalls, Jaworski "went to Haig and said, 'Not only am I getting pressure to indict, but I'm also getting pressure from my senior staff to have the president— President Ford—fish or cut bait . . . and not dangle this possibility of a pardon out there. The president needs to know that this is a call that he's ultimately going to have to make."

Later, as when Garment wanted to ensure that Ford considered his case for a pardon, he would stress the same points to Buchen.

* * *

Wanting no mistake about whose man he was now, Haig gave Helen Thomas an interview in which he denied repeated reports of friction between himself and the men around Ford. "The situation," he said, "is precisely the opposite." He cited the "cooperative spirit" between the Nixon and Ford staffs and expressed the "highest regard" for Ford's men.

"What we're dealing with today is a great deal of mythology," he said.

Blithely, almost comically at odds with the contentious atmosphere within the White House and, in particular, the open hostility between him and Hartmann, Haig's statements appeared to be aimed at three constituencies: the citizenry, which he believed needed to be reassured of a harmonious transition; those who might move to exploit his weakened position; and most vitally, Ford himself. As a combat commander in Vietnam, Haig used to tell junior officers to make sure that their fighting bunkers were properly dug and sited, and especially that the roofs—

logs, sandbags, and dirt—were "extrastrong." Haig's statements served as a rhetorical bunker, case-hardened to repel attacks on a vulnerable position and doubts about his loyalty to Ford.

"I don't suffer from insecurity pangs," he told Thomas. "In terms of my relationship with the President, I've been getting along very well. I see him every morning and I go over with him a vast number of substantive issues. He sets the tone . . ."

During their morning meeting, the *Times* reported later, Haig advised Ford of the "alarming state" of Nixon's health, cautioning him that unless he moved quickly to grant Nixon a pardon, it might be too late to avert a total collapse. (Haig denied the report.) Nixon's phlebitis was mostly quiescent, but Haig had spoken several times in recent days with Nixon, Ziegler, and Nixon's daughters and their husbands, and had become convinced that Nixon's life was at stake. He suggested to Ford the possibility of an impending "personal and national tragedy" if Nixon continued to face a threat of criminal charges.

Knowing the decision was his alone ruptured any hope Ford might have to avoid an avalanche from Watergate. That Nixon might be near death compelled him to seek a swift course of action. Yet for Haig, like Nixon, Ford's reluctance so far to end Nixon's greatest crisis augured that he might wait too long, when the obligations of being both the president and the leader of the Republican Party might make him take a more wait-and-see attitude. If Ford's ambiguity at the press conference was a trial balloon, meant to test popular opinion on leniency for Nixon, it was also a strong signal to the men around Nixon that Ford might not be the proven commodity—a "tough guy who knew how to play the game . . . a team player," Colson called him—they thought he was.

Ford's loyalty to Nixon and the degree to which he was beholden to him were firmly documented. In 1970, Ford had led an attempt to impeach liberal Supreme Court justice William O. Douglas within weeks after the second of two conservative Nixon nominees was rejected, a campaign during which Ford said famously that an "impeachable offense is whatever a majority of the House of Representatives considers it to be at a given moment in history." Nixon at first told Ehrlichman to mobilize Ford, who denounced Douglas for being "one in spirit" with the "militant hippie-yippie movement," then two weeks later abruptly ordered Mitchell to tell Ford to back off, causing Ford to look foolishly partisan. And weeks after the Watergate break-in—and before Nixon's reelection—Ford, at Nixon's urging, had been instrumental in making sure the House Banking and Currency Committee failed to investigate the source of the newly minted hundred-dollar bills found on the team of burglars. To preserve his standing with the White House and the party leadership, Ford later denied during his confirmation hearings for vice president that Nixon and his men had anything to do with his decision. That Ford chose to mislead the committee and jeopardize his confirmation attested to his priorities. "He understood that personal and political loyalty would get him further in Washington than complete testimony," Seymour Hersh noted.

Such loyalty was presumed to work both ways, and Nixon and Haig—with Buzhardt's assistance—repaid Ford by distancing him from the scandals, releasing edited transcripts of meetings where references to his role were deleted or marked "unintelligible." Indeed, thus was the status quo on August 1, when Haig approached Ford with the notion of pardoning Nixon.

Ford resisted making any new commitment to Haig now. He felt "very sure of what would happen if I let the charges against Nixon run their legal course"—a towering, overarching national spectacle, lasting perhaps years, of Nixon struggling to stay out of jail, and quite likely dying in the process, while he, Ford, faced unending pressure to end it. But he kept his thoughts to himself. To tell Haig what he might be planning, before he presented his thinking to his inner circle, would be to announce simultaneously to Nixon and Jaworski that he had adopted the monkey. As interlocutor between the White House, San Clemente, and the special prosecutor—not to mention Schlesinger and the Pentagon—Haig simply knew, and conversed, too much to be trusted.

In the twenty-four hours since the press conference, Hartmann also had gone public, trying, it seemed, to isolate and shrink Haig while goading Ford to proclaim his independence. In a *CBS News* report describing Haig as "now not much more than an operations officer," Hart-mann said, "If you'll recall, President Johnson asked all the Kennedy peo-ple to stay, and Mrs. Johnson later wrote that that was his first and greatest mistake." Hartmann possessed a huge tactical advantage—spon-taneous, near-limitless, access to the Oval Office. "I push the door ever so gently and peak through the crack and see if somebody's with him or if he's alone," he told a reporter. Knocking was unnecessary. Possessing "final word over just about everything" that came across Ford's desk, re-porter Phil Jones quoted an unnamed White House official as saying, Hartmann was "free to roam, free to get in and out of anything he pleases," and to underestimate his influence was a "grave error." Given the uncertain context—did the remarks express criticism or bravado? wishfulness or resentment? an attack or a warning?—the source of the comments could equally have been Haig or Hartmann.

Unlike Haig, Hartmann made no pretense of valuing Nixon's holdovers. "I believe this has to be answered on a case-by-case base and depends on whether they are able to adapt to the new president's ways and serve him successfully or not," he said. "That is up to them, not up to him."

* * *

Joined by Kissinger and Scowcroft, Ford met in the late afternoon with Saudi Arabian foreign minister Omar Saqqaf. They exchanged vague pleasantries through an interpreter and posed for the press. Saqqaf—a functionary who during diplomatic meetings with King Faisal "sat so far down along the hierarchy of other advisors that he would have had to shout to get the king's attention," Kissinger recalled—above all hoped to deflect American anger over the energy crisis away from his desert monarchy.

Locked in Cold War calculations, gun-shy after Vietnam, and with a "surrogate strategy" for securing Persian Gulf oil supplies that amounted to arming to the hilt repressive local regimes in Iran and Saudi Arabia, the United States could scarcely have been less prepared for the oil shock now playing havoc with the world economy. A little more than a week after Ford's swearing-in, Kissinger had briefed him on the struggle to regroup. "We have to find a way to break the cartel," Kissinger warned. "We can't do it with the cooperation of the other consumers. It is intolerable that countries of 40 million can blackmail 800 million people in the industrial world." As Kissinger outlined the joint program being discussed with the Europeans—consumer solidarity, including emergency sharing of reserves; conservation; development of alternative energy sources; and creation of a financial safety net—Ford immediately had signed on. "I'm not interested in issues," he said, "but in results."

Now, as with the rest of the Middle East cauldron, Ford left the handling of the Saudis to his secretary of state, who sought assurances from Saqqaf that Faisal would not take a hard line by opposing separate negotiations between Israel and Egypt, and would help negotiate lowering the cost of Arab-produced oil. Kissinger warned that Western patience with the Saudis, who since the end of World War II had looked to the United States to defend them against stronger, often hostile neighbors, had worn thin.

"My view," he cautioned Saqqaf, "is that current oil prices are going to create such an economic crisis in the West that other governments, whatever their view, will be driven to drastic action."

Officially, Saqqaf sounded a formal warning against separate moves toward peace with Israel. "But," Kissinger wrote, "he also left us convinced that Saudi Arabia would endorse any diplomatic progress so long as it did not have to assume responsibility for it." Persuaded that the Saudis wouldn't disrupt the peace process, Kissinger left the meeting with Saqqaf for a stag dinner in his honor at the State Department, while Ford worked in the Oval Office until after eight, then headed upstairs for dinner with Betty, who'd spent part of the day giving yet another interview to a women's magazine. Later, she chafed that she'd been asked "everything except how often I sleep with my husband," and resolved that if the question was ever asked of her, she would answer honestly, "As often as possible."

22

Friday, August 30

"A great new partnership"

Before becoming president, Ford had accepted an invitation to address summer graduation exercises at Ohio State University, where the always-hot football rivalry with Michigan had gotten much hotter since 1969, when Coach Bo Schembechler took over the Wolverines and upset Woody Hayes's number one–ranked, undefeated Buckeyes. College campuses for nearly a decade had avoided presidential visits, and vice versa. When Nixon had to cancel plans to attend his daughter Julie's graduation from Smith College in 1970 because of antiwar demonstrators and the possibility of violence three weeks after national guard troops opened fire on protesting students at Kent State, killing four, Agnew had chided him: "Don't let them intimidate you, Mr. President."

Broadcast live on national TV, Ford stood at a podium in the well of St. John Arena dressed in an academic robe—he was receiving an honorary doctorate—and warmed up an already receptive crowd of 13,500 with a gridiron story. "I still remember my senior year back in 1934," he said. "The Wolverines played Ohio in Columbus and we lost thirty-four to nothing." The crowd cheered, and Ford grinned. "And to make it even worse, we lost seven out of our eight ball games." Ford then launched a

rim shot that owed its cadences, inflection, and raised-eyebrow perplex-
ity to Bob Hope, the favorite entertainer, dinner guest, and golfing buddy
of presidents since Eisenhower. "But what really hurt was that my team-
mates after the season voted me most valuable player. I didn't know
whether to smile or *sue.*"

The crowd erupted in a long ovation that presaged several others, as
Ford used his first opportunity to talk to college graduates to lay out
broad themes about America's new role in the world after Vietnam, Watergate, the energy crisis, and stagflation—that is, after Johnson and
Nixon, whose terms, while progressive in selected areas, left many Americans, especially students and professors, feeling wounded, impotent, and
enraged. Declaring that he was "not satisfied with the progress that we
are making towards energy independence by 1980," Ford called for
novel, even radical changes in higher education. He urged converting
university classrooms into an engine of national deliverance.

"I propose a great new partnership between labor and academia," Ford
said, the crowd following closely. "Why can't the universities of America
open their doors wide to working men and women, not only as students
but also as teachers? Practical problem-solvers can contribute much to
education whether or not they hold degrees. The fact of the matter is
that education is being strangled . . . by degrees." The pun went largely
unnoticed, and indeed Ford's notion of hard hats and students—so recently at each other's throats during Vietnam—working together to lift
the United States out of its crisis was so bluntly pragmatic as to defy
ready response.

"With the war ended and the draft over," he told the twenty five hundred graduates, hair bushing out from under most of their mortarboards,
"your duty now to your country is to enlist in the campaigns currently
being waged against our urgent domestic threats, especially inflation,
which is Public Enemy Number One. Productivity, yours as well as mine,
must improve if we are to have less of an inflationary economy."

Ford spoke compellingly of his 1972 visit to China as part of a congressional delegation following up on Nixon's historic opening, and he
cast its instructional system as a kind of model. Then still in the throes

of Mao's Cultural Revolution, when workers were exalted and intellectuals not only were feverishly criticized but also physically abused, China was first starting to build momentum in industry and trade. But Ford believed its "highly motivated and disciplined" young people exemplified a commitment to national purpose that foretold a future as a world power. "We celebrate the rising capacities of the Chinese nation, a people with a firm belief in their own destiny. As Americans motivated by free competition we see a distant challenge. And I believe all Americans welcome and accept it."

Ford, applying the all-hands-together rhetoric that was fast becoming a trademark of his presidency, called on labor unions, too, to participate, shedding their guild mentality in favor of opening their "ranks to researchers and problem-solvers of the campuses, whose research can give better tools to the workman."

"I want to see a two-way street speeding the traffic of scientific development, speeding the creation of new jobs, speeding the day of independence in energy, and speeding an era of increased production for America and the world," he said.

"I want to share with you something I deeply feel," Ford concluded. "The world is not a lonely place. There is light and life and love enough for us all. I ask you and all Americans to reach out and join hands with me—and together we will seek it out."

Leaving the arena, Ford encountered about seventy-five protesters chanting: "Gerald Ford is nothing new . . . He is just a puppet too." Radicals on the left, unlike those on the right, appreciated only dimly that Ford's moves to the center were a rebuke to conservatives. Nor did they see that his appeals to unite for the good of all were opposed as fiercely, or more so, by Goldwater, Reagan, Buchanan, Jesse Helms, and in the halls of the Pentagon than in dorm rooms in Columbus and Ann Arbor. All that most of them noticed was that Nixon's plodding hand-picked successor, despite his finding inspiration in Mao and his paeans to "light and life and love," was deeply, ineffably unlike them—determinedly middle-American. The school's president handed Ford a packet of tickets to the OSU-Michigan game as he exited hurriedly to meet with a delegation of state Republican leaders and candidates at the airport on his way back to Washington.

The candidates swarmed Ford enthusiastically, delighted when he promised to come back to Ohio, probably in early October, to campaign for them. Viewed from the inside of a Republican congressional campaign, particularly in the middle of the country, Ford in three weeks had turned everything sharply around, providing a momentum all but unimaginable a month earlier. Democratic candidates had lost their best issue, the Nixon scandal, when it was shot out from under them. Many of them were young, like the twenty-eight-year-old challenger in northwest Arkansas, Bill Clinton, who'd spent a year teaching law in Little Rock and whose only experience in politics was behind the scenes, notably for George McGovern. Charismatic, able to look people deeply in the eye, Clinton quickly deduced that if he hoped to win, he had to bear down on Republican interests that, as he said, "are making a killing on inflation." But with Ford encompassing the center on the economy, such populism seemed insufficient cause to throw out a well-liked incumbent. Before Ford left, he promised the appreciative delegation that Rockefeller would also campaign in Ohio, offering the GOP hopefuls, amid what *Times* reporter Christopher Lydon called the "harsh old realities of minority status and long-term decay," their best hope in years of reuniting the venerable party symbols of Main Street and Wall Street.

Lydon wrote: "This is a ticket, virtually all Republicans and many Democrats agree these days, that only an economic disaster can defeat in 1976."

* * *

Nixon had missed a $100,000 "balloon" payment on his San Clemente mortgage and he owed $457,000 in back federal taxes, increasing public speculation about his solvency. His chief fiscal adviser told the *Los Angeles Times* in an interview that Nixon was "broke." "We won't say he's broke in the sense of you and I being broke," Dean Butler said, "but all

you have to do is look at his most recent financial statement and the payments he has had to make since then to know there is a money problem."
Agnew's New York literary agent, who also represented Haldeman, told
UPI he expected to represent Nixon in the sale of his memoirs, and that
he would ask $2 million for worldwide book and magazine rights. Nixon
thought he could do better and entered an agreement with international
superagent Irving "Swifty" Lazar, whose nickname was coined by
Humphrey Bogart after Lazar got Bogart three deals in a day on a bet,
and who arrived at Casa Pacifica in a chauffer-driven Rolls-Royce. "You
know, there is only one way you can make even more money than you
can on this book," Lazar told him.

"What's that?" Nixon asked.

"Leave your body to the Harvard Medical School."

On Thursday, Ford helped to improve Nixon's balance sheet by asking
Congress for $850,000 to cover Nixon's transition, pension, and other
expenses for the next ten months. But less than $100,000 of that figure
legally could be used to pay lawyers' fees, an amount that, according to
Butler, wouldn't come near to covering Nixon's legal costs even if he
wasn't indicted. The Mayday Tribe's civil suit subpoena augured a wave
of "crank lawsuits" that could tie him up for years. "I don't know whether
$100,000 will touch it," Butler said. "I don't know if $500,000 will."

Bill Gulley flew to San Clemente to update Nixon on the status of his
papers and tapes. Nixon's depression had lifted, albeit slightly, and the
impending negotiations over his memoirs gave him a special urgency
about how—and when—Ford would decide on the long-term custody of
his papers. Before he had resigned, Nixon famously told Kissinger, who
consolingly predicted over and over that history would judge Nixon better than his contemporaries: "That depends on who writes the history."
Kissinger had secretly shipped thirty crates of his own files, including
phone transcripts, to the bomb shelter of Rockefeller's estate in upstate
New York, safe beyond the reach of reporters, historians, and, possibly,
the courts. How Nixon could write the history of his presidency without
his materials was beyond imagining, and he importuned Gulley for his
view of what the White House would do about the problem.

"I didn't have any answers," Gulley later recalled. Discovering Nixon a "little calmer . . . less formal, less tough talking" than when he had visited two weeks earlier, he decided to lie, telling Nixon that the Fords sent him and Pat their best wishes. Gulley believed the falsehood "had an effect on him. I stressed that the difficulty I was having wasn't with Ford personally but with Jack Marsh and the lower-level people. I let him think Ford knew I was shipping stuff out to him, which Ford did not. The only thing Ford ever did was enquire about Nixon's health . . ."

One issue had been settled: Ford decided Nixon would be sent briefing papers, intelligence reports, and other documents unrelated to Watergate, and Gulley would be bringing them out personally every two weeks. Nixon asked if he would be allowed the use of military aircraft and Gulley said no, "that in fact there was a possibility he might have to pay for the planes that had been used by and for him so far."

"Well," Nixon said, "if that's what the bastards want, I'll pay."

Nixon, seated at his desk, surprised Gulley by not showing any anger, but he was eager to know who was behind the decision to charge him for the flights, asking specifically whether it was Ford or his aides. Gulley assured him Ford wasn't involved and for a moment more Nixon said nothing, then thanked him for the information.

"You know," Nixon said, "I'm really sorry I didn't spend more time in the White House talking to people like you. Bob, of course, always prevented it. But I've been thinking it over the last few days. If I had it to do over again, that's one of the things I would do differently. Talk to people like you, I mean.

"I'd like to give you a memento," he said, shuffling through his drawer, then buzzing an aide and telling him to bring in a presidential watch. Only once before, according to Gulley, had Nixon bestowed such a prize on a visitor, giving Ford a watch when Nixon made Ford vice president.

"I really appreciate your being available," Nixon said. "I'd like you to know that nothing more can hurt me, but associating with me can hurt those who do. You should always remember that, because the media aren't going to let up on me. This is not going to satisfy them. They won't be satisfied until they have me in jail. You should keep that in mind."

* * *

Ford strolled up the South Grounds from the helicopter, entered the Oval Office, and brought in Haig, who sat down across from him. Joining them soon around the desk were Buchen, Hartmann, and Marsh, who, having completed his transition tasks, had taken up duty as an all-purpose troubleshooter and the lone spoke-on-the-wheel who talked regularly to people who didn't talk to one another—the "conscience of my administration," Ford called him. As a congressman in 1967, Marsh had gone to Vietnam to witness the war firsthand and the military arranged for him to visit Haig's battalion command. The next day, they helicoptered to a rendezvous point near a supposedly pacified village and came under fire, hunkering overnight in a foxhole along with Major George Joulwan, a former West Point varsity football center who now was White House deputy chief of staff—Haig's Haig.

Ford tamped and lit his pipe thoughtfully. "I'm very much inclined," he announced, "to grant Nixon immunity from further prosecution."

No one spoke.

"Phil, you tell me whether I can do it and how I can do it," he told Buchen. "Research it as thoroughly and as fast as you can, but be discreet. I want no leaks."

Haig got up to leave, saying his presence might be inappropriate. Ford waved him back into his seat as Hartmann sneered. "[Haig's] fine sense of honor left me cold," Hartmann wrote. "It was obvious that Al wanted to be able to call upon the three of us as witnesses that he had not raised his voice as a pardon advocate."

Ford blamed himself for not having studied the issue more thoroughly before the press conference, and he believed his contradictory answers resulted mainly from his not understanding fully his role and authority. Buchen, having handled sensitive matters for Ford for more than thirty years, understood he wasn't being asked his opinion. "I could see that he had already made up his mind, and it was my job to go find out *how* he could do it, rather than *whether* he should do it," he recalled.

"Well," Buchen said. "We ought to get Mr. Nixon to settle his papers at the same time, get him to give them to the United States. As you know, we have physical custody of them, but the Attorney General's opinion is that these papers are his, by right and by history."

Buchen had received a subpoena requiring him to provide some of Nixon's tapes to the attorney for a former Democratic official whose phone was bugged in the Watergate break-in, and Saxbe's assistant Antonin Scalia, who'd been asked to look into the matter, had come to the conclusion that the White House had no authority to do so. "To conclude that such materials are not the property of Former President Nixon would be to reverse what has apparently been the almost unvaried understanding of all three branches of government since the beginning of the Republic," Scalia would write, adding as insurance, "and to call into question the practices of our Presidents since our earliest time." Though the opinion hadn't yet been released, Buchen feared it would improve Nixon's case—and limit Ford's options—when it was. Indeed, Ford could get locked into acting in accordance with the Justice Department position or else becoming himself a conspirator, obstructing the law. "Let's get that settled at the same time," Buchen urged. "We also ought to get a statement of contrition when he accepts the pardon."

Ford set down his priorities. "Do what you can to get both those things," Buchen recalled Ford telling him, "but for God's sake don't let either one stand in the way of my granting the pardon. I also want you to get from Jaworski two things—one, the list of offenses for which Nixon is the target, and two, how long after indictment might it be before he could be fairly tried."

Ford swore them all to secrecy, emphasizing that he had not made up his mind. He listed the reasons in favor of granting a pardon: the "degrading spectacle of a former President . . . in the prisoner's dock"; the pretrial publicity; the press stories that would resurrect the "whole rotten mess of Watergate"; ultimately the possibility that Nixon might be acquitted, or, if he were found guilty, that strong public opinion would arise to keep him out of jail. None of the group disagreed. "It's your decision, sir," Haig said.

Hartmann challenged Ford's timing—so soon after Nixon resigned and Ford took power, and before Ford had a clear chance to establish himself in office and become known in his own right. "What everybody believes is that you may pardon Nixon one day," he warned, "but *not* right away, and not until there have been further legal steps in the case.

"And if you do," Hartmann said, "the professional Nixon haters in the press and in the Congress will go right up the wall. You're going to face a firestorm of angry protest that will make the Saturday Night Massacre seem mild."

Ford acknowledged that there would be criticism but predicted he could survive it. "It'll flare up and die down," he said. "If I wait six months, or a year, there will still be a 'firestorm' from the Nixon haters . . . They wouldn't like it if I waited until he was on his deathbed. But most Americans will understand."

Hartmann thought sympathy for Nixon would build the longer he was out of office. "It's already begun," he told Ford. "*Newsweek* says 55 percent of the people think further prosecution should be dropped." Why not wait, he suggested.

"If eventually," Ford asked, "why not now?"

Ford wrote that after the press conference his choice had been reduced inexorably to this question. Now, his aides could offer no better solution. "We sat mute," Hartmann wrote. "Haig wiggled nervously in his chair, Buchen's scowl deepened, Marsh's frown was accentuated by a sickly pallor, and God knows how I appeared. The President's logic was unassailable, yet I felt as if I was watching someone commit hara-kiri."

Ford's phone buzzed and Haig took the occasion to leave while Hartmann dashed into his office to find a transcript of Ford's press conference. He came back, agitated, waving the papers in his hand. "Here are your own words," he said. " '. . . until any legal process has been undertaken, I think it is unwise and untimely for me to make any commitment . . .' "

"You didn't read the part about my not ruling it out," Ford protested. "I refused to make any commitment one way or another. I said that, too, every time, and I was very firm about it."

Haig aside, Ford found no enthusiasm among his inmost circle for the pardon decision but they did not oppose him, except on his sudden, enigmatic urgency to act quickly, in deepest secrecy, without discussion or attention to politics, and determinedly alone.

"I can't argue with what you feel is right," Buchen said, "but is this the right time?"

"Will there *ever,*" Ford replied, "be a right time?"

* * *

Hartmann returned alone after the meeting and pleaded with Ford, "Don't do it now." Warning him that the "public won't understand," he cautioned that a precipitous drop in popularity could jeopardize Ford's presidency as much or more than being dogged by press questions about Nixon. "I'm aware of that," Ford said. "It could easily cost me the next election if I run again. But dammit I don't need the polls to tell me whether I'm right or wrong."

Marsh, withholding his deepest concerns during the meeting, also cornered Ford alone. "I went into see him privately in that little sequestered office behind the Oval Office, and he had just finished his lunch," he recalls. Marsh, like Hartmann, thought the country wasn't ready for a pardon and he urged Ford to wait several weeks. Ford said no. Failing that, he suggested that Ford "lay the groundwork" by sounding out the congressional leadership. Again Ford refused, saying a "leak would be calamitous."

Marsh felt he needed to make sure—both for Ford's sake and for his own—that Ford understood that others in Washington, the press, and voters across the country would inevitably conflate a decision to pardon Nixon with Haig's "permutations" proposal the week before Nixon left office, once the details of Ford's discussion with Haig became known, as they surely would. "Look," Ford recalled Marsh telling him, "both of us know about the meeting with Haig that took place on August 1 . . . Although you and I understand the two are not related, will people try to connect them?"

"Maybe they will," Ford replied, "but we both know the facts."

"I don't want you to be mad, Mr. President," Marsh persisted, "but I feel an obligation to know myself that you have thought through all aspects of this, including the events of August, and that possibility that at some time the press or someone may learn about those August events and suggest there was some kind of deal."

"In effect, I was saying, 'Don't do this,' " Marsh recalls. "I wanted the president to see the linkage. I know that Jerry Ford has a naïve streak, and it is there because he trusts people and doesn't see the motives that people have."

"He said, 'Jack, I know exactly what you mean; I know where you're coming from. I have thought about that and I want to go forward.' "

It was the force of Ford's conviction that allayed Marsh's doubts. "I figured, I have raised what is a potential problem, he has considered it and does not deem it to be a problem, or is comfortable with it, and feels he can handle it. So I felt clearly that he was so *firm* about it in his own mind, and he was considering the ramifications, that in my own mind I became convinced that he never considered there was a question of a deal."

Ford had no illusions. He believed Nixon needed to step down for the good of the country, and that he—Ford—had to take over for the same reason. Haig had offered him a deal, but "it never became a deal because I never accepted," as he later told Bob Woodward. Confident of the purity of his own motives—he hadn't lusted for the presidency, hadn't pursued it, and didn't especially want it—he simply couldn't believe that others would doubt him once he explained his reasons.

* * *

Usually, after dinner, Jerry and Betty Ford sat together in the former Nixon bedroom. "She would sit on my right," he recalled, "there was a small table between us, and I would go through an hour or two of paperwork." Betty had met earlier with the chairwoman of the National Endowment for the Arts and was working on ways to promote the arts "wherever and however I can." Ford had a single meeting scheduled for the morning, with Saxbe, Schlesinger, and others to discuss Vietnam amnesty recommendations, after which he planned to play golf at Burning Tree. As he leafed through his briefing book, he told Betty he was thinking about pardoning Nixon and listed his reasons.

Sympathizing with Nixon's family, especially Pat, and realizing the "sense of morass, of instability" lingering in the wake of Watergate, Betty believed "it had to be done," though she understood the high price a pardon would carry. "I'll support whatever you decide," she said.

At about nine thirty, Becker arrived. Ford wanted him to review the law books—discreetly—to determine the scope of his authority in pardoning Nixon. His questions were mainly technical: Could a president issue a pardon before an individual was indicted for a crime? Would it bar conviction if issued after indictment but before a jury deliberated? Could a president issue a pardon without specifying particular crimes; that is, in Nixon's case, could there be an across-the-board pardon for the entire U.S. Criminal Code? What about state statutes; for instance, if Nixon were to be indicted in California, as was rumored, in connection with the break-in at Ellsberg's psychiatrist's office? Lastly, would the grant of a pardon have any impact on a possible Senate impeachment trial, if, as was being reported, some senators still sought to have him impeached?

The most junior and obscure member of Ford's inner circle, Becker found the conversation humbling; "sitting in the White House residence late at night, talking with the President of the United States about the legal implications and possibility of pardoning a former President—something no President and no lawyer had ever discussed or contemplated before," he wrote. He also believed his body language must have indicated that he was troubled by the decision, because Ford reemphasized several times that he was only considering the move and hadn't made up his mind.

After specifying his technical concerns, Ford asked Becker also to examine the more general question of what the grant of a pardon to Nixon, and Nixon's acceptance of one, ultimately would represent, not just in legal terms but in its implications.

"What does a pardon really mean?" Becker recalls Ford asking. "Am I erasing everything he did, as if it never occurred?

"Does a pardon erase a criminal act or does it only erase criminal punishment?"

23

Summer wound down across America and in Washington with the usual pre-fall migrations (families returning from the beach; politicians flying back to their districts; Ph.D.s-*cum*-bartenders-and-cabdrivers chasing one-year jobs at state colleges; geese, veering south, honking like Shriners) and Labor Day sales (Zenith nineteen-inch solid state color TVs, $398; MacGregor ash frame tennis racquets, $13.98). The Saudi government, in an agreement with Algeria, announced its refusal to lower oil prices, dealing a blow to Ford and others seeking a break in the gloom as the pace of business started back up in the months ahead. Whites in Boston, marshaled behind a group called Restore Our Alienated Rights (ROAR), threatened to turn back buses on the first day of school.

Announcing the weekend schedule, terHorst said Ford would take some time off to relax with his family at Camp David while moving ahead on inflation and, especially, on the question of allowing the return of Vietnam war resisters and deserters, which after his third full week in office topped Ford's public agenda. With the lull in fighting in Cyprus and the passing of the Veepstakes, and with Watergate in eclipse and

Nixon in seclusion, the controversy over the terms under which antiwar exiles would be welcomed home had gathered momentum as a nightly news story, with suspense building toward the announcement of Ford's plan, scheduled for the coming week.

On Friday, a dozen families of exiles—"fugitives," the *Post* called them, blurring any distinction between draft resisters and military deserters—converged on the Justice Department to request nothing less than unconditional amnesty. Saxbe preempted them with an interview on the *Today* show. "We have a pretty definite plan," he announced, that included "some probation" for everyone who returned home.

Saxbe said that draft evaders would probably have to "get a job in a hospital or some other public service area . . . This is not firmed up, but this is the worst it could be. The least it could be would be just to be a good citizen for two years. There's no prison contemplated. We're going to make it as easy as possible. But they're not going to be greeted back as heroes, and this is very disappointing to them." He went on: "They don't want to have to come back and say, 'We were wrong.' As a result, I don't think we're going to see many of them coming back under any amnesty program, even though the president is determined to open the door to them."

The families, after being allowed to meet with Saxbe's spokesman, gathered before reporters outside on the steps to voice their dismay. "That's an ugly word, the way America projects 'heroes,' " a Virginia coal miner and the father of two exiles, John Tillery, said. "I think they want to come home as citizens of a free country."

"I don't think this is for ree-al," Tillery said, denouncing Ford. "I think these words of forgiveness is to get a known criminal off the hook— Richard Nixon. Our sons are not criminals. They will never accept the fact that they should pay for something they didn't do."

Trailed by news crews, the families crossed the Potomac to the Pentagon, where Saxbe and Schlesinger were reviewing their recommendations in Schlesinger's office. An early copy of the Pentagon's own study of the problem, leaked to UPI, asserted that a "substantial majority of Americans" favored conditional amnesty and that draft evaders and deserters should have to reaffirm allegiance to the United States and work eighteen months of alternative service. The report argued that in order for any program for the return of those who had evaded service to "heal the wounds of the Vietnam conflicts, as large a majority of Americans as possible must view it as fair and just, considering both the objections to the nature of the war and the sacrifices of those who served." The family members were visibly upset after they met with Defense Department general counsel Martin Hoffman, who told them their demands were unrealistic because unconditional amnesty would mean the United States was admitting national guilt over the war.

"I do not feel that my son is a criminal. I do not feel that he should have to come back on his knees and say he is sorry to anybody," Mrs. Ed Sanders of Detroit said, sobbing.

Kissinger was away for the weekend at Rockefeller's estate in the Virgin Islands, leaving Scowcroft to conduct Ford's morning security briefing in the Oval Office. Shortly after eight thirty, Ford left for a two-hour session in the Cabinet Room with Saxbe, Schlesinger, Hoffman, ter-Horst, Buchen, Hartmann, and Marsh to listen to their recommendations and hammer out a definitive plan. That he also was working in secret on a way to grant Nixon immunity was known only to the latter three, inducing a disconnect. Viewed alone—as, say, by terHorst— conditional amnesty for draft evaders, so vehemently opposed by Nixon, appeared to be an act of healing and compassion, a piece of progress even if it fell short of acknowledging the price already paid: In the context of criminal immunity for the former president, it looked less moral and courageous, more political and sinister.

Schlesinger and Saxbe presented their combined recommendations, a six-page memo. "This program is a unique act of mercy, intended to heal the nation's wounds," the memo stated. "In no way is it intended to condone acts of evasion or desertion." Saxbe had said repeatedly on television that the exiles must "take their medicine" and "say they are wrong," yet he was also under fire from the VFW for favoring probation over prison for draft evaders. Republican senator Robert Taft of Ohio, Saxbe's home state, criticized the Justice Department for insisting on an "act of contrition," charging that an admission of wrongdoing would lay open the wounds of Vietnam rather than close them. The program aimed to promote "national reconciliation consistent with maintaining a strong military force and a viable prospect for conscripting armies in future emergencies," according to the memo. And so a deserter who had received a dishonorable discharge would receive an undesirable discharge upon completion of his civilian service; neither resisters nor deserters would be eligible for veterans' benefits.

Ford pressed for more details. He especially wanted to know how many young men fell into each category, and he was concerned that the emphasis on draft exiles and deserters was unfair to others who had resisted, such as military men who had refused a second tour of duty in Vietnam, as well as those already convicted. Ford wanted, as terHorst put it, a "program that is all-encompassing and fair to all," and he questioned Schlesinger and Saxbe closely to make sure no constituency was left out. Though relations between the three of them were strained—Ford had not forgiven Schlesinger for leaking the transition "military watch" story, and Saxbe would soon leak Scalia's opinion on Nixon's materials before delivering it formally to Ford—they were pictured by news photographers in a tableau of mutual respect and comity: Nixon's holdover secretaries of defense and justice seated, half-turned, facing each other; President Ford, standing between them, relaxed and strong, leaning in, importuning, leading, in a wide-lapeled plaid jacket and striped tie.

After the meeting, terHorst, a rare attendee at policy sessions, took questions in the pressroom. "The president has a great deal of flexibility," he said. "He has some ideas of his own which amend some of their proposals. It's not a matter of his accepting or rejecting what they give him." Ford's only firm decision was that he would not grant unconditional amnesty. Trying to defuse speculation about the recommendations, terHorst acknowledged that they included a proposal for up to eighteen months of alternative public service, but warned reporters not to make too much of that figure. Ford heard "several proposals on the length of time," terHorst said, and "the eighteen-month period was one." He noted that the report advised that the program be called "earned reentry" and "reconciliation" instead of amnesty. Asked whether the Ford program would include some form of public contrition, he said, "I can't give you any guidance on that."

A reporter asked how returnees would get jobs when so many Vietnam veterans couldn't find work. "It was the consensus of those in the meeting," terHorst said, "that it would not be necessary to create special job categories just to take care of this program."

Any press secretary is an alter ego, and terHorst had mastered the complications and ambiguities of speaking for Ford. "The mere notion of having an honest man in the White House—after a President who kept insisting he was not a criminal—was so appealing that hardly anyone bothered to worry about what Ford stood for," he wrote. Meanwhile, in the first national survey on Ford's presidency, his approval rating that morning in a new Gallup poll was 71 percent, compared with 24 percent for Nixon on August 5. George Gallup called the figure a "strong vote of confidence" even compared with the traditional honeymoon enjoyed by new presidents. What the press and public didn't know about Ford, unlike what they suspected about Nixon, only seemed to bolster his popularity. Only 3 percent of the public disapproved of Ford's performance, with 26 percent undecided.

TerHorst said Ford would take the recommendations with him to Camp David and would spend considerable time on them while he was there, trying to come up with a formula "so that nobody will be under confusion as to which category he falls in or what his obligations are."

"He really believes, as he said, that he is trying to bind up the wounds of a nation torn by war and domestic trauma . . . There should be a way for these young men to work their way back into American society and to work to rehabilitate themselves."

Asked to release further details about the meeting, terHorst demurred: "I'm going to have to stop talking about what was discussed because what was discussed is not necessarily what's going to come out."

* * *

Ford's Labor Day proclamation, announced before he left the White House, saluted "not only the 93 million men and women in the labor forces, but also the organizations which represent labor so well." As a bouquet to the unions, whose help was crucial to his voluntary crusade against inflation, it failed to reach its mark. George Meany, the powerful president of the AFL-CIO whom Ford had invited to the Oval Office for a private talk within days after he assumed office, took to the airwaves to denounce Ford's proposed wage-price guidelines as "completely unfair to the worker" and to vow resistance. "We are in a recession now and there is every indication we are going into a depression," he said. Meany predicted the downturn would be worse than the Great Depression of the thirties "unless there is a quick turnaround."

"I think Gerald Ford is what he appears to be," he said. "I don't expect any miracles from him . . . Whether they can turn [the economy] around or not I don't know. I am certainly not optimistic about it. But at least, I think, we'll have no trouble communicating with the president. I think he is open and frank. Of course, his record is very much on the conservative side."

Meany's comments reflected how far Ford had come—and how far he had to go—in taking over power from Nixon and starting to tackle the country's most pressing problems and divisions. From a standing start, he had gotten quickly up to speed, and was moving ahead across the board, captaining what remained a fractious, ad hoc team of Nixon holdovers, Ford loyalists, and irregulars pressed urgently into duty. The problems hadn't receded, but there returned a sense that they at least could be addressed. August was over—none too soon for those around Ford.

"It was a brutal month for all of us," Jerry Jones, who helped manage the transition, recalls. "Brutal . . . I've often used the squash term: The ball comes off the wall differently in the White House than it does anyplace else in the world. Things that you would never think of become problems. And until you get the hang of it, it throws you . . . Managing this monster of a government is so damn different from a congressional office. You have to change the whole way you operate, the whole way you see things, the whole way you interact with people . . . So there were a whole bunch of transformations that [Ford] had to go through, and he actually did a rather brilliant job on that."

24

Sunday, September 1

Peacemaker

Named for Nixon's son-in-law David Eisenhower by his grandfather Ike, Camp David on Catoctin Mountain in central Maryland had served as a rustic retreat from the heat and pressure of Washington until Nixon, in his first six months in office, converted it into the first of his alternative White Houses. Nixon spent $2 million from secret military funds to refurbish Aspen Lodge, once a barracks and now the president's cabin, adding a bowling alley and a new heated swimming pool, then secluded himself there three or four times a month with Haldeman and Ehrlichman—"forever plotting," as Richard Reeves wrote, "planning revolutions great and small, sometimes to build a better world, more often just coups against his own staff and cabinet."

At eleven, Ford and his family strolled out for a photo opportunity, the first time in eighteen months the press had been invited inside the gates of the heavily guarded compound. Wearing a blue blazer, checked pants, and white loafers, Ford sauntered out the front door arm in arm with Betty, who was dressed in a white pantsuit. Steve and Susan trailed behind them.

"Bright and cheery this morning, everybody? Have a good night's sleep?" Ford asked.

"How do you like it so far?" someone asked.

"Oh great . . ." Ford said.

"Beautiful." Betty nodded.

". . . nice place to work."

"Have you tried the pool yet, Mr. President?"

Ford raised his left hand in a V-sign. "Twice," he said. "Last night, this morning."

Betty fed the camp commander's pet fawn from a baby bottle as Ford, on one knee, looked on. The fawn sucked as if its life depended on it. "He seems a little hungry," Ford said. "How long does it take him to finish a bottle?" The answer: a minute. Ford chuckled. "Looks like a ham."

A reporter asked: "What are you going to do all day?"

"Play some tennis, play some golf, do a little work," Ford said. "Just take it easy."

With the TV cameras rolling, Ford turned and started—alone—back to the cabin. He swiveled on his heel, waved, walked backward a few steps to answer a last question, then waved again and twirled toward Aspen Lodge, his honeymoon still fresh enough so that even what he did on his day off was news. Looking suddenly preoccupied, Ford ducked inside for a few hours' work before heading back out to play tennis with his young house photographer, David Kennerly, who promised his former press colleagues that he would play to win against the president.

* * *

Despite his public composure, Ford set about resolving the intertwining conflicts of a Vietnam amnesty and criminal immunity for Nixon with far greater inner urgency than the country, or even the members of his family, knew. As an infant, he himself had become a party to—then, within weeks, the center of—a bitter, escalating domestic dispute when in 1913 his father, Leslie King, sued his mother, Dorothy, for divorce after they were married less than a year. The aftershocks had dogged Ford well into adulthood, molding and informing his views on life, family, law, sacrifice, and forgiveness, although the details were seldom, if ever, discussed at home. "It just didn't work out," his mother had told him. Ford never pressed her to explain.

King, a dashing thirty-one-year-old blond with blue eyes, a square jaw, and wide shoulders, accused Dorothy, then a pretty twenty-one-year-old, of "wholly disregarding her marital obligations and her duties as a wife" and of being "guilty of extreme cruelty" toward him when "without provocation" she returned with their baby, Leslie Jr., to live with her parents in Chicago several weeks after Ford was born. Alleging that she was "wholly and entirely under the influence of her mother"—who had told her "she would be living a dog's life" if she stayed with King at his parents' fourteen-room mansion in Omaha, Nebraska, where the family owned a prosperous wool brokerage—King alleged that Dorothy had "left and deserted" him.

Dorothy responded two months later with a countersuit that exposed a darker truth. Three weeks after they had been married, while they were on their honeymoon, King "became enraged" after she smiled at a man in a hotel elevator and "struck and slapped [her] in the face and about the head." Five days later, in their private room in a Pullman car, King again struck and kicked her "many times." Back in Omaha, King threatened and berated her, packing her trunk and ordering her to leave, then followed her to Chicago and demanded she return home. While she lay in bed weakened by Ford's birth, King "tore up the furniture in the house," and Dorothy, unable to sit up, had to be carried to the telephone to call the police. Feverish, her health declining, she bundled her sixteen-day-old son in a blanket and fled the King mansion.

Dorothy asked in her countersuit for custody of Ford and "sufficient reasonable" alimony and child-support payments, and in December 1913 an Omaha judge found King guilty of "extreme cruelty," awarded her sole care of their son, and ordered King to pay her $3,000 and $25 monthly in child support until their son reached age twenty-one. King refused to pay, and when the court moved to seize his assets, he turned out to have none, sending word to his mother: "I'm going to drink up every penny I get." King's father, Charles King, a self-made millionaire, had "quickly 'purchased' the couple's household goods so Leslie would have no personal wealth," historian Peter Wood notes, and it was Ford's grandfather who made the support payments himself until his death in 1930—the same year Leslie King showed up in Grand Rapids in his new Lincoln and revealed himself as Ford's real father.

The following fall—as the Depression deepened and Ford was named all-state center for the second straight year while working odd jobs and lugging varnish cans on weekends for Gerald Ford, Sr.—Dorothy Ford reopened her alimony case in Omaha. With Ford heading off to Ann Arbor, she asked the court to quadruple his monthly allowance, to $100, and though the judge agreed, King again failed to pay, forcing Ford to pay his own way through college. During the next five years, Ford borrowed money from family friends, waited tables, occasionally sold blood at the university hospital to pay his expenses—and started to think about law school. Then, in June 1937, Dorothy again went to court, to force King to pay back support for the four years of the amended agreement—about $5,600—spurring a climax of the clash that had governed Ford's life since before he was two months old.

After the judge ordered King to pay, and Dorothy won a U.S. district court order in Wyoming to obtain the money, King moved back to Nebraska, evading the Wyoming claim but finding himself back in the jurisdiction of the Omaha court. He eventually was arrested and thrown in jail before his second wife posted a $2,000 bond for his release. Afterward, King at first tried to make peace with Dorothy through their son, boarding a train for New Haven, where Ford, twenty-five, was a second-year law student at Yale. Tentatively, they agreed to resolve Dorothy's claim. Then, three weeks later, King changed his mind, threatening Ford in a letter: ". . . We are going to fight it out. You know down in your heart your mother never spent this money on you, and I am sure, you being a *King* would not be a part of getting something for nothing. I am going to fight this to a finish and I am sure it won't be very pleasant for all concerned as the publicity in all the newspapers won't do anybody any good."

King worked with his lawyers to come up with a comprehensive final motion to try to quash the order against him. In it, he argued that Dorothy was married to a "prominent businessman" and didn't need his money; that she paid less for Ford's college education than she claimed; that he, King, suffered so severely from asthma that he could not work regularly and was barely able to support his own family; and that he was willing to borrow $3,000 to repay a portion of the Wyoming court award if she would accept it "in full satisfaction of the balance due." Abruptly, he also informed Dorothy's attorney of his intention to depose Ford the following week in New Haven.

With King's offer of partial repayment, Ford's deposition became part of an emerging settlement negotiation, and, after taking the oath before a superior court commissioner, he answered each question succinctly and carefully:

Q. You have seen him very little.

A. I have seen my father from time to time—

Q. But never lived with him, is that correct? And never received any money directly from him?

A. I have never lived with my father and have never received any money from him with the exception of some $25 or $30.

Q. You have tried to act as a sort of peacemaker in this discussion between your father and mother as to the amount due under this judgment?

A. Yes, I have.

Q. And in that discussion your mother told you she would take $4,000 in cash?

A. There is something I would like to emphasize at this time, that at no time did I have direct authority from my mother to order that she would settle for a certain amount. I was trying to get her expression of what she would settle for and thereby try and clear the matter up. At all times she reserved the right to act through her attorneys and I have not been her agent in any way at all; I was simply acting as peacemaker.

Q. Did she at some time inform you that she would settle for $4,000 and that it had to be in cash?

A. That's right. I received a telegram yesterday ... saying that she would settle for $4,000 cash provided the money was in her attorney's hands Monday, June 8, 1939.

Q. Your mother told you, as I understand it, that she would not be interested in any installment arrangement; it would have to be a flat settlement. That is, when she settled it, it would have to be by cash so that it would be a final settlement on the determination of the matter once and for all.

A. Yes, that's right.

Six days later in Omaha, less than forty-eight hours before the scheduled trial, King's lawyer handed Dorothy's lawyer a check for $4,000, ending the twenty-five-year court case. "A lawsuit that had become a personal nightmare to Ford, continually reopening a chapter in his life that he had long tried to put behind him, had at last been sealed shut," Peter Wood wrote. Ford's own role in advising his mother remained unclear, but his testimony showed that in trying to mediate between his warring parents, he had brokered a deal. He may not have been, as he stated, his mother's agent, but he alone was in a position to resolve matters, and so he did. By imposing himself directly between two unforgiving adversaries and presenting them with what each felt they had to have to make the case, as lawyers like to say, "go away," he had restored a degree of domestic tranquility. After deductions for lawyer's fees, Ford received a check for $2,393, which he returned to his mother. "I didn't need it, and she was the one who endured what my father had done to her," he explained. "I was just glad it was over."

Ford's conduct, forged in the discovery that his real father was a prodigal, boozing, wife-beating deadbeat who would lie to escape the least obligation to his firstborn son, and yet also a sick man willing to settle rather than face the uncertainty of a trial and, most likely, prison, was a model of what he would try to do now to put quickly behind him—and the nation—the war and Nixon alike.

25

Back to Business

Becker studied law books all through the holiday weekend, undertaking to answer each of Ford's questions "quickly, quietly, and accurately." Immersed unnoticed at the Supreme Court library, he found that presidential pardons often were issued before indictment, but that they applied only to federal crimes, meaning California prosecutors could still bring charges against Nixon in the Fielding break-in. A pardon from Ford would have no impact whatsoever on an impeachment trial if the Senate, as was less and less likely, decided to go ahead and hold one; the Founders, fearing a return to the caprices of royal clemency, explicitly excluded impeachment cases from the president's pardon powers in the Constitution.

One 1915 ruling impressed Becker in particular. During the rough and tumble of the New York City newspaper wars in the early twentieth century, the city editor of the heavily Republican *Tribune,* George Burdick, wrote a series of articles about corruption in the customs service. The U.S. attorney subpoenaed Burdick to appear before a federal grand jury, not as a target but as a witness, and during Burdick's appearance he was asked to identify the sources who had provided him with information about rampant bribery and smuggling on the docks. Burdick re-fused, citing his reporter's privilege and Fifth Amendment right against self-incrimination. A month later, Burdick received a second subpoena, and when he again appeared but declined to testify, the prosecutor pulled from his pocket a single piece of paper. It was a blanket pardon from President Woodrow Wilson, a Democrat, for all offenses Burdick "has committed, or may have committed, or taken part in" in connection not just with his articles about the Port of New York but any other stories the grand jury might ask about. The prosecutor, explaining that since Bur-dick had been so broadly pardoned it was impossible for him to incrim-inate himself, advised him he must answer, and when Burdick again refused, he was jailed for contempt.

The Supreme Court opinion in *United States v. Burdick* answered, in effect, Ford's query: What does a presidential pardon *mean*? "The ques-tion in the case," Justice Joseph McKenna wrote for the majority, "is the effect of the unaccepted pardon." Burdick had refused Wilson's pardon because he believed not to do so would affirm that he had committed a crime. The Court agreed, clarifying that a pardon "carries an imputation of guilt; acceptance a confession of it." Burdick, in other words, didn't have to answer the U.S. attorney's questions, and he didn't have to accept forgiveness from a president. No one does. "A pardon," Chief Justice John Marshall wrote in 1833, "is an act of grace . . . which exempts the individual on whom it is bestowed from the punishment the law inflicts for a crime he has committed."

Becker believed he had found in *Burdick* a rationale for pardoning Richard Nixon that would keep Nixon from being prosecuted yet also carry an admission of guilt, and he began to warm to the idea as a solu-tion to Ford's dilemma. A pardon, unlike amnesty, instructed only that an individual would not be punished. It struck convictions from the books as if they'd never occurred and treated a person as innocent. What it did not do was forget. The controversy over amnesty for draft exiles erupted because amnesty meant not only that offenders would not be punished but also that their crimes would be forgotten. It said the gov-ernment not only forgave them but was willing to go further and overlook their alleged offenses because the war and other conditions, such as ending the military draft, that had made the acts criminal no longer existed. Becker doubted Nixon would do anything that looked as if he was confessing, but he thought Ford, by offering Nixon a pardon, could place the burden squarely on Nixon to accept or reject it.

"The pardon," Becker explains, "is an act of forgiveness: We are forgiving you—the president, the executive, the *king*—is forgiving you for what you've done, your illegal act that you've either been convicted of, or that you've been accused of, or that you're being investigated for, or that you're on trial for. And you don't have to accept this—you can refuse this."

Eager to present Ford with the strongest possible arguments, Becker set about closing all the doors. He asked to see the *Burdick* briefs and "went over and over and over them," he says. He "Shepardized" the opinion: He examined it in Shepard's Citations, books that record the volume and page number of every appeals court decision in which a law or ruling is named, each time it was tested, and found that it had been regularly affirmed. He knew that Ford as a lawyer would ask if *Burdick* was, as Becker puts it, "very much still the law."

For Ford, the power to grant pardons and the power to declare amnesty—one a specific act of forgiveness, the other a blanket "forgetting"—were the most potent methods available for advancing reconciliation after Watergate and Vietnam. Both were acts of grace, his alone to offer, withhold, or condition upon other factors. Alexander Hamilton wrote that it was better sometimes "in seasons of insurrection and rebellion" to remit punishment for insurgents or rebels in order to restore "tranquility of the commonwealth." Washington, Adams, Madison, Lincoln, Andrew Johnson, Theodore Roosevelt, and Truman all had proclaimed postwar amnesties. Reading *Burdick,* Becker came quickly to believe that by pardoning Nixon, Ford could charitably stay the movement of the law without having to condone or comment upon Nixon's offenses.

* * *

Ford returned to the White House from Camp David by helicopter to participate in a late-morning ceremony in the Rose Garden. About two hundred labor and business leaders, plus senators and representatives, surrounded him as he signed into law a mammoth pension reform act, passed overwhelmingly by both houses of Congress after seven years of debate. Spurred by what the *Post* called "countless tales of personal tragedy—of hard-earned pension benefits lost to bankruptcies, mergers, mismanagement and, in some cases, unscrupulous employers," the act provided the first federal insurance against a loss of retirement benefits, establishing a new agency, the Pension Benefit Guaranty Corporation.

"This is really a historic Labor Day," Ford said, promising the new law would "alleviate fear and anxiety of people in the production lines and people in the mines.

"I don't think I've had a happier day . . . and to have it happen on Labor Day is a tribute to the American process—a process which is good for all of us."

Paeans to working men and women aside, it seemed more and more clear, with the approach of his economic summit, that Ford already had decided upon a strategy of attacking inflation through austerity and belt-tightening. Greenspan, due to be sworn in Wednesday, was an "inflation hawk," and Rumsfeld had urged Ford to hew to his advice, saying, "Look, this is a wonderful situation. It's an absolute home-run ball. You couldn't pick a better person."

The problem was unemployment. In his last, undelivered speech on the economy as vice president, Ford had planned to call for widening the economic safety net, saying, "It serves no purpose to lecture the harassed public, especially the low- and middle-income people who have been the main losers from inflation. We are mindful that some people are suffering more than others. Certain groups—older Americans, people on fixed incomes, the unemployed—may require special help within budgetary limitations." But joblessness had jumped in August to 5.4 percent, and with the economy spinning out of control, Ford faced a reckoning. Since World War II, inflation and unemployment tended to have an inverse relationship: When one rose, the other fell, and the government could tinker with the balance. With stagflation, both problems were worsening in lockstep. Ford knew he had no new options.

Labor leaders attending the ceremony hailed the pension act, but like Meany, who glowered from the audience, they reserved judgment about Ford's intentions. Many in Washington were beginning to understand that Ford was willing to tolerate higher unemployment than the unions, blacks, and liberal Democrats—those whom he had courted so assiduously during the past weeks—were urging. Indeed, it'd begun to look as if he had cultivated them *knowing* he would soon turn against them, thinking they might be more sympathetic toward his austerity program once they got to see that he, unlike Nixon, at least listened to their concerns.

Ford's expressions of pleasure and optimism—and his quick departure after the bill signing for Camp David, where he tried to squeeze out a few more hours' rest before returning to address the challenges ahead—signaled a turning point. Eric Sevareid, more than his brethren on the other networks, noted this dividing line in his evening commentary. During the past week, since he had encouraged Leonard Garment on the question of pardoning Nixon, then watched Ford gyrate at the press conference, Sevareid, always stern, had turned sterner, less eager to extend Ford the benefit of the doubt. The economy, especially, made him gloomy. Increasingly, as his biographer Raymond Schroth wrote, the "moralist, the old fashioned patriot . . . [became] upset by his country's behavior." Sevareid, surveying Ford's early performance, now sounded less hopeful than previously: "The political guns of August fell silent, and we've had a few weeks of general benevolence in this capital—a mini-era of good feeling," he said. "For the new president, the beauty part is over already . . ."

Sevareid brooded over the divisive, difficult choices looming just ahead—"amnesty for war avoiders is a good example; defense budget cuts vs. social services cuts is another; punishment vs. pardon for Richard Nixon is another," he said. Noting the country's instant affection for its new leader, he cautioned: "Presidential popularity has to be thought of, especially by the president, as a capital fund to be used. It has to be spent, and sometimes spent away, if serious things are to be done in the long-term national interest.

"The bitter aftertaste of Watergate is about ready to rise in every throat, as the new trials begin in the courts here, and as Mr. Nixon testifies, if only as a witness," he said.

Across the country, amid the last strains of summer, TV sets cast their universal soft blue glow. Sevareid, wearing a lemon-yellow sports coat, his silver hair gleaming, and his terse delivery echoing urgent radio dispatches from Europe thirty years earlier during World War II, summed up Ford's progress so far.

"President Ford made a fast start. Nearly everyone is impressed. But it's a cross-country, long-distance event. And as always it's stamina that counts.

"And we, and he, will find out about his stamina beginning now."

A wedge of U.S. marshals flanked John Dean, Nixon's former counsel and chief accuser, as he stepped from a government car and into a churning hoard of reporters blocking the federal courthouse where Dean came to turn himself in. On August 2, Sirica had sentenced Dean to one to four years in jail for his confessed role in the Watergate cover-up, and Dean, a star prosecution witness in the upcoming trial, had returned to Washington early from his home in California to consult with Jaworski's staff before starting his prison term. Shaken and scared, he wore dark sunglasses and a sickly visage.

Reporters pressed in, microphones outstretched. "Do you feel that if the president is not indicted that even-handed justice will have been done?" Fred Graham of CBS asked.

"Fred, you know I wouldn't make a comment."

"Mr. Dean, you have to go to jail. Do you think Mr. Nixon should go to jail?"

Dean smiled weakly. "I have no comment. I'm sorry."

The fifteenth Watergate figure to be sent to prison, Dean was the first to surrender himself to authorities since Nixon resigned and the first to face the question of whether they thought their leader should join them. Among this fraternity, many of them lawyers like Nixon, most had hoped and believed that Nixon would pardon them before he left office. Charles Colson, his top political adviser who once said famously that he would "walk over my own grandmother" for Nixon and who had since found Jesus in the course of being disbarred, confessing to obstructing justice in connection with the Fielding break-in, and beginning a one- to three-year jail term, remembered Nixon telling him: "The day will come when I will wipe the slate clean." "I knew what he meant," Colson wrote, "a commander doesn't abandon his troops in battle."

Dean had no clue as to where he would be imprisoned—despite his cooperation, prosecutors had hinted only that he would be held some-where near Washington. The marshals took him inside, downstairs from the courtrooms, where he was spread-eagled, frisked, and fingerprinted, then placed in a holding cell that, he noted, "had a toilet with no seat, a sink high enough that prisoners couldn't urinate in it, and a long steel bench." Like Colson, Haldeman, and Ehrlichman, Dean was stunned and dismayed that Nixon still refused to admit his involvement in any wrongdoing. Nixon, he wrote, had been "caught in his lies, so why didn't he confess?" He guessed it was some mixture of hubris, victimization, self-pity, faith that history would absolve him, and fear of jail. He doesn't think Nixon made a deal with Ford for clemency, he says.

The marshals' service ran a detention facility for government wit-nesses at Fort Holabird, a deserted, decaying former army base just out-side Baltimore. It was housed in a soot-covered green wooden barracks surrounded by a razor wire–topped fence. Colson and two other former White House aides had been transferred there in preparation for the Watergate trial, and Dean had mixed feelings when one of his jailers told him that was where he would be held. Even before he testified publicly against Nixon during the Senate Watergate hearings, Dean's personality, long blond hair, flashy style, and place in Nixon's inner circle had marked him as a "golden boy." When he'd appeared at the hearings wearing owlish glasses and his hair conservatively cut, Colson, a blunt former ma-rine officer who'd gained a reputation in the White House for taking on unsavory assignments and who hadn't yet repented, railed at the TV. "Anger," he wrote, "would boil up in me at the mention of his name."

Most of the other inmates at Fort Holabird were informants in big organized-crime cases, and contact between inmates was supervised heavily to discourage mob hits. "Worried that defense lawyers might charge us with concocting false testimony if we were together," Dean recalled, Jaworski's office instructed him not to talk with Colson or the other Watergate witnesses—Jeb Stuart Magruder, serving one to four years for perjury and conspiracy, and Herbert Kalmbach, who had handled Nixon's secret funds and pleaded guilty to several campaign violations. Soon after arriving at Holabird, Dean was shown to his room, where a supervisor told him he would be isolated from the other inmates, he would eat all his meals by himself, and a guard would be posted at all times outside his door.

After just two hours in the barred holding cell, he welcomed the restrictions. "My apprehension," he wrote, "was overshadowed by relief."

* * *

Becker presented his findings to Ford and Buchen in the Oval Office, explaining that according to *Burdick,* if Nixon accepted Ford's offer of a pardon, he in effect would be confessing to criminal wrongdoing. If not, Nixon would place himself at the mercy of Jaworski and Sirica, shifting the monkey from Ford's shoulders. As a negotiating tool, Ford's power to pardon Nixon—at any time—of crimes he might have committed provided a whip hand that strengthened his resolve and his conviction that the country, despite a new Gallup poll that found 56 percent of Americans in favor of prosecuting Nixon, would support him. "So I had the legal authority to move ahead," Ford wrote. "I hadn't made a final decision, but it must have been obvious to Phil that I was leaning toward a pardon."

"Look," Buchen said, "if you're going to do this to put Watergate behind you, I think you also ought to let me see how far we can go to get an agreement on the papers and tapes and have that in place at the same time."

"Well," Ford said, "if you can get the papers and tapes question settled prior to the pardon, that's fine. Let's get it behind us. But I don't want to condition the pardon on his making an agreement on the papers and tapes, and I don't want you to insist on any particular terms."

"I won't condition it," Buchen told him, "but I think I can work it out so by his agreement it'll come out at the same time."

By linking a pardon to the fate of Nixon's materials, Buchen hoped to improve Ford's leverage. At the same time, he had begun sounding out Jaworski and Miller about what it would take to make the prosecution of Nixon "go away." With Ford now resolved to move quickly ahead, Buchen anticipated having to conduct, in utmost secrecy, a complex three-way negotiation in which he would be discussing two momentous issues—clemency for a former president and the fate of Nixon's records, papers, and tapes—with both the special prosecutor and Nixon's lawyer, who both were seeking ways to keep the grand jury from indicting Nixon. Meanwhile, Haig, who also spoke with both of them as well as with Nixon and Ford, would battle Buchen sub rosa. The logistics alone—with the white-haired Buchen lumbering with his canes from meeting to meeting—presented steep obstacles.

Ford was scheduled to be in the library on the ground floor of the residence to tape what was still called an "audio-video message" for the United Way of America charitable drive. Before Ford left, Becker recalls, the conversation "took a twist on Congressional action regarding presidential records and tapes." Democratic senator Birch Bayh of Indiana, a presidential hopeful, had introduced legislation requiring all elected officials to turn over to the National Archives "all papers and documents dealing with official business" within six months of leaving office. If such a law were passed, it would apply, of course, to Nixon. Meanwhile, notable historians had petitioned Congress to pass a law stating that documents prepared at public expense "cannot be regarded as private property" to be "sold, concealed, or destroyed at the whim of present and former public officials acting in their personal capacity."

Ford wanted to obtain from Nixon a deed of trust giving the government custody and control of all his records, papers, and tapes, while guaranteeing Nixon access to them, at least through the cover-up trial and until Congress had time to act. As he and his lawyers discussed the matter briefly, they realized that whatever agreement they could get from Nixon would be a holding device, a temporary stay most likely to be superseded by congressional action.

*   *   *

At his sentencing in June, two months earlier, Colson had told the court: "I shall be cooperating with the prosecutor, but that is not to say that the prosecutor has bargained for my testimony, that there is any quid pro quo: there was not. I reached my own conclusion that I have a duty to tell everything I know about these important issues, and a major reason for my plea was to free me to do so." Afterward, he announced to reporters: "I have committed my life to Jesus Christ. I can work for the Lord in prison or out of prison, and that's how I want to spend my life. What happened today is the Lord's will and the court's will, and, of course, I accept that fully."

Colson's heavily publicized conversion from ruthless hatchet man—he described his job in the White House as "to get done what the President wanted done"—to atoning, gospel-toting truth-teller and self-described "babe in Christ" attracted special attention in Washington, especially among the defendants, who had grave reason for concern. He had testified at his trial that Nixon "on numerous occasions urged me to disseminate damaging information about Daniel Ellsberg"—in effect accusing Nixon of the same crime for which he himself was convicted and sentenced. At that time, then–Vice President Ford had defended Nixon from Colson's attacks, saying, "There's a big difference between telling Chuck Colson to smear Ellsberg and ordering—or allegedly ordering—a break-in."

Having offered to testify during the impeachment inquiry, Colson appeared to be on a cleansing mission to come forward and bear witness against the sins, the corruption, known generically as Watergate. "I'm not going to try to frame a case," he told the press. "I'm sure there are guys in the White House sweating, but I'm not going to testify that way. I've made a commitment to Christ and I really believe the only commandment I have to follow is to tell the truth. I will tell the truth."

Just after dark, Dean entered the dining room at Holabird, surrounded by five marshals; none of the other inmates tried to approach him. Later, a single deputy accompanied him to the kitchen, and Colson came in, along with Kalmbach. Dean eyed them tensely until Colson, also appearing nervous, burst forward, extending his hand.

"Whatever's happened in the past, John, let's forget it," Colson said. "If there's any way that I can help you, let me know."

Dean, startled and grateful, muttered a response: "Chuck, I really appreciate that. Honest, I really do."

"Would you like to borrow my radio or something?" Colson asked. He seemed to want to test how long the guard would let them talk.

"No thanks," Dean said. "I'm fine, Chuck."

Colson kept talking. "The food is damn good here. We rotate the cooking every day and some of these fellows are terrific." Wiseguys—the killers and informants wearing "everything from Bermuda shorts to tailored suits," as Dean noted—famously prized good eating. "You'll find beef stroganoff from dinner and I highly recommend it."

"I'll try it, but I'm not too hungry tonight," Dean said.

Kalmbach, too, acted friendly. "After dinner, I'll take you around and introduce you to some of the men here."

"Well, I'm not sure we can do that . . ."

Most of the top Watergate felons had drawn light duty in prison: Egil (Bud) Krogh, Jr., for instance, a lawyer and former head of the Plumbers, helped organize a running club at a prison farm in Allenwood, Pennsylvania. But Dean was quickly adjusting to being a prisoner and didn't want to find out how he might be disciplined for consorting with other "principals," as inmates at Holabird were called.

"He can't talk to anybody. He's on restriction," the deputy said.

"Oh, I see," Kalmbach said. Dean explained the terms of his isolation and Kalmbach nodded and put his hand on Dean's shoulder. "Everything is going to be fine," he said. "Just fine. Don't worry."

"It doesn't get any better but you get used to it," Colson said.

"Thanks, Chuck," Dean said. "Thanks."

On the way back to his room with a tray of food, Dean ran into Magruder. Formerly Haldeman's assistant, Magruder had been deputy director of Nixon's reelection committee at the time of the Watergate break-in, and Nixon blamed him for ordering the burglary. In separate deals with the White House and prosecutors he agreed to testify only about the reelection committee, keeping the White House out of it. Like Dean, he had given riveting testimony before the Senate and now would be a lead witness against The Big Three and, if Nixon was indicted, the president.

"Welcome to the club, John," Magruder said. "This place looks like the White House with all of us here."

27

Wednesday, September 4

First Purge

Shortly after midnight, General Creighton Abrams, who had led U.S. forces in Vietnam until Nixon appointed him army chief of staff, died of cancer at Walter Reed Army Medical Center. A hero of three wars, Abrams had risen to the Pentagon post preeminently as a commander of troops in wartime, and while he was there his chief mission involved integrating reserve and active-duty units so closely as to make them inseparable. In Vietnam, Abrams's task had been to shift the burden of fighting to the South Vietnamese: in effect, to cover America's retreat. Faced at the Pentagon with a shrunken and demoralized force and the shift to an all-volunteer army, Abrams set about creating a military structure that would ensure "that Presidents would never be able to again send the Army to war without the Reserves and the commitment of the American people," historian James Jay Carafano wrote.

Ford and Haig had discussed privately Haig's leaving the White House, and Abrams's death, plus the newly active negotiations to pardon Nixon, impelled Ford to make a decision. Two and a half years earlier, when Haig was still Kissinger's deputy, Nixon at one point had threatened to recall Abrams, probably the most popular general in the army, from Vietnam, and replace him with Haig, who under pressure from the White House had just earned two-star rank and had commanded no force larger than a battalion in battle. Six months later, Nixon appointed Haig army vice chief of staff, jumping him over the heads of more than 240 other generals in nominating him for four stars. Despite believing Haig must have been involved in the Pentagon's spying on him and Kissinger, Nixon had quickly brought Haig up through the ranks, and Haig's ambition was to return to the army at the top. "My entire military career, despite its many twists and turns, had been spent in preparation for this post," he wrote.

Ford wanted to reward Haig for his service. "I considered Haig as Abrams' replacement, and he wanted the job, but in order to get it he'd have to be confirmed by the Senate," he wrote. Given the inevitable controversy about Haig's limited command experience and military qualifications, not to mention what Ford called his "Nixon image"—his central role in Nixon's defense—both men understood that Senate approval was impossible. Ford proposed to Haig that he think instead about becoming NATO commander, which also included overseeing more than three hundred thousand U.S. servicemen in Europe. As neither job required congressional endorsement, Ford could make the appointment unilaterally. There would likely be objections from some European allies based on Haig's hard line on Vietnam, but Ford believed he could persuade them. Haig reluctantly agreed.

A half hour after Haig left the Oval Office, Ford met alone with Rumsfeld, back briefly from Brussels, to tell him that Haig would be leaving. Ford needed Rumsfeld to smooth Haig's appointment with the NATO countries, but his real interest was in having him replace Haig in the West Wing, not as omnipotent chief of staff but as someone to coordinate White House operations and organize Ford's schedule. Rumsfeld, who could see that the sniping and disarray had only worsened in the two weeks since he'd left, bluntly resisted. "I didn't want to do it," he said later. "I'd just left Washington. I'd been here ten years. I was disappointed that the recommendations of the transition team weren't followed. The administration was having trouble just staying current. I knew what a meat grinder it was. I knew it was programmed to fail."

News of Haig's departure—terHorst had told reporters as recently as Monday that Ford wanted him to stay—no doubt would escape quickly and invite questions about what explained the sudden shift. Was he jumping or being pushed? Five minutes after Rumsfeld left the Oval Office, Ford called in terHorst, who barely concealed his frustration at being told that the situation had changed. More and more terHorst felt he wasn't being informed of major developments, and he believed it hurt his—and Ford's—credibility. A day earlier, Bush had come to the White House to discuss his China appointment, and Ford, still awaiting formal approval from Peking, told terHorst to describe it as a routine political meeting. When terHorst announced at his briefing that Ford might delay his decision on leniency for war exiles until after the weekend, several reporters openly doubted his explanation that Ford wanted to talk more with the departments of defense and justice. With the old atmosphere of skepticism and distrust spilling back into the pressroom, the "halcyon interlude," as the *New Republic*'s John Osborne called it, between Ford and the media was starting to fray.

Ford and terHorst discussed the day's announcements, a series of diplomatic and political reassignments that, along with Haig's departure, represented Ford's clearest break yet with Nixon—both at the White House and within the Republican Party. Bush, Ford said, would be going to China; replacing him as GOP chair would be a doctor's wife and mother of three, Mary Louise Smith, founder of the Women's Political Caucus in Iowa, an expert in grassroots organization and the first woman ever to fill the post. Typically, Ford had drawn from both sides of the aisle in the shake-up. Senate Foreign Relations Committee chairman J. William Fulbright of Arkansas, an antiwar Democrat, would be offered the post of ambassador to Great Britain, while Dean Burch, a Nixon appointee who had run Goldwater's presidential campaign, would be kept on as a top political adviser and architect of Ford's upcoming strategy for the fall elections.

As for Haig, obstacles barred making a formal announcement. The Dutch ambassador was threatening to oppose Haig's choice for the NATO post, which currently was filled by General Andrew Goodpaster, who wasn't due to step down for another ten months; meanwhile, Democratic senator William Proxmire of Wisconsin said he would strongly oppose any move to return Haig to active military status in a top post, warning that rewarding Haig for his political service might tempt other officers to line up with one party or the other. TerHorst would say only that Ford and Haig had been discussing possible new assignments for Haig and that NATO was one of them. Two days after declaring that Haig would stay on "for the duration," terHorst now told reporters that Haig would serve "indefinitely" as the White House chief of staff.

* * *

Betty, wearing a gold dress with an open collar and scarf, entered the State Dining Room for her first press conference since Ford took office. Facing klieg lights and one hundred fifty reporters and photographers, including much of the foreign press, she sat down on a gold upholstered chair behind a mahogany table bearing a small bouquet of multicolored flowers, beneath a large portrait of Lincoln. Recent First Ladies had met informally with reporters, usually on sofas and chairs in the living quarters, but "no one could remember when a President's wife had agreed to appear before to a full-fledged White House news conference," the *Times* reported.

Perched at the microphones, she fielded questions calmly, appearing, like her husband, to have decided that the best way to handle all subjects was to showcase an upbeat, unassuming candor. She opened with a statement that she wanted to answer all the questions that had been piling up about her views on life and the part she would play in her husband's presidency.

"I have found it a very busy life," she said. "I'm very happy. Everyone has been so generous and warm."

Questions put invariably to leaders' wives didn't faze her; instead, they offered opportunities for Betty to reinforce her image as a woman who, despite appearing conventional, enjoyed being modern, outspoken, controversial, and, especially, influencing her powerful husband—on and off the pillow. Asked what women could do to stop future wars, she said: "They can always enlist." When the laughter subsided, she added: "By becoming active in politics."

A reporter asked her position on abortion. Rockefeller as New York governor had vetoed a bill to repeal the state's liberal abortion law, which provided abortion on demand until the twenty-fourth week of pregnancy, but the state's conservative senator James Buckley, brother of right-wing firebrand William F. Buckley, Jr., had introduced a constitutional amendment to overrule the Supreme Court's year-old ruling in *Roe v. Wade*. Betty previously had said she favored abortion in certain circumstances—for unwed teenagers—but when asked whose views she was closer to, she replied without hesitation: "Definitely Rockefeller."

She also said she would campaign vigorously for the Equal Rights Amendment, adding that Ford had once joked with her about "equal rights" for women but that he wasn't joking now.

* * *

Undetected by reporters, Jack Miller arrived at Buchen's suite at the Jefferson Hotel, prepared to discuss the problem of Nixon's White House materials. On Buchen's suggestion, Miller had drafted a deed of trust for Nixon's records, papers, and tapes, under which everything would be transferred to a federal facility near San Clemente. Nixon and the government would share formal ownership, and the tapes and documents would be available for court subpoenas for up to five years, after which Nixon could do with them as he pleased. Two keys would be necessary to access the materials; Nixon would have one, the General Services Administration the other. Miller wasn't sure Nixon would accept the plan, but he promised Buchen, who'd invited Becker to join them, to present it to him.

At one point as they went over Miller's draft, Buchen interjected: "President Ford is giving some consideration to pardoning your client. It's just in the consideration stage, and . . . I don't want you or your client to get excited, because it's not a final decision yet."

Miller says he believed a "pardon was absolutely necessary: a) not only because of the question of a fair trial, but if there had not been a pardon this whole controversy would go on, and on, and on, for several years." But he had not discussed a pardon with Nixon, and he doubted that Nixon would take one, with its implication of guilt.

Buchen went on: "Look, I think it's important that there be a statement of true contrition from the former President. The President tells me we can't dictate that statement, but in the interests of both your client and the President, I hope you could persuade your client to develop something that would tell the world, 'Yes, he did it, and he's accepting the pardon because he's guilty.' "

Miller agreed that Nixon should issue a statement accepting blame, but their few meetings since Nixon hired him a week earlier had shown, according to Ford, "that the former President's ability to discuss Watergate objectively was almost nonexistent." Miller anticipated that Nixon would refuse to admit any culpability since he believed he hadn't done anything wrong. When he told Buchen and Becker he was pessimistic about getting such a statement, they replied that it wouldn't be a precondition but urged him to press Nixon for one.

"It was generally a nonproductive meeting," Becker recalls. "I'm not suggesting that Jack was being frustrating, but Jack wanted to talk about the possibility of a pardon and I wanted to talk about the records and tapes—he didn't want to talk about that because Nixon didn't want to talk about that."

Nixon's rage about not being sent his materials—and his fear that Ford might double-cross him—had intensified since his last visit from Gulley. Swifty Lazar had begun asking more than $2 million for Nixon's memoirs, but publishers wanted assurance that Nixon would recount his version of Watergate in detail and with supporting documentation. Estimates of the materials' worth ran into the tens of millions of dollars. Nixon's hopes of digging out of his financial morass, his determination to vindicate himself by writing his memoirs, his ability to prepare court testimony now and in the future and that of the Watergate defendants and prosecutors to sharpen the case *against* him—in short, his legacy, which in the end mattered to him above all else—all relied on controlling his records, papers, and tapes.

"If there is going to be a pardon at all," Becker said, understanding Nixon's urgency, "President Ford would want to move quickly on this. If you want to keep going back to California and coming to meet with us, I don't know if we're talking about months, or how long?"

Becker inserted: "But this could change. And we need to resolve the records, papers and tapes. We need to resolve the ownership issue."

* * *

Soon after Miller and Becker departed, Jaworski, who'd returned from Texas the previous afternoon, came to Buchen's suite to follow up on their earlier discussions about Nixon. Heeding Lacovara's advice that he urge Ford to pardon Nixon soon if at all—yet mindful, too, that his staff all but unanimously opposed clemency and feared it would undermine the cover-up trial—he told Buchen that Ford's statements at the press conference a week earlier put him in a "peculiar situation."

"It sounded," Jaworski told Buchen, "like he was saying that any action I might take against Nixon would be futile."

Buchen tried to clarify. As he had told Miller, Ford was considering granting Nixon a pardon but hadn't made up his mind. Buchen and Jaworski avoided discussing whether the special prosecutor planned to indict Nixon, but Ford needed to know at least whether he would object to a pardon, and Jaworski gave no signal that he would. "By words or silence," Ben-Veniste and Frampton wrote, Jaworski "intimated that as long as the pardon was based on the premise that prejudicial pretrial publicity made it impossible for Nixon to get a fair trial, [he] would not oppose it."

Ford wanted Jaworski's position on two matters—how long before Nixon could receive a fair trial if he was indicted, and what other areas of investigation into Nixon's activities he was pursuing—and within hours after returning to special prosecution force headquarters, Jaworski delivered Buchen both findings in writing. "The factual situation regarding a trial of Richard M. Nixon within constitutional bounds," he wrote in a letter, "is unprecedented," adding that the House impeachment inquiry made Nixon's legal situation "especially unique."

> The massive publicity given the hearings and the findings that ensued, the reversal of judgment of a number of members of the Republican Party following release of the June 23 tape recording, and their statements carried nationwide, and finally the resignation of Richard M. Nixon, require a delay, before selection of a jury is begun, of a period from nine months to a year, and perhaps even longer.

While the forthcoming cover-up trial would generate even more unfavorable pretrial publicity, he wrote, he had no intention of including Nixon as a codefendant, since the "unanimous adverse finding" in the House report would most likely prejudice the case against Haldeman, Ehrlichman, Mitchell, and the others.

As to Nixon's broader criminal liability, Jaworski had received a list of ten areas of investigation—besides Watergate—in which Nixon might be involved. They included a disallowed tax deduction for the gift of his pre-presidential papers, obstruction of justice in the Pentagon Papers case, concealing FBI records, wiretapping White House aides, misuse of Internal Revenue Service information, and misuse of the IRS through the initiation of audits of White House "enemies." A cover letter by Jaworski's deputy Henry Ruth summarized: "None of these matters rises to the level of our ability to prove even a probable criminal violation by

Mr. Nixon, but I thought you ought to know which of our pending investigations were even remotely connected to [him]. Of course the Watergate cover-up is the subject of a separate memorandum."

Jaworski attached a copy of the list and Ruth's summary to his letter to Buchen.

* * *

"In the career of George Bush," Christopher Lydon wrote in the *Times,* "it seems that nothing succeeds like failure."

Being Nixon's loyal protégé, despite the Townhouse Fund connection, had not hurt Bush demonstrably. Nor had his inability to win the vice presidency. In the long months of Watergate, he and Ford had often been in the same lonely position—the head of the party and the White House second-in-command trying with increasing futility to put the best face on a doomed situation—and Ford had come to admire Bush's tenacity and the murderous enthusiasm he applied to his work. Suffering reversals only seemed to spur him on.

Following the White House announcement of the shake-up in Ford's team, Bush, hands stuffed casually in the pockets of an elegant pin-striped suit, spoke at a news conference alongside Mary Louise Smith, his replacement as party chair. "This job," he said about his appointment to head the U.S. mission in Peking, "is exactly what I want to do."

Bush disguised his ambivalence with boyish optimism. After meeting with Ford for forty-five minutes Tuesday, he'd resigned himself to taking up a post half a world away from Washington. Bar, like Betty Ford, saw the assignment as an opportunity—"the answer to all my prayers," she wrote—to spend more time with her husband. China would be a sabbatical from politics, but it would also be an exile, and Bush worried that he was "running away from something."

Hoping for guidance, Bush had phoned Nixon, the "best China expert I knew," and he recorded the discussion, and his disappointment, in his diary:

He was very formal, very perfunctory. I said it would be nice to come out there. Hinted twice about being nice to chat—like very much to visit on this, and the President never responded . . . He chatted a little about China—saying that after 25 years—that it would be such a power—that [my job] would be kind of lonely and quiet—things are isolated and separated—you only see people at big diplomatic functions—but it would be a great experience . . . I gave him credit saying: "This wouldn't have been possible of course without you" etc., etc., but he never warmed up at that. The conversation was very brief . . .

Bush put a positive face on being relieved as party chair. "It's good," he told the reporters, "to have at this juncture a new chairman of the Republican National Committee. So I don't take it personally that I'm kind of being swept out in a . . . in a negative sense. I do take it very positively that this makes enormous sense from the president's standpoint, and I have nothing but respect for the choice that's been made."

Added Smith: "I think that there will be a new awareness of women in the party, because we are saying to the country, 'Look what we do, not what we say.' "

If Ford, in shuffling the line-up for his new team, showed by relieving Bush and Haig of their jobs that he was moving away from Nixon's orbit, it still remained unclear where he was headed. Politically, he'd cast his lot with the Rockefeller Northeasterners; economically, with the inflation hawks; diplomatically, with Kissinger. He was calling for women to help reshape the GOP. But presidential power emanated from a corps of close advisers, and Ford, who had staked his credibility and image upon being perceived as easygoing and accessible but ultimately his own man, now surrounded himself with a core cadre inexperienced in power and unforged by shared campaigns and battles. The four entourages that had served as his makeshift carapace in the early uncertain hours of his presidency were now one—more or less.

As ABC's Tom Jarrell summed up the changes presciently in his nightly report:

The moves represent the boldest steps taken yet by the president and his apprentice staff to show that they've gained enough self-confidence to run their own shop. One inside source said, "When they let Haig go, they cut the umbilical, ready or not." This leaves the power structure under President Ford in the hands of four men: former newspaperman Robert Hartmann; another counselor, John Marsh; news secretary Jerald terHorst, a veteran Washington reporter who knows more than the other two about the White House; and possibly, NATO Ambassador Donald Rumsfeld, whose influence is as mysterious as his unannounced meetings with the president.

28

Thursday, September 5

Renewed Conflicts

No reporters were allowed into the residence for the 6:30 A.M. photo opportunity—Ford standing at a toaster in the kitchen, waiting for an English muffin to pop. Although Betty acknowledged at her press conference that Ford no longer made his own breakfast, the act had become symbolic of what type of man, and husband, the new president was, and terHorst had arranged for film crews to witness Ford, freshly showered in a blue oxford shirt and slacks, scrape margarine from a container, then spread it to the edges. Ford sliced the muffin halves hemispherically. Two of the three networks, while poking mild fun at the artifice, aired the silent footage.

A few hours later in the East Room, twenty-eight leading economists from across the spectrum (except the far left) assembled at a long table along with Ford, his economic councilors, and eight members of Congress—four from each party—for a daylong "presummit" meeting, the first stage in Ford's escalating round of talks to forge a national policy on how to get the country going again. Rows of observers crowded behind them. Crystal chandeliers lit seminude Grecian youths and maids looking languidly from bas-reliefs high on the walls.

"This has been called a summit conference," Ford said in his opening remarks. "Maybe that title is a bit misleading." He noted that summit parleys usually involve adversaries discussing trade-offs to reduce their differences. "Around this table there are no adversaries. We come together as allies to draw upon, or to draw up I should say, a battle plan against a common enemy, inflation. Inflation is our domestic enemy number one."

"Battle strategies are usually devised in secret," Ford said. "At my insistence this is a typically American open meeting." Ford noted that skeptics had warned him that providing open microphones in a White House forum to such a normally disputatious group "would produce a spectacle something like professional wrestlers playing ice hockey." There was laughter. "But I am ready to referee this opening match."

The degree of consensus about the basic current problems was surprising, although less than unanimous. As Greenspan, seated at Ford's right, put it in his first official forecast as the government's chief expert and a key voice on managing the marketplace, the economy was "turgid" and "sluggish" and in the grip of a worrisome inflationary psychology. Consumers, he said, "clearly respond to inflation in a retrenchment way" and "become terribly concerned about being able to make ends meet when they see a rapidly rising inflation," which causes them to put off buying. Greenspan's predictions were expected to have a strong influence on federal policy. He said he foresaw a "flattened" economy in the months ahead, with some increase in joblessness, but dismissed the extreme pessimism of Meany and many Democrats.

Sworn in Wednesday by Ford, Greenspan resembled Kissinger—they'd attended the same high school in the Bronx—both in the ponderous way he put things and his ambition to rule a global balance of forces, and he stuck to analysis, refraining from partisan attacks and blaming old policies. Still, his ideological assumptions remained widely suspect, mostly due to his association with novelist Ayn Rand, who regarded government intervention as Sovietism and believed that unfettering raw capitalism was the only effective, and moral, course for society. "I'm very proud of Alan," Rand had said after Ford led her and other invited guests on a tour of the White House before Greenspan's inaugural ceremony. "His is a historic undertaking." Greenspan soon would tell another "foothill" meeting on inflation, "If you really want to examine who percentage-wise is hurt the most in their incomes, it is the Wall Street brokers. I mean their incomes have gone down the most"—bringing hoots and boos and spurring some homebuilders in Oregon to form a group called Save Our Brokers.

Ford set a relaxed, informal tone, listening attentively, smoking his pipe, taking notes, calling many of the economists by their first names, and staying through a 10:40 A.M. coffee break, when he left to meet with Kissinger. Their daily foreign policy tutorials, derailed during the Cyprus crisis, had only just resumed, and Kissinger, alarmed by the rapid reversals in Vietnam and rising calls in Congress to halt further funding for the war, took the occasion to press Ford on the issue of increased aid for Indochina.

"Without massive effort on your part," he told Ford, "we are in trouble on Vietnam. If we don't do enough, it doesn't matter how much too little you do. North Vietnam seems undecided. You might want to consider meeting with the congressional leaders next week. We are in trouble both with the restrictions and the dollar amounts . . ."

As Kissinger himself noted later, the national mood over Vietnam had turned from rage and grief to passivity and numb indifference—"as if suddenly seized by a collective obsession to extrude a past which was, in fact, inescapable . . . bent on extinguishing its witnesses, our former allies," he wrote. Even as he and Ford spoke, Senate Democrats were voting unanimously to bring Congress back for a lame-duck session to enact inflation curbs—a direct rebuke to the White House, which had been reporting that an overall anti-inflation package couldn't be ready until the start of the next session in January. With the Democrats hoping to use the worsening economy, and Republican failures to fix it, to win in November, Ford had little chance to do what Kissinger was proposing.

Kissinger persisted: "Others will see what happens to people who rely on the United States. First we make an undesirable settlement, but with the promise of unlimited aid—and then the aid is cut off within two years.

"You do have an option as a new President," Kissinger said. Ford could evacuate the last of the Americans and abandon Vietnam. Kissinger was urging Ford to blame Congress entirely for the debacle in Southeast Asia, yet if Ford failed to support further military aid, he might gain politically. "You could let it go—and not be blamed, at least through '76," Kissinger said. "I must say I think it's wrong. The liberals who would applaud it would fail you when the going was tough."

So deep had grown the disillusionment over America's most misguided and self-destructive war that Kissinger, always careful to get on record his own pleas for steadfastness, felt constrained, facing the endgame, to advise Ford that the most popular move would be to cut and run. Ford, who as the ranking Republican on the Defense Subcommittee of the House Appropriations Committee had regularly fought hard for military spending, refused to consider that option. Kissinger, the architect of the "decent interval"—Nixon's decision to leave South Vietnam to fend for itself long enough before 1976 for the war to recede as an election issue—didn't need to remind Ford that if Saigon fell to communism before then, both of them would be held to account no matter what they did.

"The end came to Indochina as it does in a Greek tragedy," he wrote, "where the principals are driven by their very natures to fulfill their destinies in the full foreknowledge of the anguish that awaits them."

* * *

Late in the afternoon, Ford huddled with Buchen, Haig, and Becker. Since the meeting a day earlier at the Jefferson, Miller had spoken at length with Nixon, who at first had opposed any offer of clemency. Nixon's "initial reaction was that he did not want a pardon," Miller said later; he "felt that if he had done something wrong, let him be indicted and go to trial." As with Jaworski, Miller had little trouble persuading Nixon, who believed his countrymen wanted to destroy him, that he could never get a fair court hearing, and he subsequently indicated to Buchen that Nixon was ready to negotiate on the papers and tapes and was willing to make a statement about his involvement in Watergate. Miller said that in order to consummate the matter, he needed to meet with Nixon in person, and he suggested that Buchen and Becker attend that meeting.

Ford was visibly pleased with the progress, telling Becker that a secret military flight to San Clemente had been readied for him and Miller, and for the next half hour the group discussed Becker's mission. Whatever doubts Ford had had about his ability to link Nixon's pardon to the disposition of his papers and tapes now had dissipated, and as always when his mind was made up, he charged ahead.

Ford emphasized his interest in the records, papers, and tapes. Haig, who'd assisted Nixon in sacrificing his presidency over the issue of executive privilege, insisted Nixon wouldn't give them up. "It will never happen," Haig said, arousing Becker to disagree. "What he was really saying to Jerry Ford, was, 'You're going to have to decide the pardon issue without any linkage,' " Becker recalls. Both Becker and Buchen agreed that Ford would not condition a pardon on Nixon's agreement to share custody of his files with the government, but they resolved to push Miller aggressively on the issue.

Near the end of instructing Becker on the deed of trust for Nixon's materials, Ford raised a suggestion urged on him by Kissinger, whose Secret Service code name was Bird. "The President advised," Becker wrote, "that the Bird had expressed concern for himself and others with regard to a public disclosure of all tapes." If not personally incriminating, the tapes were certainly embarrassing to Kissinger, Haig, and many others alike, and Ford suddenly told Becker that he should try in his negotiations with Nixon "at the very least [to] prevent public disclosure of the tapes for fifty years." Running counter to Becker's and Buchen's earlier discussions with Miller, the proposal "represented a major impediment" to a resolution of the records and tapes problem, Becker would write.

Ford authorized Becker to tell Nixon: "It's not final, but in all probability, a pardon will be forthcoming." As Becker gathered to leave, Ford walked him to the door. "I want you to look at him from a health standpoint," Ford said. "Be very firm out there and tell me what you see." Becker's assignment was to negotiate an agreement on the documents, make certain Nixon understood the meaning of a pardon under the *Burdick* ruling, and get a statement of contrition if possible, but Ford also needed him to be his eyes and ears—to evaluate Nixon's mental and physical state. At the same time, he needed Becker to voice directly, unambiguously, what Ford had to have for granting Nixon immunity.

Becker recalls: "We walked out of the office, he had his hand over my shoulder, he said, 'I will never, ever give up those records. They belong to the American people. You let President Nixon know that I feel very strongly about this.' "

* * *

Ford planned to attend as many of the economic sessions as he could, to demonstrate he was in charge and would hear all sides as the government marshaled against inflation. He returned to the East Room, where seven of the country's best-known economists delivered final statements. Harvard's John Kenneth Galbraith raised eyebrows among his colleagues by his strong opposition to easing monetary policy and by making a case for returning to wage and price controls as part of an overall strategy. Milton Friedman of the University of Chicago disagreed, saying the nation must "bite the bullet" to cure inflation, even at the cost of a recession. "The only cure for inflation," Friedman said, "is to slow down total spending." "I hope we can do better," MIT's Paul Samuelson replied, "but I don't think we will get down in the next couple of years to 3 percent inflation no matter if we bite every bullet in sight." As Samuelson warned that any attempt to do anything dramatic "would be counterproductive," Ford nodded thoughtfully.

What Ford hoped to bring to bear most compellingly on America's problems was a restored sense of confidence—in Washington, in itself—and tackling inflation, he believed, posed the greatest test of his ability to lead. Vietnam, Watergate, the energy crisis—all fed a yawning national insecurity, tearing down the country's faith and pride in itself as a benevolent, lawful, wise, and supremely powerful nation that could think and work its way out of its problems. But high inflation eroded the communal psyche, prompting gloom, helplessness, fear. People's savings—dreams—sank.

Ford thanked the economists for their advice and told them that they had set a high example for the rest of the meetings, not mentioning which, if any, of their suggestions he planned to follow. His pleasure at the progress being made with Nixon was bolstered and reinforced by the number of economists who commented that the restored "moral authority" of the presidency now that Ford had taken office was itself a weapon against inflation. Ford knew perhaps better than anyone the sheer power he held in not being Nixon. How much power would depend most likely on how soon Ford could unify the country before taking a hard stand on the economy, and whether that translated to his having political coattails in the fall elections.

* * *

On the flight to San Clemente, Becker showed Miller drafts of two documents that he and Buchen had prepared for Ford to consider—a deed of trust covering both ownership and control of Nixon's materials, and a pardon—and emphasized that Ford had yet to make a final decision on either. Soon after arriving at El Toro Air Force Base at midnight—3 A.M. Washington time—they were driven directly to Nixon's compound to meet with Ziegler, whom Miller had told about Becker's personal relationship with Ford. Watergate had showcased enough young lawyers in the White House, Congress, and the special prosecution force for Ziegler not to be surprised that Ford's emissary was young, but that he was also unknown, and showing exhaustion, gave Ziegler little reason for deference.

"I can tell you right now," Ziegler told him, "that President Nixon will make *no* statement of admission or complicity in return for a pardon from Jerry Ford."

Becker was stunned, but he says he remained calm. He suspected that he had been undercut by Haig, who he guessed must have phoned Ziegler to report that Ford wouldn't condition a pardon on a statement of blame. "It was while I was in the air," he recalls, "and it went way beyond the statement. It [the message] was, 'You don't have to give up anything, you don't have to apologize, you're gonna get the pardon.' " Faced with the fact that Nixon knew Ford's ultimate position even before they started discussions—an intolerable betrayal by Haig, Becker thought, and an impossible circumstance for any negotiator—Becker bluffed. Hard.

"Mr. Ziegler," he said softly. "I've never been to San Clemente before and for that matter I don't work for the government, so . . . I'm a bit confused.

"Can you tell me how to reach the Air Force pilot that brought me here, so that I could instruct him to take me back to Washington?

"I'll also need a car and driver to take me back to El Toro."

Miller sought to calm matters by noting that the late hour was making everyone tired. He suggested that they address the issue in the morning, after other questions had been resolved. "It seemed to work," Becker wrote. "Ziegler mellowed." For the next hour and a half the three of them talked conceptually about the problems facing both Ford and Nixon, given the current limbo of the papers, records, and tapes. Though Ziegler believed Nixon could expect the pardon on his terms, he hadn't been aware of the outstanding subpoenas for documents, or Ford's precarious legal position as a result. Becker thought he appeared surprised by the depth of the problem, and they agreed to discuss it further.

At about 2 A.M., Miller and Becker checked into the San Clemente Inn, wandered past the photographs of Nixon and his family in the deserted lobby to the cocktail lounge, and drank two draft beers apiece. They had known each other slightly through their work at the Department of Justice, and their relationship to each other, as in any negotiation, would matter as much or more than the issues at stake or the competing interests of their clients. No one noticed them as they sat watching the bar's few patrons. After an hour, Becker went to his room and, before collapsing into bed, phoned the desk clerk to ask for a five thirty wake-up call.

Becker phoned Washington at sunrise from his room and spoke with Buchen, who told him that Ford wanted to announce the pardon on Saturday, but that he had convinced Ford to wait a day to give the lawyers more time to work. Though fewer than a dozen people knew what he intended to do—all of them with a keen interest in keeping it secret—Ford worried deeply about leaks, as well he might given the press's hyperdrive and surging prestige after Watergate, and amid Washington's peak frenzy of leaking. Becker advised Buchen on the thrust of his initial discussion with Ziegler and Ziegler's "charm," and they agreed again to take the position that while a statement of contrition was not a precondition to pardon, it would be "both proper and helpful for . . . acceptance."

Becker showered, unpacked, reviewed his records, and went to the breakfast bar to meet Miller. Not long after they sat down, a *Los Angeles Times* reporter approached the table, asking Miller "what he was doing there and who was Mr. Becker," according to Becker, who excused himself and returned only after the reporter left. Miller told him he believed the desk clerk at the motel reported his comings and goings to the local press.

The meeting at Casa Pacifica started after breakfast, with Ziegler sit-

ting in for Nixon. His frequent phone conversations with Haig strengthened Nixon's bargaining position exponentially, yet Ziegler would justify
those calls as both proper and ordinary, saying, "Al Haig and I had discussions relevant to the pardon as Ford moved through the decision and
approached the decision. Primarily they were to a great extent mechani-
cal, you know, . . . what President Nixon would say in a statement, those
type of things. In other words, Al was [Ford's] chief of staff, and me as
Nixon's chief of staff had exchanges about . . . what President Nixon
would be prepared to say."

The head-butting of the night before yielded to a careful line-by-line
review of Miller's draft of a letter of agreement between Nixon and the
director of the General Services Administration, Arthur Sampson, stating that while all Nixon's White House papers, tapes, and files were his
private property, they would be "deposited temporarily" in a facility near
San Clemente. Nixon offered "to donate" the materials "with appropriate restrictions" provided no one could gain access to them without one
of two keys—one in his possession, the other belonging to the national
archivist. He agreed not to withdraw any original documents, but reserved the right to make copies and authorize others to do the same, for
a period of three years, after which they would be his "to retain . . . for
any purpose."

At each impasse Ziegler and Miller left to obtain Nixon's authoriza-
tion, sometimes for a few minutes, often longer, while Becker called
Buchen on a secure phone to report on his progress. Miller's draft treated
the tape recordings separately, and the negotiations slowed as they discussed them. These Nixon agreed to donate on September 1, 1979—five
years hence—until which time they would "remain on deposit" with
the government. Before then, only Nixon would have access—though he
might authorize access by others—and reproductions would be made
only by "mutual consent." After five years, Nixon could destroy any or all
of the tapes, which, in any event, would "be destroyed at the time of [his]
death or on September 1, 1984, whichever event shall first occur."
Becker, viewing the Nixon-Sampson letter as an interim agreement, a
"holding device," raised no objection.

And so it was settled in principle that the fruits of Nixon's secret automatic taping system, which even Haig called "Orwellian," would now be buried with him—or else could be destroyed during a year already famously equated in world literature with historical amnesia and the ability of an all-powerful state to block information and shield its crimes. Kissinger's suggestion to Ford that public disclosure of the tapes be embargoed for fifty years quietly became moot.

By noon Becker reported to Buchen that they had a deal on Nixon's materials and were preparing to discuss the twin issues of the pardon and the statement. "Stick with it," Buchen said.

* * *

It was 2 P.M. on the East Coast when the *Los Angeles Times* reporter who'd spotted Miller and Becker, and who had connected Becker's name to Ford through clippings from Ford's confirmation hearings as vice president, reached terHorst to ask what the president's lawyer was doing in San Clemente. TerHorst immediately phoned Buchen, who said Becker was there with Miller to review the disposition of Nixon's papers and tapes, which Saxbe, in his opinion to Ford released earlier in the day, now declared belonged to Nixon.

TerHorst, asked daily whether Ford planned to pardon Nixon or any of the Watergate defendants, gave his stock answer: "The President has said that when the issue is before him he'll deal with it then. And he's not going to deal with it now because it's not before him." Scarcely knowing Becker, Becker's place in Ford's inner circle, or anything about the negotiations with Miller, he took Buchen at his word, telling the reporter only what he knew. "In other words," he recalls, "I let President Ford answer for himself. It was the best I could do." With no news to report, no story was printed.

Ford at the moment was meeting alone in the Oval Office with Rockefeller—a "courtesy call," according to Rockefeller's press secretary,

Hugh Morrow, at the end of a hectic twenty-four-hour visit to Washington about which the normally voluble Rockefeller had notably little to say. After staying overnight at his Foxhall Road mansion, Rockefeller ate breakfast at the White House with Kissinger, whom Ford had told of his plan to pardon Nixon, and who'd urged Ford to move ahead quickly. The meeting was said to be a foreign policy and national security briefing. Rockefeller spent an hour speaking with the head of the Atomic Energy Commission, commenting afterward only that nuclear energy was "one of the tremendously important hopes for the future," then met again at midday with Kissinger and Soviet ambassador Dobrynin for what he would describe only as a "pleasant lunch."

Thronged by reporters, Rockefeller had no comment on any of the sessions. Asked about détente and the second round of discussions with the Soviets about limiting strategic weapons (SALT II), he ducked, saying that he was still a "private citizen," thus making it inappropriate for him to say anything. He issued the same answer to questions about inflation and the progress of congressional committees scheduled to hold hearings on his confirmation. It's uncertain whether Ford, Kissinger, or both had spoken with him about the pardon, but difficult to imagine that each, for his own reasons, had not.

Thwarted, and facing the weekly graveyard of fluff-laden Friday night broadcasts and little-read Saturday morning papers, Washington reporters and editors in newsrooms around the country scrambled to tie up other stories.

* * *

Unprompted, Ziegler brought up the subject of a statement by Nixon to accompany the pardon, declaring that a statement was proper and that he now supported the idea. He told Becker that he had outlined one and given it to a speechwriter, then offered Becker the completed document. It told of the pressures of the office, Nixon's preoccupation with world affairs, and his need to rely on the judgment and honesty of his staff. It concluded that Nixon "should have placed less reliance and delegated less responsibility to staff members," Becker wrote. "It said nothing more."

Becker restated Ford's position, much as he had earlier with the materials. "My words in San Clemente were," he says, " 'The President will fairly consider the issue of this pardon if this is executed. If this is not executed, I cannot give any insurance of consideration.' " He was not saying the statement was a condition, only that if Nixon refused to acknowledge his role, he—Becker—wasn't sure Ford might not change his mind. Just as Nixon and Kissinger calculating that Soviet doubts over America's strategic might—and how, when, and where Washington might use it—gave the Kremlin a potent incentive to negotiate arms reductions, Ford and his lawyers reasoned that Nixon's uncertainties up until the moment he received a pardon could still be used to pressure him, no matter what Haig was telling Ziegler.

Becker told Ziegler that Nixon would be better off making no statement than the one he proposed, reminding him that all thirty-eight members of the House Judiciary Committee had publicly found that Nixon had "condoned, encouraged . . . directed, coached, and personally helped to fabricate perjury." He pointed out that in contradicting mountains of damning congressional evidence, Nixon was surely inviting state prosecution, even should a federal pardon be granted. Miller concurred, and a speechwriter was called in as he began to dictate points for a second draft. Becker sat by but contributed nothing to the dictation. As Ziegler and the speechwriter left, presumably to discuss the matter with Nixon, he and Miller resumed discussing the final wording of the deed of gift.

At about 3 p.m.—as Ford, on Air Force One, was arriving in Philadelphia for a two-hundredth anniversary commemoration of the First Continental Congress—Becker received a revised draft of Nixon's statement. The fourth version, as it turned out, of the ideas outlined by Miller, it contained an acknowledgment by Nixon of poor judgment, but again no candid statement on Nixon's role in Watergate as Miller had advised.

Becker, sensing in Miller a tacit ally, postured. He bristled with impatience, repeating "for the 53rd time that day," as he would write, that although a statement was not a precondition to a pardon, an "acknowledgment of mistreatment of the so-called Watergate Affair by President Nixon after it had reached a judicial state"—in other words, that he was involved in obstructing justice—would help guarantee that a pardon from Ford would be forthcoming. After subsequent review, and further discussion with Nixon, Becker was shown a revised statement with words to the effect that Nixon "can see clearly now that I was wrong in not acting more decisively and more forthrightly in dealing with Watergate, particularly when it reached the stage of judicial proceedings and grew from a political scandal into a national tragedy."

Becker, keying on the word *forthrightly*, accepted the admission as an adequate expression of contrition. "That word is a synonym for *honestly*," he says, stretching the more common definitions: *frankly, directly, without evasion.* "That had meaning for me as a former prosecutor, because that meant obstruction of justice. Dealing with something dishonestly when it reaches a judicial proceeding—that's equal to knowledge of obstruction of justice." Becker phoned Buchen, who agreed, though Ford, expecting more, bridled when he learned about the wording. "I was disappointed," he wrote. "I was taking one hell of a risk, and [Nixon] didn't seem to be responsive at all."

With two of Becker's three contiguous missions more or less completed—he still needed to know that Nixon understood that in accepting a pardon from Ford he was acknowledging blame—Becker gathered himself to meet, and size up, Richard Nixon, alone and on behalf of the president.

* * *

Exploiting a rare dearth of momentous activity in Washington, the network newscasts turned to lighter offerings. CBS broadcast a cheeky piece by correspondent Morton Dean on the Rockefeller family empire that ran more than three minutes, showing footage of Nelson Rockefeller's vast and priceless art collection; "Grandpa" John D. Rockefeller, the world's first billionaire; Rockefeller Center and Rockefeller University in New York City; oil wells; Chase Manhattan Bank, where younger brother David Rockefeller was chairman; Rockefeller investments in Venezuela—a large supermarket chain, a milk-processing plant, service stations, as well as Rockefeller's own eighteen-thousand-acre ranch; his house in Seal Harbor, thirty-two-room New York apartment, and Fox-hall Road estate; and the four-thousand-acre family homestead in Westchester, Pocantico Hills, with its private eighteen-hole golf course decorated with outdoor sculptures—Calders, Moores—where Rocke-feller had flown to spend the weekend after his meeting with Ford. With Rockefeller's wealth and potential conflicts looming as confirmation is-sues, he was shown trying to dampen estimates of what he was worth. "We've all heard some pretty exciting stories," he said, "and I think maybe I won't be able to live up to some of the expectations."

ABC and NBC aired skeptical features on the buildup to motorcycle stuntman Evel Knievel's attempt, set for Sunday, to cross the six-hundred-foot-deep Snake River Canyon near Twin Falls, Idaho, atop a small rocket—"one of the more grotesque spectacles in our history," NBC anchor John Chancellor called it. Forty-five thousand people were expected to pay $25 each—plus another 2 million would view the stunt on pay-TV—to watch Knievel, who in twenty years or so of jumping motorcycles over cars, trucks, and hotel fountains had already broken most of the bones in his body, take off over the seventeen-hundred-foot-wide canyon at four hundred miles per hour and land by parachute about a mile away. With a percentage of every concession—there were Evel Knievel T-shirts, posters, commemorative coins, belt buckles, patches, buttons, dolls; you could even order a one quarter life-size Evel Knievel sculpture in bronze ($5,000), silver ($22,500), or gold ($150,000)—Knievel stood to gross more than $15 million.

"One gets the feeling," NBC correspondent Jack Perkins noted, "that every hype, hoopla, and hustle artist in the world is in Twin Falls this week." Knievel himself, dressed in a white Elvis-style, bell-bottom jumpsuit, led the press agentry and theatrics. "All I can tell ya is, when it comes time, I'm gonna get in it, and I'm gonna let 'em blast me, and I hope that everybody there will blow like hell behind me because I'm gonna need all the help I can get," he told reporters.

Disbelievers—sportswriters and aviation experts, mainly—dismissed the magnitude of Knievel's challenge, suggesting, despite the wreckage of unmanned prototypes conveniently littering the launch site, that the stunt involved little actual risk—as CBS's Richard Threlkeld put it, "that the whole thing is about as dangerous as John Glenn catching a commuter shuttle to Boston."

Knievel, whether because he was afraid, or irked, or concerned about a possible loss of revenue, was showing himself to be on edge. "I'm here to risk my life," he said, after shoving a cameraman. "I don't care what some of the writers say, or some of the announcers say. And you can see it, what it's doing to me. You'll do one thing for me. I do not ask for your respect, I demand it."

With less than forty-eight hours remaining, the question had become not whether Knievel would survive his dangerous attempt, but whether anyone should care. "Hero or hustler?" NBC's Perkins asked at the end of his report. "Or for Americans, are those the same things?"

* * *

Addressing an enthusiastic dinner crowd of several hundred in a packed tent outside Independence Hall, Ford invoked the nation's Founders as forebears in the war on inflation. Those who convened nearby two centuries ago at the First Continental Congress, when irate colonists organized in Philadelphia to protest the Intolerable Acts, a series of laws passed by Britain to punish the Massachusetts colony for the Boston Tea Party, were "inflation fighters before they took up arms against the British redcoats," he said. The bipartisan crowd applauded mightily.

"The tyranny of the British parliament and crown in 1774 animated our ancestors," Ford said. "The tyranny of double digit inflation is our common enemy in 1974. Inflation is the cruelest kind of taxation without representation." Again, his audience clapped hard and long.

The speech was the culmination of a two-day conference held to kick off preparations for the country's bicentennial gala, which had attracted political and governmental leaders from all thirteen original states. Jack Marsh had been pushing Ford to become more deeply involved in planning for the celebration, both to help spark the country out of its doldrums and because it coincided with the next presidential race. Stumping, Ford extracted maximum effect from the rhetorical and political parallels.

"Like the patriots who met here two hundred years ago, we may seem to move cautiously and too deliberately," he said. "But I hope no one will underestimate the fighting ability of Americans today the way some did in 1774. I warn you, as wise old Ben Franklin did, that if we do not all hang together, we will certainly hang separately.

"But we will not hang separately," Ford vowed, "nor will we fall divided. We're going after—one and all, Democrats and Republicans—the public enemy of inflation in 1974 and we will lick him before July 4, 1976."

On the return flight to Washington, Ford strolled back to talk with reporters, confirming an earlier statement by terHorst that he would establish a national review board to consider clemency for antiwar exiles, much as Truman had done for draft resisters after World War II. Ford gave no more details but announced that he would disclose his long-awaited amnesty plan on Tuesday.

* * *

Becker entered the small, spare office where Nixon sat, flanked by flags, behind an empty desk. Nothing was hung on the walls. "The famous Nixon jowls were exaggerated, the face highly wrinkled, the hair disheveled and the posture and comportment . . . reminiscent of advanced age," he noted. Ziegler had tried to bar him from seeing Nixon, but Miller encouraged it, saying it would do no harm. As Nixon rose to greet him, Becker recalled, his first impression was "unhappily, of freakish grotesqueness"—thin arms dangling from the sleeves of his dark suit, extended in a weak handshake.

Nixon slumped back in his seat. "You should be very proud of this, Mr. President," Becker said, holding out the deed of trust, heavily weighted in Nixon's favor but the best that Ford, saddled with Scalia's and Saxbe's opinion, and in his haste, hoped now to take away from the negotiations. "This is very good work . . . good staff work," Becker said. "This is good for the American people." Nixon seemed alert but distracted.

"I'm sure," Becker continued, "that Mr. Miller and Mr. Ziegler have told you that President Ford is considering a pardon, and I know they've showed you a draft of the document. Now there are certain things you should know about pardons . . ."

"Where do you live?" Nixon interrupted.

"Washington," Becker said.

"How do you think the Redskins will do this year?"

Becker repeatedly tried to steer Nixon, drifting and depressed, back to the subject before them: specifically, the meaning of pardons laid down by the Supreme Court in *Burdick*. "I said, 'The position of the Ford White House will be, if you accept this pardon, that President Nixon understood the law of pardons, and understood that he did not have to accept this pardon. And he understood that the law states that acceptance of a pardon is an imputation of guilt,' " Becker recalls.

"Uh-huh," Nixon said.

After twenty minutes of rambling circumlocution, of Becker walking Nixon through *Burdick* and Ford's interpretation of clemency while Nixon tried to change the subject and talk about trivia—he asked if Becker ever played football—Becker satisfied himself that Nixon was competent and understood what he had done and what he was agreeing to. He recalls: "He did not enjoy talking about the subject. He was uncomfortable and very anxious about it." Never having seen someone so

306 | **31** Days

openly depressed—so defeated, it seemed—Becker rose awkwardly to leave, again complimenting Nixon. "I appreciate," he said, "all the time you gave me. All the good things we did here today."

Becker was outside, about to get in the car for El Toro, when Ziegler came out to say that Nixon wanted to see him again. "My first thought," he wrote, "was that all bets were off." He could imagine no other reason for Nixon summoning him back other than to tell him that he had changed his mind, and when he returned to the office, Nixon was standing, somewhat slumped, behind his desk.

"You've been a fine young man," Nixon told him. "You've been a gentleman. We've had enough bullies." He looked away, his voice faltering.

"You've been so fair and thoughtful that I want to give you something. But look around the office. I don't have anything anymore. They took it all away from me. Everything I had is gone."

"That's all right, Mr. President," Becker said, thinking the scene pathetic and sad.

"No," Nixon said. "I tried to get you a presidential tiepin and cuff links with my name on it, but I don't even have them anymore. There's nothing left from my presidency." Nixon bent forward, opened the desk drawer, and removed two small white boxes. "I asked Pat to get these," he said. "From my personal jewelry box. There aren't any more of these in the world. You've got the last ones." Nixon handed Becker the two boxes, containing a Richard Nixon signature tiepin and a pair of generic presidential seal cuff links—almost, but not quite, the tokens he'd requested. Noting that Nixon was "inches away from tears," Becker thanked Nixon. Unable to recall ever feeling so drained, he excused himself as fast as he politely could. "I just wanted to get the hell out of there," he says.

Becker flew back to Washington with Miller, who acknowledged that Nixon indeed had tried to locate the gifts and was near to distraught when he realized he'd run out of them. The secret military red-eye landed in Washington Saturday morning, in the predawn darkness, and Becker and Miller each got home at about five. It was exactly two weeks since former Nixon adviser Richard Moore had called from Maine to sound out Miller about becoming Nixon's lawyer; ten days since Ford's press conference; nine days since Jaworski shifted the monkey to Ford; five days since Dean went to jail; and less than forty-eight hours since Haig had told Becker he would never get Nixon to release his materials or clearly state that he had done anything wrong.

D A Y

30

Saturday, September 7

A Man in Full

In his short time in office, Ford's standing was never higher, his popularity never stronger, his press never better. The *Post* ran a page-one photograph, taken at Camp David, of him jumping on a trampoline—soaring, smiling, arms outstretched like wings. A Gallup poll showed him leading Ted Kennedy almost two-to-one in a trial heat for the presidency. The *Times* reported in its lead story that Kissinger was near to concluding a deal with the Soviets to release at least sixty thousand Jewish émigrés yearly—a 70 percent increase over the previous amount—in exchange for undisclosed trade benefits, giving Ford a substantial victory over Jackson and the neoconservatives, and a card to play when Israel's Rabin, the next and last Mideast leader to visit Washington, arrived within days for talks.

In the morning, Ford played golf at Burning Tree in a foursome with Laird and two executives of the defense conglomerate General Dynamics—the first round of a weekend tournament. Since guiding Ford to choose Rockefeller for vice president, Laird and Bryce Harlow had remained part of Ford's kitchen cabinet, but Ford had excluded them both from the secret pardon team. Harlow, fearing another dangerous misstep like Ford's August 1 closed-door discussion with Haig, had devised on his own an alternative strategy for dealing with Nixon. He and Laird privately had discussed with Mississippi Democratic senator John Stennis the option of having the bipartisan congressional leadership come to the White House and urge Ford to pardon Nixon—for the good of the country. According to Laird, Stennis had encountered strong support on both sides of the aisle, and the plan was well along.

As they rounded the course, scoring well enough to put them one stroke off the lead, Ford made no mention of the pardon to Laird, one of his closest friends and confidants, even though the Harlow-Stennis plan could provide broad cover for what Ford clearly realized was a high-risk decision. It was as if, once decided, he was determined to show that he was acting out of individual courage, not political calculation, and that he was no one's man but his own—especially not that of the Democratic-controlled Congress, which had dictated his selection to Nixon. Laird thinks Ford kept him in the dark because he knew he and Harlow might succeed in convincing him to change his mind. "He knew what our plan was," Laird says. "He knew what we were trying to do."

Ford returned to the White House and, sitting alone in the Oval Office, finalized his plans for announcing the pardon. He was most concerned about Nixon's statement, which, while technically an admission that he could have been more candid and direct in addressing Watergate, in no way resembled the full-breast confession that Ford, somewhat naively, had hoped he would make. Ford thought Nixon "would be very receptive to the idea of clearing the decks." That Nixon refused to atone left Ford, in effect, out on a limb. He knew critics would say he was establishing a dual system of justice and that a pardon would prevent the public from learning the full story of Watergate. Committed to an act of forgiveness toward an unpopular malefactor who didn't admit any guilt, Ford understood that he now would be left to explain what the American people stood to gain from his mercy.

"Once I determine to move, I seldom, if ever, fret," Ford wrote of his decision to announce the pardon as soon as possible—noon Sunday on national TV. But Nixon's recalcitrance presented Ford, who had no thought of delaying, with excellent reason to worry. How could he explain to the country that giving Nixon immunity was the right thing to do, when Nixon himself refused to admit that his behavior, which had plunged the government into its worst crisis since the Civil War, was a problem? Or that Nixon shouldn't face charges when his aides, who were only following his instructions, went to jail? Or that the benefits, so one-sided in Nixon's favor, didn't simply indicate completion of some sort of deal—a pardon in return for his resignation? "Above all," Ford wrote, "I wanted it understood that my fundamental decision to grant a pardon had nothing to do with any sympathy I might feel for Nixon personally or any concern I might have for the state of his health." Now he realized, reluctantly, fatalistically, that Nixon had made that task much harder, if not impossible.

Ford rarely stewed in anger. He was sure he had made the right decision and therefore proceeded undeterred. He went to the South Lawn, where a helicopter took him to an afternoon event in Alexandria—the police department's annual picnic. Ford wanted to express his appreciation for the inconvenience he'd caused locally by keeping his residence in town after becoming president, and he brought along Dobrynin and two visiting Russian cosmonauts to feast on hard-shell crabs and hot dogs.

"We aren't going to sell our home," he told two hundred fifty officers and their families, hoisting a crab mallet, reveling, apparently, in his enjoyment at being back among his neighbors. "We're going to come back—I don't know how soon." A bushel basket of crabs steamed before him. "Out in Michigan we don't have crabs," he remarked, "but we do have a few crabby people." Goodwill extended in all directions, with Ford demonstrating to his guests how to pry open the shells, then smiling broadly as their hosts brought out a pitcher of beer and hot dogs smothered in mustard, catsup, and relish, which he recommended highly to the cosmonauts: "A very great American delicacy," he said.

"The broader we can make our relationship," Ford declared, "the better it is for us in America and for our friends in the Soviet Union."

* * *

As soon as he returned to the Oval Office, Ford met with Becker, who briefed him in preparation for a final meeting of the full pardon team at 6 P.M.

"I'm not a medical doctor," Becker reported, "but I really have serious questions in my mind whether that man is going to be alive at the time of the election."

"Well," Ford said, "nineteen seventy-six is a long time away."

"I don't mean 1976. I mean 1974."

Becker thought Nixon was an "absolute candidate for suicide: the most depressed human being I have ever met," adding, "and I didn't think it was an act." He believed Ford when he said he gave no thought to the upcoming congressional races in his decision to pardon Nixon two months before Election Day. And yet just as it could not be good for Ford and the Republicans if, after a month in office, he immunized Nixon in what appeared to be the last cynical act of the Watergate cover-up—Nixon's hand-picked successor giving him a pass legally just as his closest aides were about to go to trial—it might well be worse if Nixon died and Ford had missed the opportunity to save him from added, life-threatening punishment.

Indeed, internal pressure now seemed to drive Ford more than any pressure from Nixon, or Jaworski, or politics, as he came to view a swift and sweeping act of mercy toward Nixon not just as the right thing to do but as a redemptive release. His dilemma echoed the one he'd faced in 1939, when Leslie King, claiming to be incapacitated by severe asthma, was jailed for contempt after failing to pay Ford's child support—the act that precipitated Ford's entering his parents' bitter disputes as a "peace-maker." King died soon after the settlement without Ford ever speaking with him again. As Peter Wood points out, Nixon was not the first, or even the most important, "self-centered man from the West who had given [Ford] everything and nothing." Whatever his feelings toward Nixon, what Woods calls a "submerged but controlling personal logic" also factored into Ford's urgency to forgive Nixon before it was too late.

Haig entered, listened intently to Becker's update as if it were news, and appeared to compliment him on the statement he'd extracted from

Nixon, telling him, "What, did you put a gun to his head?"—although, given the mildness of Nixon's confession, and Haig's determination to get Nixon both a pardon and his papers and tapes on the most favorable terms possible, he might equally have been slighting the agreement. "Some of Ford's people were putting considerable pressure on Nixon to render some statement of guilt as a condition of pardon," Haig wrote, ignoring his own role in the negotiations. "Involving myself in this situation would only have made matters worse, so I stood back from it. Besides, I knew that Nixon would go to prison rather than grovel."

After Marsh, Hartmann, Saxbe, and Buchen joined them, terHorst arrived, having been informed only that Ford planned to make a major announcement and needed the press office to arrange it. According to Hartmann, terHorst first learned that Ford was planning to pardon Nixon during the flight back from Philadelphia on Friday night, when Ford called a few of his top aides up to the forward cabin to discuss plans for the announcement. TerHorst nonetheless reacted in the Oval Office with shock; in fact, he was hearing Ford's decision, and realizing how misled he had been, for the first time. "I was stunned by it, frankly," he recalls, "stunned to know that it had progressed so far that it was going to be announced the next day."

Following the frustrations of the previous week, terHorst was scarcely relieved to hear that Ford thought that by not telling him, he was protecting terHorst's relations with the press. Ford wrote that he didn't want terHorst to have to lie, nor could he afford to have him tell the truth. What was worse for terHorst, especially in light of the toxic enmity between the press and the White House under Nixon and Ziegler, was giving answers that, in retrospect, looked evasive, simply because he didn't know what the president was doing. Knowing each other for more than twenty-five years, trusting in each other's honesty, hadn't provided Ford or terHorst the least inkling of what the other felt he had to say and do regarding the most closely held of presidential secrets.

As the questions turned to terHorst, he reeled, but answered technically. "It's manageable," he said. "We can do it. I can get here early in the morning. We'll get copies made. I'll have to alert the press. It's Sunday morning so I'll have to say, 'You have to come down to the White House but I can't tell you why.' I'll say it's an important announcement."

TerHorst paused, adding, "I'm going to have to do something about *Time* and *Newsweek* because they're putting their covers to bed right now." The care and feeding of the newsweeklies was hornbook Washington media strategy, and terHorst knew implicitly that how they played the pardon story would help frame the popular narrative that would shape public opinion. Whatever the American people came to believe about Ford's motives for granting Nixon clemency so soon—less than two weeks after he pledged not to make any decision until events required him to—terHorst knew that the press reaction would be swift, hostile, and violent. Without time to lay the groundwork, he hoped at least to perpetuate the impression that Ford was acting, above all, out of conscience, in the best interest of the nation, and beyond normal Washington politics.

TerHorst raised no objection to the pardon itself. He suggested that someone other than Ford would be needed in the press room to explain the White House action, and Buchen volunteered, the logical—and under the circumstances, only—choice. In his haste, Ford had lined up no surrogates, no congressional or party elders, no cabinet secretaries or editorialists or anyone else who could rally support, blunt criticism, and share the heat. TerHorst himself, after first repeating for weeks Ford's assertion as a nominee for vice president that he wouldn't pardon Nixon because he didn't think the American people would stand for it, then saying again and again that Ford would make no decision until the matter reached his desk, which it hadn't, was plainly disqualified.

* * *

Becker and Haig left together for Haig's office to find a secure line to phone Ziegler, who since before noon had been seeking ways to water down Nixon's statement. Ziegler was pressing hard to change two essential points in what Becker considered Nixon's confession—replacing

Nixon's *I* with *the White House* and removing any reference to "judicial proceedings"—so that Nixon's statement read, "I can see clearly now that *the White House* was wrong in not acting more decisively and more forthrightly in dealing with Watergate, particularly when it . . . grew from a political scandal to a national tragedy." Becker had told Ford during their discussion about Nixon's attempts to backtrack, advising, "I'm afraid if this continues, we'll be back to square one," and Ford had instructed, "We can't tolerate any weakened statement." Now Ziegler refused to yield, even as Haig and Becker arranged with Ziegler and terHorst, who'd returned to the press office, to have Nixon's statement released simultaneously in San Clemente and the White House press room right after Ford signed the pardon. Saxbe, too, went off, leaving Ford alone with his closest advisers to discuss his announcement speech.

Ford leaned back in his chair and clasped his hands behind his head, staring at the ceiling. "He began to recite tentatively the reasons he would give for his pardon decision," Hartmann wrote. Marsh, Buchen, and Hartmann suggested alternate phrasings and pointed out misstatements of law or fact, but mostly Ford spelled out what he planned to say to the nation in his own words. Hartmann, before leaving to spend the night polishing and revising, gathered his notes, then hesitated at the doorway. "Can I ask you just one question?" he said.

"Sure," Ford said. "So long as you don't try to talk me out of it."

"No, that's not it," Hartmann told him. "I think I understand your reasoning. But one thing still bothers me, and you haven't answered it. What's the rush? Why must it be tomorrow? Why not Christmas Eve, or a year from now, when things quiet down?"

"Well," Ford said, "someone—some of the newspeople—might ask me about it again."

"But all you have to do is say you haven't decided."

"But I *have* decided," Ford said.

Ford's immovability—his staunch offensive and defensive blocking—convinced Hartmann, like Marsh, that there was no changing his mind and thus no point in trying. Becker, too, suspended his qualms in the face of Ford's lonely determination. He recalls Ford telling him before he went to San Clemente, "There have been too many decisions made in this office in the past few years because of politics. This question has nothing to do with politics. When the time is right, I'll do the right thing." Devoting oneself to serving a president often means opting to view his intransigence as steadfastness, his stubbornness as guts, and Ford, more than anything else, seemed certain that the time had come for him to act.

TerHorst was less persuaded. Driving home at dusk to Alexandria, he weighed the situation—and his options. First, there was his, and Ford's credibility, which he knew would be severely breached. "To have been left out of the loop was a clear signal that I was not to be considered one of President Ford's true confidants," he says. "It's pretty damn hard to be a press secretary after something like that. It's not what I signed on for." He was concerned in light of all the White House had done to raise the issue of welcoming back war resisters, that pardoning Nixon would taint that effort, too, and that Ford was establishing a "double standard" of justice for Nixon and the men who served him. "That," he says, "pissed me off."

When terHorst got home, his wife was meeting with a photographer they'd hired to take pictures of their family, and together they went over stacks of proofs until nearly midnight. "My heart wasn't really in it, to tell the truth," he says. "But it had to be done." Alone, finally, he explained to her that he had to return early to the White House and, trusting her to tell no one, why he had to be there.

"And what are you going to do?" she said.

TerHorst replied, "I'm resigning."

Ford awoke early and took 8 A.M. Holy Communion at St. John's Epis-
copal Church, the "Church of the Presidents" across Lafayette Square
from the White House. He prayed alone, asking, he said, for "guidance
and understanding," in pew 54, where every president since James Madison had worshipped. As he was leaving, reporters asked what he was doing for the rest of the day. "You'll find out soon enough," Ford said.

Back at the Wilson desk, he read over his speech—twice. Hartmann
had written, "It is common knowledge that serious allegations and accu-
sations hang like a sword over our former President's head." With a felt-
tipped marker, Ford inserted, "*. . . threatening his health as he tries to
reshape his life, a great part of which was spent in the service of his country
and the mandate of its people.*" Morning sun slanted through the bulletproof glass of the windows along the Rose Garden. Just before ten—
about an hour before he was to go in front of the TV cameras—Ford
phoned the leaders of Congress to notify them in advance of the pardon.

"What are you pardoning him of?" Goldwater asked. Vacationing in
California, he'd been awakened by the call. "It doesn't make any sense."

"The public has the right to know that, in the eyes of the President,

Nixon is clear," Ford said. Ford's use of the word *clear* stunned Gold-water. The right's fallen standard-bearer, whom Nixon considered a re-actionary, had watched Nixon's descent with a darkening rage, telling Nixon finally that he had to go after the tapes came out a month earlier. "He may be clear in your eyes, but he's not clear in mine," he told Ford.

Ford contacted Tip O'Neill in Harwichport, on Cape Cod. "Tip, I've made up my mind to pardon Nixon," he said. "I'm doing it because I think it's right for our country, and because it feels right in my heart. The man is so depressed, and I don't want to see a former President go to jail."

"I'm telling you right now," O'Neill said, "this will cost you the elec-tion. I hope it's not part of any deal."

"No, there's no deal."

"Then why the hell are you doing it?" O'Neill said.

Ford explained that Nixon was a "sick man" and that his daughter Julie "keeps calling me because her father is so depressed."

"Look," O'Neill said. "I know you're not calling me for my advice, but I think it's too soon."

Why now? One after another Ford's former colleagues in Congress, conservatives and liberals alike, expressed their dismay, anger, and confu-sion about his decision, but in the end their objections shrank mostly to this: It was too soon. Watergate had been a series of grave, worsening shocks—bombshells. After each, Nixon had offered some new defense, some new lie or evasion, and the country hunkered warily waiting for the next explosion. The Senate hearings, Agnew's stepping-down, the Sat-urday Night Massacre, the eighteen-and-a-half minute gap in a crucial tape, the indictments and imprisonment of top White House aides, the impeachment proceedings, Nixon's resignation—each barrage had bat-tered the White House, Washington, the country, the economy, and ul-timately the nation's confidence in itself and its leaders. Nerves were shot. Ford may have been right that if he knew he would pardon Nixon someday, nothing justified waiting, but his urgency seemed imprudent, willful, somehow more a personal statement of his need to make Nixon go away than a judicious act of state. Or else there had been a deal—an-other crushing blow.

TerHorst entered while Ford was on the phone and Ford waved him to his usual seat, a deep-cushioned yellow chair to the left of his desk that a navy steward, as always, had just plumped up. TerHorst, up all night, carried a manila envelope on which he'd written in red: "The President— Eyes Only." It contained his resignation letter. "Mr. President," he said, "I wanted to see you for a few moments before you went on the air with the pardon proclamation since I knew—"

Ford interrupted: "Everything all set? What's the time, ten forty-five?" "Closer to eleven," terHorst said. "It'll take that long to get the cameras and lights set up." Ford planned to make the rest of his calls from another office as a network crew readied the room for the announcement.

TerHorst started again more determinedly. He tore open the envelope and handed the letter to Ford, who leaned back in his outsized leather chair and began reading:

> . . . So it is with great regret, after long soul-searching, that I must inform you that I cannot in good conscience support your decision to pardon former President Nixon even before he has been charged with the commission of any crime. As your spokesman, I do not know how I could credibly defend that action in the absence of a like decision to grant absolute pardon to the young men who evaded military service as a matter of conscience and the absence of pardons for former aides of Mr. Nixon who have been charged with crimes—and imprisoned . . . Try as I can, it is impossible to conclude that the former President is more deserving of mercy than persons of lesser station in life whose offenses have had far less effect on our national well-being.

Ford had no time to consider the full implications of terHorst's choosing to make a stand based on "conscience" at that same time that he, Ford, was making one on his. "Well, Jerry, I'm sorry you feel that way," he said. "It was not an easy decision for me to make." Ford spoke evenly, solemnly, his face, terHorst wrote, "betraying no sign of emotion or surprise." "I know there will be controversy over this, but it's the right thing to do, and that's why I decided to do it now. I hope you can see that."

"I'm sorry, Mr. President," terHorst said. Ford rose and they shook hands. "I'm sorry, too," he said.

TerHorst walked back to his office to finish his preparations. Usually, the media received mimeographed copies of White House papers to be publicly released, but terHorst, fearing leaks, had decided not to make advance stencils of the texts of the four documents that would be distributed immediately following Ford's announcement: the pardon proclamation itself, Ford's speech, Saxbe's memo, and Nixon's statement. On Saturday night, Becker had given him a tentative draft of Nixon's apology, but now, with less than a half hour to go before Ford addressed the cameras, Becker advised Ford to "expect some changes." Becker and Haig had an open phone line to San Clemente, and Ziegler was continuing to backtrack. As three secretaries ran off copies of the other documents in the basement message center, a White House police officer posted at the door, terHorst wondered dismally how Ford could grant Nixon an unconditional pardon without getting in return a genuine confession.

While terHorst waited for the final version and attended to technical problems—the sound engineers were having difficulty with the wiring in the Oval Office, and the cameraman reported he couldn't find a film reel long enough if Ford went over ten minutes—Marsh entered terHorst's office visibly agitated. "Jerry," he said, "you can't do it. Please reconsider . . . even for twenty-four hours. Let me give the letter back to you.

"Don't hurt the President this way—not today."

Marsh's "utter sincerity" and "abject tone" crumpled terHorst's resolve, terHorst later wrote. Telling Marsh he wasn't changing his mind, only that he was willing to take a few hours to rethink his decision, he took back the letter, folded it, and tucked it in the inner breast pocket of his jacket. Marsh recalls: "I got him turned around." Looking at his watch, terHorst noted that it was five minutes before eleven.

* * *

The tolling of hourly church bells around Washington delayed the start of taping until 11:01, when Ford faced the camera and began to read.

"Ladies and gentlemen," he said, peering ahead, his jaw set squarely, "I have come to a decision which I felt I should tell you and all my fellow American citizens as soon as I was certain in my own mind and in my own conscience that it is the right thing to do."

After much reflection and prayer, Ford said, he had come to understand that Nixon's "was an American tragedy in which we have all played a part." He acknowledged that there were no precedents for his action, and said he'd been advised by the special prosecutor's office that bringing Nixon to justice might take a year or more. "Ugly passions would again be aroused," Ford said heavily, "our people again would be polarized in their opinions, and the credibility of our free institutions of government would again be challenged at home and abroad." He noted that if the courts ultimately decided that Nixon had been deprived of his right to a fair trial, he could be exonerated "and the verdict of history would be even more inconclusive" with respect to his role in Watergate.

"But it is not the ultimate fate of Richard Nixon that most concerns me—though surely it troubles every decent and compassionate person—but the immediate future of this great country," Ford continued. Weighing his duty to the Constitution against his responsibility to the "laws of God, which govern our consciences," he said, he'd concluded, after seeking guidance and searching his soul, that the latter were "superior."

". . . As President, my primary concern must always be the greatest good of all the people of the United States whose servant I am. As a man my first consideration is to be true to my own convictions and my own conscience.

"My conscience tells me clearly and certainly that I cannot continue to prolong the bad dreams that continue to reopen a chapter that is closed. My conscience tells me that only I, as President, have the constitutional power to firmly shut and seal this book. My conscience tells me it is my duty not merely to proclaim domestic tranquility but to use every means that I have to ensure it.

"I do believe," Ford said, "that the buck stops here and that I cannot rely upon public opinion polls to tell me what is right. I do believe that right makes might, and that if I am wrong, ten angels swearing I was right would make no difference. I do believe with all my heart and mind and spirit that I, not as President, but as a humble servant of God, will receive justice without mercy if I fail to show mercy."

Nixon and his family had "suffered enough, and will continue to suffer no matter what I do," Ford said. With that, he read a single sentence proclaiming a "full, free, and absolute pardon unto Richard Nixon for all offenses against the United States which he . . . has committed or may have committed or taken part in" during his five and a half years as president.

With a looping left hand, oddly ungraceful looking, Ford signed the document.

* * *

Less than ten minutes after Ford finished reading, Ziegler, in San Clemente, released Nixon's statement. Nixon wrote:

> In accepting this pardon, I hope that [President Ford's] compassionate act will contribute to lifting the burden of Watergate from our country.
>
> Here in California, my perspective on Watergate is quite different than it was while I was embattled in the midst of the controversy, and while I was still subject to the unrelenting daily demands of the Presidency itself.
>
> Looking back on what is still, in my mind, a complex and confusing maze of events, decisions, pressures and personalities, one thing I can see clearly now is that I was wrong in not acting more decisively and more forthrightly in dealing with Watergate, particularly when it reached the stage of judicial proceedings and grew from a political scandal into a national tragedy.
>
> No words can describe the depths of my regret and pain at the

anguish my mistakes over Watergate have caused the nation and the Presidency, a nation I so deeply love and an institution I so greatly respect.

I know that many fair-minded people believe that my motivation and actions in the Watergate affair were intentionally self-serving and illegal. I now understand how my own mistakes and misjudgments have contributed to that belief and seemed to support it. This burden is the heaviest one of all to bear.

That the way I tried to deal with Watergate was the wrong way is a burden that I shall bear for every day of the life that is left to me.

Nixon was on the road when the pardon was announced, traveling with Pat in the back of a black limousine for the Palm Desert estate of Walter Annenberg, ambassador to Britain—a "new haven of seclusion away from the heavily guarded Casa Pacifica," according to the *Times*. Located at the corner of Bob Hope Drive and Frank Sinatra Drive, the lush two-hundred-twenty-acre estate, Sunnylands, had a twenty-five-thousand-square-foot main house, private lakes, a massive swimming pool, and a nine-hole golf course. It was surrounded by seven hundred acres of desert.

"This is the most humiliating day of my life," he told her.

He had traded for the pardon and gotten it on his terms. With his materials secure, he now knew that he would be able to write his version of events, make money—begin, as he'd planned from the moment he realized he had lost all support and decided to become the first American to resign the office of president, to rehabilitate himself, perhaps even regain a role in world affairs. Unlike Haldeman, Ehrlichman, Mitchell, and dozens more of those who worked under him at the White House and ran his last triumphal campaign, he didn't face the oblivion of jail; his family could move on. He had admitted to "mistakes" and "misjudgments," nothing more.

And yet with all that, there was no assurance that he hadn't made it still harder, if not impossible, to rescue his legacy—how he would be remembered, what future generations would say about him—the verdict he cared about more than any other. Nixon had shaped the world, redefined American politics, struggled back from defeats that would have conquered anyone who didn't possess his murderous will to succeed. But that was unlikely to be how history would view him. The tapes ultimately revealed, beyond his crimes, the inner Nixon, the hater. The pardon certified the magnitude of his failure, a permanent public reminder . . . *"And then you destroy yourself"* . . . It may have looked to the world like he had won a victory, an escape, absolution, but Nixon intuited otherwise, and his depression deepened. "The reason," Stephen Ambrose wrote, "would appear to be that he realized that it did not matter that he had not acknowledged guilt in his statement: he knew that his acceptance of the pardon nevertheless acknowledged guilt."

Full, free, and absolute, a pardon was also damning and irrevocable—especially for a presumed offender who never was so much as charged with a crime. "Next to the resignation," Nixon wrote, "accepting the pardon was the most painful decision of my political career."

* * *

In Idaho, Evel Knievel was strapped into what he called the Sky-Cycle X-2, spewing steam at the foot of a steep 108-foot launching track aimed at a cloudless sky. The steam exploded through a rear nozzle, propelling Knievel up the track when, suddenly, a drag parachute designed to slow the rocket at an altitude of twenty-eight-hundred feet deployed. The chute whipped wildly in the blasting steam.

Once airborne, the vehicle, designed by a NASA engineer who stood to earn $100,000 if Knievel made it safely to the other side of the canyon, went belly up. The main chute, attached to the drogue, deployed automatically at about a thousand feet.

"A large crowd along the canyon's south rim gasped as a 15-mile-an-hour wind blew the vehicle back toward them, rocking gently in the air nose-down like a red, white, and blue Christmas ornament," the *Times* reported. Knievel struggled in the open cockpit as it appeared that he might crash into the crowd . . . until the vehicle dropped onto a boulder-strewn ledge, bounced twice, and came to rest about twenty feet from the Snake River. For several minutes there was no sign of the stuntman; then a helicopter picked him up and deposited him back among the crowd.

"I couldn't get my safety belt unharnessed," he said, recounting the danger. "I was strapped in pretty tight. Thank God I didn't go into the water. If I'd gone into the river I never could have got out." Knievel suffered cuts on his arms, knees, and face, the latter occurring when he ripped off his helmet and visor during the flight. The aborted stunt, and the recognition that Knievel's life had indeed been briefly imperiled, seemed to satisfy most of those who had trekked to Twin Falls, but many of those who paid to watch the two-hour telecast in theaters felt cheated, ripped off. Knievel himself was noncommittal about making any repeat attempts. He urged everyone to "live life as God wants you to live it" and "don't take a narcotic" and he professed his belief in God and America. "Today is the proudest day of my life," Knievel said. "I'm living a dream that nobody else thought possible. A man is meant to live, not just to survive."

* * *

TWA Flight 841 from Tel Aviv to New York stopped in Athens, then took off for a second layover in Rome. Forty-nine passengers—seventeen American; also Japanese, Italian, French, Indian, Iranian, Ceylonese, Australian, Canadian, and Israeli—had boarded the Boeing 707 in Israel and were joined by twenty more Americans and another Canadian in Greece. There was a crew of nine. The sky was overcast.

The pilot reported trouble after leaving the Greek mainland, saying he was going to try to make it to the island of Corfu because one engine was on fire. Eighteen minutes after takeoff, ground controllers lost contact with the plane, which exploded and plunged into the stormy Ionian sea. No one survived. Though a TWA spokesman in New York said sabotage was "highly unlikely," a youth organization in Beirut connected with Palestinian terrorist leader Abu Nidal claimed that it had placed a guerrilla aboard with a bomb.

As Knievel extolled his accomplishment—and moral vision—the country imbibed its first taste of a new political tactic, the first known example of a young Arab willing to go to his death to kill civilians aboard an American-bound airplane. Four years after the PLO had removed all hostages before blowing up several *empty* planes on the ground in Jordan, sparking the events of Black September, aviation officials scoffed at the idea that terrorism was involved.

* * *

At Sunnylands, Nixon stayed inside. "It was blazing hot," Ambrose wrote, "over 110 degrees; reporters and photographers hung around the place, telephoto lenses ready; a helicopter flew overhead . . ." Only a military aide and several Secret Service agents had accompanied Nixon and Pat on the trip, and Annenberg, an old friend and financial backer, was in Europe. Julie, in New York, told the AP her father had gone to the estate for a rest.

He planned to visit for about a week. In the mornings he would go out and play some golf on Annenberg's private course. His leg was feeling tender, but he believed he was OK to play. Unlike for Ford, sports and games mainly provided Nixon opportunities to test himself, a crucible: "What starts the process are the laughs and snubs and slights you get when you are a kid," he told a former aide around this time, explaining why he'd played football despite being a poor athlete. ". . . I tried and tried and tried. To get discipline for myself and show others that here was a guy who could dish it out and take it. Mostly I took it." During his first term in the White House, he'd exhorted himself on one of his legal pads: "Stop recreation except purely for exercise."

The solitary exile in the broiling California desert agreed with him. Nixon extolled what he called the "wilderness syndrome"—the phenomenon of withdrawal and return—and he liked to compare himself to other great figures who were cast out from the world after suffering shattering defeats and returned stronger for it. Thucydides, Muhammad, Confucius, Peter the Great, Garibaldi, Lenin, Churchill, de Gaulle—all had been dismissed, taken flight, and emerged transfigured. He himself had experienced the syndrome when he rose from his defeat for California governor to win the White House. As depressed as he was, he was looking ahead to being somehow back in, if not power, at least control again.

"The Watergate saga," psychobiographer James Barber wrote, ". . . took its shape from Nixon's old sense that nothing would be right unless he controlled the way of it." Indeed, it was Nixon's hubris and sense of entitlement—confusing power with control—that had caused his downfall. And just as that was evident now, it had always been there on display, even when he was being, as Elliot Richardson observed, the "architect of his times."

Even, that is, in his crowning moments. In May 1971, after reducing the business of national security to what Richard Reeves called a "two-man operation," Nixon had received word from Kissinger of a breakthrough in the SALT talks. There had been formal talks with the Soviets in Vienna—seventy-four separate sessions—but the real negotiations were between Kissinger and Dobrynin, and among those left in the dark had been Secretary of State William Rogers and the chief negotiator and head of the arms control and disarmament agency.

To celebrate, Nixon invited Kissinger, Haldeman, Ehrlichman, and Colson for a dinner cruise on the presidential yacht *Sequoia*, where after several toasts he turned from praising the upcoming announcement—a triumph, he felt, of secrecy and deception in service of getting great things done—to denouncing press leaks. "One day we will get them—we'll get them on the ground where we want them," he told Kissinger and Colson. "And we'll stick our heels in, step on them hard and twist—right Chuck, right? Henry knows what I mean—just like you do it in negotiations, Henry—get them on the floor and step on them, crush them, show no mercy."

Rogers, an old friend of Nixon, had been shattered when he found out about the agreement; he offered to resign, describing himself to Haldeman as a "laughingstock." Nixon had Haldeman explain to him that since arms control cut across all departments, "this had been handled at the highest level and it was essential that no one take credit for this except the President himself," Reeves wrote. Equating power with seizing every rein, Nixon laid down the "party line," and when Rogers called to ask what he should tell his department and Congress, Nixon returned the call personally.

After he hung up, Nixon spun his chair and looked out to the Rose Garden. "This would be an easy job," he said, "if you didn't have to deal with people."

Amid the still opulence of Sunnylands, it was not hard to see the arc of Nixon's rise and fall—it cast deepening shadows. It was the illusion that supremacy conferred illimitable power, and the destructive confusion that that had caused in Nixon's mind. "When the President does it," Nixon once said, "that means that it is not illegal."

But then he was no longer president.

* * *

Leaving the White House after recording the pardon announcement, Ford felt at once an "unbelievable lifting of a burden from my shoulders." "Finally, it was done," he wrote. "I felt very certain that I had made the right decision, and I was confident that I could now proceed without being harassed by Nixon and his problems any more." He walked down the hall to the office where Haig, Hartmann, and Marsh were sampling congressional opinion—the initial responses were good—then left by motorcade for Burning Tree.

At the clubhouse, Ford asked Laird what he thought. "We're still in this tournament and we have a pretty good chance of doing well," Laird told him. "I don't want to talk to you about the pardon now. Let's play golf, and we can talk about it later." Perhaps in part because he'd been left out of the decision, Laird thought Ford had "screwed it up," he says.

By the time Ford got back to the White House, at about seven, he could see that Laird might be right. Even as Buchen had still been briefing reporters in the press room an hour after the pardon announcement was flashed nationwide—introduced for the first time as White House counsel, Buchen sat in a chair throughout the grilling—the White House switchboard lit up with "angry calls, heavy and constant." The operators were jammed, and terHorst got word during the briefing that reaction was "running 8 to 1 against."

After the briefing, terHorst convened his staff privately and told them that he was resigning. He made arrangements to remove himself from Ford's trip Monday to Pittsburgh to speak to eight hundred delegates at a conference on urban transportation. He suggested to his deputy that Ford himself should tell the press about his resignation on the return flight to Washington, to salvage something from the détente between the White House and the press corps.

TerHorst also took a call from *Newsweek*'s chief White House correspondent, who thanked him for suggesting earlier in the day that the magazine hold its cover story on the Vietnam amnesty. As they spoke, the reporter asked if Ford's decision on the pardon had been supported by the entire White House staff, and, if not, whether anyone had resigned. Knowing that word of his resignation would be out within another day, terHorst "decided not to keep the truth" from the magazine, which, aware of its exclusive, put out a press release that was picked up by the wire services and the networks. "Within a very short time," he wrote, "the report of my decision to resign was national news."

The storm flared at once. Ever since Ford had introduced terHorst, his first appointee as president, to the press corps a month earlier as "one of yours," the press, Mary McGrory wrote, "had lost its head for Jerry Ford." Now, nearly all reporters took terHorst's side in his protest against Ford's decision. "I resigned," he told them, "because I just couldn't remain part of an act that I felt was ethically wrong." For all Ford's discussion of God and conscience, the press concluded intrinsically that terHorst's act of conscience trumped the president's. By late afternoon, as the networks prepared their telecasts, terHorst's resignation was being grafted high onto bulletins of Ford's announcement: "another shock," reported ABC's Steve Bell, who quoted terHorst's statement before recounting Ford's speech. "Mercy," terHorst said, "like justice, must also be evenhanded."

The spectacle of a top administration official resigning in protest inevitably recalled the Saturday Night Massacre. Elliot Richardson's refusal ten months earlier to fire Special Watergate Prosecutor Archibald Cox and his decision to quit instead had unleashed a torrent of public outrage so furious that it forced Nixon to hire Jaworski, triggered the first serious impeachment efforts in Congress, and set up the fatal confrontation over the tapes in the Supreme Court. "For the first time," Nixon later wrote of the firestorm, "I realized how few people could see things from my perspective, how badly frayed the nerves of the American public had become." Now, thanks to the shock of the pardon, its suspicious-looking weekend timing exactly one month after Ford's swearing-in, and terHorst, Ford was about to face a similar reckoning.

Before returning to the residence, Ford went to the Oval Office to compose a statement to give out in response to terHorst's decision. "I deeply regret Jerry terHorst's resignation," Ford wrote. "I understand his position. I appreciate the fact that good people will differ with me on this very difficult decision. However, it is my judgment that is in the best interest of our country." After routing the statement to the press office, he left to join Betty, Susan, and a friend of Susan's, Gardner Britt, who also had come along to Camp David, for Sunday supper. He knew that he would be attacked heavily, but seemed unperturbed. "Jerry was unresentful," Betty wrote. "He hadn't asked for advice from anyone."

Ford's urgent compulsion to forgive—and to expect the same from others—released him from having to worry that he might not have done all he could to keep Nixon from prison, or worse. Yet that same impulse, that self-sacrificing logic of trying to make peace by impaling himself on an explosive and haunting past, as if smothering a grenade, halted Ford's upward progress. Whether for the country's sake as he said, or for Nixon's, or for his own, his decision to act swiftly and mercifully toward his predecessor revealed an overpowering inner need to put the past behind, to bury it. Like Ford's father, Nixon had bequeathed Ford a ruinous domestic state, and Ford had closed out the matter as only he could do, by taking it upon himself to try to split the difference and then seal the record as part of the agreement.

Nixon, Ford recognized, could have helped him enormously by atoning. That Nixon refused to admit any more than that he had acted wrongly and regretted doing so saddled Ford with the very legacy that for a month he'd struggled to avoid—Watergate. And yet Ford bore those who criticized him no ill will, another quality of mercy that he now believed would lead the country to appreciate and understand his motives. As Washington's consensus candidate to replace Nixon, he had done what the other main parties of interest—Congress and Jaworski— agreed was necessary, but were unable or unwilling to do. And so Ford remained unapologetic and hopeful. It wasn't within his character to anticipate what he called the "vehemence of the hostile reaction to my decision."

"I thought people would consider his resignation from the Presidency as sufficient punishment and shame," he lamented. "I thought there would be greater forgiveness."

EPILOGUE

With a penstroke, Gerald Ford spent away almost all that he had gained simply by not being Richard Nixon—the bipartisan goodwill, the trust and affection of a divided nation that didn't know him but was willing to extend him the benefit of the doubt. His monthlong honeymoon, which he and the Republicans hoped would propel them through the fall elections, crumpled overnight. The next day in Pittsburgh, protesters booed and chanted "Jail Ford!" as he arrived downtown for a speech on inflation; a few waved signs saying "terHorst in '76." Shock, disillusion, anger—outrage—erupted from all sides. Calling the pardon a "profoundly unwise, divisive and unjust act," the *Times* lectured in an editorial: "This blundering intervention is a body blow to the President's own credibility and to the public's reviving confidence in the integrity of its Government." Conservative columnist George Will wrote: "The lethal fact is that Mr. Ford has now demonstrated that . . . he doesn't mean what he says." Ford's popularity plunged from 70 percent to 48 percent. Fewer than 20 percent of voters identified themselves as Republicans.

Pardoning Nixon when he did, the way that he did, aborted the widespread hope—both shared and promoted by Ford, his team, and most of the press—that his candor, decency, and courage could clear up the wreckage of Watergate. "His action had quite the opposite effect from that which Ford intended," his biographer John Robert Greene wrote. "Rather than ridding himself of the ghost of Nixon past, the pardon—negotiated in secret, created on advice from Ford's inner circle, and given on terms clearly in Nixon's favor—threatened to strangle any attempt to initiate a Ford Presidency . . . Ford's image was the main casualty . . . Many journalists stopped writing stories about English muffins and Ford as an average guy and began treating Ford as just another Nixon clone in the White House—deceitful, controlled by the leftover Nixonites, and in general no different than any of his immediate predecessors."

Congress, freed of the necessity of further accommodation toward an unexpectedly popular leader, bolted, as Democrats and Republicans alike calculated the cost of the pardon decision and Ford's sudden vulnerability. The day after the Pittsburgh protests, the Senate voted 55–24 to pass a resolution opposing any more Watergate pardons until the defendants had been tried, found guilty, and exhausted all their appeals. The House hurriedly passed two resolutions asking the White House to submit "full and complete information and facts" regarding how the decision was made, in particular whether Ford had discussed the pardon with Nixon, Jaworski, Saxbe, or Rockefeller. On September 24, the House voted overwhelmingly to block funding for military assistance to Turkey, the first time in two decades that Congress had initiated a foreign policy decision in direct opposition to a president's wishes. (Ford would veto the legislation twice, the House overriding him both times.) Two days later Betty Ford was diagnosed with breast cancer; promptly operated upon, she returned to the White House with her husband plainly distracted and shaken.

As Ford struggled to regain momentum throughout the fall, trying to explain and defend himself while campaigning for congressional candidates for whom he now was as much a liability as an asset, his major policy initiatives fell flat. Less than one fifth of eligible antiwar exiles signed up for his clemency plan, the "Vietnam Era Reconciliation Program," announced in mid-September. His economic prescription, following the ballyhooed anti-inflation summit, was a "placebo," *Newsweek* wrote; a thirty-one-point compromise package with something for everyone but little hard action against stagflation. The government issued, and Ford wore prominently in his lapel, red-and-white WIN buttons—an acronym for Whip Inflation Now. They "should have said PUNT," Minnesota Democratic senator Walter Mondale complained. In the crucial area of energy conservation, Ford ignored urgent recommendations from his staff to propose a ten- to twenty-cent tax increase on gasoline, in favor of largely voluntary measures from cold-water laundering to bicycling.

In mid-October, attempting to quell the upheaval and retake the initiative, Ford testified before a House subcommittee about the pardon, the first president in U.S. history to answer lawmakers' questions under oath. Marsh, Hartmann, and Buchen helped him prepare his testimony, in which he stated that the purpose of the pardon was to "change our national focus." Ford recounted his meeting with Haig on August 1, when Haig presented him with the pardon options, and his subsequent phone call the following day when he told Haig their discussion should "not be given any consideration in whatever decision the President might make." "People question whether or not in fact there was a deal," Representative Elizabeth Holtzman of New York said. Ford answered: "There was no deal, period, under no circumstances."

Without benefit of a vice president—Congress took Rockefeller's nomination hostage, prolonging his confirmation until after the election—Ford could do little to stem the furor from carrying through at the polls in November, despite delivering eighty-five speeches in twenty states during the campaign. Democrats dramatically increased their majorities on Capitol Hill, and a new class of reformers—"Watergate babies"—swarmed into Washington. Even Ford's closest allies, such as House Minority Leader John Rhodes, blamed Ford's handling of the pardon squarely for the rout, which sharply reduced party loyalty toward Ford, and his economic stewardship. Unemployment deepened through the end of 1974, as Ford, the party, and the nation started to look ahead to the 1976 presidential election.

* * *

On his third morning at Sunnylands, Nixon played a round of golf on Annenberg's private course, and although he complained of tenderness in his left leg, he seemed to a companion to be relaxed and enjoying himself. An aide noticed some swelling—enough so that, when a cardiologist arrived to examine him, Nixon couldn't pull his trouser cuff over his knee and had to drop his pants instead. By the time he returned to San Clemente a few days later, he had developed two blood clots and was, according to White House physician Major General Walter Tkach, "ravaged" with pain. "You have to go to the hospital," Tkach ordered. Nixon, his state of mind grave, refused: "If I go to the hospital," he said, "I'll never get out of there alive."

Such was Nixon's condition when he phoned Ford eight days after the pardon to say he was sorry he had caused Ford so much trouble and offered to reject Ford's act of clemency if it would help. Ford, thinking the offer no more than a gesture, told Nixon no. "I've done it, and I think it was the right decision, and I think history will prove my point."

The mystery of just how ill Nixon was—and how despondent—preoccupied the press, a confusing counterpoint to Ford's unfolding crisis. Tkach told *Newsweek*, "It's going to take a miracle for him to recover. I'm not sure I can pull him through." When Nixon finally was admitted to a hospital in late September, Ziegler told reporters: "He is not having any psychiatric problems—not at all . . . He is feeling like anyone would feel after going through a great and severe loss and after going through the uncertainty of the past forty-five days . . ." Then Irving Lazar sold the rights to Nixon's memoirs to Warner Books for $2.5 million; a few days later Nixon left the hospital, looking awful, his face sagging. "I feel great," he said, rising from a wheelchair. "Just great."

Nixon's relief lasted just briefly. With jury selection due to begin in the Watergate cover-up trial, he faced having to testify in court. Moreover, as the General Service Administration began construction on a $100,000 vault in a pyramid-shaped federal building near San Clemente for

Nixon's papers, congressional opposition rose sharply to the deed of gift negotiated by Becker and Miller. Construction of the vault was halted on October 3, and the following day the Senate voted 56–7 to direct the Ford administration to retain custody of Nixon's papers and tapes. The bill contained a flat prohibition against destroying any Watergate tapes.

Within months, Congress, reacting vehemently against what it perceived to be part of a bargain surrounding the pardon, passed the Presidential Recordings and Materials Preservation Act of 1974, directing the National Archives to seize possession and control of Nixon's papers, records, and tapes. The act specified the "need to provide the public with the full truth, at the earliest reasonable date, of the abuses of governmental power popularly identified under the generic term 'Watergate.'" Nixon retained Miller to challenge the new law on grounds that it violated the constitutional right of executive privilege. The effort failed, ultimately, in the Supreme Court.

* * *

On September 16, 1974, Ford announced the appointment of Alexander Haig as supreme allied commander in Europe, sparking unprecedented demands in Congress that Haig submit to a confirmation hearing before the Senate Armed Services Committee. "He was surrogate president during the last months of the Nixon Administration," Wisconsin Democratic senator William Proxmire said. "I'd like to put him under oath to learn his role in the Nixon pardon."

Haig escaped legal and legislative scrutiny for his role in the White House, but not the hostilities with Ford's men. On the morning before Haig's departure for Europe, Buzhardt, still working in the West Wing, phoned him at home to say that the group preparing Ford to go before Congress about the pardon had "prepared sworn testimony for the President that could very well result in your indictment," Haig wrote. Agitated, he drove to the White House, read the draft of the testimony, and, after demanding to see Ford at once and being refused, decided "this was no time for finesse" and threatened to call a press conference to expose the role people around Ford played "as part of a secret effort by Ford people to hurry Nixon out of the Presidency behind Jerry Ford's back." After being ushered into the Oval Office to meet with Ford, he concluded Ford hadn't read the testimony. "What do you want?" Ford asked him. "The truth," Haig replied, "that's all." In Brussels, he found the U.S. armed forces severely drained, as they were everywhere in the aftermath of Vietnam.

* * *

Five days after announcing Haig's departure, Ford asked Donald Rumsfeld to return to the White House to replace Haig. Ford hesitated to give him the title of chief of staff, instead appointing Rumsfeld "staff coordinator." The distinction was academic. Worse than any other single problem he faced, Ford after nearly two months in office had yet to establish that the presidency belonged to him, and not still to Nixon. And the White House, riven with disunity, disorganization, and bad blood, showed signs of coming apart at the seams. Ford's selection of Rumsfeld to replace Haig was an effort, amid the backlash following the pardon, to wrest control over his administration. Rumsfeld immediately appointed Cheney to serve as his deputy—Rumsfeld's Rumsfeld—the second most powerful person on the staff.

To replace terHorst, Ford chose NBC White House correspondent Ron Nessen. Nessen quoted Rumsfeld as telling him: "At the end of three months, the Ford administration will either have the smell of life or the smell of death. If it's the smell of death the White House is going to be torn to pieces by the press, by the Democrats, even by other Republicans who will challenge the president for the nomination in 1976."

* * *

Henry Kissinger's star, as Greene wrote, "dropped at exactly the same moment as Ford's." In mid-September, his international reputation darkened abruptly when, during Senate hearings on détente, Democrat Frank Church of Idaho assailed him for ordering the CIA to organize the overthrow of a democratically elected Marxist regime in Chile, about which Kissinger four years earlier had remarked: "I don't see why we need to stand by and watch a country go communist because of the irresponsibility of its own people." Meanwhile, the Middle East peace process collapsed. In late October, at the Rabat Hilton in Morocco, the leaders of twenty Arab states unanimously recognized the PLO as the sole representative of the Palestinian people, nullifying the Jordanian option and elevating the risk of permanent war with Israel. "Palestine is the cement that holds the Arab world together," Yasser Arafat said, "or it is the explosive that blows it apart."

As détente floundered, the anti-détente forces led by Henry Jackson, Richard Perle, James Schlesinger, and the neoconservatives challenged Ford to take a harder line against communism. Rumsfeld seized the opportunity to elevate Ford by diminishing Kissinger's power and influence. He pushed Ford to oppose Kissinger's arms control efforts while publicly disparaging Kissinger, leaking critical stories about him to the press through Nessen. Hoping to restore momentum to the Middle East peace process, Kissinger concentrated his attention on the ongoing negotiations between Jerusalem and Cairo, but with Israel asserting a hard line, his efforts petered out.

Rumsfeld also marginalized Rockefeller, curtailing his duties and access to the Oval Office on the same principle that whatever weakened the powerful men around Ford would only make Ford look stronger, more decisive—his own man.

* * *

By accepting the Nixon pardon as proper and appropriate under the Constitution, Leon Jaworski washed his hands of the Nixon prosecutorial decision. But he still faced the larger predicament of how Nixon's immunity ultimately would affect the final work of the Special Prosecution Force. In the days leading up to Ford's announcement, Lacovara had reversed himself, advising Jaworski to insist that Ford make Nixon's pardon conditional on several provisions, including an agreement not to seek public office. Jaworski thought it was too late to set conditions, and the day after the pardon was announced, Lacovara resigned, apparently in protest. Approaching jury selection in the cover-up trial, and Nixon's anticipated courtroom testimony, Jaworski, like Ford, faced rising complaints that he had undercut and betrayed the judicial process.

In San Clemente, Nixon fought the subpoena to testify against his closest aides, who contended in court papers that in the summer of 1972, just weeks after the Watergate break-in, they had urged Nixon to make a "full and complete disclosure" of the affair. Nixon argued that he was too disabled to travel and that his conversations with his advisers were protected by executive privilege, and Judge John Sirica, openly skeptical, ordered Miller to produce a medical report. Then on October 23, Nixon was readmitted to the hospital for surgery. Despite anticoagulant drugs, he had developed another large blood clot. After a ninety-minute operation to remove the clot, Nixon fainted, going in and out of a coma and suffering cardiovascular shock.

On Halloween, Ford, stopping in Los Angeles to campaign for local candidates, visited Nixon in the hospital, and the two talked briefly about politics, including the upcoming election. Ford lied: "It looks like we're going to do fine," he said. A week later, Miller delivered Sirica an affidavit saying Nixon couldn't possibly come to Washington, nor give a deposition in California, for at least two to three months. After naming a panel of three medical experts, who flew to San Clemente, examined Nixon, and determined he couldn't testify until early 1975, Sirica announced that he wanted to end the trial by the end of the year.

Thus Nixon escaped ever having to answer publicly for his role in Watergate. In private, he expressed sympathy for his men, but as Gulley observed, whenever "Nixon speaks of Watergate, it's always as a thing detached from him. It's never in the context of something he was involved in . . . He'd say, 'God, what the country has gone through with this Watergate business.' It's always in that vein, as if it had nothing to do with him."

On February 21, 1975, Mitchell, Haldeman, and Ehrlichman were convicted on various charges of conspiracy, obstruction of justice, and perjury and sentenced to two and a half to eight years in prison. A panel of circuit court judges denied their appeals, ruling that they had received a fair trial despite massive pretrial publicity.

*   *   *

The Nixon pardon handed a prime opportunity to the Republican right. After the fall electoral defeats, conservatives began to criticize Ford openly. By late 1974, Reagan stopped anguishing publicly about whether he should challenge a sitting president and began attacking Ford's policies in a weekly newspaper column.

In April 1975, Cambodia fell to the communists, and North Vietnamese forces entered Saigon, forcing the chaotic evacuation of the last Americans and 120,000 refugees—the "end of the road," Kissinger called it. Hawks blamed the defeat on the Democrats' unwillingness a decade earlier to escalate the war sharply at the beginning and do what needed doing to win it, rather than on Nixon's and Kissinger's lies, secrecy, and dissembling. Seeing the United States as locked in a death struggle with the Soviet Union that they said the Soviets were winning, conservatives and neoconservatives set out together to vanquish the "Vietnam Syndrome"—the American public's disillusionment with intervening militarily in internal Third World conflicts. "The evidence mounts," Reagan said, calling for an immediate buildup of American strength, "that we are Number Two in a world where it is dangerous, if not fatal, to be second best."

*   *   *

Fifteen months after he took office, Ford unleashed a barrage of top-level firings and hirings meant to show that he was in control of his presidency. Putting in place what he called "my guys . . . my own team" while trying to stave off a Reagan challenge for the 1976 party nomination, he fired Defense Secretary James Schlesinger and CIA Director William Colby and replaced them with Rumsfeld and George H. W. Bush, respectively. He replaced Kissinger as national security adviser with Brent Scowcroft, although Kissinger remained as secretary of state. Urged by Rumsfeld to replace Rockefeller with a conservative as his running mate in order to placate the right, Ford pressed Rockefeller to announce that he was withdrawing from the ticket. Cheney, at age thirty-five, moved up to become the youngest White House chief of staff in history.

Ford's credibility and judgment were undermined by the shake-up, dubbed inevitably the Halloween Massacre. He denied at a press conference that there were basic differences between Schlesinger and Kissinger on détente. When Goldwater asked him what qualified Rumsfeld for secretary of defense, he replied: "He was a fighter pilot in the Korean War." Although it appeared at first that Kissinger had prevailed in a power struggle over foreign policy—Ford finally had dispatched Schlesinger, Kissinger's nemesis on arms control—the ultimate winner proved to be Rumsfeld, who, despite his denials, had instigated the moves and stood to gain the most from them. Many in Washington quickly came to view Rumsfeld as a partisan opportunist willing to place his own ambitions ahead of all else in order to dispose of rivals for the vice presidency in 1976.

Rockefeller told Ford, "I'm now going to say it frankly . . . Rumsfeld wants to be President of the United States. He has given George Bush the deep six by putting him in the CIA, he has gotten me out . . . He was third on your list and now he has gotten rid of two of us." He added: "You are not going to be able to put him on the [ticket] because he is defense secretary, but he is not going to want anybody who can possibly be elected with you on that ticket . . . I have to say I have a serious question about his loyalty to you."

Though Ford, who picked as his running mate Kansas senator Robert

Dole, blamed no one but himself, he later wrote that he regretted sharply pushing Rockefeller off the ticket: "I was angry at myself for showing cowardice in not saying to the ultraconservatives: It's going to be Ford and Rockefeller, whatever the consequences."

*   *   *

At the Pentagon, Rumsfeld surrounded himself with hawks and neoconservative defense intellectuals who exaggerated the Soviet threat and complained that the CIA was gravely underestimating the Kremlin's strategic might and intentions. Ford, under growing pressure from the anti-détente right, agreed to let a team of their analysts examine the same data the CIA was using and come up with their own findings.

"It was sold as an 'exercise' in intelligence analysis, an interesting competition—Team A (the CIA) vs. Team B (the critics)," defense policy journalist Fred Kaplan wrote. "Yet once allowed the institutional footing, the Team B players presented their conclusions—and leaked them to friendly reporters—as the truth, which the pro-détente administration was trying to hide . . . The Team B report read like one long air-raid siren: The Soviets were spending practically all their GNP on the military; they were perfecting charged particle beams that could knock our warheads out of the sky; their express policy and practical goal was to fight and win a nuclear war."

Despite turning out to be almost entirely false, the Team B report became the rallying point for opposition to détente and arms control. By the beginning of 1976, as the presidential campaign got under way with Reagan and Senator Henry Jackson attacking Ford as being weak on communism, Rumsfeld and Cheney drove the SALT II negotiations into the sand at the Pentagon and the White House. Arms control had become so enmeshed with politics that Ford stopped referring to détente in his speeches and shelved further discussions with the Soviets about limiting weapons of mass destruction. The vaunted Nixon-Kissinger realism in foreign affairs was at last stalled, if not defeated.

* * *

Following an intra-party bloodletting in 1976, Ford lost the presidency to James Earl "Jimmy" Carter, Jr., an obscure Georgia governor who promised "never to tell a lie to the American people." On his first day in office, Carter announced an unconditional pardon covering all indicted and convicted Vietnam War draft resisters and nonregistrants, but excluding deserters; ten weeks later, his secretary of defense disclosed a plan to allow deserters to return home with less-than-honorable discharges. In September 1978, Israel's conservative prime minister Menachem Begin and President Anwar Sadat of Egypt met at Camp David, with Carter presiding, to sign a peace accord between the two countries—a culmination of the Egyptian option first posed five years earlier. The agreement contained a general "Framework for Peace in the Middle East," based on a five-year transitional period of civil self-rule for the Palestinians in the West Bank and Gaza, which required the agreement of other Middle Eastern countries. The framework infuriated other Arab leaders and was scrapped. Three years later, Islamic militants assassinated Sadat.

Carter served one term, during which he was plagued by rampant inflation, a second round of oil shocks, and the takeover of the American embassy in Iran by militant Islamic students, who denounced the U.S. government as "The Great Satan" and "Enemies of Islam." In 1980, Reagan defeated Carter for president, serving two terms. As his first secretary of state Reagan named Haig, who famously blurted to the press "I'm in charge" when Reagan went under anesthesia for surgery after an assassination attempt.

George H. W. Bush, vice president under Reagan, was elected president in 1988, naming Scowcroft his national security adviser. Cheney, who during the Reagan years had directed Armageddon exercises, secret planning efforts for transferring executive power during a nuclear war, became Bush's secretary of defense. Realism and restraint marked Bush's foreign policy. He declined to gloat over the collapse of the Soviet

Union, and he built a broad international coalition behind U.S. strategic goals, especially in the Persian Gulf.

* * *

Nixon lived another twenty years after abdicating his presidency, churning out eleven books in which he sought to airbrush Watergate into insignificance while he burnished his foreign policy record—his true legacy, he believed. To the end, he favored a moderate realpolitik as the "only bulwark for international stability." "The conservative policy, Nixon argued, would be belligerent without being effective, and being intellectually too 'thin,' would risk the support of American public opinion as well as that of our allies," Kissinger wrote. "The liberal position would 'sell us out' and run the risk of war imposed by a frustrated right once the American public realized that the United States was losing ground."

The Watergate tapes revealed a more complex and corrosive picture. The unambiguous verdict of the tapes is that Nixon obstructed justice and abused his power. Jaworski's worry that Nixon couldn't get a fair trial and that he might win absolution in a higher court was thus resolved by Ford's linking the fate of Nixon's presidential papers to the pardon. Nixon got his freedom, but the country got the truth. Thirty years later, Nixon's guilt—spoken in his own voice, in his own words, and available on the Internet—is indelible.

* * *

Beginning in 1996, notable critics who'd condemned Ford's decision to pardon Nixon started to revise their views. Richard Reeves, who in 1975 wrote a scathing biography in which he claimed "it is fair to say that Ford is slow. He is also unimaginative and not very articulate," now lauded Ford for his courage in an *American Heritage* article entitled "I'm Sorry,

Mr. President." The *Post*'s Bob Woodward, after interviewing Ford in 1998, concluded: "If Ford mishandled some of the details and disclosures, he got the overall absolutely right—the pardon was necessary for the nation." During that interview, Ford said about his August 1 meeting with Haig that "yes, on paper, without action it was a deal, but it never became a deal because I never accepted." When Woodward questioned Ford why he hadn't made more of the moral and legal point that accepting a pardon was tantamount to admitting guilt, Ford reached into his pocket for his wallet and, after searching around, produced a folded, dog-eared piece of paper—a portion of the 1915 Supreme Court ruling in *Burdick*. "I've got it in my wallet here because any time anybody challenges me I pull it out," he said.

In 2001, Ford received the Profile in Courage Award at the John F. Kennedy Library and Museum in Boston. Senator Ted Kennedy and liberal representative Barney Frank were among those who praised the award. Still, a few detractors remained. "Ford testified before Congress that 'there was no deal,' " National Public Radio's Daniel Schorr, a former CBS newsman, commented. "Perhaps not, but there was a premature action that left history cheated." Schorr said Ford's bravery in taking on the solitary burden of absolving Richard Nixon's sins was "shadowed by ambiguity."

* * *

In December 2000, eight years after his father failed to win reelection, former Texas governor George W. Bush became president-elect after the Supreme Court ruled 5–4 to cut off voter recounts in Florida. During the campaign, the younger Bush had asked Cheney, who between White House stints was elected to Congress and later had become CEO of the defense and oilfield services conglomerate Halliburton, to lead the search for a vice president, and Cheney, after vetting several other names, declared himself the ablest candidate. Two weeks after the Supreme Court decision, Bush selected Rumsfeld, his father's chief rival during the Ford years, to return to the Pentagon as secretary of defense. Rumsfeld appointed as his deputy Paul Wolfowitz, a leading neoconservative and former senior staff member of Team B, and he named to his intelligence team Douglas Feith, former counsel to Richard Perle, who in three decades in and out of government had become a leading neoconservative impresario.

As during the Ford years, hawks in and out of the administration set out aggressively to marginalize international diplomacy, treaties, and the secretary of state, former chairman of the Joint Chiefs General Colin Powell, a popular realist and author of the post–Vietnam-era Powell Doctrine—military guidelines for war. The doctrine, adopted under Reagan and used by Bush's father in 1991 in beating back an Iraqi invasion of Kuwait, held the need for clear goals, the backing of the American public, and the application of overwhelming force. "War," Powell had decided after his second term in Vietnam, "should be the politics of last resort."

After the United States was attacked on September 11, 2001 by Islamic extremists, who hijacked four domestic commercial jets, murdered their crews, and flew three of the planes into the twin towers of the World Trade Center and the Pentagon, Bush, with a solidly united nation behind him and extraordinary international cooperation extending from many Arab states to Cold War rivals Russia and China, declared a global "war on terror." His national security team, spearheaded by Cheney and Rumsfeld, also began planning in secret a preemptive war against Iraqi dictator Saddam Hussein. Rumsfeld formed his own "Team B" at the Pentagon, a "four-to-five-man intelligence team" to sift through raw data coming out of Iraq in search of evidence linking Hussein to the al-Qaeda terrorists who staged the attack, and to make the case that Hussein possessed weapons of mass destruction (WMD)—chemical, biological and, quite likely, nuclear—that he could use against the United States. Explaining the team's purpose to the *New York Times*, Wolfowitz cited a "phenomenon in intelligence work that people who are pursuing a certain hypothesis will see certain facts that others won't, and not see other facts that others will."

No weapons of mass destruction—nor any active programs to produce them—were found in Iraq after the U.S.-led invasion in 2003, and military investigators concluded that under pressure of international sanctions and United Nations inspections, Hussein had dismantled his programs. Nor was any link between Hussein and al-Qaeda established. Rumsfeld defended the war at daily press briefings in which he offered an ever-shifting array of rationales for the invasion, ranging from Hussein's past crimes to the establishment of a democratic beachhead in the Muslim world. He avoided any mention of Iraq's vast oil reserves, the doubling of U.S. dependence on foreign oil since 1974, or plans for permanent U.S. military bases in the region, the last of which had ignited al-Qaeda's global terrorism campaign. "Absence of evidence," Rumsfeld said about the hunt for WMD, "is not evidence of absence."

In early 2004, the war in Iraq turned substantially darker and more controversial when photographs showing U.S. troops torturing prisoners were broadcast around the world. By August, a commission headed by Schlesinger investigating the abuse or death of prisoners in Iraq, Afghanistan, and Guantanamo Bay, Cuba, reported that senior officials, including Rumsfeld, knew of the abuses but failed to fix them, yet the commission declined to call for their being held to account. Rumsfeld responded to the torture photos by blaming low-level enlistees and by ordering mobile phones fitted with digital cameras to be banned from U.S. Army installations in Iraq. He offered twice to resign, but Bush defended and retained him even as a growing guerrilla insurgency, which the Pentagon's intelligence team had failed to anticipate or prepare for, killed and wounded more than twice as many U.S. troops during the war's second year as during the first. Estimates of the number of Iraqi deaths ranged into the tens of thousands.

By June 2005, with comparisons with Vietnam increasing, public support for the Iraq war plummeted to 40 percent, from a high of 70 percent at the outset. Recalling the failure of Nixon's phased withdrawal from Vietnam, where the announcement of a schedule for bringing troops home encouraged the North to wait out the transfer to complete its takeover of the South, an embattled, second-term Bush White House resisted laying out a timetable for reducing the number of increasingly stretched, all-volunteer U.S. forces.

Within Iraq, the insurgency grew deadlier and more violent, as jihadist terrorism, and al-Qaeda, expanded worldwide. On CNN's *Larry King Live,* Cheney, the war's most forceful advocate inside the administration, said he was "absolutely certain" the administration had done the right thing in Iraq. "I think we may have some kind of presence there over a period of time," Cheney said. "The level of activity that we see today from a military standpoint, I think, will clearly decline. I think they're in the last throes, if you will, of the insurgency."

* * *

As Iraq began to subsume Bush's presidency, the extent to which Rumsfeld and Cheney had been responsible for steering the country into war by promoting flawed and misleading intelligence became clear. So, too, the aggressive role Cheney in particular played in using the September 11 attacks as part of a broader effort to reassert powers of the presidency he believed had been dangerously eroded after Vietnam and Watergate. Together they made the office of the vice president the center of strategic power in the White House, exerting an unprecedented grip on defense policy by disregarding the National Security Council's traditional leadership and browbeating intelligence officers. The cycle begun by Nixon, who joined with Kissinger to ignore Congress, the State Department, and the Joint Chiefs in forging global policies, seemed to come full circle.

With the United States facing rising casualties in Iraq—more than two thousand dead and fifteen thousand seriously wounded—approval for Bush's handling of the War on Terror plummeted. In October, Cheney's chief of staff, Lewis "Scooter" Libby, was indicted for lying to a grand jury investigating the White House unmasking of a secret CIA agent whose husband had publicly debunked prewar intelligence. Cheney, according to the indictment, had given Libby the agent's identity and counseled his staff how to handle press inquiries about her. Fearing that Libby might cut a deal, Democrats in Congress wrote to Bush urging him not to pardon anyone involved in the leak case.

The confluence of a major political scandal and a grim, unpopular and costly military occupation focused renewed attention on the reasons for going to war and on Bush, who had made personal integrity the backbone of his political appeal. Former officials depicted him as an isolated leader who didn't hear from enough people—a captive of the Rumsfeld-Cheney axis. The most potent and stinging rebuke came from Scowcroft, assumed by many to speak for George H. W. Bush, whose advice the White House ignored during the run-up to the invasion. "This was supposed to be part of the War on Terror," Scowcroft said, "but Iraq feeds terrorism. Vietnam was visceral in the American people . . . This is not that deep, but we're moving in that direction."

By December, the reemergence of the Imperial Presidency—a phrase last used to describe Nixon's presumption of being above the law—appeared complete, and there were signs that the rest of government, including members of Bush's party, were about to rein it in. News reports revealed that the administration had secretly ordered warrantless surveillance on phone calls and Internet traffic, in apparent violation of post-Watergate reforms, and Republicans in Congress vowed to investigate. Republicans in the Senate and House forced Bush and Cheney to back an amendment rebuffing Cheney's plan to legalize torture by intelligence agents. Meanwhile, a staunch conservative federal appeals judge whom Bush had considered nominating to the Supreme Court blasted the White House over the custody of a U.S. citizen deemed an "enemy combatant" by Bush and held without charges for more than three years. The Supreme Court indicated it would examine Bush's doctrine of unlimited executive power "in due course."

Cheney, the most powerful vice president ever, asserted that the doctrine emerged out of his experience working under Nixon and Ford. "Watergate and a lot of the things around Watergate and Vietnam served to erode the authority I think the president needs to be effective," he explained.

ACKNOWLEDGMENTS

I owe a great deal to a number of people for their guidance and generosity. Benton Becker, James Cannon, Leonard Garment, Phil Lacovara, Jack Marsh, Brent Scowcroft, and Jerry terHorst graciously opened doors and added insight. Dan Horowitz, Michael Gorra, and Michael Klare helped broaden my historical perspective and offered wisdom and encouragement. For help in obtaining access to rare sources and materials, and/or with navigating Washington, I am in debt to John Crewdson, Bill Dols, George Joulwan, Hank Meijer, and Loren Schoenberg. I am grateful, too, for the kind assistance I received at libraries and archives, especially from Stacy Davis and Kenneth Hafeli at the Ford Library and Pat Anderson at the National Archives. At Doubleday, I am indebted to many people, including Ronit Feldman, Nora Reichard, Pauline Piekarz, and Kathleen Fridella. I also want to thank Alice Chamberlin, Dick Evans, Lisa Hest, David Hoffstetter and Jennifer Alexander, Richard Hackel and Jennifer Hayden Merrit, Bill Seidman, Richard Levine and Jackie Austen, Dale Melcher and Bill Newman, Fred Eisenstein, Alan Sosne, David Tebaldi, and J. D. Dolan. I am blessed, as ever, to have as my editor Nan Talese, my agent Amanda Urban, my parents Hilda and Herbert Werth, and my family Kathy Goos, Emily Werth, and Alex Werth.

NOTES

DAY ONE

3 The most intriguing and authoritative account of Richard Nixon's solitary nature—and his dialogues with himself on his legal pads—is Richard Reeves's
President Nixon: Alone in the White House (New York: Simon and Schuster,
2001).

4 For details of Nixon's hasty removal from the White House, and the destruc-
tion of materials by his aides, I relied on several sources: interview with Benton
Becker, August 10, 2004; Robert Hartmann's *Palace Politics* (New York:
McGraw-Hill, 1980), pp. 173, 188; and Stephen Ambrose's *Nixon: Ruin and
Recovery, 1973–1990* (New York: Simon and Schuster, 1991), pp. 449–450.

4 For Haig's dilemma, see Roger Morris, *Haig: The General's Progress* (New York:
Playboy Press, 1982), p. 288.

3–6 I have relied here on Haig's two accounts of Nixon's last hours in office: *Inner
Circles: How America Changed the World* (New York: Warner Books, 1992),
pp. 503–505, and *Caveat: Realism, Reagan, and Foreign Policy* (New York:
Macmillan, 1984), p. 51.

5 "Haig thought": Haig, *Inner Circles*, pp. 350–351.

6 "Ford had feared": James Cannon, *Time and Chance* (New York: Harper-
Collins, 1994), p. 341.

7 "Special Watergate prosecutor Leon Jaworski": Leon Jaworski, *The Right and the Power* (New York: Reader's Digest, 1976), pp. 209–210.

7 Memo to Ford from Philip Buchen, Aug. 8, 1974, on how the transition should be managed (Gerald Ford Library).

7 "At forty-four, Donald Rumsfeld": *New York Times,* Sept. 23, 1974. For more on Rumsfeld's and Richard Cheney's scramble for power through the Nixon and Ford administrations, see James Mann's enlightening *Rise of the Vulcans: The History of Bush's War Cabinet* (New York: Viking, 2004).

8 "When Pat Nixon had heard": Ambrose, *Nixon,* p. 439.

8–9 Kissinger observed Nixon's downfall with a special keenness and interest. On the night before Nixon announced that he would resign, Nixon famously proposed that they kneel together and pray, and Kissinger found Nixon's farewell in the East Room "horrifying, and heartbreaking . . . and unavoidable. I was at the same time moved to tears and outraged at being put through the ringer once again" (Henry Kissinger, *Years of Upheaval* [Boston: Little Brown, 1982], p. 1213). See also Kissinger, *Years of Renewal* (New York: Touchstone, 1999), pp. 26–31; and David Greenberg, *Nixon's Shadow: The History of an Image* (New York: Norton, 2003), p. 235.

9 "that amazing, mammoth insight": Interview with Leonard Garment, Sept. 23, 2004.

10 An accounting of George H. W. Bush's private thoughts during the transition is contained in his *All the Best* (New York: Scribner, 1999), which includes selected excerpts from his diaries and letters. In 1997, after deciding to break precedent and order his presidential library to make his personal papers available to historians at once, Bush scrapped plans to write a much-anticipated memoir, becoming the first ex-president since Truman (excluding Kennedy) not to write an autobiography.

11 Gerald Ford, *A Time to Heal* (New York: Harper and Row/Reader's Digest, 1979), p. 39.

13 "postcoital": Interview with Steve Daley, Oct. 14, 2004.

13 To establish Haig's view of Ford as a neophyte to power, I relied on several sources: interview with George Joulwan, June 25, 2004; interview with Jerry Jones, June 23, 2004; Cannon, *Time and Chance,* pp. 360–366; memo to Ford from Haig on meeting with the White House staff, Aug. 9, 1974 (Gerald Ford Library).

14 "Watching, Bob Hartmann": Ford, *A Time to Heal,* p. 148; Hartmann, *Palace Politics,* p. 174.

14 "Ford worried": Ford, *A Time to Heal,* p. 131.

17 " 'a very complicated period' ": Interview with Brent Scowcroft, Oct. 14, 2004.

19 "Nixon could agree to leave": Ford, *A Time to Heal,* pp. 4–6.

19 "Hartmann in turn": Interview with Robert Hartmann, June 24, 2004.

21 For details of Nixon's first hours in exile I relied on Ambrose, *Nixon,* pp. 446–447; Robert Sam Anson, *Exile: The Unquiet Oblivion of Richard M. Nixon* (New York: Simon and Schuster, 1984), pp. 13–19: and Richard Nixon, *In the Arena* (New York: Simon and Schuster, 1990), pp. 12–13.

DAY TWO

23 For more on the position of the White House chief of staff, see Michael Medved, *The Shadow Presidents* (New York: Times Books, 1979).

23 Interview with Jerry Jones, June 23, 2004.

25 " 'Only a supreme optimist' ": Haig, *Inner Circles: How America Changed the World* (New York: Warner Books, 1992) p. 510.

25 Interview with Jerry Jones.

25–26 Richard Reeves, *President Nixon: Alone in the White House* (New York: Simon and Schuster, 2001) p. 542.

26 For a more comprehensive exploration of the Kissinger-Schlesinger rivalry, see Walter Isaacson, *Kissinger: A Biography* (New York: Simon and Schuster, 1992).

26–27 Gerald Ford, *A Time to Heal* (New York: Harper and Row/Reader's Digest, 1979), p. 146.

28–30 For details of the *Glomar* crisis, in particular Kissinger's role, I relied on John Pina Craven, *The Silent War: The Cold War Battle Beneath the Sea* (New York: Touchstone, 2001), pp. 220–221. Also see Sherry Sontag and Christopher Drew, *Blind Man's Bluff: The Untold Story of American Submarine Espionage* (New York: HarperCollins, 1998), pp. 258–269; and William Colby, *Honorable Men: My Life in the CIA* (New York: Simon and Schuster, 1978), pp. 413–418.

31 The conflict between Jaworski and his staff is detailed extensively by former Watergate prosecutors Richard Ben-Veniste and George Frampton, Jr., in *Stonewall: The Real Story of the Watergate Prosecution* (New York: Simon and Schuster, 1977).

31–33 Leon Jaworski, *The Right and the Power* (New York: Reader's Digest, 1976) pp. 217–220.

32 " 'issue of who should properly share' ": Richard Ben-Veniste and George Frampton, *Stonewall*, p. 299.

33 Interview with Benton Becker, Aug. 10, 2004. (Becker's interdiction of an army truck loaded with Nixon's materials has been recounted in print by Ford, James Cannon, Hartmann, Ambrose, and Seymour Hersh, all of whom also relied extensively on Becker.)

DAY THREE

36 Gerald Ford, *A Time to Heal* (New York: Harper and Row/Reader's Digest, 1979), p. 10; Sidney Schwartz, *Amway: The Untold Story*, http://www-2.cs.cmu.edu/-dst/Amway/AUS/gospelfilms.htm (Aug. 18, 2005).

37–38 Richard Reeves, *President Nixon: Alone in the White House* (Simon and Schuster, 2001), p. 306.

38 "Before Laird would take": Interview with Melvin Laird, Aug. 19, 2004.

39 Ford, *A Time to Heal*, pp. 11–13, 142–143.

40–42 George H. W. Bush, *All the Best* (New York: Scribner, 1999), p. 195; *Washington Post*, Aug. 16, 1974; Herbert Parmet, *George Bush: Life of a Lone Star Yankee* (New York: Scribner, 1997), pp. 168–171; Schweitzer, Peter and Rochelle, *The Bushes: Portrait of a Dynasty* (New York: Doubleday, 2004), p. 205.

41 "Despite the betrayal": Peter and Rochelle Schweitzer, *The Bushes*, p. 211; Bush, *All the Best*, p. 186.

41–42 "Now George W.": Peter and Rochelle Schweitzer, *The Bushes*, p. 220; Bill Minutaglio, *First Son: George W. Bush and the Bush Family Dynasty* (New York: Three Rivers Press, 1999), pp. 97, 156–161; Hatfield, J. H. *Fortunate Son: George W. Bush and the Making of an American President* (Brooklyn, N.Y.: Soft Skull Press, 2002), pp. 50–51.

42 Robert Sam Anson, *Exile: The Unquiet Oblivion of Richard M. Nixon* (New York: Simon and Schuster, 1984), pp. 26–28; Richard Nixon, *In the Arena* (New York: Simon and Schuster, 1990), p. 15.

43 David Greenberg, *Nixon's Shadow: The History of an Image* (New York: Norton, 2003), p. 154.

43–45 Brent Scowcroft first came into the White House as director of the military office. Gulley, a former marine, served as Scowcroft's executive assistant until Lyndon Johnson, looking for a "can-do guy," appointed Gulley director. The first civilian to hold the job, he was kept on by Nixon, Ford, and Carter; after retiring from the government, he wrote *Breaking Cover* (New York: Simon and Schuster, 1980), an intimate memoir of serving four presidents, with Mary Ellen Reese. All published accounts of Gulley's role in delivering White House papers to Nixon in San Clemente, including this one, rely heavily on Gulley's first-person account, as told to Reese, pp. 114–117.

DAY FOUR

46 Interview with Benton Becker, Aug. 10, 2004.

46 Interview with Jerald terHorst, Aug. 9, 2004.

46–49 For details of terHorst's grilling by the press regarding Nixon's papers, I have relied extensively on Robert Hartmann, *Palace Politics* (New York: McGraw-Hill, 1980), pp. 196–197.

48 " 'acted as if' ": Timothy Crouse, *The Boys on the Bus* (New York: Ballantine, 1972), p. 234.

49–51 Bill Gulley, *Breaking Cover* (New York: Simon and Schuster, 1980), pp. 114–117; Richard Nixon, *RN: The Memoirs of Richard Nixon* (New York: Touchstone, 1978), p. 1011; Stephen Ambrose, *Nixon: Ruin and Recovery, 1973–1990* (New York: Simon and Schuster, 1991), p. 355.

52 Jimmy Breslin, *How the Good Guys Finally Won: Notes from an Impeachment Summer* (New York: Ballantine, 1974), p. 179; Gerald Ford, *A Time to Heal* (New York: Harper and Row/Reader's Digest, 1979), pp. 133–134.

53 Ford, *A Time to Heal,* p. 126; *Washington Post,* Aug. 13, 1974.

54 " 'A lot of people' ": *ABC Evening News,* Aug. 12, 1974.

DAY FIVE

55 Henry Kissinger, *Years of Renewal* (New York: Touchstone, 1999), p. 33.

56 Ibid., p. 207.

57 Ibid., 229; *Newsweek,* Aug. 26, 1974.

57 Gerald Ford, *A Time to Heal* (New York: Harper and Row/Reader's Digest, 1979), p. 137.

58 "Cheney . . . recalled that Ford's": James Mann, *Rise of the Vulcans: The History of Bush's War Cabinet* (New York: Viking, 2004), p. 56.

59 "Haig pressed them": Walter Isaacson, *Kissinger: A Biography* (New York: Simon and Schuster, 1992), p. 468.

59 For views of Rumsfeld, see James Mann, *Rise of the Vulcans,* pp. 1–3; Robert

Hartmann, *Palace Politics* (New York: McGraw-Hill, 1980), p. 200; Richard Reeves, *President Nixon: Alone in the White House* (New York: Simon and Schuster, 2001), p. 314; Alexander Haig, *Inner Circles: How America Changed the World* (New York: Warner Books, 1992); Bernard J. Firestone and Alexej Ugrinsky, *Gerald R. Ford and the Politics of Post-Watergate America* (Westport, Conn.: Greenwood Press, 1993), p. 9.

60 "Ford loved to talk": Interview with Patrick Butler, Oct. 14, 2004.

61 "On the day Ford was sworn in": Memo to White House Scheduling from Gwen Anderson, Aug. 9, 1974 (Gerald Ford Library).

62 George H. W. Bush, *All the Best* (New York: Scribner, 1999), p. 195.

62 For details of Rockefeller's public posture and private thinking as Ford began to search for a vice president, I have relied on Joseph Persico, *The Imperial Rockefeller* (New York: Simon and Schuster, 1982), p. 244. Persico was then a speechwriter for Rockefeller. Also: interview with Robert Douglass, Sept. 23, 2004.

DAY SIX

64 I have relied extensively on Walter Isaacson's authoritative *Kissinger: A Biography* (New York: Simon and Schuster, 1992) for details about Washington's handling of the October War, especially the decision to put U.S. nuclear forces on high alert without consulting Nixon; pp. 530–531.

65 Henry Kissinger, *Years of Renewal* (New York: Touchstone, 1999), p. 196.

66 Spearheading the new coalition were the neoconservatives coalescing around Henry "Scoop" Jackson. Kissinger characterizes the relationship in *Years of Renewal*, p. 111: "Our clash with the neoconservatives was not over the nature of Communism, on which we were very close, but over the relationship of moral values to the conduct of international politics . . . The neoconservatives believed that values could be translated directly into operating programs."

66 Interview with Brent Scowcroft, Oct. 14, 2004.

67 Kissinger/Dobrynin telecon, July 12, 1974 (National Archives).

67 Richard Nixon, *RN: The Memoirs of Richard Nixon* (New York: Touchstone, 1978), p. 1031; Stephen Ambrose, *Nixon: Ruin and Recovery, 1973–1990* (New York: Simon and Schuster, 1991), p. 371.

68 Gerald Ford, *A Time to Heal* (New York: Harper and Row/Reader's Digest, 1979), pp. 138–139.

68 "Ford had been introduced": Kissinger, *Years of Renewal*, p. 365.

69 Isaacson, *Kissinger*, p. 545.

70 Kissinger, *Years of Renewal,* pp. 366–368.

71 *NBC Nightly News,* Aug. 14, 1974.

71 "Every president": John Powers, *The History of Presidential Audio Recordings and the Archival Issues Surrounding Their Use* (Washington, D.C.: National Archives, 1996).

72 Robert Hartmann, *Palace Politics: An Inside Account of the Ford Years* (New York: McGraw-Hill, 1980), pp. 244–245.

72–73 Interview with Jerry Jones, June 23, 2004.

74–75 Leon Jaworski, *The Right and the Power* (New York: Reader's Digest, 1976), pp. 222–223.

75 Interview with Philip Lacovara, Sept. 23, 2004.

DAY SEVEN

76 Gerald Ford, *A Time to Heal* (New York: Harper and Row/Reader's Digest, 1979), p. 139; Henry Kissinger, *Years of Renewal* (New York: Touchstone, 1999), p. 256.

76–77 Walter Isaacson, *Kissinger: A Biography* (New York: Simon and Schuster, 1992), pp. 611–617. I have also relied broadly on Robert Kaufman, *Henry M. Jackson: A Life in Politics* (Seattle: University of Washington Press, 2000), pp. 261–279.

78 Albert Wohlstetter, "Is There a Strategic Arms Race?," *Foreign Affairs,* Summer 1974. Also see Fred Kaplan, *The Wizards of Armageddon* (New York, Simon and Schuster, 1983), pp. 170–173.

78 Richard Nixon, *RN: The Memoirs of Richard Nixon* (New York: Touchstone, 1978), p. 562; Henry Kissinger, *Years of Renewal,* p. 250–251; Henry Kissinger, *Years of Upheaval* (Boston: Little Brown, 1982), p. 994.

79 Robert Hartmann, *Palace Politics: An Inside Account of the Ford Years* (New York: McGraw-Hill, 1980), p. 245.

80 Alexander Haig, *Inner Circles: How America Changed the World* (New York: Warner Books, 1992), pp. 340, 338.

80 Because the White House taping system remained in operation after Haig took over as chief of staff in May 1973, many of his early discussions with Nixon about Watergate were recorded. On June 4, after listening to several of his conversations with John Dean, Nixon summoned Haig to discuss the tapes. A transcript of portions of their conversation was released the following year. See Roger Morris, *Haig: The General's Progress* (New York: Playboy Press,

1982), pp. 229–235; Stephen Ambrose, *Nixon: Ruin and Recovery, 1973–1990* (New York: Simon and Schuster, 1991), pp. 158–159.

81–82   Len Colodny and Robert Gettlin, *Silent Coup* (New York: St. Martin's Press, 1991), pp. 322–332.

82   Haig, *Inner Circles*, pp. 374–375.

83   James Cannon, *Time and Chance* (New York: HarperCollins, 1994), p. 366; interview with Jerry Jones, June 23, 2004.

83   *PeopleWeekly*, Sept. 30, 1974.

84   Hartmann, *Palace Politics*, p. 246.

85   John Ehrlichman, *Witness to Power: The Nixon Years* (New York: Simon and Schuster, 1982), p. 396.

85–86   Walter Isaacson, *Kissinger*, pp. 327–331: Richard Reeves, *President Nixon: Alone in the White House* (New York: Simon and Schuster, 2001), pp. 331–339.

86–87   Ehrlichman, *Witness to Power*, p. 397.

87   "In San Clemente": Ambrose, *Nixon*, p. 452.

87   Nixon's bantering with the CBS news crew before making his resignation announcement is an extraordinary outtake, contrasting starkly with his grave public demeanor just minutes later, as he told the nation of his decision to leave office. A copy was provided to me by Leonard Garment.

88   Richard Nixon, *In the Arena* (New York: Simon and Schuster, 1990), p. 13.

DAY EIGHT

89   Richard Nixon, *RN: The Memoirs of Richard Nixon* (New York: Simon and Schuster, 1978), p. 1017.

89   For details of a possible Jordanian option in the Middle East, and Hussein's visit to Washington, see Kissinger, *Years of Renewal* (New York: Touchstone, 1999), pp. 355–365; 368–370.

90–91   Walter Isaacson, *Kissinger: A Biography* (New York: Simon and Schuster, 1992), pp. 294–299. According to Isaacson, after the eruption of large-scale fighting during Black September, Nixon told Kissinger, "There's nothing better than a little confrontation now and then, a little excitement," and instructed him to announce a major increase of U.S. forces in the region. Kissinger ignored the order.

92   "Right-wing speechwriter Patrick Buchanan . . . 'niggers' ": Richard Reeves, *President Nixon: Alone in the White House* (New York: Simon and Schuster, 2001), p. 295; Patrick Buchanan, *Conservative Votes, Liberal Victories: Why the*

Right Has Failed (New York: Quadrangle/New York Times Books, 1975), pp. 167–168.

92–93   *NBC Evening News,* Aug. 14, 1974.

93   Gerald Ford, *A Time to Heal* (New York: Harper and Row/Reader's Digest, 1979), p. 142.

93   Ibid., p. 143.

93   "Buchen met": *New York Times,* Aug. 18, 1974.

94   Ford, *A Time to Heal,* p. 110.

95   Robert Hartmann, *Palace Politics* (New York: McGraw-Hill, 1980), p. 225.

95–97   *NBC Evening News,* Aug. 16, 1974.

98–99   *New York Times,* Aug. 18, 1974; James Cannon, *Time and Chance* (New York: Harper Collins, 1994), p. 366.

99   Ford, *A Time to Heal,* p. 141.

DAY NINE

100   Gerald Ford, *A Time to Heal* (New York: Harper and Row/Reader's Digest, 1979), p. 145; Robert Hartmann, *Palace Politics: An Inside Account of the Ford Years* (New York: McGraw-Hill, 1980), pp. 222–224; James Cannon, *Time and Chance* (New York: HarperCollins, 1994), pp. 367–368.

101–103   Joseph E. Persico, *The Imperial Rockefeller: A Biography of Nelson A. Rockefeller* (New York: Simon and Schuster, 1982), p. 245; Michael Kramer and Sam Roberts, *"I Never Wanted to be* Vice-President *of Anything!" An Investigative Biography of Nelson Rockefeller* (New York: Basic Books, 1976), p. 365.

103–105   Interview with Jerry terHorst, Aug. 9, 2004.

104   *Washington Post,* Aug. 18, 1974; *New York Times,* Aug. 18, 1974.

105   Robert Hartmann, *Palace Politics,* p. 224.

105   "A year earlier, Nixon": Stephen Ambrose, *Nixon: Ruin and Recovery, 1973–1990* (New York: Simon and Schuster, 1991), p. 210.

106   Richard Reeves, *President Nixon: Alone in the White House* (New York: Simon and Schuster, 2001), pp. 567–568.

106   John Ehrlichman, *Witness to Power: The Nixon Years* (New York: Simon and Schuster, 1982), pp. 407–410.

107   Ford, *A Time to Heal,* p. 141.

108   *Washington Post,* Aug. 18, 1974; *New York Times,* Aug. 18, 1974.

108–109   Hartmann, *Palace Politics,* p. 225.

DAY TEN

110 *Washington Post,* Aug. 19, 1974.

110 Betty Ford, *The Times of My Life* (New York: Ballantine Books, 1978), p. 180.

111 Nicholas Lemann, "How the Seventies Changed America," *American Heritage,* July/August 1991; *New York Times,* Aug. 18, 1974.

111 Tom Wolfe, "The Me Decade and the Third Great Awakening," in *Mauve Gloves & Madmen, Clutter & Vine* (New York: Farrar, Straus and Giroux, 1976), p. 163.

111–112 Interview with Rev. William Dols, Jr., Jan. 25, 2005. Dols provided me with a copy of his sermon.

112–113 "The Center of the World," *American Experience* (WGBH, Boston): http://www.pbs.org/wgbh/amex/newyork/peopleevents/p_petit.html

113 *New York Times,* Aug. 18, 1974; *Washington Post,* Aug. 19, 1974.

114–115 *Newsweek,* Aug. 26, 1974.

115 " 'A total Nixon man' ": After Nixon's landslide in 1972, when Nixon and Haldeman decided who was in and who was out for the second term, Nixon again expressed his faith in Bush. "Not brains, we want loyalty," Haldeman quoted Nixon in his notes. "Eliminate the politicians, except George Bush. He'll do anything for the cause." Richard Reeves, *President Nixon: Alone in the White House* (New York: Simon and Schuster, 2001), p. 547.

115–116 Herbert S. Parmet, *George Bush: The Life of a Lone Star Yankee* (New York: Scribner, 1997), p. 172; interview with James Cannon, June 24, 2004.

116 "Laird thought they could win": Interview with Melvin Laird, Aug. 19, 2004.

117–118 *Washington Post,* Aug. 19, 1974.

118 Betty Ford has written frankly and compellingly about the hardships of being the wife of a Washington political figure. See *The Times of My Life,* p. 132: "The Congress got a Minority Leader, and I lost a husband. There followed a long stretch of time when Jerry was away from home 258 days a year. I had to bring up four kids by myself."

119 "Nixon plainly had similar feelings about [Ford]": James Cannon, *Time and Chance* (New York: HarperCollins, 1994), p. 275.

120 Reeves, *President Nixon,* p. 22; Jules Witcover, *Marathon: The Pursuit of the Presidency, 1972–1976* (New York: Signet, 1977), p. 45.

121 Betty Ford, *The Times of My Life,* p. 181.

DAY ELEVEN

125 Robert Hartmann, *Palace Politics: An Inside Account of the Ford Years* (New York: McGraw-Hill, 1980), p. 219; Gerald Ford, *A Time to Heal* (Harper and Row/Reader's Digest, 1979), p. 294.

126 Alexander Haig, *Inner Circles: How America Changed the World* (New York: Warner Books, 1992), pp. 513–514.

126 *Washington Post,* Aug. 18, 1974.

127–128 *Washington Post,* Aug. 20, 1974; *New York Times,* Aug. 20, 1974; *ABC News,* Aug. 19, 1974.

129 Stanley Kutler, *The Wars of Watergate: The Last Crisis of Richard Nixon* (New York: W. W. Norton, 1990), pp. 259–260; John Sirica, *To Set the Record Straight: The Break-in, the Tapes, the Conspirators, the Pardon* (New York: Norton, 1979).

130 "They had induced": Seymour Hersh, "The Pardon: Nixon, Ford, Haig and the Transfer of Power," *Atlantic Monthly,* Aug. 1983, p. 58.

130–132 *Washington Post,* Aug. 20, 1974; *New York Times,* Aug. 20, 1974; Sirica, *To Set the Record Straight,* p. 205; *CBS News,* Aug. 19, 1974.

132–134 *Washington Post,* Aug. 20, 1974; *CBS News,* Aug. 19 and 20, 1974; *New York Times,* Oct. 22, 2004.

135–136 Henry Kissinger, *Years of Renewal* (New York: Touchstone, 1999), pp. 481, 232; Walter Isaacson, *Kissinger: A Biography* (New York: Simon and Schuster, 1992), pp. 483, 485–486; Jeffrey Kimball, *The Vietnam War Files: Uncovering the Secret History of the Nixon-Era Strategy* (Lawrence: University of Kansas Press, 2004), pp. 186–187.

137 Betty Ford, *The Times of My Life* (New York: Ballantine, 1978), p. 181.

DAY TWELVE

138 Gerald Ford, *A Time to Heal* (New York: Harper and Row/Reader's Digest, 1979), p. 146.

139 Richard Nixon, *RN: The Memoirs of Richard Nixon* (New York: Simon and Schuster, 1978), p. 248: Ford, op. cit., p. 29.

139 Herbert Parmet, *George Bush: The Life of a Lone Star Yankee* (New York: Scribner, 1997), p. 172; Peter and Rochelle Schweizer, *The Bushes: Portrait of a Dynasty* (New York: Doubleday, 2004), p. 237; *Washington Post,* August 9, 1988; George H. W. Bush, *All the Best* (New York: Scribner, 1999), pp. 195–196.

140 Ford, *A Time to Heal,* p. 145.

141–143   *Washington Post,* Aug. 21, 1974; *ABC, NBC, CBS News,* Aug. 20 and 21, 1974.

143   "Wall Street crashed": "The Great Depression and the New Deal: 1929–1940," *Inventing America: A History of the United States* (New York: W. W. Norton, 2003), p. 759.

144   Richard Reeves, *President Nixon: Alone in the White House* (New York: Simon and Schuster, 2001), pp. 355–366; Daniel Yergin and Joseph Stanislaw, *The Commanding Heights: The Battle for the World Economy* (New York: Free Press, 1997), pp. 60–64; Leonard Ross and Peter Passell, "Mr. Nixon's Economic Melodrama," *The New York Review of Books,* vol. 17, no. 4.

144   Ford, *A Time to Heal,* p. 135.

145   *New York Times,* Aug. 19, 1974; Ford, *A Time to Heal,* pp. 151–156.

146–147   *Washington Post,* Aug. 23, 1974; J. F. terHorst, "A Transition with Frictions," *Detroit News,* Sept. 15, 1974; Robert Hartmann, *Palace Politics* (New York: McGraw Hill, 1980), p. 199; Alexander Haig, *Inner Circles: How America Changed the World* (New York: Warner Books, 1992), p. 511 (according to Haig, in a passage on the same page, the strain of the transition had grown immense: "Although I made it a point never to mention Nixon to Ford [or anyone else in the White House except as a matter of strict necessity], the weeks and months following the former President's resignation were the most difficult of my life . . . In private moments, I wondered whether I had somehow failed both my country and Nixon by not finding a way around his difficulties"); Ford, *A Time to Heal,* p. 147; Lawrence Leamer, "For Keeps: The Long Distance Race of Donald Rumsfeld," *The Washingtonian,* adapted from *Playing for Keeps in Washington* (New York: Dial Press, 1977).

DAY THIRTEEN

148   James Cannon, *Time and Chance* (New York: HarperCollins, 1994), pp. xi–xvi; Betty Ford, *The Times of My Life* (New York: Ballantine, 1978), pp. 156–157.

149–150   *ABC News,* Aug. 21, 1974; *Washington Post,* Aug. 22, 1974.

151   I have relied on J. Anthony Lukas's definitive account of the Boston busing crisis, *Common Ground: A Turbulent Decade in the Lives of Three American Families* (New York: Vintage, 1986). A discussion of *Milliken v. Bradley* can be found at the Supreme Court multimedia website, Oyez (http://www.oyez.org/oyez/resource/case/248/).

152   *Washington Post,* Aug. 22, 1974; Kissinger also noted, presciently (*Years of Renewal* [New York: Touchstone, 1999], p. 34): "As liberals veered into pacifism,

radicalism and protest, conservatives turned into crusaders . . . As containment was collapsing in Southeast Asia, some conservatives were spurred by the national humiliation into an attack not on the protest movement but on the administration the protesters were assaulting and paralyzing."

153   Ibid.; *Washington Post.*

154–155   Ibid.; *ABC News, NBC News,* Aug. 21, 1974.

155–156   Betty Ford, *The Times of My Life,* p. 181; for details about Betty Ford's struggle with alcoholism and drug addiction, I have relied extensively on her second memoir, *A Glad Awakening* (Garden City, N.Y.: Doubleday, 1987).

DAY FOURTEEN

158   Benton Becker, "The History of the Nixon Pardon," a speech delivered at the Cumberland School of Law, Feb. 3, 2000, and reprinted in the *Cumberland Law Review* (vol. 30–31), pp. 31–49; Bill Gulley, *Breaking Cover* (New York: Simon and Schuster, 1980), pp. 229–230. (After being ordered by Marsh, on Ford's behalf, not to ship any more of Nixon's materials, Gulley said he "started shipping stuff out to San Clemente as fast as it fell into my hands. In addition to papers, there were things of a personal nature—letters, mementos—in warehouses and different places around town.")

159–160   Gerald Ford, *A Time to Heal* (New York: Harper and Row/Reader's Digest, 1979), pp. 164, 165, 235, 140.

160–161   *Washington Post,* Aug. 23, 1974.

162–164   Ibid.; Leon Jaworski, *The Right and the Power: The Prosecution of Watergate* (New York: Reader's Digest, 1976), pp. 224–227; John Sirica, *To Set the Record Straight: The Break-in, the Tapes, the Conspirators, the Pardon* (New York: W. W. Norton, 1979), pp. 231–233; Richard Nixon, *In the Arena* (New York: Simon and Schuster, 1990), p. 15.

164–166   H. R. Haldeman, *The Haldeman Diaries: Inside the Nixon White House* (New York, G. P. Putnam's Sons, 1994), p. 217; Richard Reeves, *President Nixon: Alone in the White House* (New York: Simon and Schuster, 2001), p. 281; George H. W. Bush, *All the Best: My Life in Letters and Other Writings* (New York: Scribner, 1999), p. 196.

DAY FIFTEEN

167   Henry Kissinger, *Years of Renewal* (New York: Touchstone, 1999), pp. 370–374.

168 *Newsweek,* June 10, 1974.

169 *Newsweek,* June 24, 1974.

169–170 *Newsweek,* Sept. 9, 1974; Walter Isaacson, *Kissinger: A Biography* (New York: Simon and Schuster, 1992), p. 561; Henry Kissinger, *Years of Renewal,* p. 372; *Washington Post,* Aug. 23, 1974.

171–173 Interview with Robert Douglass, September 23, 2004; *Washington Post,* Aug. 24, 1974; Michael Kramer and Sam Roberts, *"I Never Wanted to Be Vice-President of* Anything!" *An Investigative Biography of Nelson Rockefeller* (New York: Basic Books, 1976), p. 365.

DAY SIXTEEN

174 Interview with Jerald terHorst, Aug. 9, 2004; *Washington Post,* Aug. 24, 1974.

175–176 For details of the Moorer-Radford affair, I have relied at length on James Rosen's article in *The Atlantic,* "Nixon and the Chiefs" (April 1, 2002)—the first account to make use of Nixon's secret tapes. For earlier investigative reports, see Seymour Hersh, *The Price of Power: Kissinger in the Nixon White House* (New York: Summit Books, 1983), and Len Colodny and Robert Gettlin, *Silent Coup: The Removal of a President* (New York: St. Martin's Press, 1991).

177 Interview with Herbert "Jack" Miller, June 22, 2004; *Washington Post,* Aug. 29, 1974.

178–179 *New York Times,* Aug. 25, 1974; *Newsweek,* Sept. 9, 1974.

179 Betty Ford, *The Times of My Life* (New York: Ballantine, 1978), p. 123.

180 " 'especially bereft' ": *Washington Post,* Aug. 25, 1974.

180 Nixon, talking politics with Haldeman at Camp David in August 1972, brought up Rockefeller and Reagan. "Reagan is not one who wears well," he said. The tape was released in late 2003, part of the tenth batch of Nixon recordings, totaling 2,109 hours, that the National Archives has released since 1980.

DAY SEVENTEEN

182 *New York Times,* Aug. 25, 1974.

183–185 Gerald Ford, *A Time to Heal* (New York: Harper and Row/Reader's Digest, 1979), pp. 321–323.

186–187 Henry Kissinger, *Years of Upheaval* (Boston: Little Brown, 1982), pp. 519–534.

186 Ibid., p. 482; *Washington Post,* Aug. 23 and 26, 1974.

187 Walter Isaacson, *Kissinger: A Biography* (New York: Simon and Schuster, 1992), pp. 483–489.

188–189 Interview with Herbert Miller, June 22, 2004.

188–189 "Lewin argued": *The New Republic,* Aug. 24, 1974.

189 "Later, Nixon in his first interview": Stephen Ambrose, *Nixon: Ruin and Recovery, 1973–1990* (New York: Simon and Schuster, 1991), p. 510. (Arranged by Nixon's agent, "Swifty" Lazar, the series of exclusive interviews with British broadcaster David Frost netted the former president $600,000, plus 20 percent of profits.)

DAY EIGHTEEN

191–192 "I talked to Haig": Gerald Ford, *A Time to Heal* (New York: Harper and Row/Reader's Digest, 1979), p. 136.

192–193 Charles Colson, *Born Again: What Really Happened to the White House Hatchet Man* (Falls Church, Va.: Conservative Press, 1983), p. 257; Alexander Haig, *Inner Circles: How America Changed the World* (New York: Warner Books, 1992), p. 529; Roger Morris, *The General's Progress* (New York: Playboy Press, 1982), pp. 305–309.

193 *Washington Post,* Aug. 27, 1974.

193 "pure Schlesinger": Interview with Brent Scowcroft, Oct. 14, 2004.

194 *Washington Post,* Aug. 27, 1974.

194 "More than 200,000": Harold Jordan, "War Resistance, Amnesty and Exile—Just the Facts," from *Youth and Militarism* (American Friends Service Committee, May 2000).

195 Explaining why he hadn't served in Vietnam, Dick Cheney told George C. Wilson of the *Washington Post* in 1989: "I had other priorities in the '60s than military service."

195–196 *CBS News,* Aug. 20, 1974; for details about *Amex,* the American Ghetto in Toronto, and Colhoun's role, I relied on John Hagan, *Northern Passage: American Vietnam War Resisters in Canada* (Cambridge, Mass.: Harvard University Press, 2001).

196–200 *Detroit Free Press,* Dec. 22, 1974, and Aug. 17, 1975; Gerald Ford, *A Time to Heal* (New York: Harper and Row/Reader's Digest, 1979), pp. 46–56; James Cannon, *Time and Chance* (New York: Harper Collins, 1994), pp. 12–32.

198 " 'unshared secrets' ": Peter H. Wood, "The Pardoner's Tale: The Personal Theme of 'Domestic Tranquility' in Gerald Ford's Pardon of Richard Nixon," *Prospects* 11 (1986): 491–539.

DAY NINETEEN

201–202 Clark Mollenhoff, *The Man Who Pardoned Nixon: A Documented Account of Gerald Ford's Presidential Retreat from Credibility* (New York: St. Martin's Press, 1976), pp. 84–88; Timothy Crouse, *The Boys on the Bus* (New York: Ballantine, 1972), pp. 250–256; Hartmann, *Palace Politics: An Inside Account of the Ford Years* (New York: McGraw-Hill, 1980), p. 250.

203 Hartmann, ibid., p. 251; Gerald Ford, *A Time to Heal* (New York: Harper and Row/Reader's Digest, 1979), pp. 156–157.

204 Hartmann's recollection of his August 2 conversation with Ford about the late night Ford/Haig phone call conflicts with Ford's, who in *A Time to Heal* wrote (p. 9): "As we [he and Betty] prepared to go upstairs, I received a phone call from Haig. 'Nothing has changed,' he said. 'The situation is as fluid as ever.' 'Well,' I replied, 'I've talked with Betty, and we're prepared, but we can't get involved in the White House decision-making process.' " According to Hartmann: "Memories are fallible, but I know what most upset me was the fact that Ford had called Haig. Why would Haig telephone the Vice-President at 1:30 a.m. just to say that nothing had changed? And why, if Ford informed Haig that night that 'we can't get involved,' did we have to go through it all over again the next day for Harlow, Marsh and me? I will have to stand by my own vivid recollections" (Hartmann, *Palace Politics*, p. 135).

205–207 Interview with Leonard Garment, Sept. 23, 2004; Leonard Garment, *Crazy Rhythm: From Brooklyn to Jazz to Nixon's White House, Watergate and Beyond* (Cambridge, Mass.: Da Capo Press, 1997), pp. 90–97.

207–209 Leon Jaworski, *The Right and the Power: The Prosecution of Watergate* (New York: Reader's Digest, 1976), pp. 222–238; interview with Philip Lacovara, Sept. 22, 2004; Richard Ben-Veniste and George Frampton, *Stonewall: The Real Story of the Watergate Prosecution* (New York: Simon and Schuster, 1977), pp. 300–315.

210–211 *ABC News* and *NBC News,* Aug. 27, 1974; Stephen Ambrose, *Nixon: Ruin and Recovery, 1973–1990* (New York: Simon and Schuster, 1991), p. 314.

DAY TWENTY

212–214 Interview with Leonard Garment, Sept. 23, 1974; *Washington Post,* Dec. 18 and 19, 1975; Gerald Ford, *A Time to Heal* (New York: Harper and Row/ Reader's Digest, 1979), pp. 159–160; Alexander Haig, *Inner Circles: How America Changed the World* (New York: Warner Books, 1992), 513.

215 *Time,* October 4, 1976; the Rev. Dr. Ward Williams, "Getting Ready," a sermon from November 30, 1997, posted on the web at http://vheadline.com. printer.news.asp?id=20916.

215–223 Ford, *A Time to Heal,* pp. 158–160; James Cannon, *Time and Chance* (New York: HarperCollins, 1994), p. 372; *New York Times,* Sept. 9, 1974; *Detroit Free Press,* Sept. 19, 1974; interview with Benton Becker, Aug. 10, 2004.

223–224 *ABC News,* Aug. 29, 1974; *Washington Post,* Aug. 30, 1974.

224–226 *Washington Post,* Aug. 29, 1974; Robert Hartmann, *Palace Politics* (New York: McGraw-Hill, 1980), p. 253.

DAY TWENTY-ONE

229 Leon Jaworski, *The Right and the Power: The Prosecution of Watergate* (New York: Reader's Digest, 1976), p. 240.

231–232 Interview with Philip Lacovara, Sept. 22, 2004; Leon Jaworski, *The Right and the Power,* p. 12; Richard Ben-Veniste and George Frampton, *Stonewall: The Real Story of the Watergate Prosecution* (New York: Simon and Schuster, 1977), pp. 288, 305–307.

232–233 *Washington Post,* Aug. 30, 1974.

233 " 'alarming state' ": *New York Times,* Sept. 17 and 18, 1974.

233–234 The extent to which Ford, as House minority leader, loyally performed political duties for Nixon is thoroughly detailed in Seymour Hersh's authoritative article "The Pardon: Nixon, Ford, Haig, and the Transfer of Power" (*Atlantic Monthly,* August 1983).

234 Gerald Ford, *A Time to Heal* (New York: Harper and Row/Reader's Digest, 1979), p. 160.

235 *CBS News,* Aug. 29, 1974.

235–236 Henry Kissinger, *Years of Renewal* (New York: Touchstone, 1999), pp. 372–374.

236 Betty Ford, *The Times of My Life* (New York: Ballantine, 1978), p. 183.

DAY TWENTY-TWO

237–240　*ABC News,* Aug. 30, 1974; *New York Times,* Aug. 31, Sept. 1, and Sept. 5, 1974; *Washington Post,* Aug. 31, 1974.

240–241　*Los Angeles Times,* Aug. 30, 1974; *New York Times,* Aug. 30, 1974; Robert Sam Anson, *Exile: The Unquiet Oblivion of Richard M. Nixon* (New York: Simon and Schuster, 1984), pp. 34–35.

242　Bill Gulley, *Breaking Cover* (New York: Simon and Schuster, 1980), pp. 230–231.

243–247　To reconstruct Ford's announcement to his core advisers that he wanted to pardon Nixon, I relied on multiple sources: interview with John Marsh, Jr., June 23, 2004; interview with Robert Hartmann, June 24, 2004; interview with James Cannon, June 24, 2004; Gerald Ford, *A Time to Heal* (New York: Harper and Row/Reader's Digest, 1979), pp. 161–162; Robert Hartmann, *Palace Politics* (New York: McGraw-Hill, 1980), pp. 258–261; James Cannon, *Time and Chance* (New York: HarperCollins, 1994), pp. 373–376.

247–249　Ford, *A Time to Heal,* p. 162; interview with Benton Becker, Aug. 10, 2004.

DAY TWENTY-THREE

250–254　*New York Times,* Aug. 31 and Sept. 1, 1974; *Washington Post,* Aug. 31 and Sept. 1, 1974; *NBC News* and *CBS News,* August 31, 1974.

254　J. F. terHorst, *Gerald Ford and the Future of the Presidency* (New York: The Third Press, 1974), p. 214.

255　*New York Times,* Sept. 1, 1974.

255　" 'It was a brutal' ": Interview with Jerry Jones, June 23, 1974.

DAY TWENTY-FOUR

257　" 'forever plotting' ": Richard Reeves, *President Nixon: Alone in the White House* (New York: Simon and Schuster, 2001), pp. 96–97.

258　*NBC News,* Sept. 1, 1974; *Washington Post,* Sept. 2, 1974.

258　Gerald Ford, *A Time to Heal* (New York: Harper and Row/Reader's Digest, 1979), pp. 42–49.

258–262　In constructing this section on the connections between Ford's inner history and his dilemma regarding Nixon, I have relied heavily on Peter H. Wood's "The Pardoner's Tale" *Prospects* 11 (1986). See James Cannon, *Time and Chance* (New York: HarperCollins, 1994), pp. 1–6, for a thorough reconstruction of Ford's parents' aborted marriage.

261–262 Court records of Ford's parents' divorce and twenty-five-year battle over child-support payments for him, including the transcript of his deposition, are on file at the Gerald Ford Library; Cannon, *Time and Chance,* pp. 25–26.

DAY TWENTY-FIVE

263–265 Interview with Benton Becker, Aug. 10, 2004. For the facts of the *Burdick* case, see 236 U.S. 79, 35 S.Ct. 267.

265 Alexander Hamilton, *Federalist,* no. 74, pp. 500–503.

266 *New York Times* and *Washington Post,* Sept. 3, 1974.

266 "In his last, undelivered": *CBS News,* Aug. 10, 1974.

267–268 *CBS News,* Sept. 3, 1975. Raymond Schroth, *The American Journey of Eric Sevareid* (South Royalton, Vt.: Steerforth Press, 1995), p. 359.

DAY TWENTY-SIX

269 *ABC News* and *CBS News,* Sept. 3, 1974.

269 "The 15th Watergate figure": In addition to the seven original Watergate defendants (Bernard Barker, Virgilio Gonzalez, E. Howard Hunt, G. Gordon Liddy, Eugenio Martinez, James W. McCord, Jr., and Frank Sturgis), seven others already had been jailed for campaign violations, political dirty tricks, the Fielding break-in, and the Watergate cover-up (Dwight Chapin, Charles Colson, Fred C. LaRue, George A. Hearing, Egil Krogh, Jr., Jeb S. Magruder, and Donald Segretti.)

270–271 Charles Colson, *Born Again: What Really Happened to the White House Hatchet Man* (Falls Church, Va., Conservative Press, 1983), pp. 258, 260; John Dean, *Blind Ambition: The White House Years* (New York: Simon and Schuster, 1976), pp. 366–368; interview with John Dean, Nov. 20, 2004.

271–272 Gerald Ford, *A Time to Heal* (New York: Harper and Row/Reader's Digest, 1979), p. 164; *Washington Post,* Sept. 3, 1974.

273–275 *Washington Post* and *New York Times,* June 22, 1974; Charles Colson, *Born Again,* 260–261; Dean, *Blind Ambition,* 370–371.

DAY TWENTY-SEVEN

276 "Faced at the Pentagon": James Jay Carafano, "Total Force Policy and the Abrams Doctrine: Unfulfilled Promise, Uncertain Future," from a paper presented at the Foreign Policy Research Institute's December 2004 conference on the future of the reserves and national guard.

277–279 Alexander Haig, *Inner Circles: How America Changed the World* (New York: Warner Books, 1992), p. 516; Gerald Ford, *A Time to Heal* (New York: Harper and Row/Reader's Digest, 1979), p. 185; Lawrence Leamer, "For Keeps: The Long Distance Race of Donald Rumsfeld," *The Washingtonian;* adapted from *Playing for Keeps in Washington* (New York: Dial Press, 1977).

279–280 Betty Ford's press conference: *New York Times* and *Washington Post,* Sept. 5, 1974.

280–282 Interview with Benton Becker, Aug. 10, 2004; interview with Herbert Miller, June 22, 2004.

282–284 Leon Jaworski, *The Right and the Power: The Prosecution of Watergate* (New York: Reader's Digest, 1976), pp. 242–243; Richard Ben-Veniste and George Frampton, *Stonewall: The Real Story of the Watergate Prosecution* (New York: Simon and Schuster, 1977), p. 308.

284–285 *New York Times,* Sept. 5, 1974; George H. W. Bush, *All the Best* (New York: Scribner, 1999), p. 197.

285–286 "Tom Jarrell summed up": *ABC News,* Sept. 4, 1974.

DAY TWENTY-EIGHT

287 *ABC News* and *CBS News,* Sept. 5, 1974.

288–289 *New York Times* and *Washington Post,* Sept. 6, 1974; Justin Martin, *Greenspan: The Man Behind the Money* (Cambridge, Mass.: Perseus Publishing, 2000), pp. 100–103.

289–290 Henry Kissinger, *Years of Renewal* (New York: Touchstone, 1999), pp. 464, 474.

290–292 *Washington Post,* Nov. 13, 1999; interview with Herbert Miller, June 22, 2004; interview with Benton Becker, Aug. 10, 2004; Benton Becker, Memorandum Re: History and Background of the Nixon Pardon Sept. 9, 1974, p. 8 (Gerald Ford Library).

293–294 Interview with Benton Becker, Aug. 10, 2004; interview with Herbert Miller, June 22, 2004.

DAY TWENTY-NINE

296–298 Interview with Benton Becker, Aug. 10, 2004. For a concise narrative of the negotiations over the Nixon pardon, see Seymour Hersh's authoritative account, "The Pardon: Nixon, Ford, Haig and the Transfer of Power," *Atlantic Monthly,* August 1983.

297 "Al Haig and I": Len Colodny and Robert Gettlin, *Silent Coup: The Removal of a President* (New York: St. Martin's Press, 1991), p. 437.

297–298 Interview with Jerald terHorst, Aug. 9, 2004; *New York Times* and *Washington Post*, Sept. 7, 1974.

299–301 Interview with Benton Becker, Aug. 10, 2004; Stephen Ambrose, *Nixon: Ruin and Recovery, 1973–1990* (New York: Simon and Schuster, 1991), pp. 458–461; James Cannon, *Time and Chance* (New York: HarperCollins, 1994), 379–381.

301–303 *CBS News* and *NBC News,* Sept. 6, 1974.

303–304 *New York Times* and *Washington Post,* Sept. 7, 1974.

304–307 Interview with Benton Becker, Aug. 10, 2004. As with Becker's August 10 interdiction of Nixon's materials outside the White House, he is the sole source for all published accounts of this private September 6 meeting with Nixon. For other versions, see Cannon, *Time and Chance,* pp. 380–381; Ambrose, *Nixon,* p. 459.

DAY THIRTY

308 *New York Times,* Sept. 8, 1974.

309 Interview with Melvin Laird, Aug. 19, 2004.

309–310 Gerald Ford, *A Time to Heal* (New York: Harper and Row/Reader's Digest, 1979), pp. 172–175; *Washington Post,* Sept. 8, 1974.

311–312 Interview with Benton Becker, Aug. 10, 2004; Ford, *A Time to Heal,* p. 172; Peter H. Wood, "The Pardoner's Tale," *Prospects* 11 (1986), pp. 529–531.

312 " 'Some of Ford's people' ": Haig, *Inner Circles: How America Changed the World* (New York: Warner Books, 1992), p. 513.

312–313 " 'I was stunned' ": Interview with Jerald terHorst, Aug. 9, 2004.

313–315 " 'I'm afraid' ": Interview with Benton Becker, Aug. 10, 2004.

314 " 'He began' ": Robert Hartmann, *Palace Politics: An Inside Account of the Ford Years* (New York: McGraw-Hill, 1980), p. 264.

315 "TerHorst was less": Interview with Jerald terHorst, Aug. 9, 2004.

DAY THIRTY-ONE

316–319 James Cannon, *Time and Chance* (New York: HarperCollins, 1994), pp. 382–384; Robert Hartmann, *Palace Politics: An Inside Account of the Ford Years* (New York: McGraw-Hill, 1980), pp. 265–267; Thomas "Tip" O'Neill, *Man of the House* (New York: Random House, 1987), p. 268; interview with Jerald terHorst, Aug. 9, 2004; interview with Robert Hartmann, June 24, 2004; interview with John Marsh, June 23, 2004.

320–323   *New York Times* and *Washington Post,* Sept. 9, 1974; Hartmann, *Palace Politics,* p. 266; Stephen Ambrose, *Nixon: Ruin and Recovery, 1973–1990* (New York: Simon and Schuster, 1991), p. 464; Richard Nixon, *In the Arena* (New York: Simon and Schuster, 1990), p. 15.

323–325   *New York Times* and *Washington Post,* Sept. 9, 1974.

325–327   Ambrose, *Nixon,* pp. 464–467; Robert Sam Anson, *Exile: The Unquiet Oblivion of Richard M. Nixon* (New York: Simon and Schuster, 1984), pp. 59–60; Richard Nixon, *Leaders* (New York: Simon and Schuster, 1982), pp. 59, 62, 313, 341; David Greenberg, *Nixon's Shadow: The History of an Image* (New York: Norton, 2003), pp. 245–255; Richard Reeves, *President Nixon: Alone in the White House* (New York: Simon and Schuster, 2001), pp. 325–326; transcript of Nixon's third interview with David Frost, *New York Times,* May 20, 1977.

327–330   Gerald Ford, *A Time to Heal* (New York: Harper and Row/Reader's Digest, 1979), pp. 178–179; interview with Melvin Laird, August 19, 2004; J. F. terHorst, *Gerald Ford and the Future of the Presidency* (New York: The Third Press, 1974), pp. 225–240; interview with Jerald terHorst, Aug. 9, 2004; *ABC News, CBS News,* and *NBC News,* Aug. 8, 1974; Betty Ford, *The Times of My Life* (New York: Ballantine, 1978), pp. 196–197.

EPILOGUE

332–333   John Robert Greene, *The Presidency of Gerald R. Ford* (Lawrence: University of Kansas Press, 1995), p. 53.

333   *Newsweek,* Oct. 21, 1974.

334–335   Stephen Ambrose, *Nixon: Ruin and Recovery, 1973–1990* (New York: Simon and Schuster, 1991), pp. 465–473; Gerald Ford, *A Time to Heal* (New York: Harper and Row/Reader's Digest, 1979), pp. 201–202.

335–336   Alexander Haig, *Inner Circles: How America Changed the World* (New York: Warner Books, 1992), p. 518.

336   " 'At the end of three months' ": Rowan Scarborough, *Rumsfeld's War: The Untold Story of America's Anti-Terrorist Commander* (Washington, D.C.: Regnery, 2004), pp. 77–78.

336   Greene, *The Presidency of Gerald R. Ford,* p. 120.

337   "I don't see why": Kissinger, June 27, 1970; *Newsweek,* Nov. 11, 1974.

338 Bill Gulley, *Breaking Cover* (New York: Simon and Schuster, 1980), p. 240.

339 Michael T. Klare, *Beyond the "Vietnam Syndrome": U.S. Interventionism in the 1980s* (Washington, D.C.: Institute for Policy Studies, 1981), p. 1.

340 "When Goldwater asked him": *Time,* Nov. 17, 1975.

340–341 Robert Hartmann, *Palace Politics: An Inside Account of the Ford Years* (New York: McGraw-Hill, 1980), p. 370; James Cannon, in an interview with me on June 24, 2004, recalled that Ford told him that pushing Rockefeller off the 1976 ticket was the "most cowardly thing I've ever done."

341 Fred Kaplan, "The Rumsfeld Intelligence Agency: How the Hawks Plan to Find a Saddam/al-Quida Connection," Oct. 28, 2002, http://slate.msn.com; James Mann, *Rise of the Vulcans: The History of Bush's War Cabinet* (New York: Viking, 2004), pp. 65–68: Jason Vest, "Darth Rumsfeld," *American Prospect,* Feb. 26, 2001.

343 Henry Kissinger, *Years of Renewal* (New York: Touchstone, 1999), pp. 48–49.

343 " 'If Ford mishandled' ": Bob Woodward, from *Profiles in Courage for Our Time,* ed. by Caroline Kennedy (New York: Hyperion, 2002), pp. 295–315.

344 " 'Ford testified' ": Daniel Schorr, "A Profile in Courage Clouded by Ambiguity," *Christian Science Monitor,* May 25, 2001.

345 For a more complete discussion of the Powell Doctrine and its roots in the Vietnam War, see Mann, *Rise of the Vulcans,* pp. 43–44, 119–120.

345 "Wolfowitz cited": Fred Kaplan, *The Wizards of Armageddon* (New York: Simon and Schuster, 1983).

346 " 'Absence of evidence' ": Donald Rumsfeld, briefing the Pentagon press, October 15, 2003.

347 " 'I think we may have' ": Richard Cheney, CNN's *Larry King Live,* May 30, 2005.

348 " 'This was supposed' ": Jeffrey Goldberg, "Breaking Ranks," *The New Yorker,* Nov. 9, 2005.

348 "Watergate and a lot": *New York Times,* Dec. 20, 2005.

SELECTED BIBLIOGRAPHY

BOOKS

Ambrose, Stephen E. *Nixon: Ruin and Recovery, 1973–1990.* New York: Simon and Schuster, 1991.

Anson, Robert Sam. *Exile: The Unquiet Oblivion of Richard M. Nixon.* New York: Simon and Schuster, 1984.

Arun, Naseer H., ed. *Middle East Crucible: Studies on the Arab-Israeli War of October 1973.* Wilmette, Ill.: Medina University Press International, 1975.

Ball, Howard. *"We Have a Duty": The Supreme Court and the Watergate Tapes Litigation.* New York: Greenwood Press, 1990.

Ben-Veniste, Richard, and George Frampton, Jr. *Stonewall: The Real Story of the Watergate Prosecution.* New York: Simon and Schuster, 1977.

Berman, William C. *America's Right Turn: From Nixon to Clinton.* Baltimore, Md.: Johns Hopkins University Press, 1994.

Breslin, Jimmy. *How the Good Guys Finally Won: Notes from an Impeachment Summer.* New York: Ballantine Books, 1975.

Buchanan, Patrick J. *Conservative Votes, Liberal Victories: Why the Right Has Failed.* New York: Quadrangle/New York Times Books, 1975.

Burleson, Clyde W. *The Jennifer Project.* College Station: Texas A&M University Press, 1997.

Burke, Bob, and Ralph G. Thompson. *Bryce Harlow: Mr. Integrity*. Oklahoma City: Oklahoma Heritage Association, 2000.

Bush, George H. W. *All the Best: My Life in Letters and Other Writings*. New York: Scribner, 1999.

Bush, George H. W., and Brent Scowcroft. *A World Transformed*. New York: Knopf, 1998.

Bush, George W. *A Charge to Keep*. New York: Morrow, 1999.

Cannon, James. *Time and Chance*. New York: HarperCollins, 1994.

Cannon, Lou. *Governor Reagan: His Rise to Power*. New York: Public Affairs, 2003.

Caro, Robert A. *Means of Ascent: The Years of Lyndon Johnson*. New York: Knopf, 1990.

Colby, William. *Honorable Men: My Life in the CIA*. New York: Simon and Schuster, 1978.

Colodny, Len, and Robert Gettlin. *Silent Coup: The Removal of a President*. New York: St. Martin's Press, 1991.

Colson, Charles W. *Born Again: What Really Happened to the White House Hatchet Man*. Falls Church, Va.: Conservative Press, 1983.

Craven, John Pina. *The Silent War: The Cold War Battle Beneath the Sea*. New York: Touchstone, 2001.

Crouse, Timothy. *The Boys on the Bus*. New York: Ballantine Books, 1972.

David, Lester. *The Lonely Lady of San Clemente: The Story of Pat Nixon*. New York: Thomas Y. Crowell, 1978.

De Toledano, Ralph. *Nixon*. New York: Henry Holt, 1956.

Dean, John III. *Blind Ambition: The White House Years*. New York: Simon and Schuster, 1976.

Ehrlichman, John. *Witness to Power: The Nixon Years*. New York: Simon and Schuster, 1972.

Ehrman, John. *The Rise of Neoconservatism: Intellectuals and Foreign Affairs, 1945–1994*. New Haven, Conn.: Yale University Press, 1995.

Firestone, Bernard J., and Alexej Ugrinsky, eds. *Gerald R. Ford and the Politics of Post-Watergate America*. Westport, Conn.: Greenwood Press, 1993.

Ford, Betty. *The Times of My Life*. New York: Ballantine, 1978.

———. *Betty: A Glad Awakening*. Garden City, N.Y.: Doubleday, 1987.

Ford, Gerald R. *A Time to Heal*. New York: Harper and Row/Reader's Digest, 1979.

Frum, David. *How We Got Here: The 70's: The Decade that Brought You Modern Life—For Better or Worse*. New York: Basic Books, 2000.

Garment, Leonard. *Crazy Rhythm: From Brooklyn and Jazz to Nixon's White House, Watergate, and Beyond*. Cambridge, Mass.: Da Capo Press, 1997.

Gergen, David. *Eyewitness to Power: The Essence of Leadership, Nixon to Clinton.* New York: Touchstone, 2000.

Gould, Lewis L. *Grand Old Party: A History of the Republicans.* New York: Random House, 2003.

Green, Fitzhugh. *George Bush: An Intimate Portrait.* New York: Hippocrene Books, 1989.

Greenberg, David. *Nixon's Shadow: The History of an Image.* New York: Norton, 2003.

Greene, John Robert. *The Presidency of Gerald R. Ford.* Lawrence: University Press of Kansas, 1995.

Gulley, Bill. *Breaking Cover.* New York: Simon and Schuster, 1980.

Hagan, John. *Northern Passage: American Vietnam War Resisters in Canada.* Cambridge, Mass.: Harvard University Press, 2001.

Haig, Alexander M., Jr. *Inner Circles: How America Changed the World.* New York: Warner Books, 1992.

———. *Caveat: Realism, Reagan, and Foreign Policy.* New York: Macmillan, 1984.

Halberstam, David. *The Reckoning.* New York: William Morrow, 1986.

Haldeman, H. R. *The Haldeman Diaries: Inside the Nixon White House.* New York: G. P. Putnam's Sons, 1994.

Hartmann, Robert T. *Palace Politics: An Inside Account of the Ford Years.* New York: McGraw-Hill, 1980.

Hatfield, J. H. *Fortunate Son: George Bush and the Making of an American President.* Brooklyn, N.Y.: Soft Skull Press, 2001.

Hersey, John. *The President.* New York: Knopf, 1975.

Hersh, Seymour M. *The Price of Power: Kissinger in the Nixon White House.* New York: Summit Books, 1983.

Isaacson, Walter. *Kissinger: A Biography.* New York: Simon and Schuster, 1992.

Jaworski, Leon. *The Right and the Power: The Prosecution of Watergate.* New York: Reader's Digest, 1976.

Kalb, Bernard and Martin. *Kissinger.* Boston: Little, Brown, 1974.

Kaplan, Fred. *The Wizards of Armageddon.* New York: Simon and Schuster, 1983.

Kaufman, Robert G. *Henry M. Jackson: A Life in Politics.* Seattle: University of Washington Press, 2000.

Kimball, Jeffrey. *The Vietnam War Files: Uncovering the Secret History of Nixon-Era Strategy.* Lawrence: University Press of Kansas, 2004.

Kissinger, Henry. *White House Years.* Boston: Little, Brown, 1979.

———. *Years of Upheaval.* Boston: Little, Brown, 1982.

————. *Years of Renewal*. New York: Touchstone, 1999.

————. *Does America Need a Foreign Policy?* New York: Simon and Schuster, 2001.

————. *Crisis: The Anatomy of Two Major Foreign Policy Crises*. New York: Simon and Schuster, 2003.

Klare, Michael T. *Beyond the "Vietnam Syndrome": US Interventionism in the 1980s*. Washington, D.C.: Institute for Policy Studies, 1981.

————. *Resource Wars: The New Landscape of Global Conflict*. New York: Metropolitan Books, 2001.

Knebel, Fletcher, and Charles W. Bailey II. *Seven Days in May*. New York: Harper and Row, 1962.

Kramer, Michael, and Sam Roberts. *"I Never Wanted to be Vice-President of Anything!": An Investigative Biography of Nelson Rockefeller*. New York: Basic Books, 1976.

Krames, Jeffrey A. *The Rumsfeld Way: Leadership Wisdom of a Battle-Hardened Maverick*. New York: McGraw-Hill, 2002.

Kriesberg, Louis. *International Conflict Resolution: The US–USSR and Middle East Cases*. New Haven, Conn.: Yale University Press, 1992.

Kutler, Stanley. *The Wars of Watergate: The Last Crisis of Richard Nixon*. New York: W. W. Norton, 1990.

————, ed. *Abuse of Power: The New Nixon Tapes*. New York: Free Press, 1997.

McQuaid, Kim. *The Anxious Years: America in the Vietnam-Watergate Era*. New York: Basic Books, 1989.

Maier, Pauline, Merritt Roe Smith, Alexander Keyssar, and Daniel J. Kevles. *Inventing America: A History of the United States*. New York, W. W. Norton, 2003.

Manchester, William. *The Death of a President: November 1963*. New York: Harper and Row, 1967.

Mann, James. *Rise of the Vulcans: The History of Bush's War Cabinet*. New York: Viking, 2004.

Martin, Justin. *Greenspan: The Man Behind the Money*. Cambridge, Mass.: Perseus Publishing, 2000.

Medved, Michael. *The Shadow Presidents: The Secret History of the Chief Executives and Their Top Aides*. New York: Times Books, 1979.

Minutaglio, Bill. *First Son: George W. Bush and the Bush Family Dynasty*. New York: Three Rivers Press, 1999.

Mollenhoff, Clark. *The Man Who Pardoned Nixon: A Documentary Account of Gerald Ford's Presidential Retreat from Credibility*. New York: St. Martin's Press, 1976.

Morris, Edmund. *Dutch: A Memoir of Ronald Reagan*. New York: Random House, 1999.

Morris, Roger. *Haig: The General's Progress*. New York: Playboy Press, 1982.

Neustadt, Richard E. *Presidential Power and the Modern Presidents: The Politics of Leadership from Roosevelt to Reagan*. New York: Free Press, 1990.

Nixon, Richard. *Six Crises*. Garden City, N.Y.: Doubleday, 1962.

————. *RN: The Memoirs of Richard Nixon*. New York: Simon and Schuster, 1978.

————. *Leaders*. New York: Simon and Schuster, 1982.

————. *In the Arena*. New York: Simon and Schuster, 1990.

Nocera, Joseph. *A Piece of the Action: How the Middle Class Joined the Money Class*. New York: Simon and Schuster, 1994.

O'Neill, Thomas "Tip." *Man of the House*. New York: Random House, 1987.

Osborne, John. *The Nixon Watch*. New York: Liveright, 1970.

————. *White House Watch: The Ford Years*. Washington, D.C.: New Republic Books, 1977.

Parmet, Herbert S. *George Bush: Life of a Lone Star Yankee*. New York: Scribner, 1997.

Pearlstein, Rick. *Before the Storm: Barry Goldwater and the Unmaking of the American Consensus*. New York: Hill and Wang, 2001.

Persico, Joseph E. *The Imperial Rockefeller: A Biography of Nelson A. Rockefeller*. New York: Simon and Schuster, 1982.

Phillips, Kevin. *American Dynasty: Aristocracy, Fortune, and the Politics of Deceit in the House of Bush*. New York: Viking, 2004.

Price, Raymond. *With Nixon*. New York: Viking Press, 1977.

Radosh, Ronald. *Divided They Fell: The Demise of the Democratic Party, 1964–1996*. New York: Free Press, 1996.

Reeves, Richard. *A Ford, Not a Lincoln*. New York: Harcourt, Brace, Jovanovich, 1975.

————. *President Nixon: Alone in the White House*. New York: Simon and Schuster, 2001.

Reich, Cary. *The Life of Nelson A. Rockefeller: Worlds to Conquer, 1908–1958*. New York: Doubleday, 1996.

Safire, William. *Before the Fall: An Inside View of the Pre-Watergate White House*. Garden City, N.Y.: Doubleday, 1975.

Scarborough, Rowan. *Rumsfeld's War: The Untold Story of America's Anti-Terrorist Commander*. Washington, D.C.: Regnery Publishing, 2004.

Schell, Jonathan. *The Village of Ben Suc*. New York: Knopf, 1967.

Schlafly, Phyllis, and Chester Ward. *Kissinger on the Couch*. New Rochelle, N.Y.: Arlington House, 1975.

Schroth, Raymond A. *The American Journey of Eric Sevareid.* South Royalton, Vt.: Steerforth Press, 1995.

Schudson, Michael. *Watergate in American Memory: How We Remember, Forget, and Reconstruct the Past.* New York: Basic Books, 1992.

Schulman, Bruce J. *The Seventies: The Great Shift in American Culture, Society, and Politics.* Cambridge, Mass.: Da Capo Press, 2002.

Schweizer, Peter and Rochelle. *The Bushes: Portrait of a Dynasty.* New York: Doubleday, 2004.

Seidman, L. William. *Full Faith and Credit: The Great S&L Debate and Other Washington Sagas.* New York: Times Books, 1993.

Sheehan, Neil. *A Bright Shining Lie: John Paul Vann and America in Vietnam.* New York: Random House, 1988.

Sirica, John J. *To Set the Record Straight: The Break-in, the Tapes, the Conspirators, the Pardon.* New York: W. W. Norton, 1979.

Sontag, Sherry, and Christopher Drew. *Blind Man's Bluff: The Untold Story of American Submarine Espionage.* New York: HarperCollins, 1998.

Steinfels, Peter. *The Neoconservatives: The Men Who Are Changing American Politics.* New York: Simon and Schuster, 1979.

Summers, Anthony. *The Arrogance of Power: The Secret World of Richard Nixon.* New York: Viking, 2000.

TerHorst, J. F. *Gerald Ford and the Future of the Presidency.* New York: The Third Press, 1974.

TerHorst, J. F., and Ralph Albertazzi. *The Flying White House.* New York: Coward, McCann & Geoghegan, 1979.

Thomas, Helen. *Thanks for the Memories, Mr. President: Wit and Wisdom from the Front Row at the White House.* New York: Scribner, 2002.

Unger, Craig. *House of Bush, House of Saud.* New York: Scribner, 2004.

Wills, Garry. *Nixon Agonistes: The Crisis of the Self-Made Man.* New York: Signet, 1969.

Wilson, Robert A., ed. *Power and the Presidency.* New York: Public Affairs, 1999.

Witcover, Jules. *Marathon: The Pursuit of the Presidency, 1972–1976.* New York: Signet, 1977.

Woodward, Bob. *Shadow: Five Presidents and the Legacy of Watergate.* New York: Touchstone, 1999.

Woodward, Bob, and Carl Bernstein. *The Final Days.* New York: Simon and Schuster, 1976.

Wolfe, Tom. *Mauve Gloves & Madmen, Clutter and Vine*. New York: Farrar, Straus and Giroux, 1976.

Yergin, Daniel. *The Prize: The Epic Quest for Oil, Money, and Power*. New York: Free Press, 1991.

Zumwalt, Elmo R., Jr. *On Watch: A Memoir*. New York: Quadrangle/New York Times Books, 1976.

ARTICLES

Hersh, Seymour. "The Pardon: Nixon, Ford, Haig and the Transfer of Power." *Atlantic Monthly*, August 1983, pp. 55–78.

Leamer, Lawrence. "For Keeps: The Long Distance Race of Donald Rumsfeld," *The Washingtonian*, adapted from *Playing for Keeps in Washington* (New York: Dial Press, 1977).

Wood, Peter H. "The Pardoner's Tale." *Prospects* 11 (1986): pp. 491–539.

INDEX